Mandela's Kinsmen

Reviews of the hardback edition

Mandela's Kinsmen

NATIONALIST ELITES & APARTHEID'S FIRST BANTUSTAN

Timothy Gibbs
Lecturer, African History
University College London

JC JAMES CURREY

James Currey
is an imprint of Boydell & Brewer Ltd
PO Box 9, Woodbridge,
Suffolk IP12 3DF (GB)
www.jamescurrey.com

and of

Boydell & Brewer Inc.
668 Mt Hope Avenue
Rochester, NY 14620-2731 (US)
www.boydellandbrewer.com

First published in paperback in Southern Africa
(South Africa, Namibia, Lesotho, Swaziland & Botswana) by
Jacana Media (Pty) Ltd
10 Orange Street
Sunnyside, Auckland Park 2092
Johannesburg
South Africa
www.jacana.co.za

British Library Cataloguing in Publication Data
A catalogue record for this book is available on request from the British Library

ISBN 978-1-84701-089-6 James Currey (Cloth)
ISBN 978-1-84701-156-5 James Currey (Paper)
ISBN 978-1-4314-1065-1 Jacana (Paper)

The publisher has no responsibility for the continued existence or accuracy of URLs for external
or third-party internet websites referred to in this book, and does not guarantee that any content
on such websites is, or will remain, accurate or appropriate.

Typeset in 10/11pt Photina MT by Kate Kirkwood

CONTENTS

Contents

Contents

LIST OF MAPS & FIGURES

ACKNOWLEDGEMENTS

Ignorance has many virtues. My research, at first narrowly focused on Transkei's chieftaincy during the apartheid era, imperceptibly morphed into a much wider project concerning the relationship between nationalism and ethnic identities. As I stumbled into the intricacies of Bantustan politics, my initial bearings were provided by two generations of excellent scholarship that have discussed this subject. I hope the book that follows clearly sets out the distinctiveness of my interests and interpretation, without short-changing these important contributions from which I have drawn much sustenance.

Another advantage of ignorance was that I was initially blithely unaware of the sheer difficulty of obtaining archival material. Ironically, the most recent era is most poorly documented, the archives of the Bantustans largely lost and scattered. I eventually put together a documentary trail that charts this history in detail by searching 25 archival collections and tracking down lost sources to government offices, from Cape Town to Pretoria via the more remote parts of rural Transkei and the Eastern Cape. In total I drove more than 50,000km in search of interviews and archival troves. This would not have been possible without the generous support provided by the Arts and Humanities Research Council, the Beit Fund and, latterly, the South African National Research Foundation's Chair in Local Histories.

Readers who comb through footnotes will note that I draw heavily on two archives. The first is the Eastern Cape newspaper, the *Daily Dispatch*, which provided incredibly detailed reporting on Transkei's politics from its news-desk in the region's main town, Umtata. The second is the archives of the apartheid government's Department of Foreign Affairs, whose meticulous reporting on 'subversion' and 'dissidence' was fuelled by fears that the Bantustan project was running out of control (as indeed it was). I would like to thank librarians and archivists who helped me navigate South Africa's archives, making special mention of the wonderful *Daily Dispatch* newspaper as well as Sandy Shell who taught me that any archive can be found if one simply phones enough people. Thembile Ndabeni very kindly translated documents for me. I am also grateful to Jeff Peires, historian, policymaker and politician, with his own deep hinterland in the region, whose advice was hugely helpful. I have also used documents and interviews kindly provided by Dunbar Moodie, Jeff Peires and Wolfgang Thomas that come from their personal archives.

My greatest debt of thanks is owed to the men and women who kindly agreed to be interviewed. Most important were the fifty-odd life history interviews I undertook with Eastern Cape based nationalist activists, who spoke about their personal connections to the Transkei chieftaincy and Bantustan bureaucrats.

Acknowledgements

The apartheid government turned the chieftaincies into self-governing, 'tribal' Bantustans as a means of fragmenting African nationalism, dividing families against each other. Nelson Mandela's fractious relationship with his nephew, Kaiser Matanzima, the Chief Minister of the Transkei Bantustan epitomised these rifts. Nevertheless, tenuous connections remained, even during the most brutal phases of apartheid, when hit-squads murdered student activists. This is a sensitive subject. If Transkei's notables were a tight-knit family, then (to stretch the metaphor) there were murdered siblings still mourned today and intimate betrayals that have not been forgotten. My book attempts to handle these painful subjects empathetically and I make no revelations that are not already found in publically accessible documents or widely discussed in ANC circles. I apologise for any mistakes and misjudgements made along the way.

I am also aware that my interest in the relationship between nationalist activists and the Bantustans has obscured other important dynamics – the significance of gender within elite family networks, the role of labour migrants, for instance. These subjects have their own extensive historiography, which I hope to explore in future projects.

Many people nourished and housed me during my travels across South Africa. I would like to especially thank: Julian Brown and his parents, Simon Brown, Tracy Carson, Andy Gibbs and Samantha Willan, Steve Innes, Andy Kerr, Sindi Magcaba, Ica Mbebe, Holly McGee, Israel Mdingi, Nolwazi Mkhwanazi, Iris Mqotsi, Justin Pearce, Kelly Rosenthal, Genevieve and Thula Simpson, and Ross Truscott, also paying respects to the late Richard Canca and Livingstone Mqotsi. Fort Hare Institute of Social and Economic Research kindly provided me with an office during an extended stay in East London, South Africa. I must also thank those whom I interviewed (named in the bibliography) who were invariably generous in their hospitality.

I started the book manuscript in the South African National Research Foundation's Chair in Local Histories at the University of Witwatersrand and finished at Trinity College, Cambridge. The first has views of Johannesburg's mine dumps, the latter immaculate lawns; both have been wonderfully supportive institutions in which to get on with the slow and silent business of writing.

I owe much to William Beinart, who grasped the essential themes of my research long before I did. Julian Brown, John Darwin, Bill Freund, Jonny Steinberg and Randolph Vigne kindly commented on various chapters. Lungisile Ntsebeza sent me a draft chapter from his own work, which helped me rethink some of my own arguments. Phil Bonner, Colin Bundy, John Iliffe, John Lonsdale and Roger Southall read different versions of the entire manuscript, sometimes multiple times. Barbara Genevaz's comments transformed a stodgy manuscript into something that is far more readable, I hope. Jeff Peires read the penultimate draft and saved me from countless errors of interpretation and fact. Juliette Genevaz read the earliest, most incoherent drafts and provided much appreciated advice and support.

A number of my arguments were trialled in an article published by the *Journal of South African Studies* 37,4 (2011) and a chapter published in book edited by William Beinart and Marcelle Dawson, *Popular Resistance Movements in South Africa* (Wits University Press, Johannesburg, 2010). I would like to thank the editors and anonymous reviewers for very helpful feedback.

Without all this help my book would be immeasurably poorer; nonetheless errors of fact and interpretation inevitably remain. These faults will be happily corrected should this book make a second edition!

A word on orthography: in recent years South African names have been changed. This is to reflect how they were said by Africans (Mthatha rather than Umtata); break the barriers of segregation (East London and surrounding townships have been incorporated into Buffalo City Municipality); and change names that symbolise apartheid history (although a surprising number of Empire Roads remain). Historians encounter these changes in all their complexity. Pondoland is now commonly spelt as Mpondoland and even Mphondoland; Kaiser Mbethe had his name spelt thus by the apartheid police who jailed him in the 1980s, but today writes his name Kaiser Mbete; his friend, Mangaliso Kenneth Jafta, is referred to in some ANC documents by his nickname, Boy Jafta. Where possible, I have chosen a catholic approach, rendering names as they were given by interviewees and documents. But there are times I was forced to simplify for the sake of clarity.

It was a year of study in Durban more than a decade ago that first brought me to South Africa. I would like to thank the Derbyshire Rotary Club – in particular, Phil Newell – who sponsored my studies, as well as friends and classmates from that golden year.

Final note: In recognition of the long history of social work and community development in the Transkei – some of which is mentioned in the chapters that follow – all royalties from this book will be donated to a number of NGOs associated with the Marianhill Order that work in the townships and informal settlements around Umtata.

ABBREVIATIONS

See Bibliography for full list of library and institutional research sources

Cape Archives Cape Town
CMT Chief Magistrate, Transkei
1/COF Magistrate, Cofimvaba
1/ECO Magistrate, Engcobo
1/FSF Magistrate, Flagstaff
1/BIZ Magistrate, Bizana
1/MQL Magistrate, Mqanduli
1/UTA Magistrate, Umtata
1/XAL Magistrate, Xalanga

University of South Africa
ACC318   Transkei Council of Churches Accession
AAS45   Transkei Government Accession

University of Cape Town, Manuscripts and Archives Centre
CKC   Carter-Karis Collection
KGC   Karis-Gerhart Collection

Alan Paton Centre, University of KwaZulu Natal Pietermaritzburg
PC2   Liberal Party of South Africa
PC86   Randolph Vigne
PC170   Magnus Gunther

University of Witwatersrand, Historical Papers
 AB1886   Anglican Church of Southern Africa, Diocese of St John's

National Archive, Pretoria
BTS1/226/1 Department of Foreign Affairs, Transkei, Political Situation
            and Developments
BAO   Department of Native Administration and Development
KGT   Commissioner General, Transkei
SADET   South African Democracy Education Project

Truth and Reconciliation Commission (online)

TRC-AD	Truth and Reconciliation Commission Amnesty Decisions
TRC-AH	Truth and Reconciliation Commission Amnesty Hearings
TRC-VH	Truth and Reconciliation Commission Human Rights Violations Hearings

Press Sources

DD	*Daily Dispatch*
SAPA	*South African Press Association*
M&G	*Mail and Guardian*
RDM	*Rand Daily Mail*

Rhodes House Library, Oxford

TLA	*Debates of the Transkei Legislative Assembly* (Umtata, 1964-76)
TNA	*Debates of the National Assembly, Republic of Transkei* (Umtata, 1977-87)

Journals

JCAS	*Journal of Contemporary African Studies*
JSAS	*Journal of Southern African Studies*
SAHJ	*South African Historical Journal*

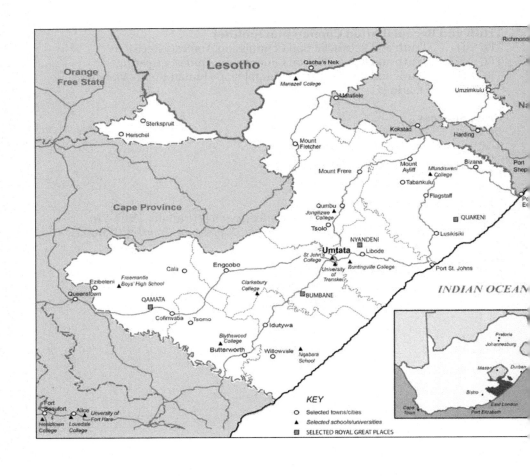

Map 1 *Transkei and the Eastern Cape*

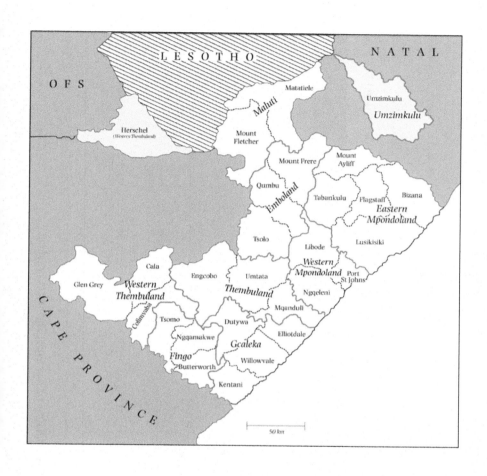

Map 2 *Transkei's Districts and Regions after 1976*

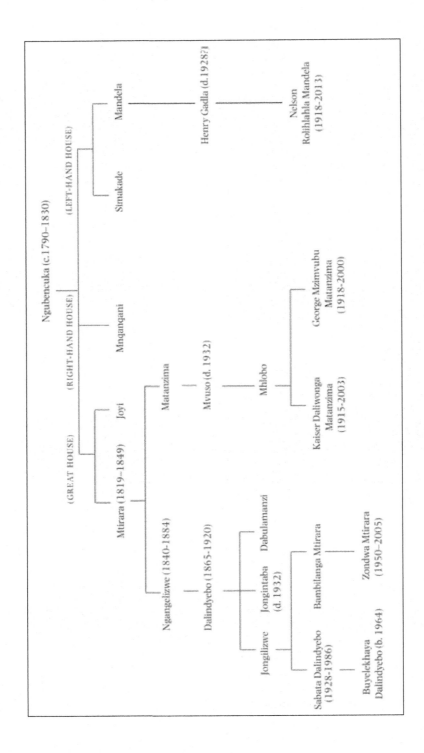

Figure 1 *Mandela's Kinsmen: A Thembu Geneaology*

Introduction
Mandela's Kinsmen

'I was born on 18 July 1918 at Mvezo, a tiny village on the banks of the Mbashe River, in the district of Umtata, the capital of Transkei... a beautiful country of rolling hills, fertile valleys, and a thousand rivers and streams which keep the landscape green.'[1] The opening chapters of Nelson Mandela's autobiography give a lyrical account of his rural childhood. The Transkei territories are an area of scattered settlements and bustling small towns situated between the Indian Ocean and the Drakensberg mountains in the Xhosa-speaking, Eastern Cape region of South Africa. Mandela spent most of his early years at Qunu, a small settlement of beehive-shaped huts built with mud walls which 'was situated in a narrow grassy valley crisscrossed by clear streams.' Only the Christian converts wore Western-style clothing, he recalled; but there were two small primary schools in the area, as well as 'a general store and a dipping tank to rid the cattle of ticks and diseases'.[2]

Nelson Mandela was aged nine when his father died and the family was separated. Being from the royal clan, Mandela was placed under the protection of Jongintaba, the regent of the Thembu Kingdom. Here he was immersed in the court life at the Great Place of Mqhekezweni. The young Mandela was fascinated by the living customs of the Thembu kingdom: a whole chapter of his autobiography is spent describing the circumcision ceremony in the mountains that brought him into manhood at the age of sixteen. Afterwards, a sheep was slaughtered and he was taken in the regent's car to one of the most prominent boarding schools in Transkei: Clarkebury College, run by missionaries whose institutions were dotted across South Africa's 'Native Reserves'. Jongintaba planned for Nelson Mandela to cap his education with a degree at the nearby Fort Hare University – an 'Oxford and Cambridge... for young black South Africans like myself',[3] remembered Mandela. However, in 1940, the young student was expelled for his role in a student boycott. Defying his guardian's instructions, Mandela fled to Johannesburg, where he became immersed in African National Congress (ANC) politics.[4]

In the first decades of the 20th century, the Transkei and rural Eastern Cape was the political hinterland of the African elite. Although it was hundreds of miles away from the cities and the histories of trade union and township protest that played a central role in South Africa's politics, it was the birthplace of many prominent African leaders. Nelson Mandela's wife and political

---

[1] N. Mandela, *A Long Walk to Freedom: The autobiography of Nelson Mandela* (London, 1994), p.1.
[2] Ibid., p.8.
[3] Ibid., p.41.
[4] T. Lodge, *Mandela: A critical life* (Oxford, 2006).

1

partner, Winnie Madikizela-Mandela (b.1936), is the descendant of a nearby chieftaincy. Mandela's closest friends in the ANC, Oliver Tambo (1917-1993) and Walter Sisulu (1912-2003), also had deep roots in the Transkei. So did his greatest rival, Govan Mbeki (1910-2001), whose son, Thabo Mbeki (b.1942), became the second president of democratic South Africa. Other rural regions of South Africa produced leaders of the same ilk as Mandela; yet Transkei was the main wellspring. A large number of biographies and memoirs show us an intricate web of regionally-focused kinship, marriage, mission school and professional links. These interlocking networks – which I refer to in shorthand as 'Mandela's kinsmen' or 'notable politics' – were the filaments that held together the African elite in the first half of the 20th century.[5]

Mandela's evocation of his rural childhood, in an autobiography published just as the ANC came to power under black majority rule in 1994, was more than nostalgic reminiscence. It was a political testament: an argument that the notable networks that shaped his early life remained intact. For as much as the apartheid era was a period of mass and class based politics, Mandela's elite, kin-based networks would remain vital to African political life.

▲ ▲ ▲

This book concerns Mandela's kinsmen inside Transkei during the apartheid years. In doing this I provide a counterweight to a number of common arguments about the nature of society and politics in apartheid South Africa. First, many histories tend to emphasise the dynamo of urban and mass-based politics.[6] When both liberal and radical historians have looked back to the late 19th century, they have argued that South Africa's trajectory was shaped by the discovery of gold and diamonds: that the politics of class and nationalism was forged within the crucible of South Africa's industrial society. Indeed, the pace of politics increased during the apartheid decades. The growth of secondary industry fostered trade union protest, starting with the 1973 Durban strikes. The 1976 student revolts in Soweto heralded a new era of township protests.[7] In the mid-1980s, as older rhythms of rural life were transformed by mass schooling and the collapse of African smallholder agriculture, a series of youth revolts swept across South Africa's Bantustans.[8] This narrative, which emphasises the modernisation of South Africa, often suggests that Mandela's kinsmen – the tiny elite from the pre-apartheid generation – were overshadowed by a younger generation, whose politics had been forged by the massification of society during the second half of the 20th century.

Second, many accounts of the apartheid era focus on the co-option of Mandela's kinsmen into the Bantustan project. Transkei was the foundation

[5] Lodge uses the term notables: see *Mandela*, pp. 19-42. Historians of Africa have tended to speak of 'elites' – C. Lentz summarises: 'Home, Death and Leadership: Discourses of an educated elite from north-western Ghana, *Social Anthropology* 2, 2 (1994), pp.149-69.
[6] See N. Worden's summary in *The Making of Modern South Africa* (1994), pp. 1-4.
[7] C. Glaser, *Bo-Tsotsi: The youth gangs of Soweto* (Oxford, 2000).
[8] P. Delius, *A Lion Amongst the Cattle: Reconstruction and resistance in the Northern Transvaal* (Oxford, 1996). I. van Kessel, *Beyond our Wildest Dreams: The United Democratic Front and the transformation of South Africa* (Charlottesville, 2000).

stone of apartheid policies of segregation, intended to divide Africans by race and ethnicity. In 1963 it was the first Native Reserve to become a 'self-governing territory' (more often called 'Bantustans' or 'Homelands'). Nelson Mandela's tribal nephew, Kaiser Matanzima (1915-2003), his closest companion at university, became the first Chief Minister of the Transkei Bantustan. In 1976, Transkei was the first self-governing territory to be granted full Bantustan 'independence' and statehood. In total, Pretoria would create ten 'self-governing territories' of which four became 'fully independent' Bantustans, although they were all so closely tied to apartheid South Africa that their sovereignty was never recognised by the United Nations.

Writing in the 1960s, political scientists and historians argued that the 'half-loaf' of Bantustan independence was a product of 'race separatism' and 'domestic colonialism'.[9] The Marxist-inspired historians of the 1970s, by contrast, provided a far more thoroughgoing critique of the political-economy of the Bantustan project. Writing at the height of apartheid, Roger Southall suggested that Transkei's elite – chiefs, politicians, civil servants and traders – were 'beneficiaries of the Bantustans' who enjoyed access to government jobs, business licenses and lucrative tenders. He argued that 'this class was the lynchpin in the web of dependence whereby the new [Bantustan] state was allowed relative autonomy by Pretoria, yet not so much as in any serious way to threaten the edifice of apartheid.'[10] Further studies, written as apartheid unravelled in the 1980s, provided ever more nuanced assessments of precisely which 'class fractions' benefited from and were loyal to the Bantustan project.[11] Some of this research also provided a sensitive account of how the growth of the Bantustan state ruptured the fabric of rural society and crystallised wider class divisions. These were the events that framed the widespread popular protests against the Bantustan state in the final years of apartheid.[12]

Third, when explaining the survival of many Bantustan bureaucrats and the reassertion of traditional authority in rural South Africa after 1994, many academics have suggested that the ANC leadership struck a compromise deal with the remnants of the old order above the heads of the grassroots insurgents. Jeff Peires provides an incisive account of how many Bantustan functionaries adeptly dropped their ties to the apartheid regime and secured their positions in the post-apartheid era.[13] Lungisile Ntsebeza argues that the 'decentralised

[9] G. Carter, T. Karis and N. Stultz, *South Africa's Transkei: The politics of domestic colonialism* (Evanston, 1967). N. Stultz, *Transkei's Half Loaf: Race separatism in South Africa* (London, 1979).

[10] R. Southall summarises his position: 'Introduction: Rethinking Transkei Politics', *JCAS*, 11,2 (1992), p.8. Cf. R. Southall, *South Africa's Transkei: The political economy of an "independent" Bantustan*, (London, 1982).

[11] The Transkei was the focus of debates concerning the Bantustans, as R. Southall summarises in: 'Rethinking Transkei Politics', pp.1-30.

[12] P. Delius, *A Lion Amongst the Cattle*. S. Marks, *The Ambiguities of Dependence in South Africa: Class, nationalism and the state in 20th century Natal* (Baltimore, 1986). C. Murray, *Black Mountain: Land, class and power in the eastern Orange Free State, 1880s-1980s* (Edinburgh, 1992). L. Ntsebeza, *Democracy Compromised: Chiefs and the politics of land in South Africa* (Cape Town, 2006). J. Peires, 'Transkei on the Verge of Emancipation', in P. Rich (ed.), *Reaction and Renewal in South Africa*, (Basingstoke, 1994), pp.192-221.

[13] J. Peires, 'The Implosion of Transkei and Ciskei', *African Affairs*, 91 (1992), pp.365-87. P. Jones, 'From Nationhood to Regionalism to the North West Province: Bophuthatswananess and the birth of the New South Africa', *African Affairs*, 98 (1999), pp.509-34.

despotism' of the chieftaincy remains unbroken. [14] Barbara Oomen and Ineke van Kessel emphasise the residual power of the traditional leadership and the pluralism of institutions in the rural regions where the writ of democratically elected, local government does not run far. [15]

▲ ▲ ▲

Neither the significance of urban and mass politics nor the dislocations of the Bantustan era should be understated, but I suggest that the notable networks that had shaped 'Mandela's kinsmen' in the early 20th century did not unravel during apartheid. In recent years our picture of the former Bantustans has changed once more. A surprising number of politicians, following the example of Nelson Mandela, re-established family homes on ancestral land in the Bantustans after 1994. Whilst these demographically dense, rural regions were poor and fractious, in general, they became an important base of ANC support and very influential in party caucuses. Even Thabo Mbeki, the urbane, second president of democratic South Africa from 1999-2008, started participating in ancestral ceremonies in the Transkei when he realised the importance of these rural votes. This trend was taken even further by the following ANC president, Jacob Zuma, South Africa's polygamous head of state who declares himself a supporter of tradition. Analysts and academics have followed these contemporary developments pointing towards the resurgence of regional elites and traditional leaders. [16]

However, very little is understood about the connections between nationalist leaders and the Homelands during the apartheid era. Such connections were difficult to trace before 1994 because the ANC underground was, by necessity, secretive. Bantustan elites also had 'a striking propensity to guard their own secrets' during the turbulent final years of apartheid. [17] Now, with the opening of apartheid era archives, this history can be told. By reading the fragmentary records in newly-opened archives and by interviewing dozens of politicians and activists, I have traced the social hinterland and political networks in which this activism was rooted. My study emphasises the hidden history of the ambiguous interconnections between the nationalist movements, the chieftaincy and the Bantustan bureaucracy.

First, I offer a new interpretation of the Bantustan state. South Africa's historians have typically highlighted the conflict between state and society, a narrative of repression and resistance. This was an understandable emphasis

[14] L. Ntsebeza, 'Democratic Decentralization and Traditional Authority: Dilemmas of land administration in rural South Africa', 16, 1 (2004), pp.69-70, quoting M. Mamdani, *Citizen and Subject: Contemporary Africa and the legacy of late colonialism*, (London, 1996), pp.22-4, 34. Cf. Ntsebeza, *Democracy Compromised*, pp.18-24, 59, 294.

[15] I. van Kessel and B. Oomen, 'One Chief, One Vote: The revival of traditional authorities in post-apartheid South Africa', *African Affairs*, 96, 385 (1994), pp.561-85. B. Oomen, *Chiefs in South Africa: Law, power and culture in the post-apartheid era*, (Oxford, 2005).

[16] *Sunday Times*, 8 August 2007. *The Guardian* 18 January 2010. J. Beall, S. Mkhize and S. Vawda, 'Emergent Democracy and "Resurgent" Tradition: Institutions, chieftaincy and transition in KwaZulu Natal', *JSAS*, 31, 4 (2005), pp.755-71.

[17] Murray, *Black Mountain*, p.7.

given the coercive power of the apartheid government and the aggrandise-ment of Homeland elites. At the same time, the Bantustans were a peculiarly rickety type of indirect rule: as soon as apartheid waned, Bantustan government crumbled. Paradoxically, the expansion of the Bantustan state created new forms of dissent within its interstices. In retrospect, one sees a process of socio-economic transformation that changed the relationship between state and society.[18] The patronage dispensed to regions preferred by Matanzima's government, for instance – schools, roads, agricultural schemes and subsidies – generated new forms of opposition amongst dis-favoured communities. By the late 1970s, a number of prominent notables (some who were linked to the ANC through kinship connections) bitterly complained about the lack of development in their communities. This politics of political brokerage and community concern would become an important language of protest as the Bantustan project collapsed under its own weight in the 1980s.

The Bantustan state also played a vital role in the formation of African elites. Whilst Bantustan bureaucracies were often synonymous with repression and self-enrichment, the Homelands also had unparalleled networks of elite schools, universities and professional opportunities for much of the apartheid era. (If we take, for example, the seven African judges sitting in South Africa's Constitutional Court in 2012, five had been educated and three started their careers in the Bantustans.)[19] Furthermore, not everyone who in some way benefited from the expansion of the Bantustan state was co-opted into the apartheid project; there was room for ambivalence, scepticism and, on the margins, active subversion. A small but very significant cohort from the younger generation who had been groomed within the Bantustans – given elite schooling, university bursaries and prestigious government employment – became involved in various forms of anti-apartheid politics. The Bantustans produced some of their best educated critics.

Clarkebury College, Fort Hare University and institutions of African local government are well known for the catalysing role they played in the intellectual, political and sociological formation of African elites in the first half of the 20th century. We require a similarly nuanced account of institutions such as the University of Transkei and St Johns College, Umtata, during the Bantustan era. These were the institutions which played a formative role for many of the contemporary elites.[20]

Second, I examine the ambiguous relationship between the Bantustan elites and the ANC, which, in many important ways, remained a nationalist

---

[18] For an older historiography that emphasises the complex relationships between colonialists and indigenous allies and opponents: R. Chandarvarkar, 'Imperialism and the European Empires', in J. Jackson (ed.), *The Short Oxford History of Europe, 1900-45* (Oxford, 2002), pp.140-2. More recent writings on state-society relationships include P. Nugent, 'States and Social Contracts in Africa', *New Left Review*, 63 (2010), pp.35-68.

[19] Constitutional Court website, 'Current Constitutional Court Judges', n.d.

[20] Research in this direction includes: P. Denis and G. Duncan, *The Native School that caused all the trouble: A history of the Federal Theological Seminary of Southern Africa* (Pietermaritzburg, 2011). M. Healy, 'A World of Their Own': A history of South African women's education* (Durban, 2013). V. Noble, *A School for Struggle: A history of the Durban Medical School and the education of black doctors in South Africa* (Durban, forthcoming).

movement built out of regional networks. From the mid-1970s, the ANC-in-exile attempted to re-enter South Africa through the Bantustans. The famed ANC leader, Chris Hani, who was born and raised in Transkei, built the nationalist underground out of the networks of local dissidence. At the same time, the ANC leadership was also talking to their brothers and sisters who had taken senior positions in the Bantustan governments. This strategy famously failed in KwaZulu, where the young 'comrades' eventually fought against the ANC's erstwhile interlocutors in the Homeland government. The Transkei offers a quieter, but equally significant counterpoint. A series of coups inside Transkei in the late 1980s produced a government far more amenable to the nationalist movements. In the early 1990s, during the perilous years of the constitutional negotiations and the political transition, Transkei became a safe haven and a stepping stone by which the ANC-in-exile returned to South Africa. These subterranean currents account for the sudden rise of Bantu Holomisa – a general in the Transkei Defence Force, trained by Pretoria to fight ANC guerrillas – who briefly became the most popular politician in the ANC after he turned Transkei over to Chris Hani's guerrillas. Bantu Holomisa was the most spectacular example of how the entwined histories of the nationalist elite and their kinsmen in the Bantustans forged unexpected alliances in the early 1990s. This was a time when the ANC, uncertain of their support in the Bantustans that accounted for perhaps 50% of the African population, needed all the allies they could.

Given the scale of violence and conflict in South Africa, we must approach this subject with great caution and attention to detail. More than 11,000 people were killed in clashes between the chieftaincy and the 'comrades' in KwaZulu and Natal alone. Whilst Transkei did not see open conflicts on such a large scale, elements of its Bantustan security forces operated hand-in-glove with apartheid murder squads right up until 1994. Notable networks were deeply ambiguous. It was through this web of educational, professional and kinship connections that a Bantustan general, Bantu Holomisa, could make a Damascene conversion to the ANC. Yet at the same time, Transkei's security police would have been schooled with some of the dissidents that they tortured and murdered.[21] The proximity of the leading protagonists made this internecine conflict extremely bitter; but there were also important instances when boundaries between opposition and collaboration, Bantustan and nationalist loyalties were blurred. We need to find a language that goes beyond the narrative of 'Bantustan stooges' and 'nationalist liberation movements' in order to incorporate the shades of grey that were so important in the apartheid endgame.

South Africa is not the only country in the region where the tangled legacies of insurgency and counter-insurgency remain a fraught subject. Recently written histories of the Mau Mau insurgency continue to trouble Kenyans, for instance. Looking even further afield, it took historians of France almost three decades to discuss collaboration between Vichy and Nazi Germany, and still

---

[21] L. Ntsebeza provides a thoughtful critique: 'The Reincorporation of Transkei into South Africa, 1987-1994: Turning against the master?' in South African Democracy Education Trust (henceforth SADET), *The Road to Democracy in South Africa* (forthcoming).

longer to write histories that broke open the dichotomies of collaboration and resistance.[22]

A third theme in this book concerns the importance of 'Africanist', communitarian ideas of political activism that were rooted in the rural areas. During the middle decades of the 20th century, African educated elites attempting to build rural support pioneered new modes of community-based activism. A handful of African socialists working in Transkei, such as Govan Mbeki, believed that co-operative self-help schemes could revive peasant agriculture, and encourage rural communities to defend their local 'moral economy' from the settler government.[23] During the Bantustan era, this ideology subtly but dramatically shifted. With the collapse of African smallholder farming, young activists increasingly saw themselves as the healers and leaders of broken and impoverished communities, using their professional skills in schools, health clinics and the like. These ideas were particularly associated with Steve Biko (1946-1977), a leading figure in the Black Consciousness Movement in the 1970s, whose projects were piloted across the Transkei and the Eastern Cape.[24] Whilst these projects were rarely successful, Black Consciousness ideas were absorbed into wider strands of political thought about the relationship between state and society. Communitarian rhetoric remains an important discourse in post-apartheid South Africa because it speaks to local debates concerning the problems of poverty and public service delivery that afflict the country's most fractious and poorest rural areas. Government ministers open health clinics in these parts of the country, hailed by grandmas who cry 'welcome our father'. Conversely, they are criticised for their selfish eating of public funds. Some of them have become political brokers accessing goods from a relatively rickety, although increasingly generous, post-apartheid state for the communities that they represent. Thus notable politics continues in post-apartheid South Africa.

Consequently, despite the ruptures of the Bantustan era, Transkei's leading families and some of the ideas that they espouse are still close to the heart of political life. The continuing importance of notable politics in the most urban and industrialised society on the African continent is at the heart of this book. This history is best understood by tracing the course of elite politics: the hinterland of Mandela's kinsmen in rural regions such as Transkei during the first half of the 20th century, and the ambiguous relationships between nationalist movements, the chieftaincy, and the Bantustan bureaucracy during the apartheid era, led to the dramatic denouement of the 1990s.

---

[22] For instance the response to D. Anderson, *Histories of the Hanged: Britain's dirty war and the end of Empire* (London, 2004) and C. Elkins, *Britain's Gulag: The brutal end of empire in Kenya* (London, 2005).

[23] C. Bundy, 'Breaking the Midnight Slumber: Govan Mbeki in the Transkei, 1940-48' (IHR seminar paper, 28 September 1998). J. Lonsdale, 'The Moral Economy of Mau Mau: Wealth, poverty and civic virtue in Kikuyu political thought', in J. Lonsdale and B. Berman (eds), *Unhappy Valley: Conflict in Kenya and Africa* (London, 1992), pp.332-53.

[24] L. Hadfield, 'Restoring Human Dignity and Building Self-Reliance: Youth, women, church and Black Consciousness community development, South Africa, 1969-1977' (PhD thesis, Michigan State University, 2010). D. Magaziner, *The Law and the Prophets: Black Consciousness in South Africa, 1968-1977* (Athens, 2010).

▲ ▲ ▲

The story of Mandela's kinsmen is also a very African one. Firstly, Nelson Mandela's countryside childhood paralleled the experience of prominent politicians elsewhere in Africa. Across the continent, many leading African leaders prospered from elite education at the mission schools that were often set up on land granted to them by local traditional leaders in the late 19th and early 20th century. 'The two principles that governed my life', growing up at the royal homestead, 'were the chieftaincy and Church,' Mandela recalled in his autobiography. [25] Similarly, Zimbabwe's longstanding president, Robert Gabriel Mugabe (b.1924) preferred the libraries of the series of Jesuit and Marist schools that he attended to the company of his peers. He then took a BA degree in South Africa, at Fort Hare University, founded by Eastern Cape missionaries in 1916. [26] The local university for Transkei's elites was one of the first such institutions on the continent; its alumni included prominent leaders from across southern Africa, as well as a many of South African political leaders. In Chapter One, I discuss the transnational ties of kinship and friendship that linked South Africa's leaders to their brothers and sisters elsewhere on the continent: one that was frequently dominated by mission educated elites, and where politics often concerned cross-cutting ideologies of ethnicity, kinship and community. [27]

There are also more painful parallels, which are discussed in more detail in the concluding chapter. The final years of apartheid, which saw near civil war in South Africa, was part of an era of conflict that consumed the southern African region. [28] In many places, internecine conflicts emerged. In Angola, where civil war continued intermittently from 1974-2002, the rival guerrilla movements never escaped their ethnic origins. Mozambique's civil war (1977-1992) brought President Samora Machel's government up against insurgents who drew support from outlying provinces. At Zimbabwe's independence in 1980, rival guerrilla movements brokered an uneasy truce, but this shattered in 1982 when President Robert Mugabe's soldiers crushed dissidence in Matabeleland. Likewise, bloody clashes between the ANC and the self-proclaimed, Zulu separatists in the Inkatha Freedom Party emerged in the early 1980s, in a series of conflicts that would claim 20,000 lives nationwide. By the early 1990s, elements of the chieftaincy inside many Bantustans mobilised against the ANC: 'tribalism' threatened to shatter South Africa into fragments.

Confronted by political stalemate and a country in crisis, the ANC engaged

---

[25] Mandela, *Long Walk to Freedom*, p.18.

[26] D. Blair, *Degrees in Violence: Robert Mugabe and the struggle for power in Zimbabwe* (London, 2002), pp.18-9.

[27] On African elites: T. Ranger, *Are we not also Men? The Samkange family and African politics in Zimbabwe, 1920-64* (London, 1995). R. Werbner, *Reasonable Radicals and Citizenship in Botswana: The public anthropology of Kalanga elites* (Bloomington IN, 2004). C. Lentz, 'Home, Death and Leadership'.

[28] J. Lonsdale summarises the voluminous literature: 'Anti-Colonial Nationalism and Patriotism in sub-Saharan Africa', in J. Breiully (ed.), *The Oxford Handbook of the History of Nationalism* (Oxford, 2013), pp.304-18.

in the politics of reconciliation. Nelson Mandela emerged from prison in 1990 as an elder statesman, who drew power from the patterns of social authority he had learnt during his youth in Transkei. He negotiated with his enemies in the Bantustans by appealing to them as kinsmen. Hundreds, probably thousands more political leaders did the same. The relatively peaceful, democratic elections in April 1994 were a minor miracle, remembered Desmond Tutu, given the violence of the previous decade.[29] When Africa is so often seen as a continent scarred by 'political tribalism',[30] the reincorporation of the Bantustans into post-apartheid South Africa (difficult and flawed as this process has been) offers an important counterpoint to the pervasive currents of Afro-pessimism.

On 8 January 1912, a small group of mission school-educated African elites, with a smattering of invited chiefs, met in Bloemfontein to found the South African Native National Congress. A century later, the ANC is a very different movement that reflects the transformation of South African society. Today it includes a bloc of leaders who rose through the trade union movement in the 1970s and 1980s, and who still sing, 'my father was a garden boy, my mother was a kitchen girl', the song of working-class assertion. It now includes veterans from the 1980s townships uprisings, today, middle-aged urban powerbrokers, such as the 'Alex mafia': a group of politicians from Johannesburg's most central township, Alexandra. Yet 'Mandela's kinsmen' also have influence in the senior echelons of the party, government, business, and the state. In the prominence of these regional elites we see the ambiguous, yet undeniable importance of the rural regions in the ANC.

---

[29] D. Tutu, 'Reconciliation in Post-Apartheid South Africa: Experiences of the Truth Commission', (Transcript of Speech, Nobel Laureates Conference, University of Virginia, November 5 1998).

[30] B. Berman, 'Ethnicity, Patronage and the African State: The politics of uncivil nationalism', *African Affairs 97* (1998), p.305.

1.   Education, Monarchy & Nationalism

The Morning Star

In 1938, during Nelson Mandela's final year in boarding school at Healdtown, 'an event occurred that... was like a comet streaking across the night sky.'[1] The school was given an impromptu holiday to celebrate the performance of a famous *imbongi* (praise poet), Krune Mqhayi. A praise poet typically performed in the court of a king; but Mqhayi was a well-educated teacher who had left a comfortable post and retreated to the hills to pursue his calling. That night Healdtown witnessed Mqhayi perform his most famous poem. First Mqhayi subversively alluded to colonial conquest. Then he danced about the stage, waving his spear, allocating stars to the different peoples of the world: the Milky Way to the nations of Europe; other heavenly constellations to the peoples and kingdoms of Africa.

> Now, suddenly, he became still and lowered his voice. 'Now come, O House of Xhosa,' he said and slowly began to lower himself so that he was on one knee. 'I give unto you the most important and transcendent star, the Morning Star, for you are a proud and powerful people. It is a star for counting the years – the years of manhood.'[2]

The hall erupted at the sight of a poet singing praises in a mission school, a colonial institution. But Nelson Mandela's autobiography also recalls his confusion. 'I was beginning to see that Africans of all tribes had much in common, yet here was the great Mqhayi praising the Xhosa above all.'[3]

Nelson Mandela's acknowledgement on the uncertainty and plurality of his identities is telling – in what sense was he a scion of the Thembu kingdom, a member of the educated, Xhosa-speaking elite, and a black South African? In time, it would mould his multi-layered sense of nationalism. This chapter considers the influences that shaped the early life and politics of the Transkei elite who would later go on to play leading roles in both nationalist and Bantustan politics during the apartheid decades. Moving into the 1940s and early 1950s, such questions of ethnic and nationalist identity would take on greater significance. During these years, the apartheid government began laying the foundation for its Bantustan policies. The apartheid vision – of attempting to fix ethnic identities into the constrictions of the Bantustan project – ran headlong into the alternate, more expansive visions of personal

---

[1] Mandela, *Long Walk to Freedom*, p.38
[2] Ibid, p.40
[3] Ibid, p.40. Cf. J. Opland, *Xhosa Oral Poetry: Aspects of a black South African tradition* (Cambridge, 1983), pp.90-5. Lodge, *Mandela*, p.7.

and political identity expounded by leading African nationalists. The debates, ideas, people and institutions of the pre-Bantustan era, discussed below, would appear again in different guises in the decades to come.

Educated elites

In one very important sense, African nationalism (like many other anti-colonial nationalisms) was fabricated by the mission school educated elites who emerged in the wake of colonial conquest. These elites were particularly prominent in parts of the Transkei and the Eastern Cape where wealthy groups of independent African traders and farmers often prospered in the backwash of colonial conquest and the frontier wars. They settled 'near mission stations at first, and very soon elsewhere as well, innovative and enterprising peasant producers appeared.'[4] In the late 19th century, Oliver Tambo's grandparents crossed the Engeli Mountains into the Eastern Mpondo districts of Transkei. We do not know the immediate reasons for their migration, but Tambo's official biographer, Luli Callinicos, notes they were probably fleeing the wars that scattered spasms of refugees across the southern African region. The Tambo family thrived as traders and transport riders. Oliver Tambo remembered that his father had three wives (polygamy was a sign of wealth) and a large homestead: 'a big kraal, as distinct from the two-hut home of which there were many'.[5]

Other scions of the ANC had similar roots. Govan Mbeki's paternal forebears were Christian refugees, colloquially known as the *Mfengu* peoples, who crossed the Kei River into the westernmost reaches of the Transkei. Indeed, the western parts of Transkei were at one time known as Fingoland because of the predominance of *Mfengu* people in these areas. Parallel processes played out in other parts of rural South Africa. Two ANC presidents, John Dube and Albert Luthuli, both hailed from communities of Christian converts and prosperous farmers in KwaZulu Natal, who were known as the *Kholwa* (Christians).

The political paths followed by African educated elites were not direct. In the 19th century, they tended to be supporters of the Crown. To the west of the Transkei there was a brutal process of settler conquest and subjugation that rumbled along the frontiers of the expanding Cape Colony, whose capital was Cape Town. In 1778 the limits of the Cape Colony lay on the banks of the Fish River. By 1871 after nine frontier wars, the Cape Colony had expanded 150 kilometres up the coast to the Kei River and the borders of Thembuland. In 1885 the Thembu kingdom was annexed by the Cape Colony. The expansion of the Cape Colony's eastern frontiers came to an end with the incorporation of Mpondoland in 1894. In total, 26 districts on the easternmost edge of the Cape Colony would be grouped together by colonial administrators in the first years of the 20th century to form the Transkei Territories, a 'Native Reserve' governed by a racially segregated system of indirect rule. During these years, a number of *Mfengu* fought with the settlers against the independent African

---

[4]   C. Bundy, *The Rise and Fall of the South African Peasantry* 2nd edn (London, 1988), p.237.
[5]   L. Callinicos, *Oliver Tambo: Beyond the Engeli Mountains* (Claremont, 2004), pp.26-8.

kingdoms during the frontier wars. Indeed, the forebears of Fikile Bam – a Robben Islander who shared a cell block with Nelson Mandela in the 1960s (of which more in Chapter Five) – received a farm in Transkei as a gift for supporting the Cape Colony in a small war against one of the African chieftaincies.[6]

From the final years of the 19th century, these prosperous African farmers were increasingly economically sidelined by segregationist policies. This process gathered pace when the Cape Colony was incorporated into the Union of South Africa at the turn of the 20th century. Moreover, they were slowly politically disenfranchised, losing the limited rights they had been granted under the provisions of the 1853 constitution.[7] This forced a reconfiguration of rural politics. 'Disappointed loyalists were [often] the bitterest 20th century rebels.'[8] The politically active *Mfengu*, who once 'would have been proud of their attributes and achievements as black Englishmen, were [now] seeking to affirm their African identities', having been chastened by racist repression.[9] Shula Marks writes that this 'era of segregation and disillusion... led to the creation of... an ethnic nationalism that coexisted in ambiguous fashion with... pan-South African black nationalism.'[10]

The exertions to define African nationalism were perhaps most prominent in the prestigious mission schools that had dotted the Native Reserves in the wake of colonial conquest. Transkei and the Eastern Cape had the densest concentration of mission schools in South Africa. The Methodists came first to Transkei. They set up half a dozen colleges, starting with Clarkebury College, the first mission station that was founded beyond the frontier in 1825 when the Thembu king, Ngubengcuka, granted them land. The Anglicans had almost as many – most notably St Johns College, established in 1879 on a bend of the Umtata River, a site that would also become the main town and administrative centre in the Transkei territories. The Catholics founded Mariazell College at the turn of the 20th century.[11] The Free Church of Scotland also had its own institution, founded in 1877 and named Blythswood after the Chief Magistrate of Fingoland. Indeed, the handsome stone house that was the home for Govan Mbeki's father was built by pupils of Blythswood College.[12] There were similar schools across South Africa: Adams College and Marianhill in Natal, for instance. The most famous school in southern Africa was Lovedale College, just outside the western borders of Transkei, in the beautiful Tyume Valley. This was alma mater to a slew of nationalist leaders because for a long time it was

[6] W. Beinart, *The Political Economy of Pondoland* (Johannesburg. 1982), p.154. Cf. C. Crais *White Supremacy and Black Resistance in pre-industrial South Africa* (Cambridge, 1992) J. Peires, *The House of Phalo: A history of the Xhosa people in the days of their independence* (Johannesburg, 1981).

[7] Bundy, *South African Peasantry*, pp.109-45.

[8] W. Beinart and C. Bundy, *Hidden Struggles in Rural South Africa: Politics and popular movements in Transkei and the Eastern Cape, 1890-1930* (London, 1987), p .8.

[9] C. Bundy, 'Schooled for Life? The childhood and education of Govan Mbeki' (Seminar Paper, Yale University, 2 December 1992), p. 38.

[10] S. Marks, *The Ambiguities of Dependence in South Africa: Class, nationalism and the state in 20th century Natal* (Baltimore, 1986). p. 111.

[11] R. Khandlhela, 'The Trappists in South Africa: A short overview', *Kleio*, 27 (1) (1995):56.

[12] Bundy, 'Schooled for Life?', p.1. Cf. S. Ngubentombi, *Education in the Republic of Transkei: Some origins, issues, trends and challenges* (Pretoria, 1989), pp.12-13.

the only school that offered an education up to university level. Just down the road from Lovedale was Fort Hare University, one of the first universities on the continent.

Missionary education was Janus faced. Though its schools had been set up to 'civilise' Africans, its printing presses also promoted a burgeoning vernacular culture. Moreover, schooling was an explosive topic because education was the domain in which the moral justifications for colonialism were stripped bare. Liberal notions that African pupils and white teachers shared a common humanity sat uncomfortably with another set of liberal ideas that lauded the superiority of white civilisations and cultures. Furthermore, demeaning ideas of segregation (dressed up as 'protecting native cultures') infused liberal pedagogy across the British Empire during the 1920s. Add to that the spartan living conditions that were the result of government parsimony, and the stage was set for protest. School riots broke out at Lovedale in 1919 and at Blythswood in 1929.[13] In reaction to British racism, Africans also self-consciously sought to renovate and promote their own cultures. Whilst he was a student at Fort Hare in the 1930s, Govan Mbeki translated Latin verse into Xhosa praise poetry. In 1936, three years after he had been elected the president of the African Teachers Association, Albert Luthuli founded the Society for the Study and Preservation of the Zulu Language and Culture at a meeting held under the auspices of the Natal Bantu Teachers Union.[14]

'It hardly needs to be said that... the emergence of nationalisms in both Africa and Europe have invariably been preceded by cultural revivals and the resurgence of patriotism and ethnic pride.'[15] However, the scale and scope of African patriotism was deeply contested by the intellectuals and politicians of the day. A number of the leading African nationalists of the 1930s and 1940s would later find themselves ensconced in the Bantustan project. Such were the restless, ambiguous nature of overlapping ethnic and nationalist identities.

African chieftaincies

If the political prominence of well-educated elites underscores the sense in which aspects of African nationalism were a colonial phenomenon, then the political journey made by Nelson Mandela offers an important counterpoint. Mandela's journey shows us how African nationalism was also rooted in a rural society that had been strained, but not broken, by colonial conquest.

---

[13] Bundy, 'Schooled for Life?', p. 9. Cf. P. Rich, *Race and Empire in British Politics* (Cambridge, 1986). A. Mager (Portsmouth, NH, 1999), *Gender and the Making of a South African Bantustan: A social history of Ciskei, 1945-59* (Oxford, 1986).

[14] Bundy, 'Schooled for Life?', pp. 39, 43. Cf. P. la Hausse *Restless Identities: Signatures of nationalism, Zulu ethnicity and history* (Pietermaritzburg, 2000), p.145. L. Vail, 'Introduction', in L. Vail (ed.) *The Creation of Tribalism in Southern Africa* (London, 1989), pp. 1-19.

[15] La Hausse, P., *Restless Identities*, p.1. Cf. H. Hughes, *The First President: A life of John L. Dube, founding president of the ANC* (Johannesburg, 2011). Marks, *Ambiguities of Dependence*, pp.42-73. H. Makoena *Magema Fuze: The making of a kholwa intellectual* (Pietermaritzburg, 2011).

Whilst many African kingdoms had been annexed and militarily defeated in the late 19th century, few were dismembered.

One significant factor for this was that colonial administrators in South Africa, like elsewhere on the continent, governed indirectly through the local chieftaincy. Historians have spilt much ink debating the nature of indirect rule. On the one hand, colonial officials tried to impose their favoured chiefs on the land and 'invent' new systems of chiefly authority that bolstered the colonial project. Moreover, the seeds of racial segregation – and ultimately apartheid – were contained in a political system that governed Africans separately. Yet at the same time, the strictures of indirect rule were not so tight – at least in the early decades of the 20th century. This was seen in the ambivalent relationship between colonial officials and the local chieftaincy.[16]

Nelson Mandela's childhood was deeply shaped by the contested nature of the chieftaincy. His father's family were members of the royal clan and councillors to the Thembu king. They traced their lineage to King Ngubengcuka (c.1790–1830), who had united the Thembu kingdom. The Thembu kingdom was a lose agglomeration of chieftaincies. Whilst chiefs within Thembuland acknowledged the paramountcy of the king (or 'paramount chief'), individual chieftaincies regulated their own affairs, operating through a lower level of headmen who, in turn, might hold autonomous authority over individual locations. The principle of power was patrilineal: paramount chiefs established their power by placing trusted kin as chiefs and headmen in key locations, binding loyalty through ties of kinship. Thus there were constant disputes over precedence within kingdoms and chieftaincies. Likewise, there was always the possibility that an autonomous chieftaincy might break away from one paramount and claim allegiance to another.[17] The interventions made by colonial officials in chieftaincy disputes added another layer of complexity to these wrangles. When Nelson Mandela was young, his father, Henry Gadla, fell foul of one such dispute when he was dismissed from his post as headman of Mveso location by the local white magistrate. Henry Gadla lost everything: his cattle, his four wives, his thirteen children. Mandela and his mother moved to live with her kinsfolk, until, shortly before his death in 1928, Harry Gadla arranged for the young Mandela to live with the Thembu Paramount Chief.[18]

The colonial system of indirect rule did not operate only through the

[16] S. Dubow 'Holding a Just Balance Between Black and White', *JSAS* 12 (2) (1983) pp.217-239. T. Ranger 'The Invention of Tradition in Colonial Africa', in E. Hobsbawm and T. Ranger (eds), *The Invention of Tradition* (Cambridge, 1983) pp. 211-259. T. Ranger, 'The Invention of Tribalism Revisited: The case of colonial Africa', in T. Ranger and O. Vaughn (eds), *Legitimacy and the State in Twentieth Century Africa: Essays in honour of A.H.M. Kirk-Greene* (London, 1993).

[17] For a description of Eastern Cape chieftaincies: Beinart, *Pondoland*, pp.9-22. Peires, *The House of Phalo*, pp.5-51. D. Hammond-Tooke, *Command or Consensus: The development of Transkeian local government* (Cape Town, 1975), pp.26-75. Contrast this to the tighter-bound Pedi, Swazi and Zulu polities: P. Delius, *The Land belongs to us: The Pedi polity, the Boers and the British in the nineteenth century Transvaal* (London, 1984). P. Bonner, *Kings, Commoners and Concessionaires: The evolution and dissolution of the nineteenth-century Swazi state* (Cambridge, 1983). J. Guy, *The Destruction of the Zulu Kingdom: The civil war in Zululand, 1879-1884* (London, 1979).

[18] Lodge, *Mandela*, p.2. Tom Lodge's biography gives Harry Gadla's death as 1928. Other biographers suggest either 1927 or 1930 – cf. D. Smith, *Young Mandela* (London, 2010), p.25.

chieftaincy. From 1895, a system of local district councils was introduced in Transkei in various stages. In 1931, all 26 of Transkei's districts were federated into the United Transkeian Territories General Council, colloquially known as the *Bunga* ('to discuss'). Every year when the *Bunga* was in session, the paramount chiefs of Thembuland, Western Pondoland and Eastern Pondoland would journey to Umtata to sit in the council, a handsome building in the centre of Umtata, whose foundation stone was laid in 1927. 78 more African delegates took part in the deliberations of the *Bunga* – some elected, others nominated according to a complex formula – along with the 26 white magistrates and the Chief Magistrate. It was responsible for agriculture and road building, funding its activities from locally imposed taxes.[19] Whilst the *Bunga* could only comment on the legislation drawn up in Pretoria that affected Africans – an indication of its impotence – Umtata became an important place of debate and discussion. It was through such networks that the Paramount Chief of Western Pondoland, Victor Poto (1898-1974), gained a wider political profile, sitting on the national bodies such as the Natives' Representative Council, along with politicians from across the country.[20]

This increasing bureaucratisation of chiefly power, centred on Umtata, drew educated elites and traditional leaders together. Victor Poto was one of the pioneers of this mode of politics. (Poto's father had sent him to be brought up and schooled by white missionaries to prevent the heir to the throne being harmed by witchcraft.) Increasingly, senior members of the chieftaincy selectively engaged with colonial society – some converting to Christianity, more sending their sons to school – in order to better preserve their own authority. In turn Poto employed a Lovedale graduate from a prominent *Mfengu* family, Tennyson Matywuku Makiwane, as his tribal secretary.[21]

Makiwane was one of a small but significant group educated elites, who used their connections to the chieftaincy to amass wealth and political prominence. He had bought land just on the outskirts of Umtata whilst teaching, then had moved to Umtata to work as a clerk in the *Bunga*, whilst pursuing market gardening on the side. 'His agricultural success might seem incidental,' writes Sean Redding, 'but the money earned from farming allowed his children to be educated and his wife to pursue her career as a social worker.'[22] Makiwane's son – Tennyson Xola Makiwane (b.1933) – would fly high in the ANC hierarchy before disagreement would bring expulsion and assassination in 1980. Another example was Columbus Madikizela, a school principal and a prosperous owner of trading stores and a fleet of buses, who was a close adviser to King Botha Sigcau, the king of Eastern Mpondoland. He sent his daughter,

[19] D. Hammond-Tooke, 'Chieftainship in Transkeian Political Development', *Journal of Modern African Studies*, 2, 4 (1964), pp.516-17.

[20] A. Paton, *Hofmeyr* (Oxford, 1964), p.432.

[21] F. Hendricks and J. Peires, 'All Quiet on the Western Front: Nyandeni acquiescence in the Mpondoland revolt', in T. Kepe and L. Ntsebeza (eds.), *Rural Resistance in South Africa: The Mpondo revolts after fifty years* (Cape Town, 2012), p.122. Cf. C. Murray, *Black Mountain*, pp.184-202.

[22] S. Redding, 'Peasants and the Creation of an African Middle Class in Umtata, 1880-1950,' *The International Journal of African Historical Studies*, 26, 3 (1993), p.535. Cf. Beinart, *Pondoland*, p.152.

Winnie Madikizela-Mandela (b.1936), to receive professional training as a social worker in Johannesburg, where she would become Nelson Mandela's second wife.[23]

▲ ▲ ▲

The other significant factor bolstering African chieftaincies in the early 20th century was the importance of land in rural politics. On the one hand neo-Marxist historians emphasised the dispossession of the African peasantry – particularly the 1913 and 1936 Land Acts – that turned the Native Reserves into labour reservoirs supplying South Africa's mines and factories with a source of cheap labour. They argued that South Africa's rapid economic growth in the industrial centres was made possible by the exploitation of the rural periphery. 'Revisionists', by contrast, offered a very different model, suggesting a far more ambivalent incorporation of rural society into the industrial economy. As much as labour migrants' cheap labour underpinned the South African economy, migrants tenaciously held onto their land and livestock in the Native Reserves, they suggested.[24] Indeed, black agricultural production increased in many of Transkei's districts during the early decades of 20th century, as migrant workers invested their wages in oxen and iron ploughs. During the 1940s almost half of the migrant labourers from one district working on the mines sent their entire pay-packet back to rural homes. William Beinart writes that one of the greatest ironies of early 20th century southern African history was that this pattern of labour migration – which would later become synonymous with the apartheid exploitation – had initially been favoured by many rural communities.[25]

Historically, the chieftaincy had derived its legitimacy from being the guarantor of African land rights. This continued after conquest with many traditional leaders presenting themselves as a bulwark that preserved African land and authority from the grasp of officials and settlers. A number of chiefs even purchased land for their communities outside the Native Reserves. As a result African communities tenaciously defended their land and 'imagined' customary laws by which they could hold the chieftaincy to account. 'Disputes of genealogy and succession were often intertwined with broader political issues. Chiefs who attracted popular following were likely to be those who resisted colonial intrusions'; though loyalists 'might have strong support in particular locations where there was a tradition of co-operation or Christian influence.'[26]

At the turn of the 20th century, rural politics was a localised affair, 'based on existing communal loyalties.'[27] By the 1920s and 1930s, a wider scale of

---

[23] Lodge, *Mandela*, p.76.

[24] H. Bradford, 'Highways, Byways and Cul-de-Sacs: The transition to agrarian capitalism in revisionist South African history', *Radical History Review*, 46, 7 (1990), pp.59-88. M. Murray, 'The Origins of Agrarian Capitalism in South Africa: A critique of the "social history" perspective', *JSAS*, 15, 4 (1989), pp.645-65.

[25] Beinart, *South Africa*, p.33. Beinart, *Pondoland*, pp.22-30, 145, 173-5.

[26] Beinart, *South Africa*, p.94.

[27] Beinart and Bundy, *Hidden Struggles*, p.33.

rural politics emerged. Victor Poto epitomises one strand of politics. He wrote a tribal history, *AmaPondo: Ibali neNtlalo* (1927), which 'strove to combine the best elements of chiefly tradition... with the most beneficial elements of European culture'. He spent one-fifth of his annual chief's stipend on a 'new Dodge car driven by a Native chauffeur'. His house was built in Cape Dutch style. He set up the Chiefs and Peoples party and founded the Nyandeni Farmers Association, although his attempts to organise an agricultural co-operative fell apart.[28]

Elsewhere, a series of protest movements swept across the South African countryside as various combinations of African peasants, educated elites and traditional leaders came together in a series of uncertain alliances protesting colonial intrusion. The Lovedale educated, millenarian preacher, Wellington Buthelezi, briefly gained great influence in a number of Transkei districts. The most organised movement was the Industrial and Commercial Union, which at its peak claimed 100,000 members. The Industrial and Commercial Union started in the Cape Town docks in 1919, and then spread rapidly into the countryside during the 1920s. It was strongest in rural Transvaal and the parts of Natal and the Eastern Cape where Africans were threatened with the loss of their land. (By contrast the ANC had little organisational presence in the South African countryside and would only become a mass organisation in the cities in the 1940s.) Leaders' stump speeches 'would declaim low wages... struggles to retain ancestral lands, the glory of great chiefs of the part – all juxtaposed in a single sentence.'[29]

In this sense, the ideas that infused the new forms of mass politics grew out of older, indigenous ideas of authority and leadership. Yet the equally abrupt collapse of the Industrial and Commercial Union in the 1930s – which rapidly fell apart after a corruption scandal engulfed it leaders – also speaks to the fissiparous nature of rural politics in the early 20th century.

'I am an African': nationalism compared

The world into which Nelson Mandela was born was one that was echoed elsewhere in Africa where regional elites were prominent in nationalist movements. This kinship was intimately felt across southern Africa as a network of friendship and familial links. The 19th century's wars and migrations gave these trans-national ties a deep history. The forebears of Govan Mbeki's wife, Epainette Moerane, hailed from Lesotho, where her great grandfather had been healer to Moshoeshoe I, who gathered the Lesotho kingdom around him in the face of the *Mfecane* and the frontier wars. At the turn of the 20th century the Moeranes had been Sotho colonists settling into an area that bordered Lesotho, Natal and the Cape Colony that was incorporated into the Transkei Territories in 1903. Elite education then strengthened these ties. Fort Hare University and the

---

[28] Hendricks and Peires, 'All Quiet on the Western Front', p.123. Elsewhere: Marks, *Ambiguities of Dependence*, pp.16-41. C. Murray, *Black Mountain*, pp.122-54.
[29] Beinart and Bundy, *Hidden Struggles*, pp.3-4. Cf. Beinart, *South Africa*, p.100.

foremost mission schools attracted the leading black students from across southern Africa during the first half of the 20th century. Black elites married across colonial boundaries; political and religious leaders attended each other's conferences. Take Govan Mbeki, whose first son, Thabo (b.1942), would pass through the best mission schools in the Eastern Cape and follow his father into ANC politics, eventually becoming the second president of South Africa in the post-apartheid era. By contrast Govan Mbeki's youngest son, Jama (1948 – 1982), who was sent to live with relatives in Lesotho at a young age, became an adherent of the Basotho Congress Party. These transnational ties made for a kaleidoscopic web of identities and connections. [30]

There were other parallels that connected South Africa's leaders with their fellows from further afield during the first half of the 20th century. First, many came from pre-colonial elites who had prospered despite the constraints of colonial rule. Economic accumulation was one source of prominence. Jomo Kenyatta, the first president of Kenya, for instance, came from the fertile, densely populated central highlands of East Africa, which became a thriving agricultural region. Likewise, Asante's cocoa growers played an influential role in Ghana's politics as a result of successful cash-cropping ventures. Educational advantage was perhaps even more important. African elites tended to invest 'in education, believing correctly that white-collar employment brought easier wealth and status.'[31] Julius Nyerere, the first President of Tanzania, for instance, was one of 26 children of a Zanaki chief, who obtained his education at the prestigious Tabora High School in the late 1930s. He later described his school as being as 'close to Eton as you can get in Africa'.[32] Many more nationalists across the continent would claim this honour for their *alma mater.*

Second, the racist underpinning of colonial rule, felt so sharply in missionary schools, catalysed black elites to conceive of a distinctly African nationalism. Albert Luthuli's Zulu Cultural Society, which he founded when a school teacher, was mirrored by countless other nationalists. A biographical sketch of Julius Nyerere notes that the Tabora school, which he attended, was 'was organised along strict and merciless hierarchical lines... The curriculum consistently stressed the white man's achievements – the obverse of which was... the black man's inadequacy.' In reaction Julius Nyerere conceived of *ujamaa* ('family-hood'): a communalist vision of African socialism. Nyerere's vision of communal African values was inspired by the Zanaki society within which he had grown up. 'He sought to synthesise these "traditional" values with Western elements in order to create a Tanzanian identity that would cut across ethnic lines.'[33] Most famously of all, Jomo Kenyatta wrote a thesis on

[30] M. Gevisser, *Thabo Mbeki: The dream deferred* (Johannesburg, 2007), pp.18-30, 447-51. Cf. Ranger, *Are we not also Men?*, pp.47-53. Z. Groves, 'Malawians in Colonial Salisbury: A social history of migration in central Africa, c.1920s-1960s' (PhD thesis, Keele University, 2011), pp.194-239.
[31] J. Iliffe, *Africans: History of a continent* (Cambridge, 1995), p.216.
[32] G. Mwakikagile, *Nyerere and Africa: End of an era* (Pretoria, 2010), p.80.
[33] V. Stoger-Eising, '*Ujamaa* revisited: Indigenous and European influences in Nyerere's social and political thought', *Africa*, 70, 1 (2000), pp.128, 143. More recently: E. Hunter, 'Revisiting

the ethno-genesis of his Kikuyu people, at the London School of Economics in the 1930s, supervised by the renowned anthropologist, Bronislaw Malinowksi. *Facing Mount Kenya* went on to become a touchstone of Kikuyu and Kenyan nationalism. Intriguingly, Kenyatta had a very different political philosophy to Nyerere. Kenyatta's conservative notion of *harambee* ('all pull together') derived from his experience of a far more competitive Kikuyu society, in which 'big men' supposedly created wealth that was shared within the community.[34]

Third, the pinch of colonial rule brought African elites closer to more popular protests. The tightening grip of the settler state provoked new political organisations in rural South Africa in the 1920s, from prophetic movements to trade unions. Elsewhere on the continent, a wave of political protests followed the Great Depression. 'Tax protests, rural revolts and millenarian movements followed, while cash crop producers organised "hold ups" directed against low prices and collusive European companies.'[35] Many African Christians left the missions to form their own independent churches. In Kenya, a bitter debate erupted over whether Christian converts should continue female circumcision practices. The underlying thread of many of these movements was a cultural nationalism of sorts: a search for distinctively African forms of 'local religion and political independence, frequently tinged with a renunciation of beliefs too closely identified with settler society' and colonialism.[36] The strictures of World War II – forced labour, crop requisitions and military conscription – followed by post-war colonial development schemes, so stringent that they were felt like a 'second colonial occupation', increased the pace of protest politics. Across Africa, nationalist leaders came to power on the back of these effervescent protests.[37]

'At long last, the battle has ended! And thus... your beloved country is free forever!' proclaimed Kwame Nkrumah at the midnight hour when Ghana became the first independent state in sub-Saharan Africa in 1957. But the course of subsequent events showed that the nation-state could not be taken for granted. Ethnic diversity – a particular theme of this book – proved a sore particular point for would-be-nationalists. Ideas of African independence from colonial interference, which had been the dynamo of many protest movements, were as likely to lead towards regionalist as towards nationalist politics. Take Ghana, where the sons of well-established families from the Asante region, known as 'Youngmen', had been supporters of the nationalist movement. But when Nkrumah took office and tried to tax Asante's rich farms to drive forward his plans of national development, the Youngmen mobilised the region against him. They drew on support from local paramount chiefs, who brought 'the

---

(contd) *Ujamaa*: Political legitimacy and the construction of community in post-colonial Tanzania', *Journal of East African Studies*, 2, 3 (2008), pp.471-85.
[34] Lonsdale, 'The Moral Economy of Mau Mau', pp.465-68. D. Branch, *Defeating Mau Mau, Creating Kenya: Counterinsurgency, civil war and decolonisation* (Cambridge, 2009), pp.117-47, 179-82, 206-7.
[35] Iliffe, *Africans*, p.220.
[36] Beinart and Bundy, *Hidden Struggles*, p.34.
[37] E. Schmidt, *Mobilising the Masses: Gender, ethnicity and class in the nationalist movement in Guinea, 1939-58* (Portsmouth NH, 2005), p.7. D. Low and J. Lonsdale, 'Introduction', in D. Low and A. Smith (eds.), *The Oxford History of East Africa* (Oxford, 1976), pp.1-64.

support of spirits and ancestors of the entire [Asante] nation'. Nkrumah was ousted by a military coup in 1966.[38]

'Once independence was achieved, nationalist sentiments, movements and parties [often] quickly faded away, leaving... a multitude of African ethnicities to fill the gap,' writes Adrian Hastings.[39] As the lustre of Africa's post-colonial independence faded, pessimists dismissed the whole transition. In recent years new histories have been written that reassess the anti-colonial movements and their legacies in post-colonial Africa. Even this writing is suffused by disenchantment: not so much reviving the hopes of the nationalist era, as considering the alternatives that were not taken.[40]

On a continent where the hopes of African nationalism were so quickly shattered, South Africa has often been held up as an exception. As William Beinart has noted, many South African historians argued that the discovery of diamonds in Kimberly in 1867 and gold at Witwatersrand in 1886 made South Africa unique. 'Mining and industrialisation have been their organising themes, together with the rise of new nationalisms, both Afrikaner and African.'[41] Indeed, the ANC had been founded in 1912, decades before comparable movements elsewhere in Africa. And the party's revival came in the 1940s when, for the first time, it developed a mass base in the overcrowded townships, during a decade of rapid industrialisation. Yet to focus solely on South Africa's burgeoning cities is to miss the importance of the 'Xhosa Nostra' and the other rural regional elites. 'I am an African,' proclaimed Govan Mbeki's most successful son, Thabo Mbeki, shortly before he became president of the newly-democratic South Africa. Thabo Mbeki's much-quoted speech spoke of a distinctly African nationalism. He drew on almost a century of political thought and practice, which connected his family's tangled history to the rest of the continent.

'The years of manhood'

In the 1940s and 1950s debates about the nature of nationalism and ethnicity took on new significance in South Africa. The new apartheid government, voted into office in 1948, categorised Africans by their racial and 'tribal' identities, turning the Native Reserves into fully-fledged tribal Homelands, as a strategy of shattering nationalist politics. Yet at the same time a rising group of African leaders, whose politics were forged in the middle decades of the 20th century, imagined alternative ways of conceiving nationalist politics. Nelson Mandela, Govan Mbeki and Kaiser Matanzima were prominent protagonists in

---

[38] J. Allman, *The Quills of the Porcupine: Asante nationalism in an emergent Ghana* (Madison, 1993), p.272. R. Rathbone, *Nkrumah and the Chiefs: The politics of chieftaincy in Ghana, 1951-60* (Oxford, 2000).

[39] A. Hastings, *The Construction of Nationhood: Ethnicity, religion and nationalism* (Cambridge, 1997), p.162.

[40] F. Cooper, 'Possibility and Constraint: African independence in historical perspective', *Journal of African History*, 49, 2 (2008), pp.167-96. J. Power, *Building Kwacha: Political culture and nationalism in Malawi* (Rochester, 2010).

[41] Beinart, *South Africa*, p.4.

these debates. Their different visions of nationalism and ethnicity would shape Transkei's politics in the coming decades.

Nelson Mandela would make his name as a lawyer and a leading member of the ANC Youth League in 1940s Johannesburg, pioneering mass based civil disobedience campaigns that revived the standing of the party in South Africa's townships. He arrived in a rapidly growing, industrialising city – at a time when colonial powers' demand for resources during World War II was transforming many of Africa's cities – and threw himself into the urbane circles of elite township society. In one sense, Mandela typified the anti-colonial politicians, described by Benedict Anderson, whose nationalism was ignited by being drawn into the circuits of the colonial/settler state.[42]

Yet Mandela's rapid rise in Johannesburg was due, in no small part, to a web of connections that stretched back to the Eastern Cape. His patron was Walter Sisulu, who was also born in Thembuland. Sisulu was prominent in Orlando Township, part of Soweto, as the leader of a choir, a member of a Xhosa homeboy association, and the leader of the local ANC branch. Sisulu acted as benefactor to the younger man, financially underwriting Mandela's studies at the University of South Africa and securing his employment as an articled clerk. From there Mandela set up a law firm with another Transkei born, ANC politician, Oliver Tambo. Practising as a lawyer in the 1940s, Mandela was in the cream of society. Just 2% of Johannesburg's African population could claim professional status. Nationwide there were just 18 qualified African lawyers in 1946. Even if there were township jokes about the pretensions of the elite 'Excuse Me', who used English terms, Mandela was not part of a middle class that segregated itself from its fellows. In South Africa's crammed townships, labourers lived cheek-by-jowl with teachers. Successful men, such as Mandela and Sisulu, ran open houses that provided shelter to kinsfolk, friends and dependents. It was a milieu in which Nelson Mandela, with his patrician bearing and talent for self-publicity, thrived. This triumvirate of Transkeians, Mandela, Sisulu and Tambo, would dominate the ANC for a generation. They came from different clans and, strictly speaking, would not have been considered homeboys in a rural setting; but the connections forged in Johannesburg had brought them together.[43]

As he moved into middle age, Nelson Mandela strengthened his connections to kinfolk in Transkei once again. Matters had once been very different. He had married his first wife, Evelyn Mase, in a simple civil ceremony in Johannesburg in 1943. But his second marriage to Winnie Mandela was very different. Her great-grandfather had been an Mpondo king in the mid-19th century, and her father, Columbus Madikizela, was an advisor to the incumbent paramount chief. When Nelson and Winnie married, they journeyed back to Mpondoland, where they were married in a ceremony that combined both Christian and ancestral rites. The ancestors had political potency too. When the ANC was derided by their rivals in the Pan African Congress for their close relationship

---

[42] B. Anderson, *Imagined Communities: Reflections on the origin and spread of nationalism*, 13th edn (London, 2003), pp.114-16. Chandarvarkar, 'Imperialism and the European Empires', p.165.
[43] Lodge, *Mandela*, pp.19-23, 28, 80.

with white sympathisers, Nelson Mandela posed in Thembu garb to stress his African identity.[44]

▲ ▲ ▲

Whilst Nelson Mandela was making his way in Johannesburg, another ANC stalwart tried to harness Transkei to the nationalist project. A winding road had taken Govan Mbeki home. In the 1930s he had refused to take up his father's headmanship, preferring instead to teach in Durban. Yet during his time in Durban, Mbeki was also writing *Transkei in the Making*, part history, part political polemic. Dedicated to 'the youth of my race', the book chastised the educated elite who attended Fort Hare on scholarships given by Transkei's *Bunga*, only to flee to the cities upon graduation. Thus Govan Mbeki returned to Transkei in December 1940, first taking a teaching post at Clarkebury College, then setting up a trading store. Rural co-operatives were much in vogue amongst some sections of the African left. In due course Mbeki would write a pamphlet extolling co-operative ideals: *Let's Do it Together*. African nationalism could be built on the communal institutions of peasant society, he believed. At Mbewuleni, Mbeki built a five-room, rectangular house and store. A contemporary recalled: '...you could see it for miles off, all whitewashed among the mud huts, like a beacon of light.'[45]

Govan Mbeki's project was also political. He got himself elected to the *Bunga* and joined the government-run, district cattle-dipping committee – an important institution in rural society where great store was placed on wealth held in cattle. Working together with local activists from the All African Convention (of which more in Chapter Two), Mbeki oversaw the revitalisation of associations which catered for well-to-do African professionals enmeshed in *Bunga* institutions. Set up in 1935 by a committee representing a broad spectrum of African organisations and chaired by the then ANC president, the purposes of the All African Convention initially had been to coordinate and promote African boycotts. By the mid-1940s, the All African Convention had taken on a life of its own. Its base was the Cape African Teachers Association which grew to 3,000 in 1952, incorporating around half of the total African teachers in the Cape. Many of the All African Convention's leaders came from the Transkei, and Govan Mbeki joined them in mobilizing their fellow professionals. Mbeki's aim was to 'draw the professional classes into better understanding of the working classes and their conditions'.[46]

Then everything went wrong for Govan Mbeki. In 1948, as the All African Convention's relationship with the ANC worsened, Govan Mbeki was ousted by his erstwhile allies, shattering his political base in the Transkei. Mbeki resigned from the *Bunga* in 1949, after an attempt to engineer a clash with government authorities on the cattle dipping committee failed. He also faced financial ruin. Colin Bundy suggests that Govan Mbeki's political activities left very little time

---

[44] Ibid. pp. 25, 76-7, photo 12.
[45] Gevisser, *Mbeki*, p.50. Cf. Bundy, 'Breaking the Midnight Slumber', pp.20, 32.
[46] C. Bundy, *Govan Mbeki* (Athens OH, 2013), p.63. Cf. Gevisser, *Mbeki*, pp. 52-4. Bundy, 'Breaking the Midnight Slumber', pp.5-16. J. Hyslop, *The Classroom Struggle: Policy and resistance in South Africa, 1940-90* (Pietermaritzburg, 1999), p.100.

to oversee the trading store. According to family legend, two calamities – a tornado then a fire in successive years – gutted the business.[47]

In the 1940s, Govan Mbeki's rural interest was marginalised within ANC leadership circles. After the upsurge of popular protest a decade earlier, the rural areas had been silent. 'Politically, [Transkei was] in a midnight slumber', Mbeki wrote to the president of the party. Mbeki's insistence that the ANC focus on rural mobilisation was not popular; he was not elected to the ANC leadership at its watershed conference in 1949. The hall was dominated by the urbane Youth League faction centred on Nelson Mandela. However, with the failure of his enterprise in Transkei, Govan Mbeki performed a political U-turn. 'The argument that such institutions [as the *Bunga*] should be used as a platform to fight the government is false,' he later wrote.[48]

Mbeki left the Transkei, eventually making his political home in the Eastern Cape city, Port Elizabeth. He arrived in a city that was a bastion of working class politics, and he threw himself into mobilising the townships and the migrant workers who came from the rural hinterlands of the region. Whilst Mandela rebuilt his relationships with Transkei's elite, Mbeki would not return to his trading store in the Transkei.

▲ ▲ ▲

Govan Mbeki's later hostility to the *Bunga* was inspired by his belief that Transkei's institutions had been hijacked by the apartheid government's project of separate development, designed to shatter South Africa into tribal fragments. In 1951 the Bantu Authorities Act established new tiers of 'tribal based' local government, strengthening the system of apartheid segregation and displacing the locally elected system of district councils. In 1955 the United Transkei Territories General Council (the old *Bunga*) accepted the Bantu Authorities system in principle. In 1957 the old *Bunga* was superseded by the Transkei Territorial Authority, largely composed of unelected traditional leaders.

Ironically, the prime advocate of separate development would be Nelson Mandela's close relative, Kaiser Matanzima. This was not immediately apparent. After graduating from Fort Hare University with a BA in Roman Law, Matanzima started his legal articles in 1940. The same year, he resigned to take up his late father's post as chief of the ama-Hala, a chieftaincy in the north-western districts of Thembuland that acknowledged the paramountcy of the Thembu king. Matanzima was the first chief in the whole of South Africa to sport a university degree. Constantly complaining about his niggardly chief's salary which rewarded hereditary rather than educational status, he got himself appointed into the old *Bunga* at Umtata in 1942. This was not satisfactory either, and he returned to his legal articles in 1944, winning the Cape Law Society prize for his results in the Attorney's Admission exam. Throughout this period Mandela and Matanzima remained in close contact,

---

[47] Gevisser, *Mbeki*, pp. 54, 67-8.
[48] G. Mbeki, *The Struggle for Liberation in South Africa* (Cape Town, 1992), p. 59. Cf. Gevisser, *Mbeki*, p. 67.

Mantanzima staying with Mandela whenever he visited Johannesburg.[49]

Kaiser Matanzima, however, never practised as a lawyer. Instead he seized hold of the opportunities offered by separate development, as the apartheid government slowly turned the Native Reserves into self-governing Bantustans. Matanzima had dabbled on the fringes of nationalist activism when he was a student at Fort Hare University, but by the early 1950s he had changed his mind. His reverse might seem opportunistic; but the ideas of African cultural nationalism, which had flourished at Fort Hare, often bounced, like a rugby ball (the game of the black elite in the Eastern Cape) in unexpected directions. 'I am a disciple of the creed of nationalism... Xhosa nationalism,' he later told a university audience. 'My heritage as a Thembu demands it.'[50]

During one painful, all-night interview, Nelson Mandela and Kaiser Matanzima formally debated their differences, with the senior speaking first, as Thembu etiquette demanded. 'I said... the government's policy was to try to put Africans into ethnic enclaves because they feared the power of African unity', remembered Mandela. 'Daliwonga's response was that he was trying to restore the status of the royal house that had been crushed by the British... He, too, wanted a free South Africa, but thought the goal could be achieved faster and more peacefully through the government's policy of separate development.' Matanzima's status as a traditional leader with a BA degree would make him a potent ally of the apartheid government, but bring him into bitter conflict with his erstwhile friend. 'We talked all night, but came no closer to each other's position,' remembered Mandela. 'As the sun was rising we parted.'[51]

---

[49] Lodge, *Mandela*, p.30. P. Laurence, *The Transkei: South Africa's politics of partition* (Johannesburg, 1976), p.5. B. Streek and R. Wicksteed, *Render Unto Kaiser: A Transkei dossier* (Johannesburg, 1981), p.111.
[50] Laurence, *The Transkei*, p.8.
[51] Mandela, *Long Walk to Freedom*, p.171.

2.   The First Bantustan
1954–1963

King Sabata and the Great Place Gang

In the 1950s, the Thembu kingdom was in the midst of a dispute – the chieftaincy split over the figure of King Sabata Dalindyebo (b.1928), the young paramount chief installed in 1954. Chieftaincy disputes were not unusual, but in the 1950s these clashes carried much broader significance. This was the decade in which apartheid government legislation laid the foundations for the creation of Bantustan self-governing territories, which followed in the 1960s. The Bantu Authorities Act of 1951 was unpopular because it established a system of Tribal Authorities: new tiers of segregated, local 'tribal' administration in which government-appointed chiefs took new powers. Most importantly, these new Tribal Authorities were used to force through rural Betterment schemes. These policies forcibly resettled scattered homesteads into concentrated villages, culled cattle and fenced in arable fields in an attempt to increase agricultural productivity. It 'constituted perhaps the most far reaching intervention into rural life since annexation and the introduction of taxes.'[1] Across South Africa, rural protests followed.

Traditional leaders throughout Transkei found themselves caught between popular protests and the apartheid government. Under these pressures many chieftaincies fractured along myriad lines. In Eastern Mpondoland a large revolt broke out against the incumbent king, Botha Sigcau, who had backed apartheid measures to the hilt. (This is discussed in more detail in Chapter Three.) In the most northern districts of Thembuland where the most powerful traditional leader, Kaiser Matanzima, had similarly aligned his fortunes with the apartheid government, local protestors were known as the Jacobins (*amayakopu*) and *Makhuluspani* (Big Team).[2]

The heart of the Thembu kingdom was different again. As the chieftaincy attempted to navigate a course between the rural protestors and the government, it splintered into contesting factions of traditional leaders and royal councillors. On the one side stood a party which looked towards Kaiser Matanzima and hoped to use the Bantu Authorities Act to undermine Sabata's authority. Against Matanzima stood various protagonists opposed to the Bantustan project, trying to influence Sabata to use his authority as the Thembu paramount chief to advance their cause. These councillors and advisers to Sabata were known as the 'Great Place Gang' by apartheid officials

---

[1] Beinart, *South Africa*, p.135.
[2] L. Ntsebeza, *Democracy Compromised*, p.187. Cf. V.Mqingwana and J. Peires, *Chris Hani Municipality Liberation Heritage Route: Icon site guide* (2008, n.p.), p.54.

– so called because the focus of their activities was Sabata's court, or 'Great Place', at his home of Bumbane, some 30 miles west of the main administrative town of Umtata.

This contest within the Thembu kingdom, and particularly the activities of the well-educated members of the 'Great Place Gang', provide us with an unusual insight into South Africa's mid-century rural revolts. Very often historians have focused on the protests *against* the apartheid government's brute imposition of state power. By contrast, this chapter contends that the connections forged between traditional leaders and *Mfengu* educated elites during the first half of the 20th century meant that conflicts within the Thembu kingdom also occurred *within* networks and institutions connected to the state. This chapter shows how Sabata's councillors connected Thembu politics into a wider web of institutions, networks and ideas – a politics of schoolrooms, law courts, and newssheets.

In 1940, Govan Mbeki had complained that Transkei was lying in political slumber. In one sense very little changed during the 1950s. Whilst many key leaders from the ANC had been born in the Transkei, the party had little political organisation here. The All African Convention was the most organised political presence in the Transkei for most of the 1950s, until it collapsed at the end of the decade, divided by an internal feud and crushed by apartheid repression. Nevertheless, if we shift our attention to the personal and political networks of the Eastern Cape elite a very different picture emerges. King Sabata's royal councillors were well connected to a wider network of African leaders from across the political spectrum. This would mean that the very localised and personalised conflicts within the Thembu kingdom would be freighted with a much wider political significance.[3]

'Uneasy lies the head that wears the crown'

From the outset, Sabata Dalindyebo's reign over Thembuland was marked by trouble. Most immediately, Sabata faced conflict within the royal clan of the Thembu kingdom. Sabata's mother had only been officially chosen as Great Wife (and thus mother to the next king) when she was found pregnant after the death of his father, King Jongilizwe. All his adult life, Sabata would suspect his brothers of harbouring ambitions of kingship. Personal conflicts intersected with apartheid policy as rival kinsmen tried to use the Bantu Authorities legislation to expand their influence. Sabata effectively blocked government plans to implement parts of the Bantu Authorities legislation that would dismember the district of Umtata – the centre of the Thembu kingdom – into four Tribal Authorities placed under the control of his adversaries.[4] Yet Sabata was unable to prevent the elevation of his half-brother, Bambilanga Albert Mtirara, to the headmanship of another Tribal Authority. 'There exists

---

[3] Focusing on the wide span of labour migrant networks, Delius makes a similar point: *A Lion amongst the Cattle*, pp.112-9, 131-3.

[4] CMT1483, 42/24, South Africa Police to Chief Bantu Affairs Commissioner (BAC), 19 August 1960, 'Minutes of Meeting held with senior chiefs', 20 September 1960. Cf. KGC88, *Reality*, March 1981, and Author interview, Mda Mda, Viedgesville, 3 November 2008.

a private vendetta' between the two, reported a government official, explaining this poisonous conflict.[5] 'Uneasy lies the head that wears the crown,' Sabata later wrote, meditating on lines of Shakespeare. 'I was only a young man from school with little life experience.'[6]

Sabata also faced the dismemberment of the districts that made up his kingdom. When the British had annexed Thembuland in the late 19th century, it was a strip of land that ran from the mountains that bordered Lesotho to the rolling hills along the Indian Ocean. These boundaries had broadly remained in place in the early 20th century, with the Thembu king the acknowledged paramount chief of six districts that lay within the Transkei territories – Cala, Cofimvaba, Engcobo, Umtata, Mqanduli and Elliotdale. (Thembuland also claimed two more districts that lay beyond the north-eastern borders of the Transkei territories, Glen Grey and Herschel.) However, in the wake of the Bantu Authorities Act, Elliotdale was broken off Thembuland and granted to the Gcaleka paramountcy.

Most worryingly for Sabata was the challenge posed by his older Thembu kinsman, Kaiser Matanzima. The Matanzima family had long been recognised as the senior chiefly line amongst the 'Emigrant Thembu' in the north-western districts of Cala and Cofimvaba. Kaiser Matanzima now argued that the Emigrant Thembu should split from Sabata's Thembuland under a separate chieftaincy. Matanzima hitched his star to the Bantustan project not least because the apartheid government had the power to make him an independent paramount chief who, under the Bantustan structures, would have almost equal stature to Sabata's kingship.

In this sense, the heart of Sabata's battle against Kaiser Matanzima was a defence of the Thembu kingdom against the Bantu Authorities Act and the apartheid government. It was crucial to Sabata's political identity that he was the legitimate heir and that Matanzima was from a subordinate branch of the Thembu kingdom. Visiting scholars were charmed by Sabata's royal touch and his fluency in the rituals of kingship. Sabata explained that the apartheid government's attempts to marginalise him would fail 'because I am in constant touch with my ancestors... Every morning I get up early... to pay my respects to my great-grandfather and ask for... protection against my enemies.'[7]

Yet at the same time, Sabata's political stance was more than a straightforward protest against state power. Sabata had close personal connections to a much wider web of councillors and advisors – African school teachers, lawyers, government officials and the like – who were embedded inside institutions of the state. This was the seedbed of the royal councillors whose influence apartheid officials feared so much.

There were four key members of the 'Great Place Gang', according to apartheid officials. We know least about McGregor Mgolombane, a teacher

[5] 1/UTA123, 1/1/5/21, Umtata Magistrate to Chief BAC, 5 June 1962. Cf. Commissioner General Transkei (KGT) to CMT, 5 June 1962, 11 July 1962, Procurer-General to S/Justice, 3 July 1963.

[6] KGT46, 1/1/3/3-1, Sabata Dalindyebo to Secretary for Bantu Affairs and Development (S/BAD), 14 July 1963.

[7] *TLA* (Umtata, 1964), p.168. Cf. CKC18, G. Carter, 'An account of a meeting with Chief Sabata, July 5, 1963'.

– only one thin file on him survives in the archives. But it is clear is that he was a 'troublemaker': a confident, well-educated man, who ambushed government officials during public meetings and consultations with pointed questions and speeches against the Bantu Authorities Act.[8] The two brothers, Anderson Joyi and Bangelizwe Joyi, were probably much closer to Sabata. The Joyi family was part of the ruling Thembu clan and held a chieftaincy in the strategically important district of Engcobo. The most important influence was Jackson Nkosiyane, a clerk and interpreter in government service who had been brought in to help with the administration of the Thembu kingdom. In his role as the Thembu king's private secretary, Nkosiyane held great power at Bumbane. He denied royal audience to contending councillors and postponed meetings of the Thembu Royal Council. Under his guidance, Sabata repeatedly delayed government plans to implement Bantu Authorities legislation.[9]

There was also a wider set of influences orbiting round the Thembu court. The ANC leadership – as represented by Thembu scions such as Nelson Mandela – had sporadic contact with Sabata. The All African Convention was far more influential. The key link between King Sabata and these wider networks of African politics was elite, secondary school education. During the late 1940s – whilst Sabata attended school – the All African Convention briefly flourished in the rural Eastern Cape, its base particularly concentrated in the upper echelons of the African teaching profession. The president of the All African Convention from 1948-59, Wycliffe Tsotsi, epitomised this professional trajectory. He had been headmaster of the prestigious Freemantle Boys High School in the rural Eastern Cape before switching to law. His close ally, Nathaniel Honono, had traced a similar path, as principal of Nqabara School, deep in Transkei's rural districts. Honono took charge of Sabata's education when, 'after a tempestuous school career', the latter was expelled from Healdtown, the century-old Methodist school. Honono became like a father to the young man; Sabata 'revered him'.[10]

Sabata never left a testament that systematically explained how he understood his relationship with the wider currents of African nationalism: we only have fragments of speeches and praise poems. But it is clear that the fused connections of family and schooling were also dear for two of Sabata's closest consorts, Bangelizwe and Anderson Joyi. Whilst studying at Lovedale College, *alma mater* to a slew of African nationalists, Bangelizwe Joyi had apparently joined the All African Convention. Anderson Joyi traced his political genealogy in the ANC from his time at Ohlange School. Many decades later, when Anderson Joyi came to give his testimony to the Truth and Reconciliation Commission, he explained his heritage in an intriguing fashion. First he recited his ancestors, from King Thembu to Sabata. Then he listed his teachers at the elite Ohlange Institute, tracing their lineage back to the founding president of the ANC, John Dube. The name of each ancestor and teacher was punctuated with the beat of his *knobkerrie* (the wooden staff which was the symbol of chieftaincy). 'Their

---

[8] CMT3/1483, 42/24/11/1.
[9] CMT1531, 56/A/11, Rose-Innes lawyers to Umtata Magistrate, 16 October 1959. Interview, Mda. CKC18, Canca, 'Memorandum'.
[10] DD 14 March 1963. Cf. R. Vigne, *Liberals Against Apartheid: A history of the Liberal Party in South Africa 1953-68* (Basingstoke, 1997), p.172; LMC, Box 1,'Dr WM Tsotsi'.

names give my story a shadow. Their names put what has happened to me in perspective. Their names say I am a chief with many colours.'[11]

'Uneasy lies the head that wears the crown,' Sabata had written, quoting lines of Shakespeare, perhaps taught to him by Nathaniel Honono.[12] In this phrase we have a hint of how elite schooling fused together the chieftaincy and educated elites, creating a web of dynastic ties that stretched far beyond chiefly lineages. This allowed a set of ideas about authority and the way society should work, which were associated with traditional leadership, to infuse the popular forms of African nationalism that took root in rural South Africa in the middle of the 20th century. Sabata was a barrel-chested man with a huge personal presence. When engaged, his charm and oratory could remind an audience of his praise name of *Jonguhlanga* (the Shepherd of the Nation).[13] Then Sabata seemed a king in the mould of a Xhosa praise poem or a Shakespearean drama. Even Professors Tom Karis and Gwen Carter – whose sharp, clear eyed, pen portraits of Transkei's leading politicians of the period are a valuable historical source – lost all academic reservations when they met him at his homestead.

> [We] were immediately taken by the person [of Sabata]. He has a curly black beard... His manner was charming, easy, hospitable, and yet very dignified... He obviously does not understand English as quickly or as well as Matanzima... [but] he seemed completely at ease, with none of the nervous tension so obvious in the former... He has an obvious pleasure at his people's response to him and they were much more outgoing than those with whom Kaiser came into contact... He has one main reaction: that he must be the mouthpiece of his people and, in addition, a very strong feeling for the dignity and role of a chief.[14]

Yet we must avoid romantic nostalgia. Mid-1950s Thembu court politics were poisoned by intrigue, as traditional leaders attempted to navigate a course between the rural protestors and the government. During meetings of the royal council, rivals traded threats. Prominent chiefs asked government officials for guns, fearing that their enemies were plotting their murder. Jackson Nkosiyane worried that Sabata was wavering.[15] Apartheid officials wrote that Jackson Nkosiyane 'played him [Sabata] like a harp,' belittling him 'in his absence when necessary to convince an audience.'[16] Thembu praise singers alluded to Sabata's troubled youth – 'his path lies strewn with broken bottles,' one sang – possibly a result of being surrounded by royal intrigue all his life. Government officials noted his various attempts to give up drinking. In 1955, the ANC in Johannesburg despatched Nelson Mandela from Johannesburg to see if he could patch together a reconciliation between his close relatives, Sabata and Matanzima. Mandela found Matanzima

[11] A. Krog, *Country of My Skull* (Johannesburg, 2002), pp.136-7. Cf. TRC-VH, Dalagube Joyi, Umtata, 20 June 1996 and author interview, Zoyisile William Nelani, Umtata, 6 November 2008.

[12] KGT46, 1/1/3/3-1, Sabata Dalindyebo to S/BAD, 14 July 1963.

[13] *DD* 14 March 1963.

[14] CKC18, 'Meeting with Chief Sabata.'

[15] 1/UTA118, N1/1/3/1, 'Notes from an interview held in Magistrate's office on Wednesday 28 June 1960.'

[16] CMT1483, 42/24, CMT to Secretary of Native Affairs (SNA), 12 December 1957.

unyielding. Sabata was in hospital, too ill (and perhaps too chastened) to talk politics. [17]

In this light, Sabata's quotation of the famous lines from the great Shakespeare play on kingship takes on a more forlorn meaning. In *Henry IV*, the young, dissolute Prince Hal is transformed by the crucible of war and responsibility into a heroic king. Sabata's political journey was far more difficult.

▲ ▲ ▲

Ultimately, Sabata had very little room in which to manoeuvre. Kaiser Matanzima's determination to secede the districts of Cala and Cofimvaba from Thembuland forced Sabata's hand. In 1956, he hosted one of the first setpiece clashes against the apartheid government at his Great Place at Bumbane. Some 30 miles west of Umtata, reached by an unmarked dirt road that wound along the side of a beautiful, steep-sided, open valley, Bumbane itself was a modest setting. Visiting a few years later, Tom Karis and Gwen Carter described the Great Place as 'a small, square run-down house', surrounded by 'three or four round huts... with people living in them in rather messy circumstances'. [18] On 10 February 1956, however, 'practically all the important chiefs and sub-chiefs in the Transkei' were in attendance at Bumbane, as well as 'a great crowd of local people'. The gathering opened with addresses from senior apartheid officials, explaining the necessity of the Betterment regulations and Bantu Authorities legislation. When their speeches were met with angry dissent and opposing orations, the senior government official in attendance 'tried to restrict the discussion... [T]he meeting ended in disarray'. [19]

A few days later, an indignant letter from the Chief Native Commissioner of South Africa in Pretoria demanded that Sabata should account for the meeting's disorder and discipline the dissidents. Jackson Nksoiyane fired off an equally truculent response. [20]

During the next few years, Sabata's councillors mustered all the firepower they could find in both legal process and customary practice in their attempts to derail Kaiser Matanzima from establishing himself as an independent chief under the Bantu Authorities Act. They submitted memoranda and petitions. They also organised a delegation, democratically elected at a meeting of the Thembu people, to go to Pretoria and protest against the implementation of the Bantu Authorities Act. An official commission of inquiry led by the Secretary of Native Affairs, C.B. Young, came to Transkei to investigate the genealogy of the Thembu kingdom. The question at hand was whether the Matanzima branch was deserving of an autonomous chieftaincy entirely independent of the main Dalindyebo stem of the Thembu kingdom. The government fiddled the rules to get their way. Sabata Dalindyebo's supporters 'decided to make a show of strength so they came to Umtata, the largest town in the region and seat of government, and camped by Fort Gale.' The government officials refused to

[17] *DD*, 14 March 1963. Cf. Mandela, *Long Walk to Freedom*, p.171.
[18] CKC18, 'Meeting with Chief Sabata'.
[19] CKC18, Canca, 'Memorandum', paragraph 36.
[20] Ibid, paragraph 37.

meet with them in the veldt. After a difficult debate, the Thembu group decided to send a delegation into the town itself. They had been outmanoeuvred. Despite bringing legal support, 'only members of the Thembu Royal family were allowed to speak' at the commission hearings. The Young Commission found in favour of Kaiser Matanzima.[21]

Finally, the Chief Magistrate of Transkei decided to cauterise the influence of Sabata's closest councillors. 'On 30 May 1958, Thembuland wakened to the startling news' that Jackson Nkosiyane, McGregor Mgolombane and the Joyi brothers 'had been deported and removed from their homes', banished to a remote area of Transvaal.[22] Three months later, Sabata was forced to install Matanzima as a fully independent chief in an angry ceremony which was only carried through with brute force. The Chief Magistrate reported:

> The proceedings went well until Sabata in his speech said 'I bring Chief Matanzima to you'... There was uproar from about 200 in the crowd of approximately 1500... A call was sent to neighbouring districts for [police] reinforcements. During the adjournment supporters of the [pro-Matanzima] chiefs armed themselves with clubs made from branches of neighbouring trees, on seeing which the malcontents withdrew and disappeared. When the additional police had arrived, order was restored and the instalment ceremony proceeded without further hitch.[23]

Rural politics – schoolhouse, courtroom, newssheet

Matanzima's instalment as an autonomous chief of Western Thembuland, with new powers over the districts of Cofimvaba and Cala was intolerable to Sabata's close supporters. 'The star of the collaborationist... ascended from nowhere to a pinnacle hardly distinguishable from that of the Paramount Chief himself.'[24] From his Great Place at Qamata, Matanzima set about stamping his authority over Western Thembuland by forcing the locations in his domain to accept land Betterment schemes. These provoked a series of local protests against state policies. Historians have focused on these rural conflicts over natural resources; on acts such as cutting barbed wire fences and torching state forests.[25] But at the same time it is also noticeable that rural Betterment policies were debated and contested in other domains – in schools, courtrooms and newssheets. And it is to these nodes and networks that we turn.

The influence of schools, courtrooms and newssheets in rural politics speaks to the importance of the connections forged between traditional leaders and African educated elites during the first half of the 20th century. This made for a dense network. Nelson Mandela recalls that even the remote village of Qunu, where he spent the first nine years of his life in the 1920s, had two small

[21] CKC18, Canca, 'Memorandum'. Interview, Mda.

[22] CKC18, Canca, 'Memorandum'. Cf. Ntsebeza, *Democracy Compromised*, pp.156-7.

[23] CMT1484, 42/27, CMT to SNA, 14 August 1958.

[24] CKC18, Canca, 'Memorandum'. A detailed account of the revival of chieftainship in Xhalanga/Cala is provided by Ntsebeza, *Democracy Compromised*, pp.131-174.

[25] J. Tropp, 'Displaced People, Replaced Narratives: Forest conflicts and historical perspectives in the Tsolo district, Transkei,' *JSAS*, 29, 1 (2003), pp.207-33.

primary schools which were presumably attached to local mission stations. Another important institution in rural life was the general trading store, once restricted by government statute to white general dealers, but from the 1940s also open to African proprietors such as Govan Mbeki. In 1932 there were 650 general trading stores dotted across Transkei. When the famous anthropologist, Monica Hunter, conducted her doctoral research on rural Pondo society in the early 1930s, she spent hours in these stores gathering stories and gossip.[26] There were also the 26 administrative towns in each of Transkei's magisterial districts. These towns were racially zoned, protecting white-owned businesses that thrived from African traffic. But small African businessmen such as Alfred Xuma (1893-1962), the president of the ANC in the 1940s, whose family ran an eating house in the town of Engcobo, thrived on the margins. The largest settlement in the Transkei Territories was Umtata, a town of 13,000 by 1956.[27]

Kaiser Matanzima clearly realised the significance of these networks in Thembuland's politics for he set about reorganising the small primary schools that were dotted around his districts, forcing them into the new administrative structures of the apartheid government's new Bantu Education policies. In turn, many of the protests against Matanzima were often led by the school principals and teachers.

To understand the interwoven nature of these protests, it is essential to consider the important role of the small primary schools in Transkei's social landscape in the early 20th century. In 1954, there were 1,430 schools and 4,300 teachers for the 171,000 African pupils in Transkei's school districts (up from 2,300 teachers and 69,000 pupils in 1932). Across South Africa, pupil numbers quadrupled from 209,000 in 1925, to 353,000 in 1935, and then to 884,000 in 1953. In the same decades, African population numbers doubled from approximately 4.7 million to 6.6 million to 8.6 million. For the majority, a few short years of schooling would be their only taste of education. Indeed, South Africa's primary schools only admitted 37% of their age cohort in 1953.[28] However, tiny schools, often mere zinc-roofed shacks, were sprouting in Transkei's rural locations. Children would run out of class to tend their cattle. After school, they 'swam in a muddy pool in the murky stream around our homes amid the cacophony of croaking frogs'.[29]

The primary school Junior Certificate exam was a passport to prestigious, white collar employment, making these the small schools dotted across rural Transkei an important focus for African aspiration. For example, Miss Mpoko in Cala district established a primary school at the Zigudu mission station in 1933, first taking teaching up to Standard II, and then slowly taking more classes until she was able to teach all the way through to the prestigious Junior

[26] E. Haines, 'The Transkei Trader', *South African Journal of Economics*, 1, 2 (1933), p.203.

[27] S. Redding, 'South African Blacks in a Small Town Setting: The ironies of control in Umtata, 1878-1955', *Canadian Journal of African Studies*, 26, 1 (1992), p.80. Cf. Author interview, Ezra Sigwela, Pretoria, 27 August 2009.

[28] BEK3, CE472, 'Bantu Education: Inspector-Supervisory field staff for Cape and Transkei regions', 11 January 1954. Cf. Bundy, 'Schooled for Life', p.11; J. Du Preez, 'The Education System in Transkei: A needs assessment' (Master's thesis, University Orange Free State, 1980), p.32; Beinart, *South Africa*, p.262; and E. Unterhalter, 'Bantu Education, 1953 – 1989', in H. Wolpe and E. Unterhalter (eds.), *Apartheid Education and Popular Struggles* (London, 1991), p.39.

[29] *DD* 1 November 1984.

Certificate exam. Her 33-year career produced 64 pupils who passed this exam and went on to become 'teachers, clerks, nurses, BA [graduates] and religious sisters'. Her most famous pupil was Chris Hani (1942-1993), the future ANC guerrilla leader (of whom more in Chapter Six). The son of a poor migrant labourer, Hani started his school career walking four hours each day to and from school.[30]

Miss Mpoko's career shows how South Africa's localised provision of education placed schoolhouses at the centre of rural communities, with the authority of school principals melded together with the power of the chieftaincy. This was not the centralised European pattern of state-building, in which a Paris-appointed teacher journeyed to remote provinces and turned peasants into Frenchmen. Instead, the South African experience was an organic, cellular affair: strong local leaders, motivated by ideologies of self-help, built a series of schools and strong communities, which together comprised the state.[31] Although the smallest school had notionally been brought under the control of the Cape Province in the middle of the 19th century, the state had only been responsible for setting examinations, inspecting schools and subsidising teachers' salaries. The successful principals of the era were benevolent patriarchs and matriarchs. They levied taxes and raised funds, often working through local chiefs in order to erect new buildings and hire additional teachers. Conversely, disputes over schooling were likely to be every bit as destabilising as those of the local chieftaincy (with which they sometimes intertwined).[32]

The Bantu Education Act of 1953 attempted to overturn this delicate model of local education provision. Most immediately, the provisions of the act allowed pro-government chiefs, such as Kaiser Matanzima, to try to exert control over school teachers in the regions where they held power. This was because individual schools were placed under the authority of newly introduced Tribal Authorities and School Boards (on which traditional leaders served). However, by tying schooling into the heart of the chieftaincy, it was caught up in the wider conflicts around the Bantu Authorities Act. Rural communities were urged to boycott all apartheid-inspired institutions. Across vast swathes of Thembuland and the rest of Transkei, school committees ground to a halt in the mid-1950s as members resigned, in fear of their lives.[33]

Moreover, the apartheid government's interference into African schools provoked deep anger within many rural communities. In one sense some sort of centralisation of control had been necessary. The inexorable growth of African primary schooling required more government funding and intervention. Few teachers were as skilled as Miss Mpoko – the renowned reputation of a few schools 'should not obscure the fact that most mission schools were poor

[30] UNISA, Ntonjeni Accession, file titled: 'MSS *Instimbi Xhosa News,'* untitled article (November 1974). Cf. J. Smith and B. Tromp, *Hani: A life too short* (Johannesburg, 2009), pp.11-4.
[31] This ideology is set out in KGT124, 12/1/5, 'Masizakhe – Alice Circuit 1967'.
[32] Author interview, Bukhosi Mabandla, King William's Town, 17 November 2008.
[33] 1/UTA167, 12/1/2-2, Umtata Bantu School Board Meeting minutes, 2 August 1956. See also /ECO6/1/1, 1/1/3, Engcobo Magistrate to CMT, 14 March 1955. Ntsebeza, *Democracy Compromised*, pp.125-6, 132-8.

primary schools with large dropout rates'.[34] However, African politicians opposed to apartheid effectively (and correctly) portrayed Bantu Education as second-rate. Not only were black pupils inadequately funded compared to their white counterparts in government schools but apartheid policy forced African children to study a segregated, inferior syllabus. 'When we speak of freedom... we mean the enjoyment of the privilege of a proper education... we mean the right to obtain extensive land', explained pamphlets the ANC issued in idiomatic isiXhosa, which found their way into Thembuland and into the files of government officials.[35]

With schoolhouses close to the heart of community life in rural Transkei, local campaigns against Bantu Education became entwined with conflicts over rural Betterment policies and the Bantu Authorities Act. This was seen at Emnxe location in the Cala district of Western Thembuland. When Betterment planning was promulgated here in the mid-1950s, it became 'the centre point of all the agitation' in the region. The issue 'became a very powerful weapon in the hands of the agitators' a government official regretted. 'They used it to sabotage... the establishment of Bantu Authorities.'. Next, they 'refused to co-operate with the newly appointed school committee' formed under Bantu Education legislation and formed a rival committee under George Msengana, the school principal. Msengana was a member of the All African Convention. His assistant teacher was suspected to be an ANC militant who organised conspiratorial meetings in the school room at nights and wrote threatening letters to their enemies.[36] Another prominent leader was Abel Ntwana, a migrant labourer who had retired to Emnxe to run a small trading store. The magistrate described him as 'fairly well educated and financially well off, and the great influence he wields amongst the residents... can be attributed to these factors.'[37] 'He has great influence of the anti-Bantu Authorities group and they obey him as if he is royal blood,' explained another informer.[38]

The localised model of school provision meant that as both sides mounted campaigns of intimidation, power leaked from one sphere into another, turning Emnxe into a morass of antagonism. Local rivals accused the other of self-interest and corruption, which threatened the local community. One dissident teacher thrashed the daughter of a rival. The child's right hand swelled up and all her finger nails fell off. Principal Msengana failed the pupils of his pro-government rivals, apparently telling them:

> Their parents are running up and down to the Great Place of Kaiser Matanzima. When he comes to Cala, all the fat stock are killed... and the teachers are not invited to those feasts... Your arse is leaking with the fat of the sheep and the cattle which are being killed for Matanzima.[39]

[34] Hyslop, *The Classroom Struggle*, pp. 8-11.
[35] KGT64, 1/9/2-1, *Izwe Lomzi*, 14 June 1961. CMT1470, 42, '*Izwe Lomzi – The year of blood and tears: 1960*'.
[36] CMT1471, 42/1, 'Affidavits re Unrest,' 1 March 1961 – both Msengana and another teacher, Dyanti, are referred to as principals of schools in the location.
[37] CMT1484, 42/27, Security Branch to Cala Magistrate, 16 September 1958.
[38] CMT1484, 42/27, Statement of George Kolaniso, 24 August 1960. Cf. Ntsebeza, *Democracy Compromised*, pp.175-94, 200; interview, Sigwela.
[39] CMT1471, 42/1, Affidavits, 1 May 1961.

In 1961, these tensions boiled over into outright violence when Matanzima's vigilantes attacked Emnxe; the violence swept through the location.[40] It was an unequal conflict. The official pro-Matanzima school board dismissed the dissident teachers without explanation. For good measure, acting in his capacity as a chief, Kaiser Matanzima also banished the teachers. Principal Msengana left for Swaziland. Abel Ntwana fled to Lesotho. The police rounded up and detained even more, crushing resistance in the district.[41]

▲ ▲ ▲

Events at Emnxe show how schoolrooms often became bound up in wider rural protests. Elsewhere in Western Thembuland, a number of Sabata's advisers who were from the All African Convention extended their influence into local politics by providing legal support to rural communities resisting Betterment policies. Indeed there was a longstanding pattern of politics in which rural communities had hired lawyers to settle local chieftaincy disputes. Just as schoolrooms had become the centres of many rural communities, so politically active lawyers hoped to make local courtrooms a focus for political mobilisation and to entwine the authority of professional lawyers with the power of local traditional leaders.

In February 1961, a serious clash occurred in Cofimvaba district when Kaiser Matanzima 'ordered the residents of Ndlunkulu, Qitsi and Qwebeqwebe locations… to remove from their old homes and settle in new areas for the purposes of land stabilisation' and betterment measures. After the communities refused to obey Matanzima, they were fined in his tribal court for 'disrespect, contempt and ridicule,' and then served with deportation orders by apartheid officials.[42] 'Ah Jonguhlanga,' announced a letter written to King Sabata. 'Sir – Thou Great One of the Thembus! Things are bad among your children [at] this end as you gave them over to the Right Hand House [of Kaiser Matanzima]. They are badly treated.'[43] Anonymous letters threatened the headman of Qitsi with death.[44] The dissident communities clubbed together and hired a lawyer from the All African Convention, Richard Canca, to defend them in court.

Canca's political path epitomises the trajectory of the All African Convention in the Transkei during the middle years of the 20th century. Born in Transkei in 1924, he had attended one of the leading mission schools in the Eastern Cape before taking a degree at the University of Cape Town, emerging as a stalwart of the All African Convention, which was strong in the city. When Canca first returned to Transkei in the late 1940s, he taught at Nqabara School

---

[40] CMT1471, 42/1, 'Report on Unrest – Xalanga,' 1 March 1961, 'Affidavits regarding unrest at Emnxe location, Xalanga', 3 June 1961. CMT1484, 42/27, statement by George Kolaniso, 24 August 1960. Interview, Sigwela.

[41] 'School board dismissed': CMT1471, 42/1, Affidavits enclosed in letter, Cala BAC to CMT, 1 May 1961. 'Teachers banished': CMT1473, 42/Q, Divisional Commander, South African Police to Chief BAC, 2 February 1962. Disappearance of Msengana and Ntwana: CMT1484, 42/27, BAC Cala to Chief BAC, 4 March 1961, 26 September 1961. 'Crushing resistance': Ntsebeza, *Democracy Compromised*, pp. 212-50.

[42] All quotations from CKC18, Vigne, 'Memorandum'.

[43] CMT1481, 42/20 Part 1, Letter to Sabata Dalindyebo, (n.d. 1961).

[44] Mqingwana and Peires, *Icon Site Guide*, p.54.

under Nathaniel Honono and edited the journal of the Cape African Teachers Association. However, the Cape African Teachers Association was shattered in 1955 when the apartheid government forced fifteen of its leading activists, including Canca, to leave the profession because of their opposition to Bantu Education policies. Like many other teachers in the All African Convention who were expelled from the profession, Richard Canca turned to law and took articles under Wycliffe Tsotsi.[45]

Richard Canca prospered as a lawyer inside the Transkei during the following decades. The administrative centres in the Native Reserves offered at least as many opportunities as Johannesburg, where apartheid's urban restrictions made for a precarious existence. Prosperous Africans, clustered in the professions around the *Bunga*, owned property in Umtata and offered lucrative opportunities for a new generation of African lawyers who took on their business. In 1946 there were only 18 African lawyers in all of South Africa; by 1960 there were 50, and from the scanty records we have it seems that at least one-third were based in Transkei at this time.[46]

Canca was part of the self-proclaimed progressive wing of the All African Convention: part of 'the new generation of African intelligentsia that [saw] their own disabilities as being inextricably bound up with the disabilities of their own people.'[47] Travelling into the areas such as Ndlunkulu, Qitsi and Qwebeqwebe on legal cases, Canca and his colleagues would be welcomed by rural communities: 'These educated people are not lost; they are truly on our side.'[48] It was a double-edged compliment. Popular epithets would mock 'the show-off, educated', for too much learning could purge the humanity out of a person.[49] On the other hand, professional learning could be used for the service of the community. Wycliffe Tsotsi, for one, was jokingly known as the 'Chief of the Thembus' for the work he did in his district. Looking for a way to explain the changing social landscape of the Transkei, Canca coined an arresting phrase: 'Chiefs have been reconciled to their position of equality with educated commoners in the leadership of their people.'[50] Other lawyers were more forthcoming: 'Lawyers have very high prestige and you will find at weddings people are anxious to please them... They invite me into their homes for advice... People take it for granted that I am a leader.'[51]

Yet Transkei's lawyers-cum-politicians were in a precarious position. Emergency legislation introduced in various guises across South Africa – specifically Proclamation R400 of 1960 for the Transkei – conferred

---

[45] Author interview, Richard Canca, Dutywa, 7 November 2008. Cf. South African History Online, 'Biography – Richard Canca', n.d., Hyslop, *The Classroom Struggle*, pp.100-5.

[46] The other centres of the African legal practice were Durban and Johannesburg. See A. Sachs, *Justice in South Africa* (London 1973), pp.209-12. L. Kuper, *An African Bourgeoisie: Race, class and politics in South Africa* (London, 1964), p.79. Lodge, *Mandela*, p.28. J. Uys, *Biographical Directory of South African Lawyers* (Johannesburg, 1970).

[47] LMC, Mqotsi, 'Tsotsi'.

[48] Interview, Mda.

[49] Z. Ngwane, 'Apartheid Under Education', in P. Kallaway (ed.), *A History of Education Under Apartheid, 1948-1994* (New York, 2004), p.278.

[50] CKC18, Canca, 'Memorandum'.

[51] Interview, Canca. Cf. Kuper, *An African Bourgeoisie*, p.126; Mqingwana and Peires, *Icon Site Guide*, p.41.

sweeping powers to individual traditional leaders. Travelling across Western Thembuland, Canca had to evade bands of young toughs, hired by Matanzima, who had 'assaulted many of the chief's enemies'. A photo from the period shows a government truck careering down a dirt road, its trailer loaded full with twenty-odd men brandishing knobkerries and assorted weapons. A 'lorry-load of Chief Matanzima's supporters', is the laconic accompanying caption.[52] As a result, 'most of the peasants [at at Ndlunkulu, Qitsi and Qwebeqwebe] were terrified to give evidence or even be seen to be talking to defence lawyers.' Moreover, Proclamation R400 allowed apartheid magistrates and police officers to arrest and detain individuals for an unlimited period. When Canca tried to meet his thirty-two clients who had been banished by Matanzima, he found that twenty had subsequently been jailed. He had to bring the others out of hiding. Fifteen days later, he brought them before the Bantu Commissioner's Court, only to see all of his clients re-arrested at the door of the court.[53] As at Emnxe, Kaiser Matanzima stifled the protests at Ndlunkulu, Qitsi and Qwebeqwebe.

▲ ▲ ▲

Political newssheets were also deeply important in Thembuland's politics. Govan Mbeki's career gives us insight into this medium, for he had played a persistent part in political journalism during the middle decades of the 20th century. In the late 1930s, when living and working in Durban, he had written for and edited the *Territorial Magazine*, later renamed *Inkundla ya Bantu* (African Forum). It was the first black-owned newssheet in the country, circulated mainly in the rural parts of the Eastern Cape and the southernmost parts of KwaZulu and Natal. When Mbeki returned to Transkei in the 1940s, he continued writing about his political activities for *Inkundla*. After his venture running a general trading store in Transkei failed in 1955, Mbeki moved to Port Elizabeth where he ran the local office of the *New Age* newspaper. He built his political base in the sprawling townships of the port and industrial city among the migrant workers from the rural Eastern Cape and the Transkei, giving him strong connections into rural politics. He regularly drove into Transkei on political business. He also gathered news stories. During the height of anti-Bantustan protests, *New Age* ran, on average, one news item on Transkei in each of its weekly issues.[54]

In one sense, political newssheets such as *New Age* were marginal compared to the white-owned, commercial press that catered for a black readership. Many of the famous missionary and independent journals, such as *Imvo Zabantsundu* (founded 1884), and *Ilanga lase Natal* (founded 1903), had collapsed or been bought out by media conglomerates during the Great Depression. By 1952, the Bantu Press (the largest media group catering for black audiences) had a stable of twelve newspapers, as well as another dozen periodicals that were

---

[52] SADET, *The Road to Democracy in South Africa, Volume I*. (Cape Town, 2004), photos between pp.356-7.
[53] CKC18, Canca, 'Memorandum'.
[54] CKC17 – Typewritten notes on the Transkei taken from issues of *New Age*.

published in eleven languages. Their premier weekly newspaper, *Bantu World*, took up one quarter of the African newspaper market, and similarly soaked up the main share of advertising revenues. By contrast, the few African political journals that survived between 1936 and 1960 were 'marginal commercial enterprises and circumscribed in terms of news coverage, distribution and numbers.'[55] The *New Age* sequence of newspapers was the most resilient, with a nationwide circulation of 50,000 at its height, yet even this publication had been repeatedly banned, appearing under half a dozen names. Most political newssheets lasted less than a year.

Nonetheless, political newssheets were a thorn in the side of Kaiser Matanzima. The local magistrate for Cala district even set up a specific file (N1/1/3-1) in his office for correspondence related to Matanzima's attempts to sue various newssheets. In one letter Matanzima complains about two articles in *Contact*: 'Kaiser Matanzima: Transkei Tyrant', and 'Transkei Tyranny'. *Contact* was a journal published by the Liberal Party of South Africa in Cape Town, another city full of Transkeian migrants. In another instance, the Chief Magistrate of Transkei investigated whether *Umthunywa* could be prosecuted for a slanderous praise-poem written in its pages.

In 1960, Matanzima pursued a court case against Richard Canca, during the time he was a director of a short-run political journal, *Indaba eMonti*, published by the All African Convention. They had published an article claiming that 'the greatest traitor belonging to the Bantu Authorities is Kaiser Matanzima.'[56] That stories published in *Indaba eMonti*, *New Age* and *Contact*, published in East London, Port Elizabeth and Cape Town, some 230km, 480km and 1200km from Umtata respectively, gave Matanzima such pain, indicates the length of these print networks.

The recollections of Ezra Sigwela (b.1940) about selling and occasionally passing-on news stories to Govan Mbeki at *New Age* give us an intimate sense of how these newssheet networks operated. Sigwela came from a prosperous, well connected family. His mother was a scion of the ruling Thembu clan. He had been schooled at Healdtown in the late 1950s, where the ANC Youth League, under the influence of Ambrose Makiwane, was initiating schoolboys into party membership in the bush at night. Sigwela's father had bought a thriving eating house in Engcobo town that had once been owned by Alfred Xuma, the past president of the ANC. Sigwela had started off by occasionally selling a stack of *New Age* magazines that were given to him by Ambrose Makiwane. At home in the school holidays, Sigwela had passed messages between Sabata's councillors, walking long distances across country or riding the rattling buses that plied their trade between Transkei's towns. Sometimes he was entrusted with a note destined for Govan Mbeki.[57]

Ezra Sigwela's foray into journalism was prompted by another bitter conflict: the apartheid Betterment policies at the neighbouring Mputi and Baziya locations in Engcobo district. It was a complex dispute, going back to

[55] I. Ukpanah, *The Long Road to Freedom: Inkundla ya Bantu and the African nationalist movement in South Africa, 1938-51* (2005), p.7.
[56] 1/XAA48, N1/1/3-1.
[57] Interview, Sigwela.

the 19th century, as to which headman in the area enjoyed precedence over the others. Many of the powerful Joyi family – which included two of Sabata's closest councillors, Bangelizwe and Anderson Joyi – were leading adherents of the anti-Betterment party. Their rivals, Absolom Yengwa and Spalding Matyile, were in favour of government policy. When the government authorities decided to enforce forestry regulations more strictly, these tensions erupted. In 1959, cattle roaming in the forest were impounded by government-paid forest guards. When a counter-raid was mounted by a group armed with battle axes, assegais and sticks, the guards shot two men dead and wounded two others. A few months later, one of the forest guards and his wife were murdered in their bed.[58] Marelane Joyi, the headman of Mputi location, told a meeting not to accept Betterment policies, urging them 'to do-away with any headman that supports it'. Joyi's rival at Baziya Mission, Absolom Yengwa, 'forbade his people to attend' this meeting. 'It was then that things started going wrong' for Yengwa, a local man explained. Absolom Yengwa's kraal was destroyed in September 1960.[59] That same month, the pro-government headman of the neighbouring Mbashe location, Spalding Matyile, was also attacked. Both men fled into Engcobo town.[60]

Staying at his father's guesthouse, Sigwela was perfectly positioned to follow local political developments in detail and pass on reports. Transkei's bustling small towns were the nerve centres of the rural districts. They brimmed full of news, stories and gossip. Many government officials who worked for the district magistrate took dinner at the Sigwela's guesthouse; some even came for breakfast. When chiefs came into town for their meetings with the magistrate, they would eat there too. Spalding Matyile had also spent some of the long hours of his exile sitting at the Sigwela guesthouse. Ezra Sigwela was in town the day that Spalding Matyile met his death in January 1961. The headman apparently could not bear to be away from Mbashe the day that the circumcised initiates returned from the mountain, so he took a car and returned home. That evening he was killed. The police responded in force, setting up camp in town, regularly raiding the surrounding locations, 'returning with a lorry full of people rounded up like they were cattle'.[61] Taking advantage of his acquaintanceship with the government officials, Sigwela attended the eventual trial of the murder suspects. He secretly reported everything he saw to Govan Mbeki and an article came out in *New Age*.[62]

There were many Sigwelas across Thembuland. With the advance of literacy – around one-quarter of the African population could read by 1951 – pamphlets and newssheets made their way into Transkei. This was not the march of mass, commercial distribution into the countryside. Rather, the political sheets were passed round by ad hoc networks of political activists. In the aftermath of the trouble at Mputi and Baziya the apartheid government prosecuted another newssheet, *Contact*. The prosecution alleged that newssheets had embittered

---

[58] 1/UTA130, 1/9/2, CMT to Umtata Magistrate, n.d.
[59] CMT1471, 42/1, Statement from Justice Mtirara, n.d., Statement Absalom Yengwa, 17 February 1961.
[60] 1/UTA6/1/11, 1/1/5-56A, BAC to Chief-BAC, 26 May 1961.
[61] Interview, Sigwela.
[62] 1UTA6/1/11, 1/1/5-56A, BAC to Chief-BAC, 26 May 1961.

local political conflicts. *Contact* reported on the events at Baziya and Mputi in great detail. The newssheet also had a vendor at Baziya Mission: a returned migrant labourer who was distributing up to 40 copies of each issue at five cents a go, earning a small living of two-and-a-half cents for each one he sold. 'We would like to congratulate you on entering the active political arena in the fight for a real and true democracy', read the pro-forma letter that the editors of *Contact* sent to such distributors. 'In this year of crisis and decision, as Africa moves forward to freedom, it is absolutely vital that *Contact* gets into every home in your area.' Through this model of distribution *Contact* had built a circulation of around 15,000 across South Africa. [63]

The influence of these papers in rural and chiefly politics also came through the pattern of their reading and circulation. Newssheets were passed around and discussed in the institutions which were at the heart of rural communities, such as schoolrooms and trading stores. One generic study of newspaper circulation suggested that, typically, each copy 'was read by five literate adults, who in turn shared its contents with illiterate friends and household members.'[64] In one district, an informer complained that there was a nucleus of lawyers and local businessmen affiliated to the All African Convention who met in each other's stores to debate political affairs and plan opposition to apartheid policies: 'They have succeeded in drawing a lot of his [the local chief's] followers into their movement.'[65] Another chief complained about the principal of the local primary school who had:

> written letters of a political nature to magazines... [and wanted] to get rid of me from my position as chairman of the school committee and secretary to the... [Tribal] Authority... When members of the School Board get drunk they divulge things I discussed at school meetings... He [the letter writer] is doing this because he is opposed to government policy... [He] is holding meetings at night to influence the people against me.[66]

The content of these newssheets was tailored to Transkei's sensibilities. Popular literacy was not a matter of private study, but of public readings, speechmaking and discussions. One newssheet, *Umtunywa*, printed praise poems written by self-styled praise singers, complete with pictures of a heroic-looking Sabata Dalindyebo in traditional costume.[67] Another printed poem, penned by Melikaya Mbutuma – who would later become a famous praise singer renowned across the Eastern Cape – accused Kaiser Matanzima of a thirst for power and love of high office. Chiefly leadership should not be based on coercion but on popular consent, the poem chided. It was particularly

---

[63] 1/UTA1/1/1/91, Case 901/62 – The State vs Peter Hjul –Statements of Salu Soyizwapi. Cf. T. Lodge, 'Patrick Duncan and Radical Liberalism' in *African Seminar: Collected Papers, Volume 1* (1978), p.117. *Umtunywa*, had a similar model of distribution: one vendor earned 1 cent for each copy he sold, selling around 38 copies in his home location – CMT1470, 42-3, statement by Mtsamane, 23 February 1963.

[64] Ukpanah, *Inkundla ya Bantu*, p.6.

[65] CMT1482, 42/23, Statement of Samuel Mnqajana, 17 November 1959.

[66] CMT1484, 42/27, statement of Gideon Ncubekezi, 11 April 1962.

[67] Cory Library, PR3669, press clippings – praise poems in honour of King Sabata in *Umthunywa*.

embarrassing because Mbtuma was a young, well-educated nephew of one of Matanzima's closest supporters. 'This *isibongo* purports to be praises of Sabata Dalindyebo... but is sarcastic and libellous', complained one of Matanzima's councillors.[68]

Once again, the repressive apparatus of the apartheid state effectively closed down open political protest. The newssheet produced by the All African Convention survived a series of libel cases brought by Kaiser Matanzima, only to fold when their editor was hit by a crippling series of banning orders. Already divided by an internal feud, the All African Convention collapsed. That was the end of its presence in the Transkei as an organised political force.[69]

By contrast, after the *New Age* was banned and its successor, *Spark*, fizzled out, Govan Mbeki set up an underground newssheet in the early 1960s. *Izwe Lomzi* (*Our Community*) catering specifically for rural isiXhosa speakers in the Eastern Cape. The logistical mastermind behind the process of printing the paper in Port Elizabeth, Harold Strachan, found it all rather bemusing. Describing himself as the 'Engels to Govan Mbeki, our reigning Marxist presence', his memoirs provide a humorous account of the trials of printing 'an unregistered revolutionary newspaper... transposed into an African pastoralist idiom.' Despite the apartheid authorities' suspicions of Govan Mbeki, 'nobody ever found out where the broadsheets were coming from.' Harold Strachan and his colleagues deadened the crashing noise of their Gestetner cyclostyle printers – 'the best technology in those primitive days' – by muffling them under a half-dozen mattresses. 'Delivery was the most dangerous part of the process, and the most punctilious: at a certain mileage along a certain road would appear an empty car with its boot open.' If the contact was more than a few minutes late, the delivery man would disappear back down the road. As the apartheid authorities clamped down on organised opposition and banned political parties, Mbeki's newspaper networks were drawn into an illicit netherworld.[70]

Petrol bombs and ballot boxes

The 1960s marked a caesura in Transkei's politics. In 1959, the Pan African Congress (PAC) broke away from the ANC, arguing the latter was too cautious and too close to white intellectuals. In March 1960, the PAC mounted mass protests at Langa Township, in Cape Town, and Sharpeville Township, to the south of Johannesburg. The police massacred protestors at Sharpeville. Shortly afterwards the apartheid government banned many political organisations. The All African Convention collapsed. However, both the ANC and PAC attempted to reinvent themselves as guerrillas.[71]

It was with the Sharpeville massacre that 'liberation politics' first arrived

---

[68] 1/XAL46, 1/1/3-1-1, Tshunungwa to BAC, 17 April 1963.

[69] Author interview, Livingstone Mqotsi, East London, 20 September 2009. 1/XAL46, 1/1/3-1-2, BAC to CMT, 30 January 1960. Bundy, 'Resistance in the Reserves', p.60.

[70] 'Engels' and 'unregistered revolutionary newspaper': H. Strachan, *Make a Skyf Man* (Johannesburg, 2004), p.41. 'Gestetner printers: ibid., p. 42. 'Delivery': ibid p.44.

[71] O. Murphy, 'Race, Violence and Nation: African nationalism and popular politics in South Africa's Eastern Cape, 1948-1970' (DPhil thesis, Oxford, 2013).

in Transkei, remembered one observer.[72] National political leaders would also recall how the violent, localised protests against the chieftaincy across rural South Africa sometimes became a motive force for guerrilla insurgency.[73] The PAC had a particularly strong presence in a number of Cape Town's townships, where migrant labourers from the western districts of Transkei worked. Kaiser Matanzima was acutely aware of their presence in Western Thembuland. 'He gave them no rest, even during their annual visits home, and was reported to have interrogated and assaulted migrant labourers from Cape Town at his palace [Great Place]'.[74] In the final months of 1962 PAC insurgents, who called themselves Poqo, organised a series of attacks. The Cape Town-based migrants killed several Matanzima-supporting chiefs. An attempt on Matanzima's life was intercepted by the police.

On 16 December 1961, the ANC announced the launch of its guerrilla wing, *Umkhonto weSizwe* (the Spear of the Nation), more often known as the MK, with a series of sabotage and petrol bomb attacks. The Eastern Cape Command of the MK, under Govan Mbeki in Port Elizabeth, was most active of all regions in South Africa. The illicit networks that Mbeki had developed in the early 1960s now retooled as guerrilla cells. Harold Strachan was in charge of the region's 'bomb-making factory' at the safe house in Port Elizabeth that had once printed copies of the newssheet *Izwe Lomzi*. Port Elizabeth was the main focus of the ANC's sabotage campaign – Tom Lodge counts 58 attacks in the city.[75] Migrant labourers such as James Kati (who will appear again in Chapter Six working for the ANC underground inside Transkei in the 1970s) played a key role mobilizing in the city's outlying townships during these years.[76] There was also an important knot of refugees in Lesotho, who were in contact with Mbeki. Qacha's Nek, a small mountain town just across the border from Transkei, was a bolthole for many from across the Eastern and Western Cape, including the families who had fled from Thembuland. Indeed, it was Abel Ntwana who was credited with showing the MK an ingenious method of sabotage. He told Govan Mbeki – a regular visitor to Lesotho – that he had destroyed cattle dips in Emnxe by burning manure to which potassium permanganate and glycerine had been added. The Regional Command's bomb-making factory was delighted. [77]

From Lesotho, the dissidents regrouped and tried to construct underground networks that would reignite unrest in the Transkei and the Eastern Cape. Conspirators travelled endlessly between Port Elizabeth, East London and Lesotho and around the Eastern Cape region, passing through Thembuland too. Government officials even suspected Sabata of being 'in touch with agitator groups'.[78] 'We were the chiefs of Thembuland [then]... because of

[72] Pers. Comm. R. Vigne, 20 February 2013.
[73] B. Magubane, P. Bonner , J. Sithole, P. Delius, J. Cherry, P. Gibbs, T. Botha, 'The Turn to Armed Struggle,' in SADET (ed.), *The Road to Democracy in S Africa, Volume I*, (Cape Town 2004), pp. 116, 120.
[74] B. Maaba, 'The PAC's War Against the State, 1960-1963' in SADET (ed.), *The Road to Democracy, Volume I*, p.274. Cf. O. Murphy, 'Race, Violence and Nation', pp.153-63.
[75] Magubane et al., 'Armed Struggle', p.124.
[76] Ibid, pp.116, 120.
[77] Ibid, p.122.
[78] TRC-VH, Joyi. CMT1470, 42-1, Chief-BAC to S/BAD, 30 October 1960.

our preaching and our influence,' Anderson Joyi later remembered, rather romantically.[79] A more realistic sense of the peripatetic, peripheral, and ultimately futile efforts made by exiles is seen in the ventures of another activist, Solomon Skotyi, a labour migrant who fled to Lesotho when soldiers swept through his location in February 1961. He had joined the ANC during the early 1950s when working at Port Elizabeth, but had lost contact with the ANC when he returned to Transkei a few years later. In Qacha's Nek he was quickly recognised by Govan Mbeki, who was trying to organise the exiles into an underground network. Drawn into a cell, ambitiously titled as a Sub-Office under the Port Elizabeth Branch of the National Action Council, Skotyi was then infiltrated back into Transkei where, for a brief period, he led an itinerant life, preaching to knots of local villagers huddled together on mountains and in sympathisers' kraals, until captured by police.[80]

Many of these hastily planned underground activities were quickly snuffed out. Indeed, it was through one of Ezra Sigwela's friends in Engcobo district, Sisa Dukada, that the Regional High Command of the MK was exposed. On their own initiative, a handful of young men had started destroying dipping tanks – 'symbols of the government authorities' – in the area.[81] This had come to the attention of Alfred Xobololo, a prominent ANC cadre in Port Elizabeth who came from Umtata district, and Sisa Dukada was sent to Port Elizabeth, where he was shown how to make a simple bomb. It was due to be detonated in the Bantu Affairs Office at Engcobo on 16th December 1961, but because of technical glitches the petrol bomb did not explode. Police soon traced Dukada because he had bought petrol from the local filling station. It 'was a serious breach of security for the MK network as a whole', Govan Mbeki later recalled.[82] Most of the senior leaders in Port Elizabeth were arrested. [83]

Across South Africa various sabotage and guerrilla campaigns ground to a halt as the result of a massive police crackdown. This culminated with the trial of some of the most senior ANC leaders in 1963-4, including Nelson Mandela and Govan Mbeki. Across the Eastern Cape, the underground networks fell silent. The PAC was even harder hit. 'Imprisonment and, above all, the execution of a whole layer of cadres, left the organisation rudderless.'[84] Exiled dissidents marooned in Lesotho returned to Transkei, journeyed further into exile, or tried to scrape together a livelihood in the country where they had been stranded.

▲ ▲ ▲

At the same time as various guerrilla campaigns spluttered out, Transkei moved towards becoming the first self-governing Bantustan territory in South Africa. In his position as Paramount Chief of Thembuland, Sabata Dalindyebo had little choice but to participate in the Transkei institutions

[79] TRC-VH, Joyi.

[80] CMT3, 1480, Statement of Solomon Bekelizwe Skotyi, 27 October 1961.

[81] Interview, Sigwela.

[82] 1/ECO1/1/1/43, 1/1/1/78, 'The State vs Sisa Allen Dukade, Case 198 of 1962'. Cf. Magubane et al., 'Armed Struggle', p.123, and Interview, Sigwela.

[83] *New Age* 19 July 1962. Cf. Strachan, *Make a Skyf*, p.44.

[84] Maaba, 'The PAC's War', p.297.

that were pushing for Bantustan self-government. In 1961 the Transkei Territorial Authority passed a resolution forming a Recess Committee to draw up constitutional proposals for Transkei's self-government. For months nothing happened; 'then events came in a rush.'[85] The Recess Committee (which included Sabata) was called to Pretoria on 3 January 1962 where they were forced to assent to a prepared set of constitutional proposals given to them by a senior government official.

The repression and disarray of many political organisations set the stage for activists from the Liberal Party of South Africa to make a remarkable foray into Transkei politics. Historically, the main support base of the Liberal Party was found amongst the prosperous, land-owning communities of African Christians in Natal. Its party leaders now saw an opportunity to expand their reach into Transkei. A few Liberal Party activists had already toured Transkei in 1960 and 1961, meeting Sabata and the Joyis. In 1962 and 1963, two of the leading liberals, Patrick Duncan and Randolph Vigne, redoubled their efforts, recruiting members into their party and making links with Sabata and his councillors.[86]

With the support of the Liberals, Sabata decided to take a stand against the new constitution when the proposals came up for debate in the Transkei Territorial Authority in May 1962. This came to nothing when Kaiser Matanzima outwitted him with a series of procedural rulings. During the second half of 1962, Sabata's advisors decided to defeat the apartheid government at their own game. They drew up alternative constitutional proposals for Transkei self-government completely contrary to the apartheid government's attempt to create a tribalised Bantustan. The centrepiece of their strategy was four large public meetings at Sabata's Great Place where the Thembu king, flanked by prominent traditional leaders and educated elites from across Transkei, officially ratified the alternative constitutional proposals.[87] But these efforts faltered when Sabata failed to force the alternative constitution through the Transkei Territorial Authority in December 1962. Once again, Kaiser Matanzima commanded the debating chamber.[88]

Soon afterwards, the apartheid government announced that Transkei would hold elections on 20 November 1963 that would open the way towards Transkei becoming a full self-governing, Bantustan territory. The November elections would choose 45 of the 109 members of the Bantustan legislature, while 64 more legislators were to be drawn from the Transkei chieftaincy. The inaugural session of this assembly would meet in December 1963 to elect the Bantustan chief minister and his cabinet.

Sabata's equivocations were seen as betrayals by more strident voices in the

[85] PC86/10/2/13/12, 'R. Vigne, 'Background to Self-Government', n.d.

[86] Vigne, *Liberals against Apartheid*, pp.165–80.

[87] Vigne, *Liberals against Apartheid*, pp.172–4. PC170/1/11/2/16. KGT46, 1/1/3-1 'Report of the Thembu Committee of 15.'

[88] CKC18, S. Vance, 'An account of the reactions of Chief Matanzima and Paramount Chief Sabata Dalindyebo to the Transkei draft constitution'. CKC17, D. Hammond-Tooke, 'Account of the 1962 session of the Transkeian Territorial Authority.' CKC 17, D. Hammond-Tooke, 'Summary and commentary on the proceedings of a special session of the Transkeian Territorial Authority called to consider the draft bill for granting self-government to the Transkei'.

ANC. Denunciations were led by Govan Mbeki *Izwe Lomzi* claimed that Sabata was 'getting the Thembus to commit suicide.' [89] Similarly, an ANC conference held at Lobatse, Botswana, in 1962 passed a resolution that there should be no collaboration with the Bantustan system.[90] But political organisations were shattered, with many leaders in jail, in hiding or in exile. In these confused political circumstances, there were no agreed party lines. Sitting in exile in Lesotho, a senior ANC leader, Joe Matthews, told Professor Tom Karis that 'The ANC does not support Sabata' outright; but that 'lots of ANC people have found it useful to join in his protest against Matanzima.' [91] Likewise, it seems that a number of members of the All African Convention – including Tsotsi, Honono and Canca – encouraged Sabata's alliance with the Liberal Party, against the protests of other party members.[92]

Sabata Dalindyebo and his supporters were put in the unconscionable position of participating in an election that they had once opposed. Moreover, the apartheid government was determined to ensure Matanzima's victory. The personal pressure must have been overwhelming, for Sabata unsuccessfully applied to the apartheid government to temporarily vacate his post as paramount chief in November 1962. The doctor's note accompanying his request cited early liver failure.[93] During this time, Victor Poto, the well-educated paramount chief of Western Pondoland, came to the fore as the leader of the anti-Matanzima faction. Poto had been cautiously drawn into the anti-Bantustan party during 1962, and had held a meeting against Pretoria's constitution proposal at his Great Place. Some of Sabata's advisers considered Poto too cautious to organise a successful 'wrecking party' for he had skilfully prevaricated during the 1950s – accepting Bantu Authorities Act and rural Betterment policies, whilst maintaining popular support in his region. Nonetheless, Poto was a shrewd and experienced politician who enjoyed the esteem of nationalist politicians, even firebrands such as Govan Mbeki.[94]

In the run-up to the November election, rival candidates claiming allegiance to either Matanzima or the Poto-Sabata slate, organised piecemeal campaigns across the Transkei. (These rival slates formed the basis of Transkei's main political parties, Matanzima creating the Transkei National Independence Party and the Poto-Sabata grouping becoming the Democratic Party in 1964.) For the journalists, diplomats and observers camped out in Umtata's packed hotels, the campaign was frustratingly elusive. 'It has been virtually impossible for any white journalist in Transkei to actually witness it or understand with certainty what is going on,' a visiting academic wrote home.[95] The journalists struggled to find the informally announced meetings that were held in guest houses, chief's kraals and school rooms. Then there

---

[89] KGT67, 1/9/2-1, *Izwe Lomzi*, May 1961, n.d.

[90] G. Mbeki, *The Struggle for Liberation in South Africa* (Cape Town, 1992), p.59.

[91] CKC18, T. Karis, 'Notes on Kaiser Matanzima compiled after a conversation with Joe Matthews', Basutoland, summer 1963.

[92] PC86/10/2/13/12.

[93] 1UTA118, N1/1/3/1, applications for leave 28 December 1960, 27 November 1962, 23 January 1963.

[94] PC86/6/1/7/3. Cf. Vigne, *Liberals Against Apartheid*, pp.171-2, 174, and Hendricks and Peires, 'All Quiet on the Western Front', pp.126, 129-35

[95] CKC17, Stultz to Carter, 16 November 1963.

was a question of finding a translator who could explain the deep isiXhosa idioms that many candidates used to appeal to their audience. As one anti-Matanzima speaker explained:

> The government has given us a closed tin and told us that in the tin there is food... But to our amazement we found a snake in one corner of the tin... We want to go to the tin, examine it, and then kill the snake. Vote for us so that we can go to the Legislative Assembly and kill the snake.[96]

Finally, many people attending the meetings kept silent because of fear. 'When asked which candidates they will support, they simply say: "polling day will come".'[97]

Nevertheless, Transkei's elections delivered a solid majority for the slate of Sabata-Poto candidates. In Thembuland, all the candidates who stood against Sabata – including his half-brother, Bambilanga Mtirara – were defeated at the polls.[98] But the victory of a Bantustan wrecking group was hardly guaranteed. The apartheid government had rigged the Bantustan legislature: elected members were outnumbered in the legislative chamber by nominated traditional leaders. Furthermore, Sabata and Poto held together a loose coalition. Umtata bristled with insinuations that Hans Abraham, Pretoria's Commissioner-General to Transkei, was winning votes for Kaiser Matanzima with promises and threats. Most notably, King Botha Sigcau was granted a government farm because of the support his chiefs provided to Matanzima.[99]

Eventually, the day of the election of the Chief Minister arrived. By 9.30 that morning, a large crowd had gathered outside the Transkei Legislative Assembly – the old Territorial Authority building, which had been refurbished, just in time, by contractors 'working nearly round the clock,' seven days a week.[100] 'Matanzima arrived early, shaking hands and telling jokes.' Then a 'line of five cars, each blowing its horn,' swept into the street. The crowd 'came to life and rushed at the lead cars ... picked up the volume and tempo of their singing and surged forward. Chief Sabata bounded out the first car with a broad smile and was greeted with a deafening salute [*Ah Jonguhlanga!*]' as he went into the chamber. Inside, visitors in the packed galleries witnessed the Poto-Sabata group win the first vote for Chairman [i.e. Speaker] of the Assembly by 56 votes to 49.[101]

The Assembly recessed for lunch and returned to find everything changed. 'Unfortunately the Potos thought they were home and dry and spent the lunch hour eating rather than preventing their voters from being subverted.'[102] An immediate vote for the vice-chairmanship of the Legislature went in favour of Matanzima, 54-48. Two hours later, Matanzima won the final, crucial vote for the office of Chief Minister at 5.45 p.m.

Not long after the decisive vote, 'Victor Poto came out of the Hall wearing

[96] CKC18, 'Transkei Elections'.
[97] CKC18, 'Chief Poto Addresses a Meeting'.
[98] KGT47, 1/3/5-2, 'Candidates who support Matanzima'.
[99] PC170/1/11/3/7.
[100] CKC17, Stultz to Carter, 10 November.
[101] CKC17, Stultz to Carter, 7 December 1963.
[102] Ibid.

a broad smile. He was vehemently cheered by the crowd. Later, Chief Sabata appeared and the crowd saluted him a loudly as they could' whilst a praise-giver sang his exaltations. Finally, Matanzima appeared on the steps of the legislature:

> As he passed down the steps, he threw out his arms and broke out into a slow run towards his car... Some cheered, many jeered, and there were many hisses. The crowd broke apart, some following Kaiser up the street... others walking slowly in the other direction. Darkness was falling quickly now, and it was still raining lightly.[103]

[103] Ibid.

3. The Second Peasants' Revolt, Mpondoland 1960–1980

Govan Mbeki's book

In 1962 Govan Mbeki languished in detention, his role as the mastermind of the sabotage campaign in the Eastern Cape having been exposed by the failure of a bomb explosion in the Engcobo district of Transkei. Whilst in solitary confinement, Govan Mbeki illicitly resumed work on what was to become his most famous book, *The Peasants' Revolt*. The book was published in Britain, thanks to the editing efforts of Ruth First, who meshed the prison manuscript, which had been written on toilet paper, together with earlier drafts.[1]

The Peasants' Revolt was a celebration of the rural revolt of the Eastern Mpondoland districts of Transkei a few years earlier in 1960. Thus far, our narrative has largely concerned the large kingdom of Thembuland, whose districts run from the central town of Umtata into the mountains that mark the north-western boundaries of the Transkei territories. Eastern Mpondoland (not to be confused Western Mpondoland – a more junior branch of the same royal stem) was the other major paramountcy in the Transkei territories. The Great Place of the Eastern Mpondo king was found at Quakeni in the south-eastern corner of the Transkei region, between the Indian Ocean and the border of KwaZulu Natal, which is a sub-tropical area of deep valleys and forests. The purpose of Mbeki's book was to remind his fellow leaders in the ANC (many of whom had spent their energies in the 1940s and 1950s organising township protests) of the significance of the revolt in Eastern Mpondoland. It was the largest of a series of rural protests that came in the wake of the expansion of the apartheid state across the Native Reserves in the middle years of the 20th century. During these years there had also been significant rural protests in Witziehoek (1950-1), Zeerust (1957) and Sekhukhuneland (1958) and also, as discussed in the preceding chapter, in the districts of Thembuland.

Not surprisingly, given the significance of the Mpondo revolt and the stature of Govan Mbeki, the events of 1960 have attracted a steady trickle of study ever since. Earlier researchers were able to interview protagonists; later historians have combed archival sources and the rich store of memories. In one sense, interpretations of the revolt changed with the prevailing fashions of historical writing. But in another sense, the general picture of the revolt has remained very similar: that this was the revolt of a rural society against government authority. Historians describe the gradual build-up of discontent against government actions such as the rural betterment schemes that forcibly changed black agriculture and the Bantu Authorities Act that co-opted chiefs.

[1]   G. Mbeki, *South Africa: The peasants' revolt* (Harmondsworth, 1964), p.9.

From the mid-1950s there was a general breakdown of government – not least the vigilante gangs against stock theft that appeared in half-a-dozen Transkei districts, dispensing justice above the heads of the local chiefs and government magistrates.[2]

These tensions exploded in Eastern Mpondoland, where King Botha Sigcau and many of his closest chiefs and advisers had been strong supporters of government policies. In March 1960, hundreds of people descended on the homestead of the king's closest councillor, Saul Mabude, burning his buildings to the ground and slaughtering his livestock. For the next months the rebels controlled much of Eastern Mpondoland. They held meetings in the mountains, taking fees from the surrounding inhabitants and summoning recalcitrant villagers before their informal courts. They commandeered provisions and transport from the local white traders and black businessmen in the small market towns. Mobile police units toured the Transkei, brutally reimposing the government writ. In June 1960, government forces surprised a meeting on Ngquza Hill and massacred eleven people. Yet dissent continued. In December 1960, another prominent chief from the Sigcau royal clan and two of his headmen were killed after clashes at another mountain meeting. The rebellion rumbled on for another few years, drawing to a close at the same time as Transkei was granted Bantustan self-government in 1963.

By the time the book was published in 1964, *The Peasants' Revolt* had an elegiac tone. That same year, Govan Mbeki and the High Command of the ANC's armed wing were jailed on Robben Island. Across South Africa, the rural revolts had been broken. Govan Mbeki made damning conclusions in the final sections of his book, writing that 'though the whip has remained in the hand of the White government, it has been the Chiefs, the new jockeys... who have applied the spurs. The Chiefs are now well in the saddle.'[3] Indeed, the notionally tribally-based system of Bantustan government invented by apartheid ideologues was, arguably, the most systematically brutal extension of the classic pattern of indirect rule, by which colonial powers ruled through local intermediaries. This view of Botha Sigcau and his chiefs as apartheid collaborators was brutally established by the support they gave to the repression of the Mpondo revolt. Apart from the people shot dead on Ngquza Hill, scores more were condemned to death and thousands held in temporary police detention camps – perhaps 5,000 people in total were arrested across the Transkei during these years. This repression would remain a lodestone in both popular memory and academic writings. The prominent historian Lungisile Ntsebza describes the chieftaincy as 'decentralised despotism' – a term that has been used elsewhere in Africa to explain how colonial and settler states extended their authority through alliance with local chieftaincies.[4]

Nevertheless, the crushing of the Mpondo Revolt did not mean that Matanzima's government would impose its authority over Transkei's rural communities during the Bantustan period. Even as he assembled his first

---

[2] J. Pieterse, 'Reading and Writing the Mpondo Revolts', in T. Kepe and L. Ntsebeza (eds.), *Rural Resistance in South Africa: the Mpondo revolts after fifty years* (Cape Town, 2012), pp.43-66.
[3] Mbeki, *The Peasants Revolt*, p.109.
[4] See Introduction, footnote 14.

government in 1964, Kaiser Matanzima complained of 'rumours spreading throughout the territory to the effect that all rehabilitation [i.e., Rural Betterment] measures have been suspended'. [5] The relationship between state and society remained fraught throughout the era. Whilst Betterment policies were never halted outright, the course of events during the Bantustan era would reveal that Mpondoland was hardly quiescent.

Chieftaincy's changing meanings

Winnie Mandela's father, Columbus Madikizela, had supported Botha Sigcau during the Mpondo revolt; now he became first Bantustan government minister given charge of the Bantustan Department of Agriculture and Forestry. In one sense, it was a powerful portfolio and a reward to Botha Sigcau and his closest supporters. On the other hand, Madikizela's principle responsibility – implementing Betterment regulations – was an impossible task.

The agricultural planners who designed Rural Betterment policies in the 1940s had imagined that government officials would impose their writ on rural society and forcibly reorder it. In one sense, the activist role designated for the state continued throughout the Bantustan era. From the 1940s to 1963, about one-quarter of the rural locations in the Transkei Territories experienced some form of Betterment Planning. By 1990, these plans had been implemented in just over half of Transkei's rural locations. [6] The policies were an attempt to increase agricultural productivity, but often they only succeeded in fragmenting rural communities, whose agricultural output in any case stagnated. One landmark study of the causes and consequences of Betterment policies was evocatively titled *Moving Together, Drifting Apart*. [7] The fruitlessness of these policies scars South Africa's landscape today. The ridges that were cut into the hillsides – a futile effort to prevent soil erosion and increase the area under cultivation, built with thousands of hours of unpaid female labour – can clearly be seen from satellite photos. Today this land lies fallow.

Yet these broad figures, which paint a picture of state intrusion into rural society, should also be balanced by an account of the ways in which communities' resistance in turn reshaped government policy. The apartheid government was already giving ground in the 1950s, cutting corners in order to reduce costs and to expedite the implementation of Betterment policies. Officials 'on the ground' found it expedient to ignore the most stringent stock-culling regulations, despite the planners' concerns that Betterment would never 'succeed without the limitation of stock numbers and the control on grazing'. [8] In the mid-1960s, the Transkei Bantustan government went even further, permanently suspending a raft of laws, regulations and circulars.

---

[5] CMT1841, 42/17, 'Press Statement by Chief Minister', 19 August 1964.
[6] *TNA* (Umtata, 1978), p.212. Department of Agricultural and Forestry (hereafter DAF), *Transkei Agricultural Development Study* (Umtata, 1991), p.91.
[7] C. de Wet, *Moving Together, Drifting Apart: Betterment planning and villagisation in a South African Homeland* (Johannesburg, 1995).
[8] F. Hendricks, *The Pillars of Apartheid: Land tenure, rural planning and the chieftaincy* (Stockholm, 1990), p.135.

Columbus Madikizela had the ticklish task of making these announcements to the Transkei legislature. 'Now the duty devolves to you and the Department [of Agriculture] has nothing to do with it. You can keep all the beasts you want, you can have ten bulls to one cow,' Madikizela joked, trying to find humour in policies that revealed the limitations of state power.[9]

Moreover, the institution of the chieftaincy – the pillars on which the Bantustan state rested, to use Fred Hendrick's apt phrase – was fissiparous and brittle, particularly in Eastern Mpondoland.[10] King Botha Sigcau presided over a large kingdom, with many dissenting chieftaincies. These rifts went all the way back to his installation as the Paramount of Eastern Mpondoland in 1937, which had been preceded by a bitter succession dispute. Botha Sigcau only won out because he had the support of the Chief Magistrate of Transkei, beating his far more popular half-brother, Nelson Sigcau. The fragility of Botha Sigcau's authority was underscored by the anger directed, very personally, against him and his entourage during the 1960 Mpondo revolt, when they were burned out of their homesteads and killed. To the chiefs' own deep shame, they had run away from their own people. How 'disgraceful and absurd it was to see a chief guarded by police [and home guards] armed with revolvers!' – they were mere hirelings, not true supporters or followers.[11] The humiliation caused by this very public rejection is seen in the wheedling letter of complaint that one government-supporting chief wrote to his home guards. 'I am in a state of melancholy because I have no people [supporters],' he wrote. 'You just laugh when you see me... I am busy trying to repair my motor car, but you do not give me a hand... It is clear you will rejoice when you hear the news I have passed away.'[12]

Given the great opprobrium directed against Botha Sigcau and the conflicts within the branches of the royal family, there were many embers of dissent in the ashes of the Mpondoland revolt. The combustible mix of popular unrest and seething royal intrigue was seen in the Flagstaff district of Eastern Mpondoland, where members of the Sigcau royal clan held major chieftaincies. Zoleka Langa, who would later join the ANC underground, was eight years old in 1960. Her father was one of the key traditional leaders supporting Botha Sigcau during the height of the revolt. The family slept out in their food garden, hidden by rows of potato leaves. 'Nobody would take us in' [not even the children] 'as their homes would have been burned down' by insurgents, she recalled. During these months of fire and arson, a neighbouring pro-government chief was murdered at Ntlenzi; then Zoleka's father suffered a heart attack and died, the old man worn down by the strain of the nights sleeping in the open.[13]

In the years following the Mpondo revolt, King Botha tried to rebuild his authority at Ntlenzi by installing a sub-chief who had been his tribal secretary and a native policeman. But the residents of Ntlenzi were unwilling to submit

[9] *TLA* (1965), p.187. T. Gibbs, 'From Popular Resistance to Populist Politics in the Transkei' in W. Beinart and M. Dawson (eds.), *Popular Politics and Resistance Movements in South Africa* (Johannesburg, 2010), p.143.
[10] Hendricks, *The Pillars of Apartheid*.
[11] *Transkei Liberal News*, April 1964.
[12] CMT1473, 42/Q-2, Chief Stokwe to Home Guards, 7 June 1962.
[13] Author interview, Zoleka Langa, Flagstaff, 9 November 2008.

to royal authority. In an ironic twist of fortune, Zoleka's brother, Babini Langa, emerged as the anti-government candidate for the chieftainship. Indeed, Babini had an impeccable lineage compared to King Botha's candidate who was not of royal blood or even from Mpondoland. After a protracted period of turmoil, the residents of the location successfully installed Babini. [14] An anonymous letter written during the campaign against Sigcau's nominee – signed by men calling themselves *Umkthonto weSizwe* (the Nation's Spear), the name of the ANC guerrilla force – reveals the extent to which this local dispute had been infused with anti-apartheid sentiment:

> You are the aboriginal of this country and you were deprived of your natural and legitimate rights of this country, like an African, by the alien white man... Now it is pain-giving to find that there are some African people who are supporting the Government in subjugating the African people...
> Your brothers in affection... *Umkhonto weSizwe.* [15]

Initially, Chief Babini maintained a discreet profile, joining the ruling party in Transkei's Bantustan Legislative Assembly. But he was forced to choose his allegiances in the most painful of public settings when Kaiser Matanzima forced the unpopular Betterment and Land Rehabilitation policies on Ntlenzi in 1969, most likely as a punishment for their role in the 1960 revolt. With three mobile police vans standing by, Chief Babini was detained under Emergency Regulations for his role in the violent protests that followed.[16] Soon afterwards, Botha Sigcau banned him from staying in the district. Babini was even shot and wounded during a dispute with a loyal nephew of King Botha. None of this prevented Babini from holding his seat in the Transkei Legislature, winning a local by-election with an increased majority in 1971.[17] Zoleka Langa remembers that it was around this time that the ANC, which was 'looking for people of influence and position,' made contact with Chief Babini. 'I was just a school girl at that time, but I would sit with him and advise him', Zoleka Langa recalled. [18] These seditious conversations were too much for Matanzima. Chief Babini was jailed repeatedly until his health collapsed and he died. The dispute became so embittered that it was a long struggle to even bury Chief Babini at his family homestead, where his body was eventually laid to rest. A few years later, now trained as a nurse at the Holy Cross mission hospital in Eastern Mpondoland, Zoleka Langa joined the ANC underground in the far east of Transkei.

Such sparks of dissidence were seen all over Eastern Mpondoland. These were conflicts that went even to the heart of the Sigcau royal family. King Botha's younger son through his Great Wife, Ntsikayezwe Twentyman Sigcau, was perhaps the most prominent dissenting voice. Ntsikayezwe Sigcau had attended Mfundisweni College, a prestigious mission school in Eastern Mpondoland,

---

[14] 1/FSF6/42, 1/1/5/6. Genealogies are discussed in 'Chiefs in Eastern Pondoland' - CMT1472, 42/Q.
[15] CMT1474, 36/4, Anonymous letter, May 1963.
[16] *DD* 19 April 1969, 24 June 1969. *TLA* (1969), p.449.
[17] *DD* 27 September 1971.
[18] Interview, Langa, 2008.

where his powerful, hearty presence had won him great popularity.[19] The archival record does not provide many details of his political activities. It is clear, however, that by the mid-1970s, he was one of a handful of young Mpondo royals who was involved in radical political circles, even making informal links with the ANC underground.[20] Installed into the chieftaincy in April 1974, when the incumbent retired of old age, Ntsikayezwe Sigcau soon became known as one of the leaders of violent anti-rehabilitation protests in the district of Tabankulu in Eastern Mpondoland. In response, Matanzima's police force was sent in to smash the recalcitrant locations, demolishing homes in the area.[21]

In the face of rural protests, often led by figures such as Chief Babini Langa and Chief Ntsikayezwe Sigcau, the Transkei Government backed further away from Betterment Planning. By the mid-1970s, government officials were forced to admit failure: 'there are no areas where the Betterment scheme has been carried out to the satisfaction of the department.'[22] The changing course of events was epitomised by Columbus Madikizela's retirement from government in the late 1960s. He was worn out, in bad health and seemingly disillusioned. Winnie Madikizela-Mandela's biographer claims that the old man 'poured out his heart' to his daughter shortly before he died, admitting she had been right to be dead set against the Bantustans.[23] This healed a family rift that had existed ever since the 1960 revolt when Winnie Mandela had unwittingly provided shelter to insurgents who had attacked Columbus Madikizela's house. In these fractious family relationships we can track some of the ruptures that followed from Land Betterment policies.

From 'Rural Betterment' to 'Community Development'

Making a partial withdrawal from Betterment Planning, Transkei's government increasingly shifted attention to a new type of rural development project in the 1970s. Funded by Pretoria, Transkei's Department of Agriculture increasingly focused on providing services to farmers, such as fertiliser and tractors. This fundamentally transformed the relationship between the state and Transkei's rural communities. A panoply of experts – both white officials with experience of working in southern Africa and Transkei-trained graduates – worked together in a cluster of government controlled parastatals linked to the Bantustan universities. They ran a slew of showcase projects: tea and sugar plantations, forestry, cattle ranching and dairy herds, irrigation schemes, and the like.

The experience of state-led development projects was often chastening. For instance, Chris Tapscott, a development expert who briefly worked in the Bantustan universities, was at one time involved in many of these government-linked schemes. Initially, he had hoped the development projects would stimulate black smallholder production, but he became increasingly disillusioned,

---

[19] Author interview, Zoleka Langa, Flagstaff, 23 September 2009.
[20] Interview, Langa, 2008.
[21] *TNA* (1979), p.23. Cf. BAO5/405, 54/1662/29, Kaiser Matanzima (hereafter KD) to S/BAD.
[22] *TLA* (1970), p.282.
[23] Mandela, *Long Walk*, p.218. Cf. A. du Preez Bezdrob, *Winnie Mandela: A life* (Cape Town, 2003), pp.88-91, 158.

and eventually wrote a damning auto-critique of his work (of which more in Chapter Six). He argued that the Bantustan technocrats implementing this policy in government parastatals, under Pretoria's direction, became a powerful collaborating group within the Transkei. Furthermore, the showcase projects were an important form of government patronage, granted to supporters of apartheid. Kaiser Matanzima's younger brother, George, had trained and practised as a lawyer until he was struck off the roll of attorneys in 1963 for the misappropriation of trust funds. This had not stopped him from following his older brother into the Transkei government, where he took a series of senior cabinet posts. Was it not surprising that he used the opportunities granted by Bantustan independence to line his pockets through a bizarre scheme that bought in tractors from an Austrian businessman? In many ways, Tapscott's arguments anticipate James Ferguson's celebrated book that critiques state-led development projects elsewhere on the continent: *'Development', De-politicisation and Bureaucratic Power in Lesotho.*[24]

A disastrous, government-run livestock project in Eastern Mpondoland epitomises the failures of this type of state-led development scheme. In 1973, the Transkei Minister of Agriculture announced that a leper colony at Mkambati, which abutted the cliffs of the Wild Coast, had been chosen to become the 'Co-operative Cattle Farming Society'. Underlying these plans was apartheid officials' enduring belief that Transkei should become the dairy herd of South Africa – particularly in Eastern Mpondoland, where the coastal plains of Lambasi and Mkambati had once been grazing land for thousands of the king's cattle. The co-operative would 'specialise in the production of cattle on a very large scale... The first of its kind in South Africa... A showpiece for Transkei.'[25] In 1976, the Transkei government took over a leper colony and farm that were situated on this land. The seaward third was turned into a nature reserve; the remainder was made into a government farm, complete with a herd of 1,400 cattle. Local youths were trained as agriculture officers, and the farm bred and sold 50 cows each year to local farmers on a subsidised basis.

Yet the Mkambati project was never a success. It never broke even. Moreover, it faced long-standing local resistance. In 1920, people living in this area had been forcibly removed to make way for the government leper colony. Ever since that time, these communities had been engaged 'in a long drawn out campaign of passive resistance. They ignored the institution's regulations and cut the fence of the reserve to allow their cattle to graze.'[26] They stole brushwood, timber and thatch. In the late 1970s, the Mkambati scheme was closed down. The remaining 900 cattle were sold at rock-bottom prices. Kaiser Matanzima's cronies probably did best from the fire sale. One of Winnie Mandela's uncles, Walter Madikizela, had been looking forward to buying the cheap cattle. He had even clubbed together with 32 friends to hire a lorry but at the last minute he was told the sale had been postponed, and missed the auction. Perhaps it

---

[24] C. Tapscott, 'The Rise of Development as a Policy Theory in South Africa, 1978-88: A critique' (London School of Economics, Ph.D. thesis, 1992). Cf. J. Ferguson, *The Anti-Politics Machine: "Development", de-politicisation and bureaucratic power in Lesotho* (London, 1996).

[25] *TLA* (1973), p.212. Cf. *TLA* (1974), p.319.

[26] T. Kepe, 'Grassland Vegetation and Rural Livelihoods', p.68. Cf. DAF, *Annual Report 1977-8* (Umtata, 1978), p.28. DAF, *Annual Report* (1980), pp.2, 4. *TNA* (1977), p.410.

was a mistake, but he suspected a plot against him. He had been detained for his role in the 1960 Mpondo revolt; and he still sat on the opposition benches in the Transkei legislature, openly against the government.[27]

▲ ▲ ▲

However, if one shifts attention away from the grandiose, showcase agricultural projects that so often left a trail of corruption and failure, to the more routine services provided by the Bantustan government, a different picture of the relationship between state and society emerges. This is seen, most notably, in the increased provision of state-run veterinary services. During the Bantustan era, Transkei's livestock were better treated than ever before. Government officers vaccinated 1.4 million cattle against the livestock disease, Quarter Evil, in the late 1970s when just 7,000 had been innoculated a decade previously. Small livestock breeding stations were dotted all over the Transkei, which bought in and sold cattle under a myriad of complex subsidy schemes.[28]

These new agricultural development policies had a paradoxical outcome. On the one hand, many rural communities were deeply suspicious of the Bantustan Government in all its forms – it was not unheard of for vets to be chased away by suspicious villagers. Moreover, these schemes failed to stimulate agricultural production and to turn Transkei into the dairy herd of South Africa, as was the dream of government planners. Most people were simply too poor and did not hold enough livestock to participate in profit-making, commercial markets (as will be discussed below). Some rural communities stopped even naming new-born babies because infant mortality rates were so high. Nevertheless, government veterinary services provided an increasingly important social welfare function, given that so many households owned livestock of some kind.[29] The increasing importance of animal welfare services for rural communities is reflected in the incorporation of veterinary practices into domestic routines. In annual reports, veterinarians noted the increasing demand for cattle dipping and livestock inoculation. When government supplies of vaccines ran out, villagers tried to buy cheaper veterinary treatments.[30] A variety of 'folk' medicines even mimicked the practices of government vets. One treatment, for instance, involved injecting a vinegary solution into the beast.[31]

It would also seem that the routines of government officials were domesticated into the idioms of rural life. In part, this was because the Bantustan state was so chaotic and corrupt. The apartheid government commissioned a number of studies in the mid-1970s that lamented the failure of Bantustan governments to establish the routines of a rational Weberian bureaucracy. These studies make troubling reading, detailing a chronic shortage of

[27] *TNA* (1981), pp.183, 200.
[28] DAF, *Annual Reports* (1964–1985).
[29] Republic of Transkei, *The Development Strategy, 1980-2000* (Umtata, 1979), pp.27-8. Cf. Hawkins Associates, *The Physical and Spatial Basis for Transkei's First Five Year Development Plan,* (Salisbury, October 1980), p.109, and *TNA* (1977), pp.69, 204, 357.
[30] DAF, *Annual Reports* (1964–1985).
[31] *TLA* (1978), p.176.

expertise and the 'limited formal education, low morale and motivation' of agricultural officers.[32] In the mid-1970s, Transkei's Minister of Agriculture worried that 'a tendency seems to be developing where everybody expects to be the boss. Productivity is in decline and authority is not freely accepted... A stable and competent civil service cannot develop under such conditions.'[33] Facing a bureaucracy that did not operate through formal procedures, many people accessed state resources by drawing on personal connections. This was a two-way street: local officials played the role of community leaders, especially as their authorities and functions often overlapped with the duties of chiefs and headmen. Using well-known patterns of communal work practices, fowls would be slaughtered and beer brewed in their honour whenever they provided services to particular localities.[34]

The Transkei Government's new role in development projects also changed the dynamics of popular protest. Increasingly, rural communities demanded state support for their areas. Matanzima's government invested heavily in Eastern Mpondoland in model farms and plantation schemes, creating jobs for 2,300 labourers in Lusikisiki district alone. However, stories still persisted that the region was hard done-by. These rumours even sparked local demonstrations that were sometimes reported in the press. During one year of drought, for instance, the women from one location mobbed the official car carrying Kaiser Matanzima as he passed through Eastern Mpondoland, demanding the government supply them with water.[35] The rumours that Eastern Mpondoland was being neglected by Matanzima also became a powerful critique of the Bantustan government by dissidents such as Chief Ntsikayezwe Twentyman Sigcau. Very few of his speeches were recorded, but the pages of the Hansard of Transkei's Legislative Assembly details one example of his oratory:

> There is undue enrichment in this land... Moneys that come from the South Africa are exploited by our own Government to the disadvantage of our lower ranks... We see farmers on the northern side [from Kaiser Matanzima's region] developing well... But the implements are not well distributed... There is no fair economic distribution here.[36]

Thus, the increasing reach of the state had contradictory effects in rural politics. Historically, the chieftaincy had derived its legitimacy from being the guarantor of African land rights, particularly during the period of colonial conquest when they had been the bulwark that had prevented settler appropriation of their people's land. During the period of Betterment planning, they were caught in a dilemma. A significant minority of chiefs, such as Chief Babini Langa, had joined their people's protests against these very unpopular measures. But most, such as King Botha Sigcau, had gone along with government policies, becoming, in the popular phrase of the day,

[32] T. Bembridge, 'Problems of Agricultural Development in the Republic of Transkei: A preliminary summary' (Research report for the Urban-Rural Workshop, Stellenbosch, 1982), p.45.

[33] *TLA* (1975), p.184.

[34] Gibbs, 'Popular Resistance', pp.145-8.

[35] *DD* 9 May 1974.

[36] *TNA* (1984), p.157.

'apartheid puppets'. Now, with the rise of government-funded development projects, a more diffuse network of notables – chiefs and other local leaders, with connections to the state – played a new role as political brokers, accessing goods from the dysfunctional Bantustan state for their own communities. In so doing, they used the ideas of personal authority associated with chieftainship. As a result, ethnic identities, once centred on smallholder production and access to land, increasingly focussed around a locality's relation to the state. Thus, there were continuities in political mentalities at the same time as there was a wrenching change in the political economy of the region. Chief Ntsikayezwe Sigcau's demands that government patronage be showered on Mpondoland tapped into this popular vein of anger.

The cattle tax crisis

It was a combined crisis of cattle dipping and taxation in the late 1970s which nudged Eastern Mpondoland to the brink of another rebellion and dramatically revealed the changing balance of power between the Bantustan state and rural communities. Cattle dipping had been one of a swathe of responsibilities handed over to the Tribal Authorities set up under the Bantustan project. The Bantustan Department of Agriculture was made responsible for supplying equipment and setting dipping regulations, while local Tribal Authorities held the budgets and overall responsibility for making sure that the livestock were dipped. In doing this, apartheid ideologues had hoped to turn local chiefs into administrators, making their Tribal Authorities organs of local government.[37] Chaos resulted.

The Tribal Authorities collapsed under the weight of three interrelated problems. One was rural poverty. Cattle dipping had always been a rickety operation run by the lower levels of local government on a shoestring budget. But during the Bantustan era, rising dipping costs far outstripped the ability of the Tribal Authorities to raise revenue. Second, the very illegitimacy of the Tribal Authorities hamstrung the system. It was often far easier to overlook rather than to properly enforce the livestock dipping regulations that were stipulated by government. Third, many chiefs were corrupt or incompetent. Apartheid planners had placed financial accounts in the hands of Tribal Authorities. 'No-one understands it, the treasurers least of all', wrote one official trying to implement the administrative changes. 'The more sensitive keep threatening to resign because of the suspicion cast upon them through being unable to explain what the balances are.'[38] Auditors found they could not balance any one of the Tribal Authorities' financial accounts they had inspected. 'The less educated chiefs and headmen are not quite sure...what

---

[37] *TLA* (1972), p.424.

[38] 1/MQL6/1/103, 11/1/2, BAC Mqanduli, to Chief BAC, 8 September 1961. Cf. Office of the Auditor General, *Report of the Auditor General on the Appropriation and Miscellaneous Accounts and on the Accounts of Lower Authorities in the area, 1966-7* (Umtata, 1967). *Report of the Auditor General* (1977). TNA (1978), p.117. BAO5/515, 109/1294, 'Report – Meeting of the chiefs in the Thembu Region', 26 May 1964. .

they can eat,' explained one auditor. [39] Consequently receipts that should have been paid into the public purse were often consumed (or 'eaten') by local chieftaincies. The Bantu Authorities system might have been authoritarian but it was also remarkably brittle.

Whilst livestock disease was dormant, no one much cared that the Tribal Authorities and the cattle-dipping system were in disrepair. But when stock disease returned to southern Africa in the mid-1970s, the inadequacies of the Tribal Authorities were exposed. Pretoria worried that Transkei's diseased livestock would infect the herds of apartheid South Africa. They demanded that the Transkei government take action, or they would take their own punitive measures. Transkei's officials hastened to explain how there had been a slow decline in dipping controls. Noxious dipping chemicals sometimes 'overflowed the banks and spread on the grass' because cattle-dipping tanks were in such disrepair.[40] In other locations, livestock were poisoned when sheep and cattle were dipped together in an inept attempt to save costs. Matters became so bad that, by the mid-1970s, four coastal districts – including Bizana and Lusikisiki in Eastern Mpondoland – were incapable of dipping their cattle during the summer months when tick-borne diseases were most virulent. 'Various districts ran out of money and so did not purchase dip or had no money to repair dip tanks leading to a breakdown of the programme.'[41] The most painful sign of the crisis was the sight of emaciated cattle covered by blood-engorged ticks.

Intriguingly, for once a number of ANC-linked dissidents agreed with the apartheid government. They too wanted the Bantustan government to further intrude into the affairs of rural communities. Two anti-government politicians sitting in the Transkei legislature, Alfred Xobololo and Jackson Nkosiyane, proposed a motion calling on the Bantustan Department of Agriculture to effectively take over cattle dipping operations.[42] Xobololo was a longstanding ANC supporter who had endured a long period of house arrest because of his involvement with Govan Mbeki's rural sabotage campaign in the early 1960s. Nkosiyane had been banished and then served a term of imprisonment because of his opposition to Kaiser Matanzima. The thrust of their demands was significant. During the 1960 rural revolts, ANC leaflets had called on rural communities to sabotage cattle dipping tanks as these were symbols of government oppression.[43] Now these ANC-linked activists were asking the Bantustan government to reach deeper into rural society, taking over cattle dipping operations from inept and insolvent Tribal Authorities. Facing a clamour of protest, the Transkei Department of Agriculture did exactly this. Within a year the number of livestock deaths caused by tick-borne diseases declined by 40%.[44]

---

[39] *TLA* (1973), pp.360-1. Cf. 1/MQL6/1/100, 11/1/4, BAC Mqanduli, to Chief BAC, November 1962.

[40] *TLA* (1972), p.273. Cf. *TNA* (1982), p.154.

[41] *TLA* (1974), p.196. DAF, *Annual Report* (1975), p.3. Cf. Gibbs, 'Popular Resistance', pp.149-50.

[42] *TLA* (1976), p.52.

[43] On Xobololo and Nkosiyane: *DD* 16 June 1966, 2 June 1992. On the ANC sabotage campaign: CMT3, 1480, Statement of Elija Gxona, 3 November 1961.

[44] *TLA* (1972), p.273. Cf. DAF, *Annual Report* (1975), p.3. DAF, *Annual Report* (1978), p.2, and Gibbs, 'Popular Resistance', p.150.

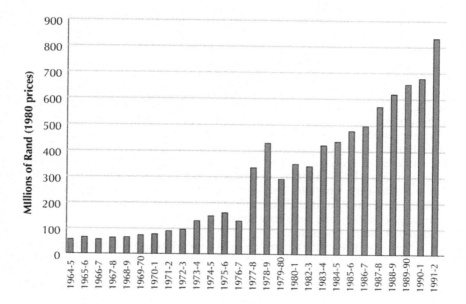

Figure 2 *Transkei Bantustan Government Expenditure*

Source: Transkei Auditor General, Estimates of Expenditure (Umtata, 1964-91)
Note: Transfers from apartheid South Africa to the Transkei Bantustan remained relatively constant as a proportion of total spending, ranging from around 75-85% of the Transkei government's total expenditures – as a result the apartheid government's commitments dramatically rose in the late 1970s and 1980s.

▲ ▲ ▲

The cattle dipping crisis symbolised a much broader transformation in the relationship between the Bantustans and apartheid government. Historically, the Native Reserves had been financially self-supporting. Indirect rule through local chieftaincies, as generally practised across Africa, was government on the cheap. In addition, the Bantustans had long supplied low-paid, migrant labourers to South Africa's goldmines. But apartheid's promises to turn Bantustans into self-governing territories carried additional financial commitments that were beginning to become apparent in the late 1970s. (Figure 2 indicates the dramatic increase in both the expenditures of the Transkei state and the financial transfers made by the apartheid government.) Some of these expenses were the gaudy trappings of statehood, such as airports and grand government offices; but most significant were the increases in Bantustan in education, public works and agriculture budgets, which account for the vast majority of expenditures.[45] The growing number of agricultural development projects and the Transkei Bantustan government's take-over of cattle dipping responsibilities epitomised this broad shift.

[45] W. Beinart, 'Beyond the Homelands: Some ideas about the history of African rural areas in South Africa', *SAHJ*, 64, 1 (2012), pp.13-14.

59

The growth of Bantustan government expenditure provoked bitter debates in both academic and government circles. On one hand, these flows did little to overturn the deep spatial inequalities in South Africa between the poor rural peripheries and the rich industrial centres. Certainly, it was clear that the education, health and infrastructure expenditures allocated to the Bantustans were never enough to make to make inroads into rural poverty. Another key question was whether the 'cheap labour' of Bantustan migrants working in South Africa's industries subsidised the apartheid government, in effect cancelling out the financial transfers sent from Pretoria to Umtata.[46] On the other hand, the increase in Bantustan government expenditure was significant. The underlying figures were clear. The Transkei Government ran up shortfalls every year from 1976 to 1979, turning a budget surplus of almost R16 million into a deficit of R1.5 million. This sense of crisis was aggravated by the erosion of financial controls and planning inside the Transkei Bantustan government. Transkei's civil servants were only paid in 1979 because of a last-minute, R70 million bail-out by Pretoria.[47]

The growth of Bantustan government expenditures took apartheid South Africa into novel political territory. With the apartheid economy in recession in the late 1970s, white voters were demanding that the Bantustan experiment begin to pay for itself. The rapid economic growth that had been part of the apartheid 'success story' of the 1960s was fading away. For one, the apartheid government's policies that aimed to turn South Africa from a producer of primary commodities into an economy that manufactured secondary goods were falling apart. On top of that, South Africa was particularly hit by the 1970s global economic downturn. With the apartheid government fiscus under strain, Pretoria leaned on the Transkei treasury. Kaiser Matanzima was forced to make swingeing emergency cuts to the Bantustan government budget, throttling the spending commitments of large departments such as the Department of Agriculture.[48]

It was at this point that Transkei's agricultural planners dusted down an old plan of introducing a livestock tax. The logic was deceptively straightforward. The tax would increase Bantustan government revenues. Moreover, the tax would kick start the agricultural economy. Rural households would be forced to sell their livestock to raise money to pay the tax, which in turn would commercialise cattle keeping. The documents written by government officials were tinged with exasperation. They estimated that eight-tenths of Transkei's land was suitable for pastoral farming, which could be worth R40 million per year. Yet less than 5% of Transkei's livestock were sold at commercial cattle auctions – statistics that were shockingly low when compared to the rural areas of Zimbabwe. Finally, a veiled threat lay behind these calculations: Pretoria argued it would only give more financial aid if Transkei raised more revenue.[49]

Yet when the livestock tax was proposed to the Transkei legislature in March 1977, 'it was greeted with shocked whistles.'[50] Even members of

---

[46] Ibid.
[47] *RDM* 16 October 1979.
[48] Ibid.
[49] Gibbs, 'Popular Resistance', p.152.
[50] *Cape Times* 24 March 1977.

Matanzima's party railed against it. Quite simply, most rural households were not in a position to pay additional taxes by engaging in profit-making farming activities. Agricultural production had flatlined, whilst Transkei's resident population doubled to 2.9 million by 1985.[51] The consequences were complex, but the painstaking research done by a generation of anthropologists, who did intensive stints of fieldwork in the rural communities scattered across the hills of the Eastern Cape, provides us with some clues. Researchers would ask old men about the livestock they herded in their youth, checking memories against government records. Around half of Transkei's households still held cattle (a proportion not much changed since the 1930s), and increasingly people kept goats, chickens and other small stock. But livestock were now mostly held as assets, to sell when a child needed a new school uniform, or to slaughter when father returned home from the mines at Christmas, rather than for productive farming purposes.[52]

Both the physical and social landscape of Transkei had been transformed in a generation. Aerial photographs from the 1940s show relatively few homesteads scattered across the ridges of the hills with fields laid out in the valleys between. This was the 'beautiful country of rolling hills and fertile valleys... [irrigated] by a thousand streams that keep the landscape green,' which Nelson Mandela's autobiography evokes so lyrically.[53] Three decades later, the aerial photographs show more homesteads, increasingly built with mud bricks and tin roofs rather than wattle-and-daub and thatch. These dwellings were clustered closer together, separated by smaller, enclosed gardens. The old fields largely lay empty. By the late 1970s very few people held large herds of more than eight cattle, which was the minimum considered necessary to have a surplus that could be sold to market to pay the stock tax.[54]

Tensions were particularly high in Eastern Mpondoland which, as one of the main cattle-keeping areas in the Eastern Cape, would be hardest hit by the proposed stock taxes. When government officials went to King Botha Sigcau's royal residence to explain the new taxes, they faced uproar. One explained:

> [At the Great Place] where the Paramount Chief had called us [for a general meeting] ... a discussion arose where the Honourable [Government] Minister said it was essential for these taxes to be paid. When we had gone through the agenda the Pondos howled at us... We did our best... pointing out the tax had been lowered... We pointed out we were a free country, that if the Transkei is to be developed we would have to raise our own revenue... Even then they were not satisfied. They instructed us to come and explain the position to the legislature and have the taxes reduced again.[55]

[51] Beinart, 'Transkeian smallholders and Agrarian Reform', *JCAS* 11, 2 (1992), p.182.
[52] Patterns of livestock holding are complex, with great variations between neighbouring districts and locations. An overview is provided in *Transkei Agricultural Development Study*, pp.9, 55. Cf. W. Beinart, 'Agrarian Historiography and Agrarian Reconstruction', in J. Lonsdale (ed.) *South Africa in Question* (Cambridge, 1988), p.138, and F. Hendricks, 'Preliminary Notes on Land and Livestock in Libode' (Carnegie Conference paper 294, Cape Town, 1984).
[53] Mandela, *Long Walk to Freedom*, p.1.
[54] Bembridge, 'Aspects of Agriculture', p.19. Cf. M. Andrew and R. Fox, 'Cultivation Trends in the Transkei and Ciskei, 1940-96', (Conference paper, Fort Hare Institute of Social and Economic Research, 2003). TNA (1977), p.309.
[55] *TNA* (1977), p.334.

Regional representatives railed against the unfairness of the government. They also gave dark warnings of rural uprisings: 'In Mpondoland the ordinary man, if you have gone too far, will cut your neck,' explained one traditional leader, Cromwell Diko. 'They will tell you: "we sent you to parliament to put right our affairs and now you have decided to join Matanzima".' [56] (His comments about the prevalence of violence proved prescient as he was murdered a few years later by a hired assassin during a local chieftaincy dispute.) The Transkei Government hurriedly revised its plans and the tax was reduced once more. This was not enough. During the winter of 1977 rumours of rebellion spread throughout the Mpondo region.

Mpondoland's smothered revolt

The rumours of revolt over the livestock tax became powerful because it coincided with ructions within the heart of the Bantustan government. If the Transkei Government's delicate relationship with rural communities revealed one aspect of the fragile edifice of the Homeland state, Kaiser Matanzima's fraught relationship with the Sigcau family points towards another. Although Botha Sigcau was hardly a 'chief by the people', it is a gross oversimplification to think he was therefore a 'chief of the government', in other words, that there were only these two centres of authority, as historians sometimes suggest. [57] Whilst the Bantustan state might have established suzerainty over the rural regions, it never achieved hegemony. The Sigcaus and Matanzimas came from branches of the two most powerful regions within the Transkei territories, Mpondoland and Thembuland. The complex plots and counter-manoeuvres between regional potentates and their supporters within the Transkei Government would reveal exactly how the Bantustan state was made up of dysfunctional clusters of antagonistic personal networks and institutions.

For most of the 1960s and 1970s, Matanzima carefully manoeuvred around the interests of his powerful supporters. He once told a confidant, 'if he did not provide for the Pondos he would not last a day'. [58] Indeed, during the first crucial election campaign of 1963 that would decide whether Transkei would accept Pretoria's offer of self-government on the apartheid government's terms, Botha Sigcau held the tie-breaking position. As king, he controlled the votes of 15 unelected chiefs from Eastern Mpondoland, who sat in the Transkei Legislative Assembly by virtue of their royal blood. The apartheid government granted him the gift of a 3060 hectare farm; a few months later, Sigcau's votes secured Matanzima's victory. [59] The enduring power enjoyed by Transkei's regions had been written into the very birth of the Bantustan state.

As a reward for supporting Matanzima's Government, some of Sigcau's

---

[56] *TNA* (1977), pp.71, Cf. *DD* 7 July 1986.
[57] For instance, D. Coplan and T. Quinlan, 'A chief by the people: Nation and state in Lesotho, *Africa*, 67 (1997), pp.27-60.
[58] BTS10, Robert du Plooy, RSA Trade Representative in Umtata, to the Secretary, RSA Department of Foreign Affairs, 23 May 1978.
[59] Carter, Karis and Stultz, *South Africa's Transkei*, p.148. Cf. Streek and Wicksteed, *Render Unto Kaiser*, p.235.

supporters were raised from being headmen to sub-chiefs, then chiefs – a process that involved a government ethnologist pruning and grafting royal branches onto the king's genealogical tree. As part of the process of establishing Tribal Authorities, ten headmen were raised to sub-chiefs in the early 1960s. At least eight more sub-chiefs were created in the following decade. Officially described as 'an endeavour to link the people... more closely to their Paramount Chief', its effect was to pay off Sigcau's allies with increased salaries and powers over their localities.[60] In 1976, when Pretoria granted the self-governing territory the status of an independent state (although Transkei's 'independent' statehood was never recognised by the international community), Botha Sigcau was granted the honorific office of Bantustan State President.

More importantly, Botha Sigcau's close circle was given great power within the Transkei Government. Sigcau himself never took a seat in the cabinet. It was not becoming for a true king to grubby his hands in the business of government. But a succession of his allies played key roles in the cabinet. After the aging Columbus Madikizela stepped aside in 1969, one of Botha Sigcau's new favourites, Curnick Ndamse, was brought into the heart of the government.

The spectacular rise and fall of Curnick Ndamse reveals the fragility of the Bantustan state. Ndamse had been sacked from a lectureship at Fort Hare University in the mid-1960s because of his trenchant criticisms of the preponderance of Afrikaner academics. Matanzima brought him straight into government, despite complaints from Pretoria, in an attempt to signal that the Bantustans were not beholden to the apartheid government. Ndamse's cautious criticisms had won him plaudits and Matanzima wanted the reflected praise. Just as importantly, Ndamse's inclusion in the cabinet was intended to break the stranglehold that white officials – seconded from, paid for, and presumably answering to Pretoria – held over Transkei's government. Indeed, the Bantustan state was riven by racial hierarchies. White officials held onto the levers of power and the markers of their superior status. Black officials' promotion was also held back by the lack of training and opportunity – a legacy of white rule that continued throughout the Bantustan era.[61] The desire for African advancement, in the face of racist intransigence, quickly led to the balkanisation of the bureaucracy, torn by cliques, mistrust and suspicions.[62] Curnick Ndamse's rapid promotion was yet another thrust in this conflict that was destabilising the very centre of government.

However, there were soon rumours of a rift between Matanzima and Curnick Ndamse. The explanations offered by local politicians involved mutterings of plotting and intrigue, a feature of a culture of politics that thrives when regional and familial loyalties enmesh a fractured state. Ndamse thought it was because Kaiser Matanzima's younger brother believed his

---

[60] CMT1472, 42Q-1, 'Report of the Departmental Committee of Enquiry into Unrest in Eastern Pondoland', 9 August 1960.

[61] CKC17, White to Carter, 26 July 1963. *TLA* (1971), p.80.

[62] *DD* 12, 26 September 1968. Pretoria National Archives, Transkei Commissioner General, Box 13, File 1/1/4/1-1, (hereafter KGT13, 1/1/4/1-1), KD to the M/BAD, 17 September 1968. KGT112, N11/3/2/5/T, Under-secretary in the Transkei Department of Education to the Secretary of the department, 24 January 1974.

position as heir presumptive to the Prime Ministership was threatened.[63] Lurid rumours circulated that Adina Ndamse had contrived her husband's success by engaging in a love affair with Matanzima. What is more certain is that the Ndamses made a play for power, taking advantage of Botha Sigcau's position as a regional powerbroker.[64] Matanzima bided his time, then dealt a series of crushing blows. Curnick Ndamse was demoted in cabinet in 1970, and then ejected in 1971. He was humiliatingly evicted from his ministerial residence. Adina Ndamse, one of the top educationalists in the Transkei, was dismissed from her job. The couple rebuilt their life once more. Curnick Ndamse took a job as the manager of a furniture store in Umtata. Adina Ndamse renewed her contacts with radical students in the Black Consciousness Movement (of which more in Chapter Four). Ndamse regained the trust of his son who was heavily involved in student politics and deeply suspicious of anyone involved in the Bantustan system. Curnick Ndamse told a visiting researcher that their reconciliation was 'the sweetest news he had ever heard'. [65] Then Ndamse suddenly took ill and died in hospital – an event inevitably shrouded in suspicion.[66]

King Botha was appeased by the rapid elevation of his daughter, Stella Sigcau, who was made Minister of Education at the same time as Curnick Ndamse was sacked from the cabinet in 1971. Born in 1937, she was the first woman to hold ministerial office in South Africa's Bantustans or in the apartheid republic. Predictably, newspapers hailed her appointment as 'possibly the greatest success story of any South African woman'.[67]. Nevertheless, there was no love lost between Kaiser Matanzima and Stella Sigcau. Their differences could be traced back to student politics. When Stella Sigcau had been at Fort Hare University in the late 1950s she had been very active in the ANC Youth League. Matanzima had then been associated with their rivals, the All African Convention. Because of her political involvement, Sigcau had struggled to find a job as a teacher in the Transkei in the early 1960s. It seems she blamed Matanzima for her persecution. She taught instead in Natal at her *alma mater*, Ohlange High School. Here she briefly married another school teacher, Ronald Tshabalala, who died in 1964, leaving her a widow with two young children. A few years later she returned to the Transkei after her father had found her a seat in the Bantustan legislature, on the government benches.

As much as Stella Sigcau had benefited from her father's patronage and told newspapers about her love of her children, cookery and knitting, she was no shrinking violet. When she met a visiting researcher, Professor Tom Karis, in the mid-1970s, he was struck by her 'dramatic, white, wool-knit, evening gown' that was set off by a large belt with Ndebele-type patterns. Sigcau told Karis that she visited her children in Natal every weekend – an eight-hour round trip – breaking South African speed limits in a breakneck, cross-country drive. 'It was very difficult to press her regarding Matanzima... She doesn't seem to like Matanzima – he is aloof and cold and

[63] KGC2, Interview, Curnick Ndamse.
[64] *DD* 21 July 1970, 11 April 1971.
[65] KGC2, Interview, Curnick Ndamse.
[66] KGC3, 'Miscellaneous Transkei Conversations'.
[67] 'A Woman in Government', *South African Scope*, (December 1974), p.6.

maybe worse', noted Karis. This 'very big and handsome woman, with close cropped hair... a forceful person... seems very ready to take advantage of her position.'[68]

▲ ▲ ▲

Stella Sigcau bided her time, then struck out against Matanzima when relations between the Transkei Government and Eastern Mpondoland fell to another low point, due to the new livestock tax of 1977. The long decline and death of King Botha Sigcau in 1978 was another factor in the changing relationship between the Bantustan government and the Mpondo chieftaincy. Kaiser Matanzima clearly sensed that he had to quash the influence of the Eastern Mpondo group in parliament, and he struck first when he forced Stella Sigcau to resign from the cabinet in October 1977. The conflict that followed revealed the extent to which the dynastic networks of the Mpondo chieftaincy were intermeshed with the structures of the Bantustan state.

It was the birth of a royal child from a love affair between Stella Sigcau and another government minister, Chief JD Moshesh, which forced her out of office. Sigcau's surprise resignation from government was followed by rumours that she had been at loggerheads with Matanzima and was also pregnant. Both stories were eventually confirmed by the birth of her child in December 1977.[69] Three months later, in March 1978, the Transkei legislative assembly erupted when a member dared raise these issues publicly. 'Miss Sigcau, who attended parliament for the first time this session, sat... in stony silence.' She then told the assembly '"I do not want my name to be bandied about as if it were a toy"... The House sat in stunned silence and then adjourned for the day.'[70] A fortnight later, 'shaking with anger', Kaiser Matanzima told the legislature:

> I warned ministers to have no love associations with Minister Sigcau... No sooner did I make this warning then I discovered Miss Stella's movements with another Minister... When it became clear to the general public that Miss Stella was in an advanced state of pregnancy, I advised her to resign from cabinet to avoid scandal.[71]

Matanzima claimed that the codes governing the conduct of public officials overrode customary practices regarding marriage and family. When Stella Sigcau had been the Minister of Education, her department had forced mothers to resign from government service. But Stella Sigcau was a princess, and the claims of custom were defended against the impositions of central government. Many people in the region believed that the local *ngena* (levirate) tradition allowed a widowed woman to sire children out of marriage.[72] Even government supporters from Matanzima's region acknowledged, 'the manner

---

[68] KGC3, T. Karis interview, Stella Sigcau, New York, 2 November 1974.

[69] *DD* 10 October 1977, 14 November 1977, 9 December 1977.

[70] *DD* 21 March 1978. Jeff Peires also notes that Stella Sigcau had antagonised Matanzima by attempting to grant Transkei citizenship to a white businessman – pers. comm. 30 January 2013.

[71] *TNA*, (1978), p.53.

[72] Author interview, Veli Ntsubane, Libode, 19 November 2008.

in which he has treated a member of the royal family must be shocking to them [the Mpondos].'[73]

For a short time it seemed that the fragile regional coalitions that held the Transkei Government together would unravel. Matters moved swiftly after the clash in the legislature. A day later, six members of the Legislature from East Mpondoland crossed to the opposition benches. More defectors from the East Mpondo chieftaincy followed, and in May 1978 they formed a breakaway grouping, the Transkei National Progressive Party.[74] Matanzima replied by rewriting the constitution so that the breakaway chiefs were excluded from the Legislature.

The father of Sigcau's child, Chief JD Moshesh, was also drawn into the imbroglio. Moshesh represented the Sotho-speaking, north-eastern area of Transkei that abutted the mountains of Lesotho. This region was not as large or important as Eastern Mpondoland but if anything, its gripes against Matanzima's government were even more complex. Linguistic communities crossed Bantustan boundaries, and Matanzima had long feared that a number of senior chiefs in the region had been plotting to secede from Transkei and link themselves to the Sotho-speaking Bantustan of Qwa Qwa. Moshesh was put on trial for undermining the authority of the state, although he claimed that he merely wanted 'full recognition... [that] the Sotho... [were] a nation within the Transkei'.[75] In this politically febrile atmosphere, the veteran journalist, Leslie Xinwa, wondered: 'How long will Matanzima remain in power? Suddenly this has become a question some Transkeians are speculating on.' Transkei's regions threatened to spin away from Matanzima's grasp.[76]

Stella Sigcau artfully portrayed her break from Matanzima as part of the broader battle against apartheid. Rumours circulated that 'while alive, her father was a stumbling block... to her activities.'[77] Now she reminded journalists of her ANC Youth League credentials. The *Daily Dispatch* reported that 'the political reasons for the breakaway seem to be displeasure with the ambiguous stance the [Transkei] Government has taken against apartheid. In certain spheres they feel the Government has the ear of Pretoria too close.'[78] Stella Sigcau's close relationship with her brother, Chief Ntsikayezwe Twentyman Sigcau, was a definite benefit as she tried to build a broad coalition. Through Chief Ntsikayezwe's contacts, she was able to make a wider alliance in the Transkei legislature with well-known, ANC-linked dissidents.[79] In reply, Matanzima used the full force of the state against his rivals in the chieftaincy and the Eastern Mpondo region as a whole. Ntlenzi erupted in revolt once more in 1979, when another member of the Sigcau royal family was arrested after 'a skirmish... between police and Mpondos' that left two dead. The battles were so ferocious that the police deployed a helicopter to comb the neighbouring

---

[73] *DD* 12 May 1978.
[74] *TNA* (1978), p.234.
[75] *DD* 7 August 1975. Cf. 3 September 1976, 27 October 1976, 9 April 1980.
[76] *DD* 19 May 1978.
[77] KGC3, 'Miscellaneous Transkei Conversations'.
[78] *DD* 11 April 1978.
[79] *DD* 28 March 1979.

gorges and ravines during mopping-up operations that led to 137 arrests. [80]

With the death of Botha Sigcau, the struggles to control the Eastern Mpondoland paramountcy became central. Kaiser Matanzima plotted to break the power of Stella Sigcau by trying to remove her closest brothers, Ntsikayezwe and Mpondombini, from their positions in the chieftaincy. In September 1979, the police mounted a dawn raid on the homesteads of seven of the leaders of the Sigcau breakaway. [81] Twelve rifles and two revolvers were found. Stella Sigcau's elder brother, Mpondombini appeared in the magistrate's court on a charge of holding unregistered firearms – a charge which, had it stuck, might have opened the path for the government to depose him under the Transkei [Tribal] Authorities Act. [82] Stella later told her colleagues in the Transkei Legislature how:

> The Great Place at Quakeni was surrounded by 19 police vehicles... Women were sjamboked [beaten]... A very tall lieutenant [said]: "I am used to arresting even Paramount Chiefs. I can apply all the force I want to get information from you"... If he can adopt that attitude at the Great Place, how much more violent will he be in dealing with ordinary people? [83]

The government also tried to convict Chief Ntsikayezwe of misconduct for saluting Mpondombini ahead of Prime Minister Matanzima at an official function. But the government's case was defeated in court: 'the judgement greeted with great joy, excitement and ululating from the big crowds gathered outside'. Later that night, 'a victory celebration was held at the Quakeni Great Place.' [84]

The key battleground in this struggle was the East Mpondo kingship. With the death of Botha Sigcau, the contest for the throne was open once again. Stella Sigcau's brother, Mpondombini, as son and heir of King Botha, seemed to have the most direct claim. But Chief Majority Zwelidumile, the son of King Botha's old rival, Nelson Sigcau, stepped forward with a rival claim. [85] With Matanzima's government backing Chief Zwelidumile, to even mention these matters might unleash the full force of the state. Stories circulated that security policemen had detained people simply for discussing the succession dispute on the streets of Eastern Mpondoland's bustling towns. [86] The Quakeni Regional Authority – the council of the King of Eastern Mpondoland that was officially recognised by the Bantustan government – held firm against this intimidation. At a meeting in December 1978, Mpondombini was unanimously appointed as the king; at a second gathering in February 1979, he beat Zwelidumile by 22 votes to three. But the Transkei Bantustan

---

[80] *RDM* 12 December 1979.

[81] *DD* 21 September 1979.

[82] *DD* 21 September 1979. D. Ndima, *Law of Commoners and Kings: Narratives of a rural Transkei Magistrate* (Pretoria, 2004), p.58.

[83] *TNA* (1980), p.417.

[84] Ndima, *Commoners and Kings*, p.58.

[85] Nelson Sigcau had sired Majority Zwelidumile through *ngena* custom with the Great Wife of his father, King Madlonke, to strengthen his claim that the sire would officially be the true heir to the throne. See *DD* 12 December 1978, 9 December 1983, 14 January 1984, 26 May 1984.

[86] *TNA* (1979), p.132.

government refused to accept the results of the vote. [87]

Over the next months, the rival factions tried to manipulate customary procedures to give their own man the kingship. The Transkei Government argued that the vote in favour of Mpondombini was not valid because the Quakeni Regional Authority had become a political faction rather than councillors to the king: they 'were all members of the opposition party under... the guidance of Miss Sigcau'.[88] Instead the government demanded that the king of Eastern Mpondoland be chosen at a series of meetings in the region's towns. Initially, Mpondombini demurred: 'the dignity traditionally accorded to the office of the Paramount Chief will be permanently eroded by the appointment... by way of elections instead of the customary manner of succession.'[89] After laboriously fulfilling his customary obligations by taking a wife whose bridewealth was paid by the people, and digging the first sod of his father's grave, he feared the throne would be snatched from his grasp. But Mpondombini's qualms were unfounded. He won a series of snap votes held in Transkei's towns during the winter of 1979. These were appealed in the courts, but the Transkei government could not delay the people's will on Mpondoland indefinitely.

Matanzima finally installed Mpondombini as king in March 1980. At the ceremony he made a speech asking if 'the Pondos had learnt their lesson during the 1960 rebellion'. Matanzima made the charge that the leaders behind the unrest in Mpondoland were 'self-appointed individuals, greedy for power, hypnotised by leftist political ideologies foreign to Transkei traditions'.[90]

A family squabble?

The prospects of an above-ground political opposition were very limited in 1980. 'They would have to come up with a workable plan to make Transkei more independent of South Africa if they hope to use that [their anti-Bantustan opposition] as a political platform', opined the *Daily Dispatch*.[91] This was an almost impossible proposition, given the hegemony of the apartheid government in the region. Moreover, the unrelenting grind of state repression orchestrated by the Transkei police exhausted all but the hardiest dissidents. Stella Sigcau returned to the ruling party in August 1980, followed by most of her breakaway group. Only Chief Ntsikayezwe's small knot of supporters stayed on the opposition benches. Stella Sigcau was almost immediately given a cabinet post. Chief JD Moshesh also benefited from the political reconciliation, becoming the Bantustan government's diplomatic consul in Durban. These individuals were apparently wooed back with the soothing argument that the conflict had signified nothing: it had only been a squabble within the tight-knit family of Transkeian notables.[92]

[87] *DD* 19, 25 January 1979, 29 February 1979, 9 May 1979, 10 August 1979, 3 March 1980.
[88] *DD* 9 May 1979
[89] *DD* 29 February 1979. Cf. *DD* 19, 25 January 1979, 10 August 1979.
[90] *DD* 3 March 1980.
[91] *DD* 11 April 1978.
[92] *DD* 8 August 1980.

Even so, this second, smothered Mpondo revolt of the late 1970s suggests that despite the increasing reach of the state into rural communities, the Bantustan government did not hold the whip hand. First, rural communities successfully redefined their relationship with the state in their terms. Matanzima replaced the proposed livestock tax with a less onerous General Stock Tax. Even then the rate of tax collection declined in rural areas for much of the 1980s.[93] Second, Bantustan government expenditures increased exponentially (as a result of Pretoria's subsidies) throughout the 1980s. This never seriously dented the swingeing poverty in Transkei's rural communities, but it was a drain on Pretoria's fiscus that the government could ill afford, as economic crisis mounted in the final decade of apartheid.

Moreover, the Transkei Government had been revealed as a fragile coalition that was forced to maintain a delicate relationship with regional potentates. A small but influential minority of chiefs, such as Ntsikayezwe Twentyman Sigcau, developed anti-apartheid politics, which straddled their roles as members of the chieftaincy, prominent politicians in the Transkei state, and individuals linked to prominent ANC families. There was also a much larger group of malcontents clustered around Stella Sigcau. In 1987, she would briefly take power after a successful coup brought down the Matanzima brothers – which in turn would set off a train of events leading to the ANC's return to the region. Govan Mbeki had castigated Botha Sigcau in his famous book, *The Peasants' Revolt*; but Winnie Mandela would keep channels open to her kin the Mpondo chieftaincy.

---

[93] *TNA* (1978), p.117. *TNA* (1979), p.147. Cf. *Report of the Auditor General* (1977-85).

4. The Old Mission Schools 1963–1980

The Children of Soweto and Transkei's elite

Above all, it was the mission schools dotted across the Native Reserves that shaped the African elite during the middle decades of the 20th century. The story is most easily told in the figures. In 1940, the year after Nelson Mandela left Healdtown College, there were only 5,800 African pupils in secondary school in the entire country. Two decades later, when Thabo Mbeki sat his school exams at St Johns College at Umtata, secondary schooling remained an elite concern. In 1960 only 4% of African teenagers attended a secondary school; even fewer graduated. That year, there were 47,000 African pupils in secondary school, of which just 957 sat the Senior Certificate exam that marked the end of school education. Consequently, African political elites were linked together by close-knit kinship, friendship and rivalries. [1]

In one sense, apartheid marked a generational watershed. During the Bantu-stan era the pre-eminence of the tiny network of mission schools – mainly based in the Eastern Cape – was largely overshadowed by the 'massification' of South African society. The centre of gravity in youth politics largely shifted from the old mission colleges to the burgeoning township schools. By 1980 one-third of African teenagers attended secondary school. The number taking the school leaving exam nationwide climbed from 957 in 1960 to 774,000 in 1980. (This 800-fold increase far outstripped the demographic growth rates, with the African population increasing from 11 million to 21 million in the same period.) Transkei's school enrolments followed national trends: from 1964 to 1980, secondary school pupil numbers grew from 9,500 to 151,000, whilst population numbers doubled. The numbers in Transkei taking the exams that marked the end of schooling rose from 167 to 7,600 over the same period. [2]

At the same time, the apartheid government's Bantu Education policies – legislated in 1953 – legally enshrined the second class education provided to Africans.[3] Schools were often the focal points of white domination and student anomie: they were institutions simmering with unrest. There were three great waves of pupil protest. Soweto's townships, to the southwest of Johannesburg, made headlines around the world in 1976 when pupils from its secondary

---

[1] K. Hartshorne, *Crisis and Challenge: Black education, 1910-90* (Oxford, 1992), p.43. Unterhalter, 'Bantu Education', pp. 37, 39.

[2] Unterhalter, 'Bantu Education', pp.39, 42. Hartshorne, *Black Education*, pp.43, 128. Beinart, *South Africa*, p.262. Transkei Department of Education, *Annual Reports* (Umtata, 1964-1994).

[3] J. Hyslop, '"A Destruction Coming In": Bantu Education as a response to social crisis', in P. Bonner, P. Delius, D. Posel (eds), *Apartheid's Genesis, 1935-62* (Johannesburg, 1993), pp.393-410.

schools led a boycott and demonstrations that turned into the first revolt that broke a decade of silence. In 1980, a less iconic but more far-reaching school boycott spread from Cape Town to South Africa's other main cities, as well as across the Western and Eastern Cape. Another round of school revolts in the mid-1980s would radiate even further into the rural areas, causing a nationwide conflagration.

The exiled South African writer, Mbulelo Mzamane, was teaching in Botswana in the late 1970s as the teenage refugees from the Soweto uprising fled across the border. A few years later he produced a fictionalised treatment of the 1976 revolt, *The Children of Soweto*. In Mzamane's book, the young students are heralds of a modern society in which the grievances of an angry, youthful generation, alienated by their experiences of inferior Bantu Education, would dominate the political landscape of South Africa.[4] A classic example is Tsietsi Mashinini (1957-1990), a student leader at Morris Isaacson School in Soweto, who became the figurehead of the revolt. He typified the transformation of South African society. His father was a labourer, his mother a domestic servant. Both parents had poured their energies into educating their offspring, only to see their children consumed by the Soweto uprising. 'These were not members of the political elite', writes the family biographer, Lynda Schuster. They were 'the foot-soldiers... the story of black South Africa in a microcosm.'[5]

But if the Soweto revolt epitomised the mainstream of mass protest, this chapter contends that there were also significant counter-currents in the Bantustans. By 1980, Transkei's schools were in the throes of rebellion. Here was a profoundly different pattern from the township revolts. In the Transkei it was the long-established elite educational institutions that were the focus of the protests. The best school in the territory, St Johns College, founded by the Anglican Church in 1879, was at the centre of events. The story of *The Children of Soweto* and the mass youth revolts of the 1980s – in both urban and rural areas – are well told in fiction, journalism and history writing, but far less is known about the elite Bantustan schools during the apartheid era. This chapter argues that, paradoxically, the 'massification' of South African society – particularly the youth revolts that followed the expansion of African schooling – reinforced elite networks. Facing huge uncertainties, well-to-do parents strove to secure their family fortunes, and for much of the apartheid era the best educational and professional opportunities were found in the Bantustans. Schools such as St Johns College attracted pupils from across South Africa.

The Bantustan state would play a vital and very ambivalent role in the formation and politicisation of African elites. On the one hand, schools such as Jongilizwe College for the Sons of Chiefs and Headmen had been explicitly designed to educate the future officials and leaders of the Homeland state. At the same time, schools like St Johns College would produce some of the best educated opponents of the Bantustans. The politically ambiguous, interwoven

---

[4] M. Mzamane, *The Children of Soweto* (Harlow, 1987).
[5] L. Schuster, *A Burning Hunger: One family's struggle against apartheid* (London, 2004), pp. 2-3. Cf. Glaser, *Bo-Tsotsi*, pp.159-183. For the rural areas, see Delius, *A Lion Amongst the Cattle*, pp.155-65.

ties of kinship, educational and professional connections would matter as much for the generation that came of age in the 1970s and 1980s as it had done to Nelson Mandela and Kaiser Matanzima, who had been educated together in the 1930s.

Lazy teachers, school scandals, community collapse

The survival of Transkei's elite secondary schooling during the Bantustan era was far from obvious to contemporaries. In the middle of the riots and boycotts that afflicted Transkei's schools in the 1970s, African parents feared that the golden age of elite missionary education, which they had enjoyed during the first half of the century, was now finished. Stella Sigcau was Transkei's Minister of Education, thanks to her birth as the daughter of the powerful Paramount Chief of Mpondoland and her education at Fort Hare University. She so distrusted Transkei's schools that she would have sent her children out of the country to an exclusive, multi-racial school at Waterford in Swaziland, if only she had been able to afford the fees. The need to secure a family's future through education could even override bitter political differences. Nelson Mandela had first met his cousin, Chief Kaiser Matanzima, at Fort Hare University in the 1940s. Now Mandela was imprisoned on Robben Island and Matanzima was the leader of the Bantustan government in Transkei; yet they set aside these rivalries to help each other's children gain precious scholarships to foreign schools and universities.[6]

When the African elite contemplated the crisis of schooling, they most often mourned the demise of the grand old mission schools in the old Native Reserves. In the late 1950s, the apartheid government starved mission schools of financial subsidies for refusing to comply with the Bantu Education Act. Rather than conform, most missions relinquished control of the schools, which were taken over by the apartheid government and subsequently transferred to the new Bantustan governments. Only the elite Catholic schools held out, fortified by subsidies from Rome. As early as 1959, Govan Mbeki was writing articles predicting 'the rape' of the mission schools. In the 1970s, the Transkei Government used its self-governing status to have some of its schools opt out of the second-rate, Bantu Education curriculum offered to Africans.[7] However, they were fiddling at the margins.

The heart of the matter was the ill-planned, underfunded expansion of secondary schooling during the apartheid era. Rural society was fundamentally transforming in the Bantustans. Youths who would once have herded cattle in their teenage years now entered school *en masse*.[8] In one sense, the Bantu Education system was an attempt to provide mass education to a mass society. The mission school system, which was only partially subsidised by the state and depended on voluntary contributions from the church and parents' fees,

---

[6] Karis interview. Sigcau. Lodge, *Mandela*, p.80.
[7] S. Ngubentombi, *Education in the Republic of Transkei: Some origins, issues, trends and challenges* (Pretoria, 1989), p.58. Gevisser, *Thabo Mbeki*, p.103.
[8] Delius, *A Lion Amongst the Cattle*, pp.155-7.

had been cracking at the seams. However, the apartheid government never adequately funded African schools. [9] In the townships, and particularly in the Bantustans, there were always shortages of classrooms, books, and trained teachers. This dearth was most painfully felt in the most marginalised schools, typically found at the end gravel roads in the remote mountains; but to varying degrees the rot also infected many of the better schools.

One consequence of this disastrous expansion of secondary schooling was a crisis of staffing and educational standards that spread throughout the entire system. The percentage of teachers with a university degree declined in the Transkei. A cohort of ill-qualified primary school teachers took promotion and joined secondary schools. Following the advice of apartheid policy planners, the Transkei Government attempted to fill the breach by instituting a bewildering new range of teacher training courses, but there was still a fundamental shortage of staff. The graduates from Transkei's teacher training institutions were able 'to meet little more than the expected annual loss [of teachers] through death, retirement, illness and resignation'. [10] As a result, low morale was endemic, even in the highest echelons of the educational system. 'One [teacher training] college principal taught 35 periods a week', noted a government report, 'because many of his staff could not... meet the academic demands.' [11] When the staff started skipping class, they were, in turn, followed by the trainee teachers.

Desperate for academic achievement in a demoralised educational system, pupils and teachers bent the rules and cheated in exams. This was dramatically evident in a Transkei-wide, examination cheating scandal in 1978. It surfaced when an inspector caught the boys from the prestigious St Cuthbert's School cribbing an exam paper. 'The boys threatened to stab him. The invigilator appealed to the police for protection and the boys were arrested.' Next, the Transkei Department of Education received information: 'pedlars were making a fortune in the streets of our two largest towns and in the countryside, through the sale of examination papers.' [12] The Department called in the police. During the course of the following year, a series of trials of the teachers and principals involved in the fraud uncovered a network of complicity. Many came from the most prestigious, former missionary schools. At least 25 teachers and bureaucrats were jailed. Far more striking than the details of bureaucratic corruption was the sheer desperation for exam success that had led to the fraud. The principal of one school claimed that he feared demotion if he did not produce good exam results, so he gave a leaked exam paper to a pupil, who organised secret evening study classes. The rot quickly spread even to schools that enjoyed relatively good academic results, including St Johns College, whose principal was sacked for his complicity in the scandal. His *mea culpa* was that pupils in his school had pleaded to be given sight of the

[9] Hyslop, 'Bantu Education', pp. 397–401.
[10] A. Donaldson, 'Aspects of the Economics of Education in Transkei' (University of South Africa, MA thesis, 1984), p. 230.
[11] S. Ngubentombi, 'Teacher Education in Transkei' (University of Natal, Ph.D. thesis, 1984), p. 212. Cf. Du Preez, 'The Education System in Transkei', p. 89.
[12] *TLA* (1979), p. 234. Cf. *TLA* (1980), pp. 297, 323. Also see *DD* 13, 14 June; 12, 14, 15 September; 5 December 1979.

exam papers. Since '99.9% of the pupils were in possession of the papers... it would be unfair to those that did not have them.'[13]

The decay of buildings and institutions was another consequence of an underfunded educational system. The conditions in the boarding hostels were a particular flashpoint, given that so many pupils boarded in Transkei because they lived so far away from the nearest school. In one sense, this was not a new problem. There had been persistent complaints about inedible food and spartan living conditions during the period of mission control during the first half of the 20th century. (Thabo Mbeki was expelled from Lovedale College in 1959 for his role in a school strike that demanded 'no more rotten food.')[14] The situation dramatically worsened during the Bantustan era as the Transkei Government had neither the capital to immediately take over the hostels or the finances to properly subsidise them. The hostels were gradually transferred to the Transkei state over the course of two decades until only three remained under mission control in 1980.[15] During this time, many of these underfunded boarding institutions unravelled. The government issued statutory guidelines to improve conditions in the hostels after repeated outbreaks of disease, but angry speeches and government regulations were not enough. Quite simply, private and church-run hostels were unable to raise boarding fees to maintain their quarters when so many African parents struggled to pay even the most basic charges.

Most records of these schools have rotted away along with the fabric of the buildings, but we do have the startling comments made by a delegation of government officials who visited Clarkebury school in 1976, following an outbreak of typhus which hospitalised 215 pupils and staff.[16] The sewer system barely functioned and the water supply was contaminated by refuse. An educational researcher who visited Clarkebury fifteen years later found conditions no better. It was a place of 'decay and despair'. A new men's hostel had been built on campus two years ago, but was already showing signs of disrepair and the blocked drains stank. Four male students shared each double bunk in tiny rooms, although this was still better than the old dormitories which housed 60 women. Ablution facilities were so bad that students defecated in the bushes. The only patch of brightness was the perimeter fence, which 'sports a colourful variety of [drying] clothing each day.'[17] It was a sad state of affairs for the Methodist Church's oldest institution in Transkei and the *alma mater* of Nelson Mandela.

Nyanga High School, just outside the town of Engcobo, provides the most detailed example of how the erosion of educational institutions produced a new type of student protest. Actually, it was one of the better secondary schools in Transkei. It the early 1970s it was one of only a handful of schools that could boast that half-a-dozen teachers held a university degree. King Sabata, the

---

[13] *DD* 14 June 1979. Cf. *DD* 23, 28 August 1979.

[14] Gevisser, *Mbeki*, p.102.

[15] *TLA* (1980), p.301. ERD346-1, 6/1/1, Letter to Regional Director Bantu Education, 31 July 1959.

[16] *TLA* (1976), p.184.

[17] Both quotes in F. Barron, 'The Trouble with Teacher Training in Transkei' (University of Cape Town, Honours thesis, 1991), pp.48, 51.

Paramount Chief of Thembuland, sent one of his sons, Mimi Dalindyebo, to it in the late 1970s, as did the Suffragan Bishop of Cape Town. In the early 1980s, it was achieving excellent exam results.[18] But the hostel accommodation 'was so overcrowded you would be surprised it can hold so many scholars.'[19] Eight mud and thatch rondavels had been jerry-built to accommodate some of the school's 700-odd pupils. Other parents were forced to trust their children to an ad hoc variety of lodgings. Pupils might stay with relatives, sympathetic householders, or in various types of privately rented accommodation. But the best laid plans went too easily awry. One might 'take a child to [live with] relatives near the vicinity of the school' only to discover they had been set to work, and 'made to brew beer, instead of going to school.'[20] At times, parents feared that all authority might break down. One complained: 'I have known secondary schools where boys and girls are accommodated indiscriminately in rural locations, bundling into groups, exchanging places of abode... It is not love play when men with beards take advantage of the situation.' Others feared that many of 'these children did not want to be under any control.'[21]

Enterprising businessmen and charlatans, such as Sizwe Mahati, the Principal of Nyanga High in the early 1970s, were quick to seize these lucrative opportunities. Mahati amassed a small fortune by building a private boarding hostel that was attached to the school. He milked his pupils, fitting four boarders into each bunk-bed, cutting their food rations and forcing them to purchase their books and bedding from the supermarket he owned in town. Principal Mahati also fiddled the books. As chair and treasurer of the school committee, he forbade teachers to make out receipts for any financial transactions, not even for the large charitable donations given to sponsor pupils. Over a four-year period, his assets grew fourfold: he acquired an eating house in town, a large fleet of tractors, a sports utility vehicle and a luxury car. The details of the scandal came out when he was jailed for the theft of funds of more than R37,000 in 1974. 'Abuse of trust is a feature of life here... [and] I don't understand how the Department of Education let you operate these businesses,' noted the judge when sentencing Mahati. [22] But his conviction came a year too late to save Nyanga High from the student's anger. They rioted and set fire to their school in 1973, leaving a mournful shell of a burnt-out building that could be seen from the road beside it for years to come.[23]

One more consequence of the erosion of school institutions was that it gave pupils a great amount of autonomy. Students often remember the most positive aspects of the buccaneering conditions of school life they enjoyed in the boarding hostels: choosing their own prefects and enforcing their own rules; the deference shown by younger pupils to older students initiated into

---

[18] For graduate teachers: *TLA* (1972), p.294. For Mimi Dalindyebo and the Suffragan Bishop: *DD* 23 August 1980. For exam results: *Laborateur*, 2, 1 (1984), p.20. *Laborateur*, 3, 1 (1985) p.22.
[19] *TLA* (1972), p. 223. Cf. *TLA* (1974), p.153
[20] *TLA* (1972), p. 77.
[21] Both quotes *TLA* (1976), p.134.
[22] *DD* 23 November 1974. Cf. *DD* 19, 20, 21, 22 November 1974 and also *DD* 14 September 1979, 5 February 1982.
[23] *TLA* (1975), p.165.

manhood through circumcision.[24] Certainly, young men living together in the most prestigious of Transkei's schools enjoyed a close, robust companionship, forming friendships that often endured for life. Nevertheless, the Transkei Government worried at 'the increasing number of cases of assault, stabbing and drunkenness that is occurring amongst students in schools and hostels.' When 'two pupils started playing and ended up fighting' at one elite school, the defeated boy took a knife from under his bed and stabbed his rival in the back. Another time, one student tragically killed his close friend during 'a bout of fisticuffs... While this type of rough and boisterous play is frowned upon, it is all too common', lamented the school's principal.[25] Gangs of students from the Transkei government's flagship training institution, the Tsolo College of Agriculture regularly raided the girl's dormitory of a rival school. On one occasion they brandished knives and fought off a posse of prefects and boarding masters who chased them back home over the hills.[26]

These living conditions led to a novel type of politically charged protest as students struggled to defend their new-found autonomy from school and government authorities. (It was very different from the school strikes of the first half of the 20th century, which had been against the propensity of teachers to discipline and punish.)[27] Kenny Jafta was a pupil at Mount Frere School when he fell foul of a boarding master's personal grudge. The previous hostel master, despite being a supporter of Matanzima, had been popular with the boys because he allowed them to elect their own representatives; but the new boarding master insisted he would rule the hostels. One evening, when the students elected Jafta as their representative and then sang songs of protest, the new hostel master took his revenge. Later that night, when the boys were in bed, the police broke down the door. They had been called by the master, who had falsely accused the pupils of vandalising the school. Jafta was handcuffed and severely beaten, then the boys were taken outside and roughed up. When light came the next day, the pupils were cleared of wrongdoing, but their encounter with the police had tainted Jafta with political suspicion. He was not an obvious rebel, for he came from a prosperous trading family and was expected to do well in exams and gain entrance to university. The sympathetic headmaster of the school privately explained to the young student that this incident might attract the attention of the security police. The headmaster suggested that it was time for Kenny Jafta to move on. He left school to take his exams elsewhere, and a few years later joined the ANC underground. The incident at Mount Frere School was a watershed in his political life.[28]

---

[24] Author interview, Kenny Jafta, Dutywa, 10 November 2008.
[25] MTA7, 12/1/4, 'Extract from monthly circular N8/69 – 31/10/69' ('stabbing and drunkenness'). Principal, St Johns College to Circuit Inspector, 9 February 1966 ('stabbed a rival'). Principal, Blythswood College to Transkei S/Education, 4 March 1971 ('a bout of fisticuffs').
[26] Principal, Dilizintaba Secondary School to Inspector of Education (hereafter I/Education), 14 September 1966.
[27] On discipline, punishment and the racism implicit in mission schools: Bundy, 'Schooled for Life', p.9. Mager, *A Social History of Ciskei*, pp.196-213.
[28] Interview, Jafta.

'The clenched fist of Black Consciousness'

By the 1970s, many of Transkei's old mission schools were primed for unrest. Student militancy spread to Transkei's schools by night, conveyed by a small network of Black Consciousness activists from Fort Hare University.[29]

Above all, Black Consciousness was a movement born in the burgeoning universities. Over two decades the number of Africans at university grew from 752 in 1961, to 3,850 in 1974, and to 8,175 in 1981.[30] The expansion of tertiary education had been shaped by apartheid segregation. In 1959 and 1960, the apartheid government created two new government-run universities, the University of the North and the University of Zululand. At the same time, the apartheid government restricted black admissions into the 'White' universities and took control of Fort Hare University, redesignating it as a 'Xhosa institution' that would only take students from the Eastern Cape. In many ways, Black Consciousness was a challenge to the racialism and tribalism inherent in such apartheid policies. In 1968, black students, led by a young medical student, Steve Biko, split from the National Union of South African Students (NUSAS), which they perceived to be dominated by students from the white universities. A year later, Biko was instrumental in forming the South African Students Organisation (SASO). In 1972 SASO activists formed the Black People's Convention, an umbrella body for various related groups. In these years, it was 'more an intellectual orientation than a political grouping... represented by a scattering of proponents and small organisations.'[31] Black Consciousness ideologies found a ready home in the burgeoning high schools in Soweto. Because Black Consciousness was also a challenge to the ambivalent political and cultural direction of the African elite – not least those co-opted inside the Bantustans – it also had great appeal in the old mission schools in the Eastern Cape.

In the cold, unheated concrete outbuildings behind the old Transkei Legislature in Umtata, to which the Bantustan Government archives have been haphazardly banished to make way for a museum celebrating Nelson Mandela, an anonymous box file provides tantalising details of these protests. A slim folder describes – from the authorities' point of view, at least – student protests at Blythswood, one of the grand old mission schools. Blythswood Institution had been founded in 1877. A few years earlier, local *Mfengu* communities in the Butterworth district had asked for 'a child to Lovedale College' (then the most famous African school in the country) to be built in their area. Captain Blyth, the magistrate of Fingoland, had promised to match their fundraising with donations from the Free Church of Scotland. In total, the local communities raised a staggering £4,500 out of the total £7,000 of costs. An imposing, two-storey building in 'Scottish Baronial' style was built in the rolling hills. The

---

[29] Delius notes that students at the University of the North politicised surrounding schools in Sekhukhuneland in the 1980s: see *A Lion Amongst the Cattle*, pp.181-2.

[30] South African Institute of Race Relations, *A Survey of Race Relations in South Africa* (Johannesburg, 1963), p.240; later edition: (1974), p.369; later edition: (1981), p.379.

[31] Beinart, *South Africa*, p.216.

school went on to become one of the leading educational institutions, its fate deeply entwined with the fortunes of the region's African elite. When Govan Mbeki returned to the Transkei in the 1940s, he had Blythswood's pupils make him a set of handsome wooden furniture in their carpentry workshop, for his own home.[32]

In the 1970s, almost a century after its foundation, Blythswood was in turmoil, hard hit by the erosion of elite education during the Bantustan era. In the account left by the school's principal, C.K. Smart, he blamed 'visits by outsiders' from Fort Hare, who indoctrinated 'the sons and daughters of the [region's] elite... Cars visiting Blythswood came... to disseminate information on Black Power' four months before the most serious strikes started in 1975. [33] A year earlier, 'a spokesman for the students' had been bold enough to 'ask for the introduction of a Student Representative Council.' He was summarily expelled, suspected of being a political activist and having links to the South African Student's Organisation (SASO). After that, student discontent became synonymous with subversion. They anonymously 'made remarks on the blackboard, identifying themselves with Black Power.' And 'whenever there was entertainment' or a social function, 'some girls and boys appear in a black uniform suggestive of Black Power – black polo neck sweaters, huge black bowties, black shirts, black bottomed pants.' Others 'occasionally raised clenched fists.' The students were, in turn, encouraged by a clique of African teachers who made no secret at their anger of being passed over for promotion to principal of the college in favour of C.K. Smart, a white man. (Transkei's old mission schools were being gradually turned over to African principals, but the pace of change was slow.) They accused Smart of being a 'stooge of Matanzima'.[34] The infiltration of Black Consciousness ideologies into the student hostels was facilitated by the students' control over the dormitories. 'During the blackout, boys, carrying such weapons as sticks, broken bottles, sharpened iron rods, take control of activities in the institution.' [35] In defiance of school rules, they spent 'all night listening to the radio' – quite possibly tuning in to Radio Freedom programmes broadcasted by the ANC in exile. Another night, a gang of boys broke into the girl's dormitory through a toilet window, 'ensuring silence by threatening student witnesses with a knife. Their object and purpose was to get their girlfriends to sleep with them', but the girls 'scorned their importunities and either hid in their rooms or chased their suitors away.' The principal tried to fight back, drafting in teachers to make regular night patrols in order to 'thwart and quash subversion at unholy hours.' Yet the pupils were winning: 'the stranglehold of fear and pressure' had

---

[32] Bundy, 'Schooled for Life'. A. McGregor, *Blythswood Missionary Institution, 1877-1977* (KingWilliams Town, 1977).

[33] MTA7, 12/1/4/17, 'Unrest... Recommendations by the Department' ('visits from outsiders' and 'remarks on the blackboard'). Letter from Principal, Blythswood Institution, 7 June 1976 (a spokesman for the students'). 'Commission of inquiry: Disturbances in Blythswood Institution' ('raised clenched fists' and 'black bowties').

[34] MTA7, 12/1/4/17, 'Incidents after Commission's visit'

[35] MTA7, 12/1/4/17,'Commission of Inquiry' ('iron rods' and 'stranglehold of fear'). 'Recommendations by the Department' ('listening to the radio'). 'Report on Disturbances' ('they felt threatened'). Principal to Transkei I/Education, 11 October 1974 for quotes regarding girlfriends.

the 'consequence that the teachers are now refusing to do hostel duty.' A few teachers attempted to impose discipline by brute force, beating a prefect who had failed to stop the students' rebellious singing. But the prefects mutinied en masse, threatening to resign because 'they felt threatened by both the boys and the hostel authorities.'

By this time, a network of politicised students dominated Blythswood. In 1974, Smart suspected that a SASO committee 'continues to function underground'. A year later, he believed this had developed into 'an underground movement in school called "The Right Brothers", who... are untouchables'. They labelled their enemies as 'spies' – a polarising term of abuse. At least one prefect was assaulted in his dormitory with iron bars and knives by this gang of students. 'The incident created such a pressure among scholars that we [the school authorities] had to prevent an intended exodus by the most junior scholars.' The conflict finally erupted into a series of strikes, open confrontations and riots in the spring of 1975. It was heralded on Sunday 7 September, when the column of pupils marching from their hostel to the church hall sang 'war songs' instead of hymns. A week later, students plunged the college into darkness by throwing bed sheets over the power lines in the early evening hours:

> All boys in the junior block [then] gathered in the quadrangle... Staff intervention to restore order was met with violence... Mr Rapiya was attacked and stabbed and Messrs Ndleleni and Mayekiso were stoned [sic] back into their rooms. The boys ran berserk and during four tense hours they ran riot until police intervention found them huddled together between the junior block and the kitchen in trembling solidarity. [36]

The spate of unrest flowed unchecked for the next six weeks. Seven days later, the pupils rioted again, this time 'a girl masked with black stocking and armed with a knife' intimidating prefects and wavering pupils. With students now deserting Blythswood for the safety of their homes, the principal suspended a group of 56 alleged ringleaders on the 8 October in an attempt to bring peace. Even then, the Department of Education was reluctant to physically punish the ringleaders, as this might 'expose its officers to the risk' of pupils who 'decide to take revenge.'[37] Twelve days later, 'the suspended scholars were reinstated... due to a wave of intimidation of the students.' The school prize giving ceremony was then cancelled on 23 October after a rumour circulated 'that some students... would rather hold their own "picnic" where they would "put the spies right".'[38] Only the end of the school year and the long summer break quelled the worst of the protests.

When Mvula Mthimkulu, then a 14-year-old teenager, arrived at Blythswood in 1976, he found the institution was still an unhappy place. His father was a prosperous doctor in Umtata. Mthimkulu was shocked by 'the awful food and

[36] All narrative quotes in this paragraph are from MTA7, 12/1/4/17, 'Further report on Blythswood', Principal to I/Education, 11 October 1974.

[37] MTA7, 12/1/4/17 ('Departmental Meeting on student disturbances at Blythswood, Annex B)' ('a girl masked') and 'Report on a meeting with parents' ('pupils... take revenge').

[38] MTA7, 12/1/4/17, for: 'Incidents after Commission's visit' ('a wave of intimidation') and 'Further Report' ('put the spies right').

terrible ablution facilities' at secondary school that 'made militants of a lot of us.' His elder cousin-brother had been expelled during the previous round of rioting, so Mthimkulu was under suspicion of 'bringing in this influence'. There were troubles again at Blythswood in 1976 and 1977. In 1978, Mthimkulu joined a small group of pupils who planned a protest march to the local circuit inspector's office:

> Most of us were 15 or 16 years old. We had to travel from Blythswood to Butterworth [a long journey of 30 kilometres] on foot. We did it at night... and that humiliated them... They could not understand how we outmanoeuvred them, so they thought there were outside forces... I still think they responded so brutally because we scratched their egos... We were crushed and eight of us were expelled. [39]

Kicking his heels back at his family home, banned by the government from attending schools in Transkei for one year, Mthimkulu had plenty of time on his hands to meet other well educated, dissatisfied youths. Through three friends with links to the South African students' movement, he came across proscribed political literature such as the Freedom Charter, penned by the ANC in 1955. They would organise informal discussion sessions to debate these ideas. Looking back Mthimkulu smiled wryly at the youthful naivety of their heated arguments. They were a long way from the centres of student politics. Nevertheless, these informal circles would lead him towards university politics and from there into the networks of the ANC underground.[40]

'Our sin is we are Black'

If the angry pupil protests that fractured many of Transkei's secondary schools were one manifestation of the Black Consciousness ideologies spreading out of Fort Hare University, other strands of the movement emphasised ideas of African self-renewal. In the mid-1970s, a loose grouping of youthful activists spread throughout the Eastern Cape and the Transkei. The foremost example was Steve Biko, who had studied medicine for three years, his education sponsored by his local community, for his father died when he was still a child. Similarly, the memoirs of his close collaborator and lover, Mamphela Ramphele, a trained doctor, stress the community work undertaken by Black Consciousness leaders. They drew on an amalgam of ideas in their work. They combined the Africanism of the mid-century political movements with a sense of black pride and self-assertion that was espoused by 'Third World' thinkers such as Franz Fanon (who also practised as a doctor). The South African colleges that trained the black clergy – not least Federal Theological Seminary which was based next door to Fort Hare – were also important incubators of a 'liberation theology' that grappled with the problems of apartheid.[41]

Education was a particular priority for Black Consciousness activists.

---

[39] Author interview, Mvula Mthimkulu, East London, 13 November 2008.
[40] Ibid.
[41] Hadfield, 'Restoring Human Dignity'. Magaziner, *The Law and the Prophets*. M. Ramphele, *Mamphela Ramphele: A life* (Cape Town, 1995). Denis and Duncan, *Federal Theological Seminary*.

Pondering the crisis of elite education, Vuyani Mrwetyana, an activist and editor of a weekly newssheet that he printed in Umtata, pleaded: 'We want schools with prestige and an African curriculum... and not the patched up shacks that honour the glory of separate development.'[42] Mrwetyana's prose captured the frustrations that followed the erosion of the mission schools. Might not it be possible, speculated Black Consciousness activists, for distinctively African solutions to be found for the troubles in Transkei's schools. Adina Ndamse had been senior educationalist in the Transkei bureaucracy and her husband had been a cabinet minister. But after Kaiser Matanzima drove her husband out of government, Adina became an officer in the Black Community Programmes women's division. She toured the Transkei, telling the Catholic Women's Congress that: if corrupt principals-turned-businessmen looted school funds, then business associations had a duty to 'root out the evil rivalry... and plan long term benefits for the community at large... We can rehabilitate the Black Community's lost self-image... [with] a lot of hard work, devotion, sacrifice and seeking of God's guidance and help.'[43]

In the early 1970s, Kaiser Matanzima tried to co-opt the youthful energies of Black Consciousness activists into the Bantustan project. Steve Biko's refrain – 'Black man you are on your own' – seemed to suggest there might be some points of contact between them. Pretoria complained that 'when South Africa banned the Black People's Convention, the Transkei Government was instrumental in assisting the organisation in Transkei in getting back the R 30,000 in their bank account [which had been] liquidated' by the apartheid government.[44] Another report grumbled that two leaders of South African Student's Organisation were openly conducting their business in Transkei.[45] Matanzima once tried the clenched-fist salute of Black Power in the unlikely setting of the Transkei Legislative Assembly – much to the bewilderment of most onlookers.

To a certain extent, Matanzima succeeded. In the early 1970s, the Revd Hammington Qambela had started off as a fiery SASO activist at the Federal Theological Seminary which had a formidable reputation for producing politically minded church leaders. (Indeed, Hammington Qambela's militancy had caused bitter conflict with more cautious, moderate student leaders, such as Njongonkulu Ndungane, a future archbishop of Cape Town.) From there, he progressed into the upper echelons of the Black People's Convention, where he worked on the building of schools, boarding hostels, health clinics and churches across the rural Eastern Cape. In the mid-1970s, Revd Qambela was persuaded to leave the Black Consciousness Movement and take money from the Transkei government. Enjoying this state patronage, his 'philosophy of self-help spread widely' throughout Transkei. His projects were 'seen by many people as a God-sent salvation to their dilemmas.'[46]

---

[42] *Isizwe*, 1 June 1979.

[43] AAS45, file named 'Transkei Three'. Mrs A.N. Ndamse, 'Working Towards Self-Sufficiency as a Local Church – speech to Catholic Women's Congress held in Qumbu'.

[44] *DD* 30 November 1979

[45] KGT64, 1/9/3-1.

[46] *DD* 6 January 1978. Cf. *DD* 19 June 1971 and AB1886 F1.1 'Memo... from the Revd. Crispin Harrison'.

The equivocal relationship between young Black Consciousness activists and the Bantustan establishment – not least because of the social proximity of the leading participants – is captured in a reception organised for a visiting academic, Tom Karis, in the mid-1970s. It was hosted by Lennox Mlonzi, one of the founding members of the Pan African Congress, who subsequently made his peace with Kaiser Matanzima. 'He seemed anxious for me to meet critics of the Transkei Government,' Karis wrote home to a colleague. 'Yet he made a speech at the dinner party... [where] he praised the great achievements of our wonderful Transkei.' Karis also noted:

> Another notable guest... was CM Kobus, a lawyer of about 65, who was... [the] national secretary to the All African Convention ... The party also included Nimrod Mkele... [who] seems an unhappy and guilt ridden man, torn between wanting to go back to South Africa [where he had been imprisoned for political sabotage] and staying in Transkei – [apparently he was] inquiring into the purchase of a hotel in Umtata. He does not like moral dilemmas, he says...[47]

The most surprising guest at the party was the young Reverend Mcebesi Xundu, a Black Community Programmes officer and Anglican priest, who was wearing old blue jeans and a crucifix. He made a rollicking speech – how 'he was pro-black'... [almost] dancing as he spoke... Mkele slouched in a chair with a drink... muttering 'blasphemy, blasphemy, blasphemy'.[48]

Yet it was impossible for Matanzima to find common cause with a small knot of the Black Consciousness activists, who preached a politically charged message of spiritual renewal. The first big clash came when the Federal Theological Seminary (Fed-Sem) relocated to Umtata in 1975. The theological college had been forced out of the university town of Alice by the Bantustan government of the neighbouring Ciskei Homeland, because of their students' involvement in the political ferment at Fort Hare University. Bereft, they were granted temporary refuge by the Bishop of Umtata, whose patch of land in the bend of the Umtata River housed the Anglican Cathedral, St Johns College, and the tiny theological seminary of St Bede. 'The sons and daughters of Africa' felt like Israelites arriving in Canaan as they crossed the River Kei into Transkei, claimed one of the exiled students. 'They came into their own land, given [to the Anglican Church] by the old Kings, the proper owners of the land!'[49] But the 100-strong student body soon strained the cosy life enjoyed by the local Anglican hierarchy. For a start, the diocese was desperately over-stretched. St Bedes turned into a shanty town: students were 'housed in mobile homes, tents,' and sheds.[50] All meals were eaten in the open air. Then there was the unruly behaviour of the students, which shocked the local Anglican hierarchy. Women were allowed to visit the men's quarters during daytime. Some made noise after 11.30pm. Large numbers of the students enjoyed a drink at the Transkei Hotel in town.

---

[47] KGC1, T. Karis interview, PS Fadana, 2 October 1977.
[48] Ibid.
[49] AB1886, F1.1, Gcuma to Bishop of Umtata (n.d. 1975).
[50] Streek and Wicksteed, *Render unto Kaiser*, p.274. Also see AB1886, F2.5, 'SOS – Urgent –St Bedes FedSem'. On 'unruly behaviour': AB1886, F.1, 'Memo in Response to the letter of 9 July 1975 from the Bishop of St Johns.'

Some of the theological students were also bringing politics into Transkei and subverting pupils in the elite schools. There was an imbroglio over a supposedly seditious sermon given by a young trainee minister to Buntingville School, the second oldest Methodist educational institution in the Transkei. The new Warden of Buntingville, Revd Gaba, insisted the sermon was merely 'an examination service, set for probationer ministers'. The students had been seated fifteen minutes before the service began, 'as is the rule of the institution', and had simply greeted the trainee Minister with the fashionable clenched fist salute.[51] But there had been politically-charged protests at Buntingville College the year before, after which 'twenty-two male pupils – among them sons of highly respected Transkeians' – had appeared in court 'on charges of malicious damage.'[52] So when news of the seditious clenched-fist salute reached Kaiser Matanzima, he immediately instructed the Minister of Education to ban Fed-Sem students from Transkei's schools.[53]

The local Anglican hierarchy was also worried. 'We... have not wished to interfere with the internal political debates which take place in Transkei,' the Canon of St Bedes, Robin Briggs, assured Kaiser Matanzima. He had been shocked to see that 'some students used the clenched fist greeting in town.'[54] And Robin Briggs was appalled by the youthful ebullience of a small group of Fed-Sem students who protested at a graduation ceremony, attended by government ministers, 'by occupying VIP chairs and refusing to move. I saw them... indulging in an excessive amount of fist-waving and shouts of "Black Power". In Alice, this might go down well; in this situation, the implied militancy of the group disturbed me.'[55]

The breakpoint came on 24 March 1975, when a small group of SASO-orientated students held a well-attended Heroes' Day church service. It was a template of the commemorations held across South Africa that mourned the 1960 Sharpeville Massacre in which at least 69 peaceful protesters had been killed by apartheid police. The organisers read out 'a long list of heroes who have given their lives... in the course of liberation for the black people.'[56] Then the congregation sang the hymn, *Senzeni Na.*

What have we done?
Our sin is that we are black
Our sin is the truth
They are killing us
Let Africa return.

Kaiser Matanzima was particularly infuriated by the text of a pamphlet

[51] Above quotes from AB1886, F1.1, 'Verbal Report made by Reverend Gaba – Warden of Buntingville.'
[52] *DD* 23 October 1974.
[53] AB1886, F1.1, Harrison to Schuster, 21 July 1975. Cf. AB1886, F2.5, Matanzima to Briggs, 16 June 1975.
[54] AB1886, F.1, 'Memo in Response'.
[55] AB1886, F3, Briggs, 'Confidential Memo'. Cf. AB1886, F5, Briggs to Matanzima, 5 March 1975.
[56] AB1886, F.3, 'A Digest of the Investigations of the Four Churches into the Service at Ngangelizwe'.

handed out after the service: 'The oppressors have never been in the habit of handing out freedom to a subjugated people... in the form of separate development... [Transkei] remains an ethnic pigsty.'[57] The Government's response was swift. 'The seminary came to Umtata not for the purpose of learning theology, but for the purpose of engendering ill-feeling', Matanzima told a packed Transkei legislature. 'I am satisfied that... they are people who are determined to incite the black people... by revolutionary means.' He threatened: 'my government will use any weapon at its disposal to get rid of the arbiters of this horrid affair... My government... will expropriate St Bedes College if it continues to harbour these people.'[58] In July 1975, the Bishop of St Johns Diocese told Fed-Sem to pack their bags and leave.

The second decisive clash between the Black Consciousness movement and Matanzima's Government came shortly after Steve Biko's brutal killing by the apartheid police in September 1977. His politicised funeral mobilised thousands of students across South Africa. In Transkei, the Revds Mcebisi Xundu and Prince Ntlintili sent a dozen buses, packed with pupils from the elite colleges, to attend Biko's funeral. They also organised a 400-strong memorial service in Umtata, attended by the pillars of the Transkei state – 'the Commissioner of Police... magistrates, top civil servants and lawyers.' Their sermons provocatively claimed: 'the congregation had come to identify with the ideals of the pursuit of liberation of the black people of Azania [Africa].'[59]

Kaiser Matanzima was clearly worried that the Black Consciousness activists had managed to gain the sympathy, not only of young students, but also of many senior professionals. Just one month after Steve Biko's death, he took decisive action: 'we shall sweep them out like dirt,' he announced.[60] In October 1977, the offices and homes of Black Consciousness officials were searched by security police. The organisation was liquidated; their project materials looted by the security forces. Ten days later, the organisers of Steve Biko's memorial service were detained. The same night, police searched the house of Adina Ndamse. Even the unhappy Nimrod Mkele – who just a few months previously had been debating whether or not to throw his hand in with the Bantustan government – was caught in the police sweep.[61]

Elite schooling survives

Although Black Consciousness activists lamented the collapse of African education, Transkei still had some of the best schools in South Africa. Many of the mission schools that had educated the African elites in the first half of the 20th century maintained their reputation, relatively speaking, even during the era of Bantu Education and government control. Ironically, the overall erosion of the schooling system reinforced the small circles of educational

[57] AB1886, F.3, 'The Ngangelizwe Incident'. Cf. AB1886, F.1, 'Memo in Response'.
[58] Matanzima's speech: *TLA* (1975), pp.252.
[59] All quotes in this paragraph are from *DD* 19 September 1977.
[60] *DD* 17 October 1977. Cf. *DD* 25, 28 October, 30 November 1977.
[61] Arrest of Ndamse and service organisers: *RDM* 13 October 1997. Arrest of Mkele: *The Star* 3 December 1977.

privilege. Realising the importance of educational success, parents struggled to get their children into the better schools. For many African parents, trying to find a means for their children to succeed in the broken school system created by apartheid, the former mission schools often offered them the best hopes of social success. This was particularly so after 1976, when many township schools descended into chaos. [62]

St Johns College, the school founded by the Anglican Church at Umtata in 1879, established a reputation as one of the best schools in South Africa during the Bantustan era. It more or less successfully survived the transfer from missionary to government control, unlike Lovedale or Healdtown, whose prestige rapidly declined. Even so, it did not have the ebullient spirit of its missionary founders. Arriving at St Johns College in 1979, an idealistic young teacher, Glen Fisher, found an institution that was shocked and humiliated. The school's principal had been summarily sacked for his role in Transkei's examination fraud scandal. Fisher organised the school's centenary celebrations almost singlehandedly. The teachers were listless; they thought the event would only 'symbolise sadness'[63]. But over the coming months, Fisher made the surprising discovery that even if the institution was frayed at the edges, the school's foundations were still firmly in place.

About half a dozen teachers, approximately one third of St John's staff, were excellent and experienced educators. Most of them were older women in their fifties, university graduates and polished products of the old mission schools. Perhaps the most treasured of the male teachers was Victor Mzimba: a dapper dresser in red socks and a blazer, who had Mozart blaring out of his office during his free periods, and who would regale colleagues with stories about his experiences as a political activist in the Cape African Teachers Association, many decades earlier. Glen Fisher would later reflect that these teachers 'almost saw themselves as guardians and protectors of the people... The [Bantu Education policies of the] apartheid government had set out to destroy African society, but they stood in the way.' Then there were the famed educational standards of the St Johns pupils. The College was an oversubscribed, selective school, attracting African children not only from the Transkei region, but from across the whole country. Transkei cabinet ministers were always trying to wheedle their children into the school, but by-and-large the school's meritocratic principles held firm.[64]

While some of the grand old mission colleges quite literally rotted away, others more or less survived. Some even claimed that St Johns College was among the top half dozen schools in the country during the apartheid era. Then there was a group of newer schools – such as Jongilizwe College for the Sons of Chiefs or Matanzima High School – which through government favour or good fortune established a good reputation, attracting relatively well qualified teachers. Andrew Donaldson, a young economics lecturer working in the Transkei, wrote that it was a dozen or so 'older, more established schools

---

[62] This was mentioned by many interviewees and is also referenced by J. Dlamini, *Native Nostalgia* (Johannesburg, 2010), pp.86-7.
[63] Author interview, Glen Fisher, by telephone, 1 October 2009.
[64] Ibid.

[that] attain[ed] the better scholastic results.'[65] It is difficult to gauge the exact importance of schools such as St Johns College because the fragmented, dysfunctional education bureaucracies created during the apartheid era did not collect statistical data systematically. Yet the few shards of evidence that remain suggest that the circles of privilege were still extremely small. It was these schools that drew in the majority of university educated teachers: in 1972, one-third of the 155 teachers in Transkei who held a university degree taught in just eight schools. These schools dominated the school league tables. For instance, in the 1984 Standard 8 examinations, St Johns pupils accounted for seven of the twenty best results.[66]

Schools such as St Johns College were central to the process of elite formation. The biography of Pathekile Holomisa (b.1959), who would become a prominent ANC parliamentarian as leader of the caucus of traditional leaders, illuminates how tight-knit family networks were linked into educational institutions. His grandfather, Chief Bazindlovu, was the leader of the Hegebe Traditional Authority in Thembuland and sat on the government benches of the Transkei legislature. Pathekile Holomisa grew up far from home in the household of Chief Douglas Ndamase, who was married to one of his aunts. Douglas Ndamase was a well educated, senior traditional leader and businessman in Western Mpondoland who joined Matanzima's government in the 1970s. Holomisa remembered that 'a lot of traditional leaders took their own children to be brought up with him' – away from the intrigues that inevitably surrounded a royal heir – 'because he was a stern personality'. Initially, Holomisa attended the local village school. 'We herded cattle like all other boys in the village, we tilled the lands, cultivated crops, harvested them. We milked the cows, we fed the pigs and fowls and everything else.'[67] Education was an equally important part of the training provided by Douglas Ndamase. Holomisa won a scholarship to St Johns College; then his law degree at the University of Natal was paid for by the Hegebe. Thus the upper echelons of the chieftaincy provided one means of ascent. 'Don't lay a hand on him [Pathekile Holomisa]', a fellow staff member warned Glen Fisher during his first weeks teaching a St Johns College: 'His is royal blood.'[68]

The experience of elite education during the Bantustan era knitted together a network of young notables who were the scions of the chieftaincy and professional families. Oyama Mabandla, one of Pathekile Holomisa's closest friends at St Johns College is an example. He came from a prominent family of professionals who had returned to Transkei from Cape Town in the mid-1970s, when his father took a position in the Bantustan bureaucracy. This well paid post provided them the means to live in the prosperous, once segregated, Fort Gale suburb of Umtata. Nevertheless, political sympathies and family connections crossed Bantustan divides. Mabandla was related to Tennyson Makiwane, who was prominent inside the ANC in exile in the 1960s and early 1970s. His father had driven the family to attend Steve Biko's funeral in 1977.

[65] Donaldson, 'Aspects of Education', p.211
[66] *Laborateur*, 2, 1 (1984), p.20. *Laborateur* 3,1 (1985), p.22.. *TLA* (1972), pp.294-5.
[67] This narrative from P. O'Malley interview with Pathekile Holomisa, 22 August 1993, 16 October 1996.
[68] Ibid. Interview, Fisher.

Mabandla's family often talked about these intertwined personal and political matters when they were together.[69]

Within this tight-knit milieu, Transkei's top schools provided a fertile ground for politically charged debates, in which a small coterie of students were often influenced by an older generation of teachers from leading Eastern Cape families. Despite the *en masse* resignation of many teachers during the 1950s in protest against Bantu Education, there were still some politically engaged teachers active in Transkei's schools. Perhaps the most startling glimpse into these circles is given in the memoirs of Dumisa Ntsebeza, who today is a senior advocate (i.e. barrister) and public intellectual based in Johannesburg. Ntsebeza was born in a district of Transkei where, historically, the writ of the chieftaincy did not run far. (Indeed, his distrust of traditional leaders is a constant theme in his memoirs.) His father had founded a secondary school in Transkei; his mother and sister were teachers too; and his younger brother, Lungisile, would later become a professor at the University of Cape Town. Yet Dumisa's first post was in 'the modern white buildings of Jongilizwe College' which had been built 'in the rolling green hills' of Tsolo to educate the sons of chiefs.[70] Dumisa was given the job largely because of the formidable reputation of his family. 'If you are half as good a teacher as your mother, I'll be happy', Ntsebeza was told by the school principal on his arrival.[71]

Jongilizwe College was a creation of apartheid, designed to turn the scions of the chieftaincy into competent Bantustan administrators. Nevertheless, Ntsebeza – known as Cat to his pupils – was a popular figure because he encouraged debate and dissent. He stocked the school library with subversive books. His class studied *A Man for All Seasons*, the Robert Bolt play that explored the fraught relationship between an autocratic monarch, King Henry VIII, and a man of conscience, Sir Thomas More. The moral dilemmas of the Tudor monarchy surely raised pointed questions for the children of the Transkei chieftaincy.[72] Thus Ntsebeza became a mentor to a significant number of the young students who would become prominent politicians.

On Sunday evenings, a menagerie of friends and favourite pupils would gather in Dumisa Ntsebeza's room to discuss politics. One favourite was Bantubonke ('Bantu') Holomisa (b.1955), a son of Chief Bazindlovu and uncle to Pathekile Holomisa – although, as is typical in large polygamous families, uncle and nephew were almost the same age. Another regular guest, Matthew Goniwe, soon to become a famous ANC political activist, was then well known as a dynamic teacher at Holomisa High School, named after Bantu Holomisa's father, Chief Bazindlovu. Goniwe came from Cradock, 400km away on winding roads. His mother was a domestic servant; yet he had risen to prominence via his hard-won education in the best Eastern Cape schools. In this sense, the African elite was relatively open, at least for bursary students who could climb up through the education system.[73] Dumisa's Ntsebeza's rooms were the place

---

[69] Author interview, Oyama Mabandla, Johannesburg, 1 September 2009.
[70] 1/UTA118, 1/1/1, Jongilizwe Prospectus, 1962.
[71] T. Bell and D. Ntsebeza, *Unfinished Business: South Africa, apartheid and truth* (London, 2003), p.128.
[72] *Sunday Independent* 11 September 1997.
[73] Author interview, Bantu Holomisa (BH), Pretoria 2 September 2008. Ntsebeza mentions BH in

where all sorts of people with all sorts of views gathered. It typified the swirling political currents of the 1970s.

The ANC in the old mission schools

The ANC underground began to secretly infiltrate Transkei's top schools during the final years of the 1970s. A far more subversive type of politics was in the air. The ANC guerrilla commander, Chris Hani, was based in Lesotho, and many of the men who had been imprisoned on Robben Island now returned to Transkei on their release (as will be discussed in Chapters Five and Six). Trusted comrades smuggled pamphlets and propaganda across the border; the older men started drawing well educated youths into discussion circles, bringing some of them into underground structures.[74] Indeed, the intellectual hothouse in Umtata, St Johns College, would produce some of the leading cadres of the ANC movement during the 1980s.

During the long Christmas vacation in the southern-hemisphere summer of 1979-80, the ANC stepped up its recruitment campaign. Alfred Xobololo, a longstanding member of the ANC underground, approached a handful of senior school and university students who were at home on holiday around Umtata. On the 15 January 1980, the core group of students announced to the Transkei press that that they had formed a youth league attached to the Transkei Democratic Party that opposed Kaizer Matanzima in the Bantustan legislature. (See Chapter Five for more on the Democratic Party.) A young journalist, Zola Dunywa, was its president. The vice-president, Teddy Mpahlwa, was the son of a former boarding master at St Johns College. (Teddy's younger brother, Mandisi Mpahlwa, would become a cabinet minister in the ANC government.) The Youth League's secretary, Ndima Saliwa, and its treasurer, Kaiser Mbete, were both pupils at St Johns. Their friend, Mazwi Yako, a Fort Hare student, educated at one of South Africa's top schools in Natal, was chosen as Chairman.[75]

Mazwi Yako later wrote a biographical account for an ANC vetting committee, giving us a flavour of the times. He had been born in Umtata in 1959, the son of two teachers. They had sent him off to school when he was only a tiny four-year-old, much smaller than his classmates, who were three years his senior. He had thrived at school, moving up through the classes much faster than his contemporaries.. Yako passed his Standard 6 primary school examination with flying colours in 1973, before travelling outside Transkei to board at St Francis College (also known as Marianhill High) in Durban. This made Mazwi Yako one of the lucky few: Marianhill was reputedly one of a handful of elite African schools whose reputation had more or less survived the traumas of the Bantu Education system. With this prestigious background, it was not surprising that, when Mazwi returned to Transkei for the long

---

[(contd)] *Unfinished Business*, p.129. For Matthew Goniwe's hinterland, see J. Seekings, *The UDF: A history of the United Democratic Front, 1983-91* (Oxford, 2000), p.310.

[74] KGC2, G. Gerhart interview, Oyama Mabandla, Johannesburg, 19 August 1996.

[75] *DD* 15 January 1980. Mazwi Yako, *Molotov Cocktail*, 4, (March – May 2008), pp.34-5.

Christmas holiday in the summer of 1979, having completed his first year at Fort Hare University, two childhood friends looked him up. Within a few weeks he had been recruited into the ANC underground and was preparing to launch the Youth League.[76]

The inaugural event of the Youth League, held in the final week of January, was a revelation. 500 students attended the two-day conference. The packed meeting in a hall at Umtata boldly resolved: The youth would be 'the brains trust and power station' of opposition politics in Transkei. The league would 'identify itself and work hand in hand with other liberation organisations in southern Africa'. [77] The new formation survived a few days: then the entire leadership was swept into Transkei's jails. It was a stark reminder of the crushing repressiveness of the Bantustan state.

Despite the arrests, the circles of dissent did not fall silent. A loose network of youths circulated political literature – some obtained from the ANC in Lesotho – around Transkei's leading secondary schools.[78] A few months later, the first wave of politically motivated school strikes swept through Transkei's elite schools. On the 29 May 1980, George Matanzima told a shocked Transkei Legislature that these had been inspired by the subversive activities of Fort Hare students. St Johns College in Umtata was the epicentre:.

> Students had threatened to boycott classes... The boys started singing Azanian songs and went to the girl's hostel and forced the girls to join them. The police came to the hostel and defused the would-be strike. Two banners were seized and police are busy investigating who are the authors of the banners. The contents of the banners are political in that they mention Steve Biko, Robert Sobukwe and Nelson Mandela.[79]

On 5 June 1980, the Transkei Government declared a State of Emergency. It 'imposed drastic curbs on the movements and activities of... scholars and students at any [educational] institution.'[80] The results were terrifying. At one high school, 95 students were sentenced by the Transkei Police Commissioner under the Emergency Laws to be caned for holding a meeting at school without his permission. Another interviewee recalled how he had walked the long distance home after his school had been closed down by the riots, sleeping in the bush at night, like hunted game, because Transkei's police would brutally beat any student they caught breaking the curfew imposed during the Emergency.[81]

At St Johns, Glen Fisher was more sanguine. His school had not faced violent vandalism, an indication that the protests there were very different from the self-destructive violence that consumed so many other institutions. The pupils had simply 'packed their bags and gone home'.[82] Even so, the Transkei Government was right to suspect political subversion. Oyama Mabandla

[76] Ibid.

[77] 'Brains trust': *TLA* (1981), p.54. 'Work hand in hand': *DD* 28 January 1980. Cf. *TLA* (1980), p.156. Gerhart interview, Mabandla. Author interviews: Junior Saliwa, Umtata, 21 September 2009, Kaiser Mbete, East London, 25 September 2009.

[78] UTA Case 15/1982, Affidavits of Lieutenant Phindile Fatman and Detective Sergeant Bongani.

[79] *TLA* (1980), p. 438.

[80] *DD* 6 June 1980,

[81] Author interview, Israel Mdingi, Bizana, 4 April 2008. *DD* 4 August 1980.

[82] Interview, Fisher.

was one of the ringleaders at St Johns. Earlier that year he had attended the Youth League launch, where he was recruited into the ANC underground by two school friends, Kaiser Mbete and Junior Saliwa. 'I was organising these [political] discussion classes,' he later recalled. 'I was so young and foolish! ... I got hold of these contraband documents... and they landed with this woman, then someone ratted on her... And we knew it was only a matter of time [before] they came for us.'[83] All this took place in the middle of Oyama's matriculation exams: he was only 17. In desperation, he turned to his school friends who had recently been recruited into the ANC underground. Less than a week later, Oyama crossed the Orange River at three o'clock in the morning, taken into exile in Lesotho by senior ANC cadres.

That year, during the wave of school strikes that consumed the Eastern Cape's schools and Fort Hare University, scores more students from the region's elite slipped out of South Africa and fled to Lesotho. This generation of young students, bound together by close-knit friendships and rivalries, would go on to play a leading role inside the ANC, thanks to the elite education they had received inside the Bantustans.

[83] Author interview, Mabandla.

5.   The Comrade-King
Bantustan Politics 1964–1980

The dispute on Robben Island

The rural unrest in the Mpondo districts of Transkei and the school revolts pointed towards deep discontents within the Bantustans, but for most of the 1960s and 1970s, the official opposition parties, who opposed Matanzima within the Transkei legislature, struggled to find their voice. For one, there was the problem of finding a political ideology and language that appealed to the diverse splinters of dissent. The young protestors in Transkei's schools made the most noise, but their schools were islands of anger. They had an uncertain relationship with more cautious, prosperous professionals, who made a good living inside Transkei's towns, but still disdained the racism inherent in the apartheid project. The well-educated dissidents were fully aware that they were a minority and that the most dramatic challenge to Matanzima's rule had not come from them but from the rural regions. Then there was the vexed question of how Transkei's political ideologies might link to the wider strands of black politics. The ANC had not returned to South Africa in any force since it had been crushed in the early 1960s. Black politics was in flux; a kaleidoscope of ideas, activities and projects. Finally, Kaiser Matanzima was notorious for ruthlessly squashing individuals whom he suspected of subversive dissent. Only a few academic researchers and journalists ventured off the main roads and down rutted tracks to speak to Transkei's dissidents who had been repeatedly imprisoned and banished into remote rural areas. They found a handful of men and women who spoke repeatedly of personal hardship, political setbacks and, worst of all, of their isolation.

The ANC was also torn over the approach they should take to Bantustan politics. On Robben Island these debates were particularly bitter. Govan Mbeki and Nelson Mandela had never been on good terms, not least because the older man could not accept Mandela's unspoken leadership of the ANC's High Organ on Robben Island. They argued over all manner of policies, but most of all they argued over how the ANC should approach the Bantustans. This issue summed up their contrasting approaches to politics. The disputes were compounded because many prisoners on Robben Island had close family and friends inside the Bantustans, making the political bitterly personal. Govan Mbeki and his many supporters thought that 'the ANC should oppose them [the Bantustans] entirely, and give them no legitimacy at all.'[1] Mbeki saw revolutionary potential in the smothered protests inside the Bantustans. He

---

[1] P. O'Malley, *Shades of Difference: Mac Maharaj and the struggle for South Africa* (Johannesburg, 2007), pp.154-6. Cf. Bundy, *Mbeki*, pp.126-32.

believed that by its very definition the political parties that were allowed to exist inside the Bantustan system must be unreservedly compromised. On Robben Island, Nelson Mandela and Walter Sisulu were the foremost advocates for making alliances inside the Bantustans. In debates, they spoke of strategic collaboration with surrogates; in practice, they were willing to speak to almost all-comers. They did not share Govan Mbeki's Marxist and somewhat Manichean view of politics, where 'progressive' forces and revolutionaries were in eternal struggle with 'reactionaries'. Moreover, they realised that the ANC needed to find allies and sympathisers wherever possible, if they were to prevail inside South Africa.

Subsequent historians have leaned towards Govan Mbeki's arguments. This is because the final years of apartheid were dominated by 'black-on-black' violence, which claimed more than 20,000 lives, when elements of the chieftaincy in many Bantustans clashed with the 'young lions' of the liberation movements. Yet events in Transkei offer a much quieter but equally important counterpoint. Here, it was Nelson Mandela's younger kinsman, King Sabata, the Paramount Chief of Thembuland, who would provide the fulcrum for various currents of dissent. By the time of his death in 1986, Sabata would be well known as the Comrade-King, for he lived with the ANC in Lusaka after he fled Transkei in 1980. But for much of his adult life, Sabata was buffeted by the swirling political currents that eddied through the Transkei. His personal journey also reveals much about the ambiguities of the era and the diverse threads of African politics during the decades that the ANC was either imprisoned on Robben Island or exiled abroad.

Quo Vadis?

Most political parties that tried to oppose the Bantustan ruling parties and the apartheid project within Bantustan legislatures withered away into irrelevance. For a decade and a half, this seemed to be the fate of the Transkei Democratic Party which was formed in April 1964 from the loose coalition grouped around Sabata Dalindyebo and Victor Poto. They faced the repressive weight of Matanzima's state. Just as importantly, the Democratic Party was uncertain of its political direction. The one bond that held the new party together was that its members had all opposed Kaiser Matanzima's inaugural election as Chief Minister of the new Bantustan government in 1963.[2] The Great Place Gang – the small knot of conspirators who, from the late 1950s, used Sabata's throne as a rallying point to campaign against Bantustan self-government – still had links to the ANC in prison and in exile. Yet, troubled by personal ailments, Sabata was offstage for many years, and the vast rump of the party, associated with Victor Poto, was socially conservative and politically cautious.

During the 1960s, politically cautious members dominated the Democratic Party. This group favoured a genteel form of liberal multi-racialism which they hoped might preserve chiefs and rural notables from the ravages of apartheid. Victor Poto, the Paramount Chief of Western Mpondoland, was the foremost

---

[2] *DD* 19 May 1964.

advocate of this grouping and he was also the official leader of the Transkei Democratic Party during the first part of the 1960s. By this time, the Liberal Party of South Africa, which had briefly played a prominent role in Transkei's politics in the years leading up to Bantustan self-government (see Chapter Two), had been crushed by apartheid repression. However, more cautious forms of liberal politics still survived in apartheid South Africa. Poto's group held talks with the South African Progressive Party, which sat on the opposition benches in the apartheid legislature. It was a 'natural liaison,' they believed. 'Both parties... rejected nationalism – whether it was white or black.'[3] In the 1950s, African liberalism had flourished amongst the prosperous black Christian communities who owned freehold titles to land in rural Natal. While there was no freehold land title in the Transkei, there was an equally well-educated and prosperous elite, of which Victor Poto was an exemplar. Indeed, he had extensive connections to prominent South African liberal politicians, having sat on a wide range of their committees and councils since the 1940s.

Yet Transkei proved to be far stonier soil for liberal politics. Most immediately, Kaiser Matanzima enjoyed impunity. His acolytes turned their areas into no-go zones for the Democratic Party.[4] The most blatant intimidation came in 1966 when security police arrested five members of the Democratic Party's senior leadership on suspicion of treason. Three turned state witnesses, leaving the other two – Citibunga Nogcantsi and Jackson Nkosiyane – to face a seven-year jail term. The prosecution alleged witchcraft: that Nogcantsi made a 'medicine from his wife's favourite fowl' which, if buried in Matanzima's yard, 'would bring about his death.'[5]

The repression deepened the rifts inside the Democratic Party. Shocked by the arrests, Paramount Chief Victor Poto unexpectedly resigned his leadership. Radicals in the party were hopeful, telling the *Daily Dispatch* that 'the leadership of the party was too moderate... [and] a change has to be made.' Their hopes were disappointed. At a party congress held at Poto's Great Place over an April weekend in 1966, King Sabata 'declined leadership for which he was earmarked.'[6] Instead he backed Knowledge Guzana, a prosperous Umtata lawyer, who was a confidant of Chief Victor Poto. Almost immediately, Knowledge Guzana faced dissent. The 1968 elections to the Transkei legislature were a disaster. In one stroke, 'the heart of the Democratic Party opposition was torn out – only two of its glittering front bench returned'[7] and the number of their elected members of the Legislative Assembly almost halved. In the 1973 elections, the party's presence in the Assembly was reduced to twelve.[8]

The Democratic Party's decline had been foreseeable, given the power of Matanzima's government, but dissenting party activists claimed that Knowledge Guzana's elitist brand of liberal politics was disastrous. 'The majority of [party] members... lost confidence with their leader' within the year,' protested a colleague. 'He is a man of very high standards, who has no

---

[3] *DD* 4 April 1964.
[4] *DD* 29 May 1967, 27 May 1970.
[5] *The Star* 23 April 1966. Cf. *DD* 23, 24 March, 16 June 1966.
[6] 'The leadership too moderate': *DD* 1 April 1966. 'Declined leadership': 15 August 1980.
[7] *DD* 13 March 1969.
[8] Southall, *Transkei*, p.119.

time for people who are illiterate.' Party activists claimed that Guzana had preferred to attend world conferences of the Methodist Church instead of fighting Transkei's parliamentary elections. Party organisers were no longer 'organising the rank and file into politics' because the money set aside to pay them was lost.[9] The final straw came when Knowledge Guzana expelled three rivals who had close connections to King Sabata. They ran as independents against the Democratic Party and won seats in Transkei's parliament, weakening Guzana's position within the party even further. In January 1976 the dissidents forced a showdown, and Knowledge Guzana was voted out of office. However, it was not Sabata Dalindyebo who stepped into the breach: he was standing off the political stage, troubled by personal ailments. Instead a 32-year-old clerk, Hector Ncokazi, became leader of the party[10]

Hector Ncokazi's ambition was to bring the Democratic Party closer to the young student activists in the Black Consciousness Movement who had influenced an emerging generation across the Eastern Cape from Fort Hare University. In many senses Ncokazi was a typical son of the Eastern Cape elite. He was connected by birth and marriage to the most prominent Thembu dynasties; he had been educated at a mission school and smattered his speeches with literary allusions. He was also alive to the youthful, radical impulse of Black Consciousness politics. Aged only 16, Ncokazi had joined the rival party to the ANC, the Pan African Congress, in 1959, the year it was formed. He seems to have formally left the movement when it was banned by the apartheid government in 1960. His political path then led him to Steve Biko's nascent Black Consciousness movement and to a leadership position in the Black People's Convention. He knew many of the student leaders who had caused ructions in Transkei's schools in the early 1970s.[11] Now, in taking on the leadership of the Democratic Party, he was taking a stand in Transkei's politics. '*Quo Vadis?*' he asked Knowledge Guzana during a leadership debate.[12] For both men – mission school educated and lay preachers in the Methodist Church – the Biblical allusion was obvious. As Jesus had foretold of his own sacrifice, so Ncokazi boldly proclaimed he would stand up to Matanzima and that he was willing to face Transkei's prisons.

The Democratic Party faced a critical juncture. On 26 October 1976, Transkei became the first self-governing Homeland in South Africa to receive full Bantustan 'independence' from Pretoria. The ANC in exile vigorously opposed any form of constitutional change that would deny blacks majority rule in a united South Africa. Yet there was a group of influential South African liberals – including the newspaper editor Donald Woods, who would eventually be forced into exile because of his exposés of apartheid brutality – who believed that the federalism inherent in the Bantustan project might possibly loosen the stranglehold of Afrikaner politicians on the South African state. Woods dreamed of turning the clock back to the late 19th century when South Africa was a

[9] Both above quotes from PC2/12/1/1. *DD* 15 January 1974.
[10] *DD* 5 January 1974, 11 March 1974. BTS1, 'Foreign Political Situation', (n.d.), p.56. KGC3, 'Miscellaneous Transkei Conversations'.
[11] Interview, Nelani. KGC3, 'Miscellaneous Transkei Conversations'. *DD* 6 January, 10 July 1976, 29 May 2004.
[12] *DD* 26 July 1974.

patchwork of independent African kingdoms, English colonies, and Afrikaans republics. Moreover, Kaiser Matanzima hoped Bantustan independence would extend Transkei's boundaries, thus making him the Prime Minister of a Great Xhosa-land straddling the Eastern Cape.[13]

Transkei's forthcoming independence was a moment of great political fluidity because it offered the prospect of redrawing the map of apartheid South Africa. It provoked frantic lobbying from within the tight-knit group of African politicians that had kin connections with Transkei's chieftaincy. Winnie Madikizela-Mandela held a two-hour private meeting with Kaiser Matanzima. As his 'tribal-aunt' through her marriage to Nelson Mandela, she had demanded that Matanzima reveal 'his innermost thoughts' on Transkei's independence, she later explained.[14] Matanzima sought to bring Transkei's opposition parties and influential traditional leaders into his camp. To some extent he succeeded. A group of politicians close to the late Paramount Chief Victor Poto crossed the floor of the Legislature, picking up prime government postings. Knowledge Guzana took part in the committee that drafted the constitution for Transkei's independence, and then formed his own political party, taking with him most of the remaining opposition members in the Legislative Assembly.[15] However, Matanzima was publically embarrassed when Sabata refused the offer of high office as ceremonial president of the new Transkei Republic. Moreover, leading white liberals and African Homeland leaders, such as Donald Woods and Mangosuthu Buthelezi, rejected Transkei's Bantustan 'independence', compounding Matanzima's humiliations.[16] They argued that he had conceded too much to the apartheid government.

Matanzima fell back on the argument that an electoral victory in the legislature elections in September 1976 would give him a sufficient mandate to take Transkei to full Bantustan independence. Hector Ncokazi refused to contest Transkei's independence elections, telling journalists that his goal was not 'the mayor-ship of a village, but the freedom of the black man in South Africa.'[17] These comments carried a whiff of treason, and he was soon swept into Transkei's jail system. By contrast, other Democratic Party activists campaigned in the areas of Thembuland that were still strongholds of support for King Sabata. Just weeks before Transkei went to the polls, Matanzima jailed them too.[18] Matanzima won a sweeping victory in the polls, but Transkei's borders were only extended with two more rural districts; and economically the territory was still in hock to Pretoria. Moreover, Transkei's independence was not recognised by the United Nations or any major government. The dissidents had trumped Matanzima and the apartheid government.

The following years of repeated imprisonment seem to have broken Hector Ncokazi. He spent the rest of the decade in and out of detention, struggling

---

[13] D. Woods, *Asking for Trouble: Autobiography of a banned journalist* (London, 1980), p.217.

[14] *DD* 28 July 1976.

[15] *DD* 11, 20, 26 March 1976.

[16] Black Community Programmes, *Transkei Independence* (Durban, 1976), p.18.

[17] *DD* 26 July 1974. Cf.*Pretoria News* 16 January 1976. *DD* 11 March 1974, 23 August, 16 December 1975, 10 February 1977. BTS10, Ambassador, Transkei to Secretary of the Department of Foreign Affairs (hereafter S/BTS), 3 January 1978.

[18] *DD* 27 July 1976. SAPA 22 February 1977.

against deteriorating health as 'his kidney trouble [was] aggravated by the cold stony floors of prison.' He told reporters that his life was 'a dreary struggle to stay out of jail.'[19] Worse, he played Judas. In a separate development, he turned state witness in a court trial against a small group of young professionals based around Umtata who had formed a subversive, supposedly treasonous, reading and discussion group. His evidence was instrumental in four of the accused – Dumisa Ntsebeza and his brother Lungisile, Matthew Goniwe and Godfrey Silinga – serving jail sentences. Stories soon spread that a petty ideological feud led to this betrayal. Others, who had witnessed the burdens of imprisonment, would later wonder what pressures had forced Ncokazi to turn against his fellow dissidents.[20]

With Hector Ncokazi sidelined, the effective leadership of the Democratic Party fell into the hands of Sabata's old allies from the Great Place Gang, particularly Alfred Xobololo, Anderson Joyi and Jackson Nkosiyane, all of whom had taken seats in Transkei's Legislative Assembly. With his allies now running the Democratic Party, King Sabata took over its leadership. 'The wrangle for the leadership... has caused great confusion within the party and amongst supporters,' Sabata told a reporter from the *Daily Dispatch*. 'I, as King of the Thembus and a member of the [Legislative] Assembly... will now take a stand in reorganising the party.'[21] After a long period of decline, his health was on the mend. 'He is better now because he is drinking less,' gossiped Stella Sigcau.[22]

Sabata threw himself into politics, not just in Thembuland, but across the Transkei. In the final years of the 1970s, he deftly brought the fragmented factions of the Democratic Party back together into a newly named Democratic Progressive Party. He followed up this success with overtures to Stella Sigcau's Mpondo dissidents. Sabata still rarely spoke in Transkei's Legislature: like many politicians in South Africa, he was not comfortable with the procedures and poses of parliamentary debate. Instead, opposition activists toured Transkei's rural districts, making speeches at local gatherings. (This tactic sometimes backfired. One man left the party after activists used his late wife's memorial ceremony to make speeches against Matanzima.)[23] Even as a young man, Sabata had been a formidable orator at the ceremonies and gatherings that were part of community life. Suddenly, Matanzima faced a serious opponent.

In the late 1970s, Professor Tom Karis journeyed with a local journalist into in rural Thembuland in search of one of King Sabata's councillors, Samson Fadana, who had been recently released from Matanzima's jails. They set out on a fine Sunday morning, spending hours jolting along untarred roads, taking directions first from a trading store, then at another 'house and store where... hymn singing was going on.'[24] After 'long and complicated directions' – which the journalist guide ignored entirely – they located the junction leading to Fadana's church. 'Shortly, a woman in her thirties, carrying a Bible and a hymnal' walked past the car, 'followed by Fadana, dressed in a blue suit

[19] 'Stony floors': *DD* 23 March 1978. 'Dreary struggle': *DD* 23 August 1981. Cf. *DD* 10 July 1976
[20] Gerhart interview, O. Mabandla. Author interview, Dumisani Mafu, King Williamstown, 19 October 2008. Bell and Ntsebeza, *Unfinished Business*, pp.126-9.
[21] *DD* 29 March 1976.
[22] Karis interview, Sigcau.
[23] *DD* 14 June 1978.
[24] All details in paragraph from KGC1, T. Karis interview, P.S. Fadana, Umtata, 2 October 1977.

and tie'. They all drove back to Fadana's smart, 'stucco-mud, modern shaped house', surrounded by 'huts and sheds'. Most prominent inside the house was a framed certificate on the wall: a prize Fadana had won in a ballroom dancing competition, when he was imprisoned on Robben Island in the 1960s.

For more than a decade King Sabata was silent whilst many of his trusted councillors were dispersed. Now with Robben Islanders such as Fadana returning to Thembuland and Sabata's health and spirits revived, the pace of politics accelerated.

Rural politics – chiefs, community development, comrades

King Sabata was a threat not so much because he was the leader of a political party: the Thembu king was hardly a typical parliamentarian. Rather, Sabata's strength drew upon the political networks embedded in his Paramountcy that remained potent. Writing about the Sekhukhuneland region in the rural northern districts of South Africa, Delius has argued that the chieftaincy's links to the wider political movements largely withered away by the late 1970s.[25] In Transkei, however, things were very different.

Kaiser Matanzima's strategy to control Transkei had always been concerned with reducing the power of Sabata's kingship. Pre-colonial African kingdoms (or paramountcies) in the Eastern Cape were an assemblage of independent chieftaincies that acknowledged the over-rule of a Paramount Chief, so there was always the possibility of division and secession. In the 1950s, the apartheid government had manipulated these customs in order to shear off three districts from Sabata's Thembuland. Two districts were turned into a semi-autonomous unit, called Western Thembuland, under the independent chieftainship of Kaiser Matanzima; the third district was lost to the Gcaleka paramount chief. In the mid-1960s, Matanzima raised himself to the rank of Paramount Chief, attempting to consolidate his power over the rival region of Western Thembuland (sometimes known as Emigrant Thembuland) and make himself Sabata's near equal. This proved more difficult. 'What has happened to the Transkei Legislature Assembly's controversial resolution to elevate the Chief Minister, KD Matanzima, to Paramount Chief of Emigrant Thembuland?' commented an editorial in the *Daily Dispatch*, written during 1966. [26] 'Word is going round that the State President [of apartheid South Africa] has either vetoed the decision or is reluctant to approve his designation.' In fact the government was so scared of popular protest that festivities to celebrate the recognition of Matanzima's Paramountcy had been delayed. It was only in January 1967 that he was finally installed.[27]

Matanzima always struggled to justify the independence of his paramount chieftaincy from the main stem of the Thembu kingdom. Matanzima was willing to acknowledge that he was junior to Sabata Dalindyebo, at least in ritual terms. For instance, he attended the marriage of Sabata to his Great Wife,

[25] Delius, *A Lion Amongst the Cattle*, pp.172-5.
[26] *DD* 5 March 1966.
[27] KGT47, 1/1/3/5-2, Cofimvaba Magistrate to KGT, 28 September 1966. *DD* 3 January 1967.

which would establish the heir to the Thembu kingdom. Matanzima even 'gave away the bride... thereby tacitly acknowledging his [Sabata's] pre-eminence.'[28] However, Matanzima's argument was that he was politically distinct and independent of Dalindyebo, and thus deserving of an independent paramount chieftaincy. Matanzima was therefore always vulnerable to genealogical claims that suggested otherwise: for instance, the subversive verses sung by praise poets or a chiding letter written by Nelson Mandela.[29] Matanzima even snatched back a manuscript stored in the archives of Rhodes University, entitled *Who are the Thembu and where do they come from?* Giving the Vice-Chancellor only a few hours' notice of his visit, Matanzima's ministerial entourage swept into the university, parking their cars in front of the clock-tower designed by Sir Herbert Baker, the quintessential architect of empire. Matanzima strode across the lawn and into the library, 'accompanied by equally smartly suited bodyguards, whose suits bulged at the armpit, barely concealing holstered weapons'.[30] They were delayed by the librarian, Sandy Rowoldt-Shell, in 'the most ostentatious and time-consuming tea drinking and welcoming ceremonies'. In the basement her colleague, Zweli Vena, a long-standing supporter of the Dalindyebo chieftaincy, desperately copied the original documents.

King Sabata was a threat to Matanzima because his political influence was strengthening from his base in rural Thembuland. Three of the original members of the Great Place Gang, Jackson Nkosiyane, Anderson and Bangelizwe Joyi, remained faithful councillors to the king, despite repeated detentions and banishments. In the 1970s, they were joined by ANC veterans such as Samson Fadana. In all, some 30 ex-Robben Islanders returned to Transkei during this period. 'Some did not want to go underground' after their experiences in jail, but others 'became a nucleus and used the Democratic Party' as a vehicle for their political activism.[31] Newspaper reporters focused mainly on the party political activities of the Democratic Party; but this was just the tip of the iceberg. Political activists held influence in Thembuland because of their prominence in local communities. They spoke at funerals, set up farmers' associations, and ploughed their neighbours' fields. Joyi 'became prominent, especially as an orator', remembered a neighbour. 'Because of his presence all the [younger] men of my age became his followers.'[32] This was a more disparate, diffuse type of politics, which could not be neatly labelled. George Matanzima turned to Biblical imagery when he told his supporters of the threat that Sabata's consorts posed. The 'fallen angels of the Democratic Party under their Lucifer [King Sabata]' are a group of 'ever-marauding political jackals... [who] always want to cause trouble.'[33]

▲ ▲ ▲

[28] BTS10, Du Plooy to S/BTS, 23 May 1978.
[29] For instance, NMPFA3, 8, Mandela to Matanzima, 14 October 1968 (undelivered).
[30] All quotes from: author interview, Sandy Shell, Cape Town, 16 May 2008. The manuscript that caused the trouble: CO PR 3664 06, E.G. Sihele, *Ngobani na abaThembu, bevela phi na?*
[31] Gerhart interview, O. Mabandla.
[32] TRC-VH, ECO171/96, Zoyisile William Nelani, Umtata, 20 June 1996.
[33] *DD* 26 November 1975.

The Biblical imagery used by George Matanzima was apt given the influence of Christian ideas in Transkei's politics. The odyssey made by Ezra Sigwela provides an example of how wider political ideologies were woven into these strands of chiefly and Christian politics. Related to Sabata's royal clan and recruited into the ANC in the Eastern Cape mission schools in the 1950s, Sigwela endured two terms of imprisonment. In the early 1960s he was detained in Transkei's jails, ostensibly for possessing seditious literature, but in fact because the police knew of his involvement in Govan Mbeki's sabotage campaign. In the late 1960s he was jailed on Robben Island, together with his maternal uncle, Twalifeme Joyi, after they had attempted to set up a general workers' union in Transkei, which the security police suspected was a front for an underground cell organised by the ANC in exile. After his return from Robben Island in the late 1970s, Sigwela took a job as a fieldworker for the Transkei Council of Churches which had just started to engage in community development projects. Here he found his vocation and also an institutional base that would give him influence not only in Thembuland but all over rural Transkei.[34]

Ezra Sigwela was a devout Christian, and at the Transkei Council of Churches he found himself at the centre of a web of Christian social action. By the mid-1970s, a network of Christian-based, community development organisations spanned the Transkei. There was a great variety: the Transkei Council of Churches, influenced by radical liberation theology; offshoots from Steve Biko's Black Community Programmes; Reverend Hammington Qambela's government-funded projects; and also the hundreds of small *Zenzele* self-help groups run by church-going women. Whilst there were sharp disagreements, in practice everyone talked to each other. Hammington Qambela built churches to the glory of Matanzima's government and officiated at weddings of the leading Bantustan dynasties. However, Qambela also received funding from Ezra Sigwela, and provided a job for Hector Ncokazi when he was suffering political persecution.[35]

An increase in charitable funding during this period allowed this loose web of Christian community development groups to spread even further into Transkei's rural areas. International aid trickled into Transkei through anti-apartheid-aligned organisations. The Transkei Council of Churches' annual reports boasted that almost one-quarter of the 160 families under their care, were 'widows of men executed for political crimes, widows whose husbands had died on Robben Island, and widows whose husbands died on release from prison.'[36] At the same time, South Africa's mining corporations funded community development projects in the rural areas where labour migrants' families lived.

It is difficult to gauge the influence of all this charity. One government-commissioned report was sceptical, finding that the Transkei Council of Churches only supported 20-25 projects at a time, of which perhaps only two or three were really making progress.[37] The archives of the Transkei Council of

---

[34] TRC-VH, ECO191/96, Ezra Sigwela, Umtata, 20 June 1996. Interview, Sigwela.
[35] TCC, File 7.5.49
[36] *DD* 14 July 1983. Cf. Hawkins Associates, *The Physical and Spatial Basis for Transkei's First Five Year Development Plan* (Salisbury Zimbabwe, October 1980), p.265. TRC-VH, Sigwela.
[37] Hawkins Associates, *Five Year Development Plan*, p.265.

Churches provide a counterpoint, revealing a lively correspondence between the Council of Churches and many scores of small organisations across Transkei. These in turn spoke to a wider web of local health workers, teachers, agricultural officers and chiefs. The expansion of primary education in the middle years of the 20th century had brought the teacher and the preacher, whose authority overlapped with the powers of the local headman, into many rural communities. Now the growth of the Bantustan state strengthened this group of black professionals; a new wave of local notables and community leaders.

In this web of correspondence, meetings and conversations, we can see the changing ideals of community and political leadership in Transkei's rural areas. One example is Mrs Miriam Maloko, 'stationed at Upper Cabuzana', who attended the women's prayer meeting every Thursday and organised one or two talks a week 'on the importance of growing vegetables, keeping fowls, and occupying oneself with home industries.'[38] She led a campaign to encourage people to erect toilets by their houses (people still commonly defecated in the open, in fields, bushes and ditches) with the help of local agricultural and health officials and the women's prayer groups. She had a local black doctor lecture young mothers on the importance of hard work 'which helps women from partaking in gossip.' But she worried about the older, idle men, who spent most of the day drinking, the 'infiltration of shebeens into the area and the sale of Jabulani cartons of liquor at vantage points on the main road'. Many activists were godly, middle-aged women, but the reports written by male leaders speak of similar aspirations and concerns, if they were perhaps more focused on masculine matters such as cattle breeding and tractor ploughing. Another woman, a local nurse, explaining the credo of her profession, painted the picture of a perfect community leader in rural Transkei: [39]

> She carries out demonstrations... she teaches home economy... She often finds one or two toddlers with even a TB case in the family... She has to find solutions to these problems in varying degrees... She is the Community Florence Nightingale... She studies the community... and promotes self-help.
>
> Even in social activities like church gatherings she is inundated with questions... She answers these questions with a smile which often attracts all... She is easily approachable to patients who exalt her to the highest ranks of mankind... She is the only one known to her community. She enjoys full respect, which is becoming rare to find.

Sadly, this devout Christian action did not transform Transkei's rural communities into prosperous cells of self-help and smallholder agricultural production. For the same reasons that the Transkei Government failed to promote agricultural development (see Chapter Three), the church-based, community organisations made little impact on the swingeing poverty in the rural areas. Moreover, like many organisations in Transkei, the Council of Churches struggled. 'Their organisation was haphazard and their resources

---

[38] This narrative from TCC File 7.4.5.
[39] This account from 'The Role of the District Nurse as seen by Senior Professional Nurse, CB Notyalwa', *Transkei Nursing News*, 2 (Umtata, 1983) – in AAS45.

stretched to the limit.' One rural project supported by the Council of Churches had been run by a one-man-whirlwind, and when he died the scheme collapsed. An internal evaluation later revealed that most of the money had been used to pay field staff; and the project workers had made requests for huge grants, despite having already received an R18,000 donation from Oxfam.[40] Even the best intentioned efforts could go awry.

Nevertheless, the doctrines of community development remained important in the 1970s. Some of the most cosmopolitan political activists kept their fingers in the soil. One such example is Fikile Bam, born in 1937 in Transkei, who had been schooled at Holy Cross School in Mpondoland when his father was tribal secretary to Victor Poto. Whilst at the University of Cape Town he was arrested, tried and imprisoned on Robben Island for his membership of an underground movement that was an offshoot from the All African Convention. After Robben Island, he started as a lawyer in Transkei. Fikile Bam threw himself into rural development too. He became a director of the Black Community Programmes.[41] He also started a grassland development project on his farm, a gardening scheme intended to teach: 'soil sense; interdependency and the law of return [to the land]; soil and water conservation; fighting soil erosion in all known ways.'[42] It was hoped it would beome self-funding by selling vegetables to boarding school hostels, traders and city markets. The Transkei Council of Churches praised the eloquence of Fikile Bam's funding reports, which charted the tribulations of the project. While all the residents had collectively benefited from using a tractor owned by the scheme, there was little enthusiasm for communal work. Planting was delayed because no one could be found to fence the land allocated for the vegetable plots:

> Call ups for people to come and work are adroitly evaded by excuses that show all that communal business is placed rather low in the list of priorities. Personal business comes first and, as yet, the ploughing of a vegetable garden in winter seems to be regarded as a communal obligation on the same level as putting up a new hut for the school – something that will have to be done in due course, but not yet.[43]

▲ ▲ ▲

If devout activism seldom resulted in 'community up-liftment' (to use a phrase of the time), social activists sometimes played an influential role in local politics. This provoked intense conflicts in parts of Thembuland in the late 1970s, when Matanzima feared the authority of the chiefs and magistrates loyal to him might be undermined by interfering social activists. This occurred in the area of Mpeko, a location that had been bitterly disputed by King Sabata and the local chief for decades. When Hammington Qambela set up a range of self-help projects in the area, he was drawn into a complex dispute. His schemes became a powerful local force at Mpeko. He started a boarding hostel for school

---

[40] C. Moreku, 'Community and Church during the Apartheid Era: A focus on the projects of the Transkei Council of Churches' (UNISA, MA thesis, 2003), pp.11, 19, 42, 169.
[41] BTS9A South African Embassy, Umtata to S/BTS, 8 November 1977.
[42] TCC File 7.5.18.
[43] Ibid.

pupils and a sewing project that made school uniforms. He was busy erecting a school and also a joint health clinic-cum-community hall, with money from Anglo-American and a local community levy. However, his prominence provoked the local magistrate and chief. They fined his aunt in the tribal courts, claiming the sewing scheme was corrupt – an easy charge to make given the chaotic financial and organisational records. They forced Qambela to hand over the community hall to the Tribal Authority. The chief then stamped his authority on the location, arresting 'most of the educated people for failing to contribute R1 [each] toward the opening ceremony of the... community hall'.. King Sabata took Qambela's side, while students in the local secondary school rallied against their corrupt principal and the local magistrate. It seemed that politics might engulf the self-help schemes, but Qambela backed down, and moved his organisation into another district. At the end of the affair, only the school principal was jailed, after it was found he had stolen money from the school funds..[44]

The Baziya region of Thembuland was brutally divided by a similar dispute. The area had been a hot-spot of unrest since the 1950s, and matters reached boiling point when Matanzima decided to break the power of the locally powerful Joyi family in the late 1970s. Matters reached a head when Chief Marelane Joyi was deposed as headman in 1978 for giving his support to Sabata Dalindyebo.[45] Bangelizwe Joyi was next in line, but refused to take the post – a move that would implicitly condone Matanzima's actions. In his place, Mvuso Zwelidumile Joyi, a school teacher and a leading member of the ruling party, became headman of Mputi location. To consolidate the government's grip on the area, Matanzima created a new sub-chieftainship, which was filled by Mvuso Joyi.[46] Now returned from Robben Island, Twalifene Joyi mobilised opposition to Mvuso Zwelidumile. The dispute escalated. One rainy day, while he was ploughing a neighbour's field on the banks of the Mbashe River, Twalifeme Joyi was murdered apparently by a local policeman. His swollen body was found in the shallows downstream a few days later. When a worker from the Transkei of Council of Churches went to investigate the killing, he was detained.[47]

The trouble thickened. Anderson Joyi held secret meetings at night, supposedly plotting to kill the sub-chief. Matanzima struck back. 'Transkei police besieged and invaded the Mputi location... More than 200 men were taken in police vans to Umtata police camp.' Eighteen dissidents were detained for six months. In 1980, the Transkei Government struck a mortal blow against the 'hard core' who still supported King Sabata. Eight families, including Anderson and Bangelizwe Joyi, were permanently expelled. 'Graders were used to knock them [the houses] down, after thatched roofs had been set alight... Government trucks stood by, ready to remove each family's belongings after the demolition.'[48] They were taken to Cofimvaba District, a region ruled by Kaiser Matanzima.

---

[44] TCC File 7.5.49. *DD* 5 February 1982. Interview, Mkhangeli Manford Matomela, East London, 30 October 2008.
[45] *DD* 4 November 1978.
[46] *TLA* (1978), p.508. *DD* 18 March 1981.
[47] TRC-VH, Nelani.
[48] *DD* 25 September 1979, 18 November 1980. *TLA* (1978), p.53. BTS10, Ambassador, Transkei to S/BTS, 21 March 1978.

With their homesteads destroyed, life for the exiled families was hard. By contrast, Chief Mvuso was rewarded for supporting Matazima. Under his rule, the Mputi area prospered through a number of government development projects. In the year that Mvuso was upgraded and installed as a full chief, the community received piped water, diverted from a mountain stream. A few months later, extensions were built onto the medical clinic at Baziya.[49] Chief Mvuso's flock of 100 sheep proclaimed his wealth and political good fortune.

The curse of corruption

With his followers crushed, the mantle of kingship no longer provided any practical protection for Sabata Dalindyebo. In July 1979, his arrest finally came. The imposition of state power at the moment of his arrest was a starkly symbolic invasion of the King's royal domain. Eyewitnesses saw 'a fleet of police cars' surround Sabata's Great Place.[50] To his supporters, it seemed a Christ-like sacrifice. Followers at court drew weapons to help their King, just like the disciples in the Garden of Gethsemane. But 'Sabata told the people to allow the police to do their job.' Witnesses claimed they heard Sabata tell his captors that 'he was willing to go to jail in order to gain freedom for his country.'[51] He was taken to Umtata and charged with the crimes of 'subverting Transkei's sovereignty' and 'injuring the dignity' of Kaiser Matanzima.[52]

The charge sheet against Sabata detailed the pungent comments that he had made at one of his stump speeches, in the district of Qumbu: 'That he [Sabata] was the Paramount Chief of Matanzima, having been born his senior, and will remain for ever so... [that Matanzima] has an abundance of the necessities of life while his people have to live on excreta... that the Republic of Transkei is a pigsty.'[53] This was not the usual critique of the 'Bantustan system' that one would find in contemporary academic debates or in the doctrinaire statements of political activists, which tended to use Marxist jargon to explain Transkei's 'dependence' on apartheid South Africa. Rather it was a potent religious-moral analysis of Kaiser Matanzima's personal misrule. This rhetoric appealed as much in the rural locations as to the respectable, Christian social activists and the youthful protestors influenced by Steve Biko's doctrine of Black Consciousness.

The arrest of King Sabata provoked a flurry of dissent that was reported in national newspapers, giving us a rare glimpse into the ideas of rural politics during the Bantustan era, whose informal speeches and debates were rarely recorded.[54] For Sabata it seems that the heart of the matter was his dynastic struggle with Matanzima which went all the way back to when they were both young, newly installed chiefs in the 1950s. Sabata indicted Matanzima's group

[49] *DD* 5 November 1983, 22 December 1984. TRC-VH, Joyi.
[50] *DD* 27, 28 July 1979.
[51] *TNA* (1980), p.136. Interview, Nelani.
[52] *DD* 19, 21, 27 March 1980.
[53] Streek and Wicksteed, *Render unto Kaiser*, p.326.
[54] Before 1963 government magistrates had taken legal statements from and made notes of the meetings they held with traditional leaders, but the archives of the magistrates from the Bantustan era are largely lost.

of cronies as upstarts: jumped up chiefs with no legitimate authority. Because of apartheid legislation, 'chiefs in rural areas were [now] legislators and administrators [of a Bantu Authorities system] never employed anywhere in any recorded history... The people are not prepared to accept this because they know who their real leaders are,' he told a reporter from the *Daily Dispatch*.[55] Throughout the course of the trial and the subsequent legal wrangles, Matanzima and Sabata disputed each other's accounts of Thembu royal history. Matanzima claimed that Sabata had been a dissolute youth, expelled from school several times for misbehaviour, whose accession to kingship was surrounded by controversy. (Sabata responded that the only reason he had failed to get into Lovedale College was because Kaiser Matanzima had forgotten to put in the application.) Matanzima claimed that Sabata had always conspired against his chieftainship, calling him a 'spy and a good boy for the Republic of South Africa'. Sabata's reply was equally plaintive:

> I want the world to know that I have been persecuted for my political convictions... and have been ridiculed and humiliated even by junior chiefs who were government supporters. When I was installed as Paramount Chief, I became King of the Thembus from Lady Frere to Elliotdale – seven districts ... I have ended up with only three districts and all of my councillors have been in and out of prison. All along I have kept quiet but I cannot take anymore.[56]

These disturbances at the heart of dynastic politics rippled through the chieftaincies causing ructions that were felt throughout society. This was particularly the case in the late 1970s, with Matanzima crushing dissident communities in Thembuland, Mpondoland and elsewhere in Transkei. Rural elders commonly held that a responsible, mature adult man was master of his own house; therefore when Matanzima deported his opponents and ruined their livelihoods he was also destroying the fabric of society. This was certainly the case in Mputi location. While Chief Mvuso Joyi prospered from rural development projects as a reward for his support of Kaiser Matanzima, the deported families experienced only hardship. One had harvested a record 106 bags of grain from his fields just months before he was banished. The bags of grain rotted away outside the makeshift homestead to which he was deported. 'I had a big house... [with] so many rooms that could occupy all my family [back home]; but now... [we were] just occupying one room with such a big family... On the second day when I arrived there, there was a big hailstorm and the house was flooded.'[57] Another deportee's wife died in exile. She 'was denied the respect' of having her funeral at her ancestral home, but instead 'was buried in the ruins' of their Cofimvaba homestead:

> Can you imagine what it means for your brother to destroy your *kraal* [home]?... For seven years, [Mvuso] Zwelidumele was ploughing and enjoying my *mielies* [grain] – for seven years – the produce from my fields... It is difficult for me to say I would forgive those who have done this to me.[58]

[55] *DD* 4 November 1978.
[56] Streek and Wicksteed, *Render unto Kaiser*, p. 310 – also see pp. 312, 330-1.
[57] TRC-VH, Joyi.
[58] Ibid.

The criticism of Matanzima's misrule – that he destroyed the households of his enemies whilst his cronies prospered – was also a wider critique of the Bantustan system. The quickest route to wealth in the Bantustans was through business licenses, contacts and connections. This was not an anonymous process of class formation, but barefaced corruption: a myriad of dissolute decisions taken by a clique connected to Kaiser Matanzima by a web of kinship connections. Sabata Dalindyebo and many others explained the deepening inequalities within the Transkei in terms of status and personal aggrandisement. The trouble was, they concluded, the curse of 'corruption' or 'undue enrichment' – both terms that occur in many speeches. Just as powerful was their sense that these misdeeds were evil: an accusation with a long history in Transkei's politics. The historian Sean Redding has written on the prevalence of these ideas in Transkei during the early 20th century, when taxation had been bitterly opposed.[59] Intriguingly, it seems that these ideas were reshaped when they were taken up by young, well educated, Black Consciousness activists in the mid-1970s. If virtuous Christian social activists gained prestige from their good works of community development, then corrupt government ministers secretly roamed the shadows. During his detentions, Hector Ncokazi had spoken of:

> These Transkei leaders are living in luxury getting thousands of Rands a month when the masses are floundering in poverty. They roam about under the cover of darkness with women, using government cars without public consent... They have unduly enriched themselves and when we ask why they do these things, they react by locking us up in their prisons... [This is] a government that is scandalously corrupt and is prone to suppress the Democratic Party which always castigates them for their corrupt deeds.[60]

The broken pledges of Transkei's Bantustan 'independence' doubled the drum beat of opposition. If man was the master of his own household, then national independence should offer the same self-mastery. During the stump speeches that Sabata had made against self-government in 1963 (one of the few times when his speeches were reported by journalists), he warned that: 'the freedom you are getting in the Transkei is a fowl-run [chicken coop]. A cattle *kraal* [enclosure] would be better.'[61] His metaphor was well chosen. Many men left their rural homes for most of the year and worked as labour migrants in apartheid South Africa, returning home only at Christmas and Easter. They slowly saved for decades, hoping to retire to a bustling rural homestead full of goats and cattle bought with their wages. Bantustan independence in 1976 only brought trouble for Transkei's labour migrants; during the economic recession in the final years of the 1970s, apartheid officials restricted the flow of black migrant workers into South Africa's cities. Transkeians felt particularly vulnerable because they were now passport-carrying foreigners. In his speech at Qumbu, Sabata had apparently urged labour migrants to return their

---

[59] S. Redding, *Sorcery and Sovereignty: Taxation, power and rebellion in South Africa, 1880-1963*, (Athens OH, 2006).
[60] *DD* 31 December 1976.
[61] *The Star* 10 August 1963.

worthless passports to the Bantustan government. These criticisms became too much for Matanzima to bear. Sabata was arrested not long after he made the stump speech at Qumbu, where he told the crowd: 'I would not accept the position [of Transkei President] while the rest of the people are living in excreta.'[62]

In arresting King Sabata, Kaiser Matanzima had taken a huge risk. Organisations such as the Transkei Council of Churches issued prophetic warnings against the government: 'God says: "I hate and despise your feasts and I take no delight in your solemn assemblies" [most likely a reference to the Transkei Legislature]... What Christian can rest and sleep with a clear conscience when... greed and exploitation of men by men are the daily experiences of so many.'[63] Half a dozen young students and bureaucrats secretly printed pamphlets on a duplicating machine at a government hospital, denouncing 'Matanzima [as] a poisonous brother serpent' whose skin 'is black, but he is spiritually white.'[64] Four times during the summer and autumn after Sabata was arrested, Umtata woke up to find hundreds of their loose-leafed pamphlets littering the street. There was also a major crisis inside the highest levels of government. It was one thing to imprison Sabata's councillors, but quite another to harm a king. The head of police, Elliot Cwele, resigned, apparently because he refused to arrest Sabata, and was promptly replaced by Brigadier Martin Ngceba, whose career had included a stint with apartheid's Bureau of State Security (better known as BOSS). Umtata bristled with rumours of plots. Cliques within the ruling party sat under the jacaranda trees outside government offices, writing anonymous letters denouncing their enemies. Burglars broke into the attorney general's house, ransacked his private papers, but took nothing. Then Martin Ngceba detained Elliot Cwele, leading to press reports of a smothered coup attempt planned by eight members of the Bantustan government, who were unhappy with Matanzima.[65]

The drama that Sabata would provoke, were he to be tried for treason in Umtata, was demonstrated when thousands of Thembus gathered outside the magistrate's office in town. Sabata's praise singer lamented: 'All is not well in Transkei. We call upon the ancestors to come and arbitrate', while the crowd chorused the king's name in response. When 'George Matanzima... descended the steps of the Palace of Justice... one of Chief Sabata's wives... caught hold of his hand, knelt, and asked him "*Umzimvubu* [George's praise name], where is my husband, *Jonguhlanga?*'[66] A flustered Matanzima said he could not answer such questions in the street, and escaped to his waiting ministerial car. With office workers rapidly gathering on the busy streets during their lunch hour, the police quickly arrested the ring leaders in the crowd. Four days later, Sabata's praise singer was 'detained at St Johns College, whilst he was singing praises to

[62] *DD* 19 March 1980. Cf. Streek and Wicksteed, *Render unto Kaiser*, p.326.
[63] *DD* 15 March 1983. Their acts of dissent: Hawkins Associates, *Five Year Development Plan*, p.265. Moreku, 'Transkei Council of Churches'. *DD* 14 July 1981.
[64] BTS12, 'Duty to the Youth'. For more pamphleting: *DD* 26 August 1980. TRC-VH, Nelani. BTS12 untitled pamphlet, September 1979. UHC, Case 168/80, State vs. Magxinga and Nelani.
[65] Streek and Wicksteed, *Render unto Kaiser*, pp.306-7 Cf. Streek and Wicksteed, *Render unto Kaiser*, pp.353-5. *DD* 7 March 1980.
[66] *DD* 31 July 1979. Streek and Wicksteed, *Render unto Kaiser*, p.314.

mark the school's centenary celebrations.'[67] Sabata's trial was moved to Port St Johns, 90 kilometres away from Thembuland.

Sabata's ill health repeatedly postponed his appearance in court as the year of 1979 came to a close. Doctors diagnosed hyper-tension, bronchitis and kidney trouble. When proceedings finally started in Port St Johns in March 1980, he was ailing and often close to tears. He told the judge that the ancestors were angry and had told him in a dream 'to go to Kaiser Matanzima and tell him the place that where I was [a prison cell] was not suitable for a man of my status.'[68] Another time, he explained the core of his opposition to Bantustans was that 'we were given independence by the Whites on their terms, without consulting our people, especially the enlightened ones.'[69] At times, he seemed like a shrivelled relic of a bygone political age – so different from the young, virile, student dissidents, who appeared in most political trials of the era. Even so, Sabata's criticisms of Matanzima's misrule struck a reverberating chord. His achievement was to find a political language that wove together the ideas of dissent within Transkei's rural regions with the incipient ideologies of opposition emerging from within the swelling ranks of the region's educated youth. Even as a young man, Sabata had been a formidable orator, who, when stirred, could make speeches that lived up to his praise name, *Jonguhlanga* (Shepherd of the Nation). Now Sabata had become the sacrificial lamb, and the drama of his trial gave his words new weight.

The making of the 'Comrade-King'

The great paradox of Sabata's trial was that Matanzima would never have moved against the Thembu king had he not judged that he could ride roughshod over Sabata's supporters in the chieftaincy. Yet at the same time, Sabata's political martyrdom provoked great fear of mass demonstrations. When Sabata went on trial in Port St Johns, police threw up road blocks, cutting off entrance to the town, and the army was mobilised and sent into the surrounding hills. The local magistrate banned all gatherings and public meetings.[70] Sabata's familial connections to ANC leaders and the coverage of his cause in national newspapers connected him to wider networks that stretched across the Eastern Cape and South Africa, giving him new prominence as the 'Comrade-King'.

King Sabata's celebrity owed much to the coverage he received from the newspapers. In Transkei a handful of newssheets – *Imvo, Intsimbi, Isizwe* and the like – circulated around Umtata. Sometimes typed and printed, otherwise handwritten and produced on duplicating machines, they were labours of love, whose editors faced censure and sometimes jail for their pains. They broke scandalous stories and achieved local fame around Umtata, but the success of Matanzima's campaign to suppress them is seen in that only a handful of copies survive in South Africa's libraries. The big change was the penetration

[67] Streek and Wicksteed, *Render unto Kaiser*, p.319.
[68] *DD* 21 March 1980. Cf. *DD* 9, 10 November 1979, 19 March, 2 April 1980. Streek and Wicksteed, *Render unto Kaiser*, pp.320-32.
[69] *DD* 27 March 1980.
[70] *DD* 5, 8 November 1979.

of commercial newspapers into Transkei. Their success was epitomised by the *Daily Dispatch*, which had transformed its operation under a dynamic young editor, Donald Woods, in the mid 1970s. He covered forced removals and black opposition politics in the Eastern Cape Homelands. He employed more black journalists than ever before, who used their contacts to break these stories. He produced *Indaba*, a weekly supplement in English and isiXhosa. Most scandalous was the desegregation of the news pages which announced births, marriages and deaths. Circulation figures dropped from 21,000 to 18,000. But then a new black readership – which accounted for perhaps half the paper's circulation – took figures to 33,000. Transkei readership accounted for one-fifth of the newspaper's total circulation, and advertisements placed by the Bantustan Government proved a lucrative source of revenue.[71]

The *Daily Dispatch* was so much a part of Transkei's politics that the militant young activists who anonymously leafleted Umtata sent copies of their tracts to the newspaper for publication. 'Don't fear Master', one conspirator had written, in a letter to the editor, which he naively signed. 'Do me one favour in your life: publish it [the pamphlet] as it is... Maybe you have got a fear that your newspaper will be banned in Transkei... By publishing appeals like this one, you will be popular with the public. There will be good sales.'[72]

The journalists working in Umtata were at the heart of Sabata's trial. It was the newspaper reports of Sabata's speech in Qumbu that were the immediate cause of the treason trial. Reporters from the *Dispatch* and *Imvo* were subpoenaed to appear as state witnesses. Their evidence would be crucial in corroborating the police reports on Sabata's supposed subversive comments. They promptly received death threats from anonymous supporters of the Thembu king. In the build up to Sabata's trial the *Dispatch* extensively reported the widespread uncertainty at the heart of the Bantustan government. 'Many senior government officials were dismayed by what they see as the biggest blunder ever made by the Matanzimas in arresting Sabata Dalindyebo – an event which would have serious repercussions for the government.'[73] Trying to quell the negative reporting, Kaiser Matanzima was often found at the newspaper's headquarters in East London, threatening to withdraw the Homeland Government's advertisements – a lucrative source of revenue – from the paper. Eventually, the entire Umtata bureau of the *Dispatch* was locked up when they investigated reports of an assassination plot against Kaiser Matanzima at Qamata. It was a crude but effective tactic.[74]

Sabata also became famous throughout the Eastern Cape region because his trial symbolised the dissent that connected the politics of Thembuland to the ANC in prison. His supporters started a legal defence fund to hire the top anti-apartheid lawyers, collecting R50,000 within hours at a rally held in Mdantsane, the second largest township in South Africa, just outside East London.[75] Sabata's legal team was studded with leading lights of the anti-

[71] Woods, *Asking for Trouble*, pp.170–9.
[72] Case 168/80, Exhibit I: Magingxa to Farr.
[73] Streek and Wicksteed, *Render unto Kaiser*, p.314.
[74] Author interview, Richard Wicksteed, Cape Town, 12 June 2008. Streek and Wicksteed, *Render unto Kaiser*, p.297.
[75] Streek and Wicksteed, *Render unto Kaiser*, p.316.

apartheid movement. Nelson Mandela's advocate, Ismail Mohamed, led the defence team. Then there was a younger generation of attorneys, including Griffiths Mxenge, the Eastern Cape born, Robben Islander, whose assassination by apartheid killers, some years later, would make his name known across South Africa.[76]

Most important were Sabata's kinship connections to Nelson Mandela. From Robben Island, Mandela took a keen interest in the inter-related concerns of family matters, Thembu affairs and Transkei's politics. When Mandela's mother died in 1968, Sabata had stepped into the breach, 'undertaking the strenuous task of organising the funeral' attended by a crowd of 800 people. Shortly afterwards, Mandela wrote a letter (which was not delivered) to Kaiser Matanzima, thanking him for attending the funeral, although he chidingly reminded his old friend that 'your brother... *Jonguhlanga*' was the 'head of the Royal House.'[77] When George Matanzima visited Robben Island in 1973 to bring news that Transkei was seeking full Bantustan independence, Nelson Mandela criticised the plan in some detail. Even so, they were 'obviously very pleased to see each other and a lengthy greeting took place followed by enquiries about one another's health and all the family'.[78]

The fraught politics of Transkei's independence increasingly strained family relationships within the Thembu Royal House. Nelson Mandela repeatedly refused to meet Kaiser Matanzima: 'your contemplated visits, even if intended to be of a friendly or family nature, are no longer my personal affair', but instead were 'being handled by my organisation', the ANC High Organ on Robben Island.[79] With Sabata's arrest and detention, relationships within the Thembu Royal House chilled further. Winnie Madikizela-Mandela journeyed to Transkei to seek a family reconciliation but was rebuffed. Nelson Mandela even asked Sabata's cousin-brother and pretender to the throne, Chief Bambilanga Albert Mtirara, to come to Robben Island, presumably to warn him not to depose the Thembu king.[80] Sabata's legal team tried to have Nelson Mandela give evidence at the trial in Transkei. 'Mandela's presence will be a determining factor in whether Sabata will be acquitted or not... He must be cross examined in court [as he would provide evidence related to] family history and land in the area of Umtata', argued the defence lawyers. Both the Bantustan and the apartheid governments feared Mandela's presence, and refused the request.[81]

The dense thickets of legal expertise provided Sabata Dalindyebo with some defence. In April 1980, the presiding judge found Sabata guilty only of injuring the Head of State's dignity and fined him a mere R700. But the Matanzimas were determined to hound him from the Thembu chieftaincy. George Matanzima directed the Thembu Regional Authority to discipline Sabata's misconduct. In

[76] Ibid, pp. 317, 321.
[77] NMPF A3, 8, Mandela to Guzana, 19 October 1968, Mandela to Matanzima, 14 October 1968 (both letters undelivered).
[78] NMPF A4, 13, 'Visit to Prisoner No 466/64 Nelson Mandela by Honourable Minister of Justice, George Matanzima', 3 January 1973.
[79] NMPF A4, 17, Mandela to J.A. Zeka, (n.d. 1977) – refers to a letter Mandela wrote to Matanzima on 21 November 1977.
[80] DD 15 September 1979. Mandela, *Long Walk*, pp. 495-6.
[81] DD 15 September 1979. NMPF A5, 18, A.M. Omar to Commanding Officer, Robben Island, 21 August 1979.

July 1980, the first time the Thembuland Regional Authority met, they held firm, emerging from a four hour meeting with a large majority in favour of simply fining him R100. Only Mvuso Joyi and Bambilanga Mtirara had called for the deposition of the king.[82] It was not enough for the Matanzimas. They overruled the Regional Authority and dismissed Sabata themselves. Three weeks later Sabata disappeared, smuggled into exile.

▲ ▲ ▲

After a sojourn as guest of the Swazi king, Sabata settled with the ANC in Lusaka. The ANC capitalised on his presence. At his first press conference in Lusaka, Sabata made a speech that was faithfully reprinted in the ANC press, claiming: 'Matanzima's army, police and civil service are all split in half.'[83] His critique of Matanzima's misrule suggested that the Bantustans were brimming with resentment. The ANC underground found that the Thembu king was a galvanizing force. 'We would even phone up [Cape Town's townships] and tell people to do things; not using the name of the ANC, but using the name of Sabata.'[84] He was also a smash hit at the ANC's conference in 1985, held in Zambia, where he made a speech in idiomatic isiXhosa that had the delegates on their feet. Sabata told journalists, 'I am not in exile; I have just found myself a new home.'[85] But he seemed bored, and played cards incessantly to pass the time. Occasionally, he wept when friends from Transkei visited him. Sabata would die in exile in 1986, far from his ancestral home.[86]

With Sabata in exile, the Thembu Paramountcy no longer provided a refuge for anti-Matanzima opposition. Bambilanga Mtirara took over the Paramount Chieftaincy of Thembuland, officially acting as a regent to Sabata's son, Buyelekhaya. Rumour soon spread that Bambilanga Mtirara wanted to install his own son on the Thembu throne. Indeed, Buyelekhaya Dalindyebo was not returning to Transkei in the near future: he had fled into exile and was being schooled by the ANC in Tanzania.[87] The Democratic Party also fell apart as party numbers collapsed. A lame and aging Jackson Nkosiyane abandoned political activism in 1980. 'I have no choice,' he told a reporter. 'The founder member, Sabata Dalindyebo, my Paramount Chief, is said to be missing.'[88]

Nine years later, at the age of seventy-five, Nkosiyane was killed whilst staying with relatives in Soweto, where he had been seeking medical treatment. 'He was shot dead while he slept', when the home was attacked by apartheid police during a security sweep.[89]

---

[82] NMPF A54, 107, Sabata to Mandela, 27 April 1980.
[83] *Drum* March 1983.
[84] Interview, Lindi Ndabeni, Johannesburg, 31 August 2008.
[85] *Drum* March 1983.
[86] Interview, Velile Ntsubane, Libode, 19 November 2008.
[87] NMPF 46, 94, Pathekile Holomisa to Mandela, 13 September 1989.
[88] *DD* 3 October 1980.
[89] *Weekly Mail*, 4 July 1989.

6.   Chris Hani's Guerrillas
1974–1987

Hani's Transkei hinterland

In 1974, Chris Hani illicitly travelled across South Africa to Lesotho. His mission was to 'establish a political and diplomatic presence there'.[1] It was through frontline states such as Lesotho and Swaziland – known as the Island and the Bay – that ANC guerrillas in *Umkhonto weSizwe* (MK) would return to South Africa.

The ANC-in-exile believed they would return to South Africa through armed struggle. Just as Fidel Castro's forces had survived in the Cuban countryside whilst support for Batista's regime had ebbed away, so insurgent forces inside South Africa would detonate a popular struggle against the apartheid regime. However, the ANC had difficulties returning to South Africa for much of the 1960s and 1970s. Apartheid was supported by settler regimes in Angola, Mozambique and Zimbabwe (then Rhodesia). Namibia was a UN mandate territory governed by South Africa. Moreover, Lesotho, Botswana and Swaziland were landlocked states with limited room to manoeuvre, given their economic ties to South Africa. In the Wankie and Sipolilo campaigns in 1967 and 1968, the ANC attempted to send detachments of guerrillas through Rhodesia into South Africa, but they were cut up by General Ron Reid-Daley's Rhodesian counter-insurgency forces. In 1971, a plan to land 50 men in Mpondoland ended in fiasco when the ship bound for Transkei's Wild Coast suffered engine failure only a few hours after setting off from Dar es Salaam. (Perhaps the planners of the operation had read Govan Mbeki and were hoping to reprise *The Peasants' Revolt*.)[2]

Hani's journey to Lesotho in 1974 marked a slight shift in ANC thinking. With the dissolution of the Portuguese Empire in the mid-1970s, the ANC swung its attention to newly independent Mozambique and the 'frontline' states of Botswana, Lesotho and Swaziland that ringed South Africa. Now it would infiltrate smaller groups of cadres into South Africa via the Bantustans that shared a border with these frontline states.[3] In the early 1960s, Lesotho had been a waypoint for refugees during the unsuccessful ANC sabotage campaign. Thereafter Lesotho had been a political entrepot, hosting exiles, dissidents and spies. From the mid-1970s, Lesotho's borderlands would become central to the ANC's strategy to return to South Africa.

---

[1] T. Simpson, 'The People's War of Umkhonto we Sizwe' (PhD thesis, University of London, 2006), p.135. Smith and Tromp, *Hani*, p.126.
[2] Simpson, 'The People's War', pp.114-18, 134. H. Barrell, 'The Turn to the Masses: The ANC strategic review of 1978-9', *JSAS*, 18, 1 (1992), p.69.
[3] Barrell, 'The Turn to the Masses', p.77.

▲ ▲ ▲

Chris Hani's ascent through the ranks of the ANC to an important post in Lesotho provides a penetrating insight into how regional networks still counted inside the ANC-in-exile. Unlike his rival, Thabo Mbeki, he did not come from one of the privileged families that dominated the nationalist leadership in the early 20th century. His father, Gilbert Hani, was a migrant labourer from Western Thembuland, who worked as a hawker in Cape Town. In the 1950s, Gilbert Hani had made his name as amongst Transkei's migrants as a local-level ANC leader in Cape Town's townships.[4] Chris Hani had been able to break into the ranks of the educated elites, winning scholarships to Lovedale and Fort Hare, emerging with a law degree and ANC membership card in 1962. His education had been sponsored by missionary teachers in Thembuland and subsequently he was supported with a bursary granted by the Transkei Territorial Authority. Education offered him an immense opportunity, given that only a handful of Africans held a university degree. With these credentials, Chris Hani found employment at a law firm in Cape Town. He was also recruited into the secretive, elitist South African Communist Party.[5]

While Gilbert and Chris Hani's search for employment and political involvement had taken them to metropolitan Cape Town, they also had a deep hinterland in Western Thembuland and Transkei. In particular, they had a long-standing feud with Kaiser Matanzima. During the unrest in Thembuland in the late 1950s, Chris Hani almost lost his scholarship to Fort Hare. Matanzima's Tribal Council had tried to revoke his bursary, arguing:

> Gilbert Hani... is strongly opposed to the Bantu Authorities and has been disseminating belittling information about the working of these authorities in Emigrant [Western] Themubuland and elsewhere. These bad influences are being spread by him in Cape Town... I know [Chris] Hani to be a politically minded youth... We cannot sharpen that axe that will fall on our necks.[6]

When many political organisations were banned by the apartheid government in 1960, both father and son became increasingly involved in the ANC's underground networks. A year later, Gilbert Hani was accused of murdering a black policeman in Cape Town, and was banished home, to live under Matanzima's rule: instead he fled to Lesotho. In 1964, as the underground ANC unravelled in the face of apartheid repression, Chris Hani also left South Africa, making his way to the main body of ANC exiles in Zambia.[7]

Despite these tribulations, the Hanis prospered in exile. Certainly, Chris Hani did not enjoy the advantages of Thabo Mbeki, whose father was a senior leader in the ANC imprisoned on Robben Island. As a favoured son of the ANC,

---

[4] Smith and Tromp, *Hani*, p.41.
[5] Op. cit. pp.36, 38, 41, 45.
[6] 1/XAL242, N11/12/21, 'Meeting of the Emigrant Thembuland Regional Authority', 20 November 1959.
[7] Smith and Tromp, *Hani*, pp.129-30. CMT3/1481, 142/20, BAC Western Cape to S/BAD, 20 November 1962, Matanzima to BAC Salt River, 13 March 1962, S/BAD to Chief BAC Transkei, 30 October 1962.

Thabo Mbeki received a scholarship to study at Sussex University. By contrast, Chris Hani made his name as a guerrilla, at great personal risk, in the Wankie Campaign in 1967.[8] Even Chris' name was a marker of the danger he faced. He was actually born Martin Thembisile, but took the name of his brother, Christopher, to confuse the authorities when on the run. And it was as 'Chris Hani' that he earned the fame which eventually earned him command in Lesotho, where he was able to link up with his father again. By the mid-1970s, his father was running a trading store in Lesotho and had sired a second family with Elizabeth Mafikeng, another trade unionist who had been banished from the Cape. Gilbert Hani had also remained involved in exile circles, so he could introduce his son to political contacts.[9] In due course, Chris Hani married a Lesotho national, Limpho Sekamane, whose connections carried the ANC even deeper into local politics.

In 1976, Chris Hani and his colleagues were arrested and tortured by Basotho security policemen who suspected that the ANC was involved in Lesotho's internecine struggles. Limpho Hani's brother was a senior leader in the Basotho Congress Party, which had started a guerrilla wing, the Lesotho Liberation Army, after the incumbent government had refused to cede power to them in a disputed election. Chris Hani was briefly suspected of channelling money to the insurgents.[10]

Yet diplomatic relations were delicately poised: Lesotho's relationship with the apartheid government was cooling, and senior ANC officials quickly secured Hani's release. Shortly afterwards, Lesotho's head of state, Leabua Jonathan, granted the ANC official recognition. This ploy would win Leabua Jonathan plaudits on the global stage and prop up his regime with a World Bank aid programme. (It would also push elements of the Lesotho Liberation Army into the arms of the apartheid government.) Chris Hani became the Chief Representative of the ANC in Lesotho in 1976. Hani's prominence earned him promotion to Army Commissar and a seat on the National Executive Committee of the ANC in 1975. Together with his rival, Thabo Mbeki, they were youngest members of this powerful institution.[11]

Then there was the matter of the Hani family's entanglement in Transkei's politics. Rumours spread that Gilbert Hani's favourite pastime was to make harassing phone calls from Lesotho to Kaiser Matanzima. 'An audibly angry Matanzima would respond with threats of coming to Maseru to beat up Gilbert.'[12] Instead, it was Chris Hani's MK which was carrying the war out of Lesotho to Transkei, and from there into South Africa.

The 'country bumpkins'

Based in Lesotho and in command of the Cape region, Chris Hani rebuilt the nationalist underground, drawing on longstanding networks of local

[8] Gevisser, *Mbeki*, p.229.
[9] Gerhart interview, O. Mabandla. Smith and Tromp, *Hani*, pp.41. 130.
[10] Smith and Tromp, *Hani*, pp.132, 134.
[11] Ibid.
[12] Op. cit., p.130.

dissidence. Heuristically, one might speak of two distinct pools from which Chris Hani drew his cadres. First, he recruited from those who had been involved in Govan Mbeki's underground networks in the late 1950s and early 1960s. Second, there was a younger generation, who came of age in the Bantustan era, and had most likely been involved in student dissidence either at university or in the elite schools dotted across the Eastern Cape in the late 1970s.

Tata (Father) James 'Castro' Kati (1924-2006) was at the centre of the ANC underground in Transkei during the 1970s. Kati had joined the ANC when he was a migrant worker in Cape Town in 1949, and was first arrested in 1952 for his role in the Defiance Campaign. In the late 1950s, he had moved to Port Elizabeth for work, where he collaborated with Govan Mbeki in the MK underground, for which he was sent to prison on Robben Island. When released in 1970, James Kati was banished to his home district of Thembuland, a long way from the cities where he might cause trouble. His restriction order expired and he returned to Cape Town, only to be sent back to Transkei in 1977 for 'instigating the youth and recruiting them for training outside the country'.[13] Back in Thembuland, James Kati became involved on the peripheries of anti-Matanzima politics, and was mentioned as a councillor to King Sabata Dalindyebo. More importantly, he worked for the ANC underground and established a network of arms caches and safe houses around his home in Luheweni, an area of Umtata district that had been a centre of resistance against the apartheid government's agricultural 'Betterment' policies in the early 1960s. One of Kati's closest allies in the Transkei underground was Ezra Sigwela (b.1940), his well-educated nephew who had also been imprisoned on Robben Island.[14]

By contrast, the second core constituency of Chris Hani's underground were typically young men (less often women) born in the 1950s and early 1960s who had been involved in political unrest in the Eastern Cape's elite schools or at university. One of Chris Hani's most trusted MK commanders, Dumisani Mafu, was typical. Mafu attended St Johns College, Umtata, before taking a Transkei Government bursary to study law at Fort Hare University. Here he joined the ANC underground, playing a leading role in the strikes that closed down the campus in 1980. He briefly worked as an assistant magistrate in Transkei's bureaucracy. But Transkei's security services were tracing students involved in the ANC underground and the 'net was closing';[15] so he left Transkei for Lesotho, joining good friends whom he knew from school and university, who would also rise high in the MK.

Within the tight-knit circles of the ANC in exile, the social prestige and connections obtained at a top school like St Johns College carried great weight. Oyama Mabandla, who also fled into exile in Lesotho during 1980, did not know of Chris Hani until they met in Lesotho, yet they soon found they had many things in common. 'We came from the same part of the world and spoke the same language... [And] Chris Hani had attended Lovedale

[13] TRC-VH EC0309/96, James Kati, Umtata, 18 June 1996. Cf. Magubane et al, 'Armed Struggle'. pp.116-7, 120, 127. *DD* 29 July, 3 August, 5 November 1982.
[14] Interview, Sigwela.
[15] Author interviews, O. Mabandla, Mafu.

114

and Fort Hare just like my father too ... That does bring you closer.'[16] Then there was the matter of Chris Hani's famed intellectualism and his habit of quoting Latin verse. He often spent time in the backyard of the Lebentele family, 'a famous rendezvous [for debates and discussions] in the suburbs of Maseru', where students and exiles lived together in 'a clutch of shacks'.[17] Yet independent thought was only treasured up to a point. After four months in Lesotho, Oyama Mabandla joked that the sour milk in their coffee must have come from the Soviet Union. One comrade 'became very serious and sombre... "This is not a jocular matter"... Everyone was listening; the atmosphere was tense.' Fortunately, his youthful indiscretion was quickly forgiven. A few days later Hani invited Mabandla to join the elite and secretive South African Communist Party. 'I was thrilled.'[18]

▲ ▲ ▲

Chris Hani's recruitment of well-educated young men from the Eastern Cape gave him a significant powerbase within the MK and the ANC-in-exile. Hani 'rarely missed an opportunity to push the brightest and most promising into key positions, gaining a reputation as the patron and godfather of many of the best cadres.'[19] This was deeply significant given the prevailing difficulties inside the MK. After the student uprisings of 1976, 1980 and 1984, its ranks swelled with youngsters who had fled South Africa for exile. Vladmir Shubin, a USSR official tasked with supporting southern African liberation movements, later wrote about the low standards in the MK, which he attributed to the deleterious effects of the Bantu Education system and the sustained township revolts. On passing an advanced training course in Odessa, one MK cadre thanked his Russian instructors by telling them, 'Thank you comrades; now we know how to rob a bank.'[20] Other memoirs mention how easy it was to identify an ANC man, supposedly operating underground, '...in the discos of Manzini [in Swaziland] and Maseru [the capital of Lesotho]. He was the one with the fashionable clothes and the BMW who boasted of his trips abroad.'[21] Under these circumstances, the Eastern Capers who came from the better ex-mission schools were likely to rise high in the MK and the ANC-in-exile.

There was also an ethnic dimension to Chris Hani's pattern of recruitment of Xhosa-speaking Eastern Capers, which cleaved to the heart of ANC exile politics. They were a vital part of Chris Hani's support base in his disputes with Joe Modise. Born in 1929, family poverty had forced Modise to leave school early and take work as a driver in Johannesburg. Obituaries would speak of his determination to pursue education through night school. Other accounts describe him as a 'former street-fighter from Alexandra [township]' who had made his name by providing security for Nelson Mandela during the 1950s

---

[16] Author interview, O. Mabandla.
[17] Smith and Tromp, *Hani*, p.130.
[18] Gerhart interview, O. Mabandla.
[19] S. Ellis and T. Sechaba, *Comrades Against Apartheid: The ANC and the South African Communist Party in exile* (London, 1992), p.122. Sechaba was Oyama Mabandla's pen-name.
[20] V. Shubin, *The ANC: A view from Moscow* (Bellville, 1999), p.173.
[21] Ellis and Sechaba, *Comrades*, p.140.

township campaigns.[22] Involved in the ANC sabotage campaign in the early 1960s, Modise had gone into exile and become the commander of the MK in 1965 after the imprisonment of Mandela. Because he was head of the MK, Modise was the lightning-rod for complaints, blamed for the failure of the Wankie and Sipililo campaigns in the 1960s and the frustrations within the guerrilla camps. Yet Modise, and his coterie of supporters who came from Johannesburg, held onto power despite Chris Hani's relentless promotion of his supporters.[23] (Indeed, Modise would become Minister of Defence in post-apartheid South Africa.)

Disheartened by these tensions, Oyama Mabandla exiled himself from the ANC and become a dreadlocked student at San Diego University. He co-authored an exposé on the patronage politics of the ANC-in-exile. The book alleged: 'Hani's blatant championing of Xhosa-speakers from the Eastern Cape... created ethnic tensions which persist.' His collaborator, Stephen Ellis, later explained that:

> [Mabandla] had become disillusioned... Patronage is used to keep fiefdoms intact. Various rewards/punishments that patrons could dispense, besides career advancement and good/bad transfers, included scholarships... [and the] taking/not taking [of] wives and girlfriends. In exile the constituency for the ambitious would-be leader is quite small, only the few thousands in the camps... Most party members are so dedicated that even if they fall out they believe their last duty in the cause is to keep silent. Anyone who squeals is called an agent.[24]

In the battle for the control of the MK, the exiles traded smears. The Johannesburgers 'attacked Chris Hani's personal vanity... criticised his flamboyant lifestyle... [and] spread ugly rumours about his wife.' At the same time they claimed that Chris Hani's protégés were Country Bumpkins (*moegoes*) – a name that was generally used against people from the rural areas, but was particularly applied to Transkeians.[25]

▲ ▲ ▲

The contrast between the rivalries over power and prestige in exile and the experience of underground work inside South Africa was stark. Some estimates suggest that almost one-fifth of the 100 or so cadres infiltrated into South Africa in 1977-78 were captured or killed.[26] There was also a high attrition rate amongst members of the ANC underground based inside the country. One such was Mazwi Yako, the Fort Hare student recruited into the ANC underground in Transkei, when he formed the Democratic Party Youth League in 1980. In an autobiographical essay he later wrote for his handlers (a strategy they used to weed out spies), he recalled the events of 1980:

[22] S. Ellis, 'The ANC in Exile' *African Affairs*, 90 (1991), p.443. South African History Online, 'Biography – Joe Modise', n.d..

[23] Ellis and Sechaba, *Comrades*, p.128.

[24] KGC1, G. Gerhart and T. Karis interview, Stephen Ellis, London, 1 March, 1991. Cf. Gerhart interview, O. Mabandla.

[25] Ellis and Sechaba, *Comrades*, pp.178-80.

[26] Shubin, *The ANC*, p.198.

[When] the students started to boycott classes... a state of emergency was declared by KD [Matanzima]. I rushed to Comrade Kati and we were certain that we were once more going to be arrested... [So] we decided to visit Maseru as we already had a few recruits.

In Maseru I met Comrade Chris Hani and we discussed at length... transporting material, people and [finding] accommodation. After two weeks I returned home and luckily got a job in a bank [in Umtata]...

This is the time I was recruited to the [Communist] Party. At the same time I was recruiting youth for military training. [Then] I was arrested because most of my friends from Fort Hare had disappeared [abroad]... and I was detained till October...

When I was released [I went] to Maseru to report... [and] I was given the task of checking [Martin] Ngceba [the head of the Transkei Police], in preparation for an assassination attempt. I did this and everything was arranged, but unfortunately the comrades missed him. A week after this, almost all the people who were active were arrested... I was released in January 1981. I again visited Maseru to report... [and was involved in transporting] military material to East London and Port Elizabeth. During this time I formed a propaganda unit in Durban Medical School... During this time I was having party discussions with Comrade Kati and Ezra Sigwela.[27]

In August 1981, James Kati's network was eventually rolled up. Security police tracked down an MK unit, suspected of a series of bombings in the Eastern Cape and Natal, which had been hiding-out in Transkei. The men shot their way out of the first ambush, killing a Transkei policeman; but later that day, fleeing to Lesotho, they were caught at a roadblock. The entire MK unit was killed and their bodies were secretly buried.[28] The rest of James Kati's network was soon undone. Some fled to exile. Mazwi Yako sneaked out of the back door of his bank, whilst police waited outside. From Lesotho, he was sent to study in the USSR, later rising high in ANC exile structures and making his fortune after 1994. Others were not so lucky. Kati and half a dozen others were captured and taken to East London, where they were severely tortured and interrogated by security policemen. In 1982, Kati and his colleagues were put on trial and jailed for seven years. This was one of half a dozen security trials that disrupted the ANC underground across the rural Eastern Cape.[29]

In one sense, these desperate actions were of little military consequence, fought by a score of men; but occasional incidents suggest the depth of tacit sympathy that martyrdom could arouse. James Kati's wife died in 1981 whilst he was in detention. Almost 2,000 people attended her funeral at Luheweni. From Lusaka, King Sabata Dalindyebo smuggled R1,000 across the border to pay for the ceremony. James Kati was allowed to attend the gathering in handcuffs, escorted by a convoy of five police cars.[30]

[27] *Molotov Cocktail*, 4 (March – May 2008), pp.34-5.
[28] Interviews, Matomela, Saliwa. *DD* 12 April 1997. ANC Press Release, 9 June 1997.
[29] Umtata High Court, HC Case 15/1982. TRC-VH ECO0121/96UTA Mkangeli Manford Matomela, Umtata, 19 June 1996.
[30] *DD* 5 October 1981, 9 December 1982. TRC-VH, Kati.

University dissent – communitarians and class analysis

In the mid-1980s, whilst James Kati was in jail, the ANC underground re-established itself in Transkei. Their activities increasingly centred on the newly built University of Transkei. Opened in 1980, the university would have a student population of around 3,000 by 1984.[31] The university would also provide a forum for ideological debates, which would show the extent to which the communitarian ideas associated with Steve Biko's rural self-help projects in the 1970s had entered the currency of ANC debates in the 1980s.

At first glance, the new brick and concrete campus of the University of Transkei, perched on the hills overlooking Umtata, was not the most likely place for intellectual debate and dissent. In one sense, Transkei's university was just another 'Bush College' – as the segregated universities for African students located on rural campuses in the Homelands were derisively known. Transkei's new institution joined the University of Fort Hare, the University of the North, and the University of Zululand in providing a tertiary education for African students who were expected to staff the Bantustan state. 'The university's position was basically to... provide a fairly cheap, higher education to the... civil servants and teachers in the region,' an old professor would recall, rather self-deprecatingly.[32]

Living conditions at the University of Transkei were tough. One survey claimed that only 3% of students had 'no difficulty in obtaining proper meals'. There was also a perpetual shortage of student accommodation – only 1,480 places in total, with 120 beds available for 800 applicants in 1983. As a result, student squatters moved into the already cramped dormitories allocated to their friends, making a messy nonsense of university rules. They were the lucky ones. The vast majority lived off campus, renting from slumlords, forced to share beds as four or five students were crammed together in small rooms.[33] The campus social life also required street-smarts. The first graduation ball descended into a mass brawl when students got fighting drunk at the free bar.[34] Thriving in the university's chaotic teaching environment required an equal measure of guile. The Head of Department in the Economic Sciences Faculty constructed a three-year graduate degree which had only seven texts on the course reading list – 'two of which had been written by the learned lecturer himself.'[35] Results were so poor in 1980 that one staff member drafted a memorandum with the plea that students should not be accepted 'unless faculty had a chance to see a record of students' school performance'.[36]

[31] *DD* 25 October 1982, 9 October 1984.
[32] A. Habib, *Structural Constraints, Managerial Ineptitude and Stakeholder Complicity: A study of the institutional crisis at the University of Transkei* (Pretoria, Human Sciences Research Council report, 2001), p.9.
[33] *DD* 25 October 1982, 2 February, 10 November 1983, 19 September 1984. R. Morrell, 'Books and Batons', *Work in Progress*, 34 (1984), p.5.
[34] *DD* 29 April 1980.
[35] Author interview, Rob Morrell, Durban, 8 September 2008.
[36] W. Thomas, 'Faculty of Economic Sciences – Proposal for steps to improve student performance', (draft memo, February 1981).

Moreover, 'the University of Transkei was his [Kaiser Matanzima's] own little fiefdom.' Some lecturers complained that 'any attack on the University of Transkei is seen as an attack on the state... It is part of his personal aristocracy [that] he [Matanzima] is trying to build out of his Paramount Chieftainship, as Head of State and Head of the university.'[37] Indeed, the university had little institutional autonomy: it was just 'another line item on the budget of the Transkei Department of Finance.'[38] Matanzima tried to ensure that his supporters held senior managerial positions inside the university. He also pushed one of his favourites – Liston Ntshongwana, a civil servant, taking part time university courses after office hours – into the post of Student Council President. Liston Ntshongwana ran the Student Representative Council as his sub-fiefdom, stifling student activity.[39]

Matanzima's treatment of the University of Transkei as his patrimony was supported by Pretoria's policies. The apartheid government had a long-running strategy of placing loyal Broederbonders in positions of university leadership, turning a blind eye to their peccadilloes. The university's Vice Chancellor, Professor Van der Merwe, employed his wife as a personal secretary even though she could not type. Senior university staff siphoned off petrol for their own private gain, gave lucrative contracts to friends and family, and even removed building material for their own personal use.[40] Lecturers who made allegations of corruption to the police found their affidavits fell into the hands of the university authorities, and they instead were charged with misconduct.[41]

Even so, university education was still an elite enterprise, relatively speaking. Only 5,200 Africans attended university in 1977, rising to just over 8,300 in 1981 and 18,400 in 1984. (Although there was a rapid growth in the student body, they numbered less than half a percent of their age cohort.)[42] Within the University of Transkei, there were a number of young, well-educated and highly motivated students – not least some of the students on Bantustan government bursaries, who had started their degrees at Fort Hare and brought their taste of student politics back to Umtata.

Moreover, even if the University of Transkei was run in a patriarchal, repressive fashion, there was still some space for dissent. Anxious to gain credentials as a reputable university, it 'was having a little bit of a Prague Spring'.[43] The university's hiring policy brought in an eclectic, effervescent mix of lecturers. There were around a dozen young academics who had been involved in left-wing politics at South Africa's 'white' universities in the 1970s.[44] The

---

[37] BTS20, Umtata Ambassador to DG DFA, 2 November 1984.
[38] Habib, *University of Transkei*, p.9.
[39] Interview, Morrell. Morrell, 'Books and Batons', p.6. *DD* 13 September, 31 May, 7 November 1984. Habib, *University of Transkei*, p.9.
[40] *DD* 31 May, 3 August 1984 – quoting a Commission of Inquiry. BTS20, Umtata Ambassador to DG DFA, 2 November 1984. BTS20, untitled document produced by an unnamed University of Transkei member of staff, 6 July 1984.
[41] *DD* 31 May, 13 September, 7 November 1984.
[42] S. Badat, 'The Expansion of Black Tertiary Education', in Wolpe and Unterhalter (eds.), *Apartheid Education*, p.80 – this figure excludes students taking correspondence courses through the University of South Africa.
[43] Author interview, Chris Tapscott, Cape Town, 7 September 2009.
[44] Interview, Morrell.

University of Transkei also hired a significant group of African lecturers who were heirs to the mission-educated intelligentsia. This included Xoliswa Jozana, one of Kaiser Matanzima's daughters, well known for her disapproval of her father's policies. The ANC also infiltrated a few cadres onto the campus. Mzolisi Mabude was a lecturer with a complicated past. His late father, Saul Mabude, had been a prominent supporter of King Botha Sigcau and was derided in popular songs that were well known across Mpondoland. However, Mzolisi had worked on the fringes of the ANC, as a student in Sweden and a lecturer in Nigeria, before returning to Transkei to take a senior post in the bureaucracy and then a lectureship at the university. He was playing a double game: some parts of the ANC encouraged his return to Transkei, hoping he might prove 'a source of information for them.'[45]

For politically-minded young students, the University of Transkei's lecturers opened new horizons. In the Transkei, where any sign of opposition had been repressed and political materials were banned, dissidence was an intellectual adventure. Marxist reading groups flourished amongst the staff. Lecturers circulated socialist pamphlets amongst their students. Charismatic teachers gained a popular following. Herbert Vilakazi, the son of a noted scholar of African languages, had written an article for the prominent American publication, *Monthly Review*, which suggested that Karl Marx was a black man. His lectures at the University of Transkei were always packed.[46]

▲ ▲ ▲

For many students and lecturers, Marxist theory provided the clearest answer to the problem of what was to be done in the Bantustans. In the 1970s, the Black Consciousness movement, with its eclectic ideas about the politics of identity and community, had held sway amongst university students. This was changing in the 1980s. The ANC-in-exile – which used Marxist theory as a prism to frame the discussions of its official documents – was now recruiting students. Trade union protests in South African cities also increased the purchase of socialist ideology across the country. Class analysis had become the global language of intellectual conversation: from the beginning of the 1980s, academics based on campuses around the world produced a series of books, theses and articles on the Bantustans. The University of Transkei was plugged into these debates. Xoliswa Jozana, for instance, wrote an article eviscerating 'The Transkeian Middle Class' in *Africa Perspective*, one of the many excellent journals produced by 'engaged' South African intellectuals. (She neatly skipped the problem of her membership of Transkei's elite by focusing on the bureaucrats, politicians and businessmen who benefited from state patronage, ignoring teachers and professionals such as herself.)[47]

---

[45] Interview, Sigwela. Gerhart interview, O. Mabandla. Cf. Ellis and Sechaba, *Comrades*, p.65. BTS12, Untitled Report, 4 May 1979. Nordic Documentation Centre on the Liberation Struggle in Southern Africa interview with Mzolisi Mabude, Mbabane, Swaziland, n.d.

[46] H. Vilakazi, 'Was Karl Marx a Black Man?', *Monthly Review*, 33, 2 (1980), pp.42-58. Author interview, Sakhela Buhlungu, Johannesburg, 26 August 2009. Morrell, 'Books and Batons', pp.4-5.

[47] Xoliswa Jozana, 'The Transkeian Middle Class: Its political implications', *Africa Perspective*, 1,

Yet at the same time, communitarian ideas infused students' socialist ideals. Bathandwa Ndondo, the scion of a teaching family and one of the most prominent student leaders at the University of Transkei, was involved in the Health Care Trust in his home district of Cala.[48] Kenny Jafta, the son of prosperous rural traders who later joined the MK, was teasingly named *Umngqusho* (a dish of maize and beans) by his friends because he always argued that South Africa would only be free when rural children had full bellies. Mvula Mthimkulu, who was working for the ANC underground at the University of Transkei, had previously studied at the University of the North, where he had made his name in student politics by organising food parcels for poor rural communities that surrounded the student campus. [49]

The Institute of Management and Development Studies, founded at the university in 1980, provided the most structured forum for debates about models and concepts of community development in the Transkei. What is most noticeable is the heterogeneity and ambivalence of these ideas. Although its first director, Wolfgang Thomas was a critic of the apartheid system, he had intended that the institute work in tandem with the Bantustan government, bringing services such as water and health care to rural communities. Intriguingly, the most penetrating critic of this ideal of community development was Chris Tapscott, who also worked at the Institute of Development and Management Studies. He had come to Transkei in 1980, hoping that government-backed development projects would stimulate black smallholder production. He became increasingly disillusioned, and eventually wrote a damning auto-critique of his work. He argued that the Bantustan technocrats who were implementing this policy in government parastatals, under Pretoria's direction, became a powerful collaborating group within the Transkei. [50]

Nevertheless, the Institute of Management and Development Studies ran a wide variety of different types of community development programmes. Their projects were most successful when they played a palliative role and tapped into the concerns of local social activists: supporting the communal gardens of *Zenzele* women's groups, for instance.[51] The Insitute staff criticised chiefs and headmen, claiming the absence of locally elected committees often stifled grassroots rural development projects. They also ran seminars that provided a forum for longstanding critical voices: one such was Adina Ndamse, the director of an NGO, Vusisizwe Development, who had been detained for her role as a Black Consciousness activist in the 1970s. (See Chapters Three and Four). 'Grassroots development is a crucial task', Adina Ndamse told a conference held at the University of Transkei: [52]

(contd) 7&8 (1989), p.96.

[48] C. Tapscott, 'Village Health Worker Project,' *Transkei Development Review*, 1, 2 (1981), pp.74-5.

[49] Author interviews, Kenny Jafta, Dutywa, 10 November 2008, Mvula Mthimkulu, East London, 13 November 2008.

[50] Author interview, Wolfgang Thomas, Cape Town, 11 September 2009. Tapscott, 'The Rise of Development'.

[51] W. Thomas, 'The Hawkins Report: First of a new type of planning report' (Typescript, February 1981), p.13. C. Tapscott, 'Nkanga Rural Development Project Outline', *Transkei Development Review*, 2, 2 (1982), pp.60-66.

[52] Tapscott, 'Nkanga', p.60. A.N. Ndamse, 'Meeting the Challenge of Rural Development', *Transkei*

Groups such as Mothers' Unions have unduly emphasized spiritual matters...
Practical matters, such as literacy training and cooking, must not be neglected...
Our standards, values, beliefs and attitudes are instilled in us by our communities...
They pose a challenge to those who are concerned about developing a nation, or a
rural community.

The work of the Institute of Management and Development Studies took
on an even more subversive role when they hired Mvula Mthimkulu. With the
tacit support of some senior staff, he ran an underground cell in which visiting
guerrillas masqueraded as development consultants. It was perfect cover: 'you
could go anywhere in the rural areas armed with a clipboard.'[53]

For students at the University of Transkei, the Catholic Students Association
was the other important nexus of dissent and debate. It involved many of
the undergraduate student leaders, including Bathandwa Ndondo.[54] Their
great supporter was Father Cas Paulsen, a maverick priest from America,
who had been briefly thrown out of South Africa in 1971 for preaching a
heady mix of Liberation theology and community self-empowerment.[55] His
ideas resonated with the Black Consciousness-inspired theology that was
prominent in institutions such as the Federal Seminary. 'Our aim was not to
clap our hands for Jesus, but corrupt young minds with the social teaching
of the Church,' he recalled.[56] Father Cas held retreats where the student
activists made contact with figures such as Ezra Sigwela, who combined his
involvement in the ANC underground with work for the Transkei Council of
Churches.[57] (The community development work of the Transkei Council of
Churches is mentioned in Chapter Five.) Thus the young radicals of the 1980s
imbibed the ideas of class analysis while at the same time articulating a more
communitarian mode of thinking.

▲ ▲ ▲

Under the influence of the Catholic Students Association, the pace of student
politics increased at the University of Transkei. In 1982 and 1983, there were
'sports trips' to other universities – most notably the National University of
Lesotho – where students made contact with the ANC. Underground operatives
based in Transkei, such as Ezra Sigwela and Mzolisi Mabude, formed individual
students into underground cells.[58] Then an unexpected set of events galvanised
the student body. Vice Chancellor van der Merwe suffered a freak accident,
breaking his back when he fell off a ladder. At the same time, a series of student
murders in the centre of Umtata provoked 'great unease' in the student body,
'who began to demand that a ceremony be held to appease the ancestors...
This was an implicit attack on the state and university administration.'[59] The

---

(contd) *Development Review*, 1,1 (1981), p.37.
[53] Interviews, Mthimkulu, Tapscott.
[54] Interview, Buhlungu.
[55] Author Interview, Father Cas Paulsen, Umtata, 21 September 2009.
[56] Ibid.
[57] Interview, Buhlungu.
[58] Interviews, Buhlungu, Sigwela.
[59] Morrell, 'Books and Batons', p.6.

deaths occurred off campus and could have been avoided if student life had not been stifled by the corrupt student council, they argued.

During the seven months of van der Merwe's sick leave, the Deputy Vice Chancellor, Wiseman Nkhulu, launched a series of investigations against his boss, stirring up the student body even more. One pamphlet denounced the 'internal corruption within the university administration, which has a strong link with the state.' [60] The corrupt Liston Ntshongwana was turfed out in student elections. Perhaps two-thirds of the new Student Representative Council were members of the Catholic Students Association. [61] They produced the first student newspaper, *Progress*, and refused to deal with an unpopular Dean of Students, who had been a notoriously authoritarian residence director. Student activists also extended their reach over campus politics by organising a series of food boycotts. 'These ... were notable feats of organisation, since both the residence directors and the phony house committees did their best to prevent them,' noted a sympathetic lecturer. [62]

Van Der Merwe hurried back from sick leave, still on crutches. Although Wiseman Nkhulu was forced out of the University of Transkei in February 1984, the genie was out of the bottle. [63] This was dramatically brought home by an incident in April 1984 in which a carful of young men was arrested after a grenade accidently detonated inside their vehicle. It transpired that they had been carrying an ANC cadre to the Lesotho border. Two of the youths were university students – one of them the son of a Bantustan government minister. [64] Van Der Merwe used his speech at the university's graduation ceremony to attack the Marxist professors who were infecting his institution. The student dissidents got wind of his speech and dashed off a pre-emptive pamphlet on copying machines owned by the Institute of Development and Management Studies. 'You are going to cover up your corruption by mounting an attack on the Student Representative Council... by accusing them of being agitators and communists... Tell your bosses to come for a crackdown on us. We are ready for them. But should they touch us, you are in [the] shit.' [65]

It was the students who were crushed. Hundreds were detained, the subversive lecturers deported, and the campus closed down until the worst storms had passed. A handful of student leaders were smuggled through road blocks by a sympathetic lecturer. They were hidden by Father Cas and other sympathisers until the hue and cry had died down. [66]

---

[60] Morrell, 'Books and Batons', p.6. Cf. Interview, Morrell (who served on Nkhulu's committee). *DD* 8 December 1982, 16 July 1983. BTS19, ASAZO pamphlet.

[61] Interview, Paulsen.

[62] Morrell, 'Books and Batons,' p.6. Cf. BTS19, telex from Umtata to Pretoria, 29 May 1984.

[63] *DD* 8 February 1984.

[64] *DD* 21 August, 19 September 1984. Interview, Buhlungu.

[65] Morrell, 'Books and Batons', p.8. Cf. BTS20, Untitled Document, 6 July 1984. *DD* 7 May 1984. Interview, Buhlungu.

[66] Morrell, 'Books and Batons', p.9. Interviews, Morrell, Paulsen. *DD* 8, 27 June, 21, 29, 31 August, 18, 22 September, 24 October, 1, 3 November 1984. BTS19, 'TBVC Afdeling'.

The intimacy of insurgency

While Transkei's security police had smashed organised student politics within the university, the unrest had also caught the attention of the ANC-in-exile. After the university boycotts in 1984, 'approaches from the ANC [underground were] popping up all over the place,' one student leader recalled.[67] Chris Hani, promoted away from Lesotho to be the Commissioner of the MK, was escalating the ANC's armed campaign against South Africa. Transkei was a vital transit point and students were drafted into the front line.

There was a brutal intimacy to this insurgency, for the students-turned-guerrillas came from same families as their enemies inside the Bantustan state. It made the conflict exceptionally bitter, but there were also moments when boundaries between opposition and collaboration, and ethnic identities and nationalist loyalties proved extremely permeable.

In the mid-1980s the strategic thinking of the MK had shifted again towards planning for a 'People's War'. MK attacks increased from around 50 in 1984 to 230 in 1986. 'No one ever believed that MK was going to march in Pretoria with its banners flying', Stephen Ellis and Oyama Mabandla have argued. Nevertheless, 'the series of bomb, grenade and rifle attacks' – coming at a time when apartheid South Africa faced sustained township revolts, industrial unrest and international isolation – 'had a marked [propaganda] effect'.[68] The front-line states and the Bantustans on the border played a critical role in the new strategy:

> Expensive and difficult though it was to send cadres into the country one or two at a time... there was a steady trickle of trained saboteurs infiltrating the country. Cadres would fly from the camps in Angola to Lusaka, and from there to Lesotho or one of the other forward areas. They slipped across the border... and received weapons at a point pre-arranged by the Ordinance Department.

As a result, the conflict between security forces and dissidents within Transkei intensified in the mid-1980s. This was a family affair. At various times, three senior MK commanders operated inside Transkei; all were Chris Hani's protégés and had attended St Johns College, Umtata. The official commander of the area for much of the period was Mazizi 'Pieces' Maqhekeza. He was a close friend of Dumisani Mafu, who also operated out of Transkei at various points. Both men had been bursary students together at Fort Hare in the late 1970s, training to work for the Transkei judiciary, before they had fled into exile. Mzawandile Vena was the other St Johns College graduate-turned-senior cadre; he was behind an operational spectacular that blew up Umtata's fuel depot on 25 June 1985, sending a plume of smoke high above the town. In response, an apartheid hit-squad assassinated the Transkei student leader, Bathandwa Ndondo, who had been rusticated for his involvement in the campus protests in 1984. Kaiser Matanzima gave a speech soon afterwards, claiming (incorrectly)

[67] Interview, Buhlungu.
[68] All quotes in paragraph: Ellis and Sechaba, *Comrades*, p.173.

that he had been linked to the fuel depot bombing. Ndondo's family made informal inquiries. Their discoveries were shocking: one of the leaders of the hit squad was Gladstone Mose, a man well known to the ANC and another alumnus of St Johns College. He had fled into exile and joined the MK but had later been captured, tortured and turned by the apartheid security forces.[69]

Such revelations were not uncommon. The secrets and betrayals typical to all insurgencies in this instance fused onto the close-knit networks of the Eastern Cape elite. The elimination of Tennyson Makiwane by MK cadres in 1980 was another such moment. Makiwane was the scion of a prominent Transkei family who had flown high in exile with the ANC in the 1960s, until disagreements about the strategic direction of the movement had brought about his expulsion in the mid-1970s. At a loose end, Makiwane applied for a UN post in Swaziland, but the ANC obstructed his appointment. 'Destitute, he moved to Lesotho and there was contacted by an official in the Transkei Government who persuaded him to return home.'[70] Some years later, an ANC operative based in Transkei was briefly detained and 'confronted with questions... that [apparently] could only have been provided by Tennyson Makiwane,' whom he knew well through family connections. 'Acting on its own initiative,' an MK unit based in Lesotho killed Makiwane. In Lusaka 'Oliver Tambo was furious, and condemned the murder;' but he took no action and publically denied ANC involvement.

These ambivalent relationships went to the heart of the Bantustan state. Prince Madikizela had been involved in the ANC underground for decades, partly as the result of the influence of his aunt, Winnie Madikizela-Mandela. He was also married to another of Kaiser Matanzima's daughters, Camagwini Matanzima, who was known to be close to her father. This relationship had allowed him to visit Robben Island with his wife on "family business". Nelson Mandela later wrote Camagwini a letter addressed to 'my darling Mzakulu'. Some in the ANC underground also remembered that 'the police would not detain Prince because they knew they would be in trouble – so we used him a lot.'[71] However, by the mid-1980s Prince's Madikizela's marriage was falling apart. One night he came home late and caught Camagwini kissing a man from Transkei's security forces. Shortly after he separated from his wife, he was brought to court to face charges of domestic violence. Prince Madikizela won the case, but Kaiser Matanzima then banished him to a remote rural area, acting on allegations of his underground activities. One of Nelson Mandela's lawyers unsuccessfully tried to intervene, filing a protest that this political persecution was motivated purely by a family feud.[72]

However, there were many other times when the ANC took advantage of their close relationships with the Bantustan establishment. In 1986, Dumisani Mafu used an inside contact in the Bantustan bureaucracy to

[69] Bell and Ntsebeza, *Unfinished Business*, pp.143-9. TRC-AH, Gcinisiko Dandala, Umtata, 17 June 1998. Interview, Sigwela.
[70] Ellis and Sechaba, *Comrades*, p.65. Cf. Truth and Reconciliation Commission (hereafter TRC), *Truth and Reconciliation of South Africa: Report, Volume Two* (Cape Town, 1998), p.335.
[71] Interview, Junior Saliwa. Mandela's letter: NMPF A54, 107, Mandela to Camagwini Matanzima, 15 November 1981.
[72] *DD* 11 April, 30 June, 11, 12 October, 8, 12 December 1984.

plant a bomb in the centre of government: the eleven-storey Botha Sigcau Building in the centre of Umtata.[73] Searching for hiding places, MK cadres used their old-boy networks, looking up school and university friends who had often joined the Bantustan bureaucracy. Government housing became guerrilla hideouts. Pieces Maqekeza cached weapons in staff housing at Jongilizwe College for Sons of Chiefs – the school especially set up to train the future Bantustan leaders. When he was hiding out in the staff accommodation, Maqekeza would catch up on gossip about old school friends and homeboys who were rising through the Bantustan judicial system – the very career path he had left behind when he joined the ANC in exile.[74]

Oliver Tambo even attempted to place sympathisers inside the Bantustan system. He instructed Pathekile Holomisa to take the Hegebe chieftainship on his grandfather's death and even to join Kaiser Matanzima's governing party. Pathekile Holomisa baulked at this prospect. Some of his old friends from St Johns College had joined the ANC underground, and he too had been involved on the periphery of activism when a student at the University of Natal in 1984 and 1985, handing out political pamphlets. Holomisa feared his friends would disown him if he took up the chieftaincy. He chose instead to work as an attorney and joined the ANC-aligned National Association of Democratic Lawyers in East London, only later returning to Transkei to train as an advocate (barrister) in 1989.[75]

Two bombs placed by MK cadres at Cala Post Office and the Wild Coast Casino in Eastern Mpondoland in 1986 signalled the arrival of an even more bitter phase of the insurgency inside Transkei. The Cala blast caused no injuries, but the latter, placed by Ndibulele Ndzamela and Pumzile Mayaphi (the second yet another St Johns College and Fort Hare graduate who had fled South Africa in 1980) killed a young black boy and a white pensioner. It was too much for Lusaka: the ANC denied responsibility for the attack.[76] That year the MK also attacked the police station in the centre of Umtata. 'It was a very bold attack... Three comrades came in just as the guard was changing.'[77] Eight security police were killed and five more injured; but a ricochet severely injured one of the MK cadres, Solly Talakumeni.

In desperation, the guerrillas fell back on their trusted networks, asking sympathisers such as Chris Tapscott, Father Cas and Ezra Sigwela to find a doctor. It was of no use: a few days later Solly Talakumeni died. The sympathisers were now roped in to help with the burial. 'It was a pure Graham Greene moment', Tapscott later remembered. He found himself driving Father Cas' car down dark roads into Ngato Forest, with the dead body in the boot.

---

[73] TRC-AD, AC/2000/240, Dumisani Mafu.

[74] Transkei Supreme Court, Case 34P/89, 'Affidavit of Ronald Vumile Bikitsha'.

[75] Gerhart interview, O. Mabandla. Author interview, Pathekile Holomisa, Cape Town, 18 September 2009.

[76] ANC, 'Further Submissions and Responses by the ANC to Questions raised by the Commission for Truth and Reconciliation – Appendix Four, Appendix Five'. The Wild Coast bombers argued they had not intended to kill because they placed the bomb in the toilets rather than the foyer of the casino – *DD* 23 March 1989.

[77] Interview, Paulsen. Cf. TRC-AD, Mafu.

One of Tapscott's former students was beside him and a couple more comrades sat in the back. They were all armed and ready to shoot their way through any police roadblocks.

> They were all pretty strung out and on alcohol to an extent. [We had] a little light in the dark [forest]... The valedictory [went]: 'We do not mourn our fallen comrade; we pick up his gun,' or something like that... There was a heroic romanticism about these guys: they had attacked the Police Station on 29 July because it was the anniversary [of the founding] of the Communist Party...They mostly all gave their lives [in the end].[78]

'Things were OK for a while, but then... it all unravelled.'[79] Chris Tapscott fled to London. The Institute for Management and Development Studies closed down. Ezra Sigwela escaped to the USA. Father Cas and Mvula Mthimkulu were caught up in the security force dragnet, along with other MK cadres and sympathisers. They spent months in detention, but were lucky to avoid the spate of security trials that swept away so much of the MK networks in Transkei.[80]

▲ ▲ ▲

More broadly, the MK was in trouble in Transkei and South Africa because its rear bases were unravelling in Lesotho and the frontline states. 'South African military chiefs took MK very seriously, despite of its small size and modest achievements, because they knew its potential if it were ever to build up proper supply lines.'[81] Throttling the MK, therefore, was a matter of winning back the frontline states. In the 1980s, apartheid forces repeatedly hit ANC bases. Lesotho's capital of Maseru, for instance, was raided by apartheid commandos in 1982 and again in 1985. Diplomatic pressure was even more effective. In March 1984 Mozambique signed the Nkomati Accord with the apartheid government. South Africa undertook to cease its support to insurgents fighting in Mozambique; in turn the Mozambique government expelled the ANC from its territory. This led to an influx of 400-500 ANC cadres into Swaziland, creating great tensions in a territory that had recently signed a security co-operation pact with the apartheid government. The skirmishes that inevitably followed severely depleted the ANC's operational capacity. In January 1986 the Government of Lesotho, which had offered the ANC support for almost a decade, was toppled in a military coup backed by the apartheid government. 'Thus began the retreat of the ANC from Lesotho.'[82]

The same month as the military coup in Lesotho, apartheid security forces

---

[78] Interview, Tapscott. Cf. TRC-AH, AM6362/97, Bongani Wana, Umtata, 27 March 2000.
[79] Interview, Tapscott.
[80] Interviews, Paulsen, Sigwela, Tapscott.
[81] Ellis and Sechaba, *Comrades*, p. 111.
[82] Ibid. p.166. Simpson, 'The People's War', pp.203-6.

caught up with three senior MK cadres based in the Transkei, Dumisani Mafu, Pieces Maqekeza and Mbulelo 'KK' Ngono. They had been staying at a trading store run by Kenny Jafta, which was owned by his parents. At dawn on 21 January 1987, the security forces surrounded the trading store. Pieces Maqekeza and Dumisani Mafu were away from the store. Kenny Jafta was quickly caught. KK Ngono stood his ground and engaged in a thirty-six hour shoot-out with a joint force of Transkeian and South African police before escaping in the confusion. [83]

The black policemen took their revenge on the university-educated elite dissidents, destroying the Jafta family's prosperous trading store after the gun battle. Jafta's mother later told the Truth and Reconciliation Commission that she thought her son would become 'a responsible man' by running one of the family stores. Now she experienced social mortification. Her husband was arrested and taunted by the security police:

> One of the policemen said, 'This man has got no problems – he has got three children at university and the other one is in a high school'... The second [police]man said 'he is much better than you... this man has two shops... You see, Jafta, I am going to make you starve. You will not be proud any more. You are going to starve until your children starve as well. You are going to be just like other people...'
>
> [Then] there was a command from Umtata saying: 'destroy everything,' and these boys [the police] now were very happy... When I got back home... everything was destroyed... I had nothing left... all my valuable things; everything I had collected in all my life was destroyed. When I got into the garage three of these [my] cars were vandalised... When I came to my shop it was worse... They looted my shop... That is how much we lost.[84]

It was worse for the MK cadres and their close sympathisers. Dumisani Mafu, KK Ngono and Pieces Maqekeza fled Transkei for Lesotho; but they were later trapped at a police roadblock run by Basotho security forces loyal to the new regime. Ngono escaped the roadblock, but then disappeared, presumed killed. Maqekeza was wounded in the shootout and taken to Maseru hospital. Here he 'was killed by unknown gunmen on 15 March 1987, while recovering under police guard.' Only Dumisani Mafu and a few more ANC cadres got out of Lesotho alive. 'Those who had offered assistance to [the] guerrillas... were subsequently arrested and tortured.' [85]

A Bantustan coup

The frontline states collapsed underneath the MK, but the ANC underground's intimate connections to their brothers and sisters in senior positions in the Bantustans took on a new significance in the late 1980s. Internecine conflict within many Bantustan governments offered new opportunities for the ANC to establish a foothold inside South Africa.

[83] Interview, Jafta. TRC-AH, Wana.
[84] Interview, Jafta. TRC-VH, EC0329/96, Enid Jafta, Umtata, 18 June 1996.
[85] TRC, *Report, Volume Two*, pp.433-4.

Events in the Transkei typified this scenario. The factors behind the disintegration of Matanzima's government are discussed in more detail in Chapter Seven. The crucial consequences, insofar as apartheid officials were concerned, was the possible return of the ANC. Two possibilities were most often mentioned. One was that the Bantustan state was in danger of collapsing under the weight of corruption; in the midst of the confusion MK guerrillas might then operate on Transkei soil with impunity. The other was that Kaiser Matanzima's rivals inside the government were attempting to outmanoeuvre him by making connections to the liberation movements in exile. Such rumours mounted in the 1980s. Transkei's Minister of Justice, T.T. Letlaka, who had once been a member of the Pan African Congress, reduced the sentence of political prisoners in Transkei's jails, reversing Kaiser Matanzima's policy that 'terrorists' should serve the full tariff. A number of Transkei officials even tried to hold talks with the political prisoners in Umtata jail – mimicking the apartheid government who were talking to Mandela.[86] The ruling Transkei National Independence Party slowly crumbled. Then in September 1987 a coup overthrew the Matanzima brothers.

In early October the ruling Transkei National Independence Party held its first ever open election contest to choose the new Prime Minister. Stella Sigcau won the leadership race when one of her rivals, Chief Ngangomhlaba, who represented the Kaiser Matanzima's supporters, threw his weight behind her. This was a move that Kaiser Matanzima very soon came to regret, as Sigcau cautiously began to open doors to the ANC. On the prompting of the ANC underground, Sigcau allowed Prince Madikizela and a dozen other banished activists to come back home. Furthermore, she gave speeches stating that Govan Mbeki (who was released from Robben Island in 1987) would be welcome to return to the land of his birth in Transkei. The ANC underground also attempted to revive the Democratic Party – Transkei's long-standing, anti-Matanzima political party – as a front for ANC recruitment. Chief Ntsikayezwe Twentyman Sigcau was taken to Lusaka to meet Chris Hani and the ANC leadership. Apartheid officials were clearly worried.[87]

The coup that brought Stella Sigcau to power marked an important caesura. From the 1970s, when the ANC had returned to the frontline states that ringed South Africa, the Bantustans on the border had gained new prominence. Yet the MK's military campaigns had brought limited returns. Underground networks were repeatedly smashed and MK operatives often captured within months of being infiltrated across the border. Transkei's sudden coup in 1987 showed how everything could change so suddenly. With apartheid South Africa informally talking with the ANC, Bantustan leaders were also reconsidering their political alliances. With so many senior Bantustan officials who had maintained connections to their relatives inside

---

[86] On Pretoria's fears: BTS15, Commander General, Department of State Security and BTS17, Telex, Umtata Ambassador, 29 April 1983. On the treatment of political prisoners: Interview, Mbete. On T.T. Letlaka: Tapscott, 'The Rise of Development', pp.248, 267.

[87] Author interviews, Ntsubane, Ndabeni, Daniel Ganyile, Bizana, 5 April 2008. Gerhart interview, O. Mabandla. TRC-VH, Joyi. BTS24, 'Meeting minutes with Transkei Ambassador', 7 January 1988. BTS24, 'Minutes of meeting with Stella Sigcau', 29 February 1988.

the nationalist movements, bewildering political realignments were possible. The Bantustans – significant on the national stage because they were home to 50% of the African population – now hung in the balance during the final years of apartheid.

7. The Apartheid Endgame 1987–1996

'A military intelligence project that went wrong'?

String-pulling and elite political manoeuvring worked both ways. A counter-coup against Stella Sigcau's Bantustan government was brewing within the Transkei Defence Force. Her 'apparent ANC sympathies' were causing 'considerable consternation'. On the penultimate day of 1987, a young officer, Brigadier Bantu Holomisa, toppled Sigcau. The interregnum had lasted less than 90 days. A week later, Kaiser Matanzima telexed the apartheid government in Pretoria: 'Military takeover peaceful. South Africa citizens safe and happy. Transkeians joyful.'[1]

Tumbled into power aged only 33, Bantu Holomisa's meteoric rise owed much to the militarisation of Bantustan politics. He rose through the ranks of the Transkei Defence Force at a time when Pretoria's securocrats were constructing a formidable array of African armed forces to fight the black liberation movements and solidify apartheid rule, not only in South Africa but across the southern African region. During the 1980s, a web of Bantustan armies and security police, African vigilante groups, and secretive 'Third Force' proxies had fought a low key counterinsurgency against the liberation movements in the Homelands. By the time Holomisa came to power, these conflicts had exploded into the open. A state of near civil war consumed some Bantustans, particularly in KwaZulu and Natal, where political violence would claim over 11,000 lives. Nevertheless, having come to power with the benediction of Kaiser Matanzima, Holomisa achieved the astonishing feat of changing horses in midstream. He switched his support, becoming one of the most popular politicians in South Africa when he turned Transkei into a stronghold that supported the liberation movements. Holomisa's meteoric rise was framed by southern Africa's insurgencies and counterinsurgencies. His equally rapid fall from grace some years later, would also reveal much about how the post-apartheid dispensation was shaped by the fragmented legacies of these conflicts.

In the immediate aftermath of Bantu Holomisa's fall, adversaries would insinuate that he had once been an apartheid front-man: a 'military intelligence project that went wrong' when he double-crossed the apartheid counterinsurgency forces.[2] With the benefit of hindsight, perhaps it is now possible to take a more ecumenical view of the turbulent forces that framed the apartheid endgame.

---

[1] BTS23, KD to RSA State President, 5 January 1988. BTS24, 'Meeting minutes with Transkei Ambassador'.

[2] African National Congress, *The Rise and Fall of Bantu Holomisa* (Johannesburg, 1997).

Bantu Holomisa's rise and southern Africa's civil wars

Bantu Holomisa's political success revealed the ambiguities inherent in apartheid's attempt to construct a Bantustan state from the chieftaincy. He was a child of the Bantustan state; a prime beneficiary of the project of 'ethnic modernisation', by which apartheid tried to build a Bantustan bureaucracy from elements of a chieftaincy. Holomisa (b.1955) was a junior son of Chief Bazindlovu, who was in any case a relatively minor traditional leader in Thembuland. Furthermore, Holomisa was not expected to become a traditional leader – that role was reserved for Chief Bazindlovu's grandson, Pathekile (b.1959), who grew up in another royal household. When Bantu Holomisa's mother left Transkei for Johannesburg, looking for work as a nurse, he was placed in the care of an Anglican preacher. His path to prominence instead came through the growth of Transkei's government bureaucracy. He was given a subsidised education at Jongilizwe College for the Sons of Chiefs (see Chapter Four), where he was school rugby captain and Deputy Head Prefect. After leaving school in 1975, aged 20, having passed his Matriculation exams, Holomisa briefly joined the Postal Service, before entering the new Transkei Defence Force in one of the first batches of trainee officers. He later claimed he joined the army simply because he wanted to play rugby and the recruiters were looking for sportsmen.[3]

Initially, Transkei's Defence Force was something of a backwater – the ideal career, perhaps, for sports-loving young man. Granted as a gift to Kaiser Matanzima when Transkei was given 'independence', the Transkei Defence Force rapidly deteriorated when the apartheid government withdrew support during a diplomatic spat in the late 1970s. Kaiser Matanzima had been disappointed by the terms of Bantustan 'independence', so throughout the late 1970s he tried to assert Transkei's sovereignty. He pursued a series of grandiose infrastructure development projects backed by foreign impresarios that never got beyond the drawing board. Senior members of the Transkei Defence Force were even entangled in a hare-brained arms deal as they tried to break free from Pretoria. It made good copy for muck-raking journalists, who portrayed Transkei as a banana republic. During this period, the Transkei's Defence Force's 'equipment was destroyed and allowed to deteriorate, soldiers terrorised the citizenry, and drunkenness was rife.'[4] However, the fortunes of the army were revived at the start of the 1980s when rapprochement between Umtata and Pretoria brought funding back to the beleaguered force. Now the apartheid government was beginning to build up Bantustan armies, proxy

[3] O'Malley interview, Pathekile Holomisa, 22 August 1993. KGC89, Bantu Holomisa (hereafter BH) press clippings. BH was the son of Chef Bazindlovu by his second most important wife (the Right Hand House). Pathekile was the grandson and heir of Chief Bazindlovu from the Great House. BTS30, BH's CV. B. Holomisa and R. Meyer, *A Better Future: United Democratic Movement towards a winning nation in ten years* (Pretoria, 1999), pp.1-12.

[4] K. Grundy, *Soldiers Without Politics: Blacks in the South African armed forces* (London, 1983), p.238. Cf. Streek and Wicksteed, *Render unto Kaiser*, pp.170-233, 255-71. BTS1, Ambassador Du Plooy to S/BTS, 20 December 1979. TRC-VH, E.R.G. Keswa, Lusikisiki, 26 March 1997.

units and vigilante groups as part of its war against the MK.

Holomisa rose through the ranks of the Transkei Defence Force at a time when it was being drawn into wider counterinsurgent networks that spanned southern Africa. To preserve the fiction that Bantustans were fully independent countries, the apartheid government did not want to directly command Transkei's Defence Force. Instead, Ron Reid-Daly, the former Officer-In-Command of the infamous Rhodesian Selous Scouts, was brought in to lead the Defence Force in 1981. Reid-Daly's professional hinterland was telling. Born in Rhodesia, he served an apprenticeship fighting communists in Malaya, under the command of British Special Forces during the last decades of Empire. The interlocking insurgencies of the Cold War era had subsequently brought him back to southern Africa. In Rhodesia, in the 1960s and 1970s, he had fought ANC guerrillas as well as Zimbabwean insurgents . Fairly soon after Zimbabwe gained independence in 1980 he moved onto Transkei. Indeed, many of the personnel 'who were to emerge at the heart of the underground war against subversion [in South Africa had] served in Rhodesia.'[5]

Ron Reid-Daly's brief was to reshape the more tractable parts of Transkei's Defence Force into an elite, counterinsurgency infantry battalion. Bright, young, black officers rose rapidly under the direction of their Rhodesian trainers. In 1981, Holomisa was raised to Second-in-Command of the infantry battalion. Promoted twice more, he was sent to the Staff College of the South African Defence Force in 1984. Holomisa and his peers were among the first handful of black soldiers to undertake this intensive training course.

Holomisa also benefited from a purge of the older army officers, which reveals much about how the upper echelons of the chieftaincy were enmeshed in the workings of this new, militarised version of Bantustan rule. The apartheid government feared the loyalties of senior Transkei Defence Force commanders had been compromised during the hiatus in the late 1970s. As a result, the young officers chosen for rapid promotion in the early 1980s were often the sons of Thembu chiefs loyal to the Bantustan regime. A number had attended Jongilizwe College for the Sons of Chiefs and Headmen. They included Zondwa Mtirara, the son of Chief Bambilanga Albert Mtirara, who had wrested the Paramountcy of Thembuland from King Sabata. Another rising star was Themba Templeton (better known as 'T.T.') Matanzima, whose elder brother was a protégé of Kaiser Matanzima. Tensions mounted inside the Transkei Defence Force as the senior commanders, who feared the influence of the 'young princes', directed their intelligence units to gather information on their young rivals. 'One morning during 1980, anonymous pamphlets appeared in the Transkei Defence Force's Headquarters' calling on the army command to stand down in favour of Zondwa Mtirara.[6] Days later Kaiser Matanzima demanded the resignations of the older generation of commanders.

There were other good reasons for apartheid securocrats to build Transkei's Defence Force from Thembu officers whose families were close to Kaiser Matanzima. The late 1970s had seen rumblings of dissent against Matanzima

---

[5] Ellis, 'Third Force', p.268. Cf. 'Obituary, Lieutenant Colonel Ron Reid-Daly', *Daily Telegraph* (online) 20 September 2010.
[6] This narrative from TRC-VH, Keswa. Cf. *DD* 21 May 1987.

in Sabata Dalindyebo's portion of Thembuland, Eastern Mpondoland and the Sotho-speaking regions in north eastern Transkei. The training exercises run by Ron Reid-Daly reveal the apartheid government's fears of how the Bantustan project might unravel. In Exercise Crocodile Tears, for example, Transkei's security forces had to stop Eastern Mpondoland from falling into the hands of ANC insurgents. The war-game scenario listed a nightmare conjunction of circumstances – 'tribal' faction fighting, aggravated by MK guerrillas, supported by a renegade Defence Force commander who had abruptly staged a coup and seceded Mpondoland from Transkei.[7]

This was the central paradox of the counterinsurgency: whilst the Bantustans had been designed to make Transkei's Bantustan elite solid supporters of the apartheid project, securocrats feared that armed 'tribal' units might spin centrifugally out of control. Indeed, the 1980s saw a series of insurgencies and counterinsurgencies fought across southern Africa's porous borders. One example is the convoluted conflict in Lesotho, next door to Transkei, where linguistic communities crossed state boundaries. The Lesotho Liberation Army, an offshoot of a political party originally formed with the help of South Africa's black nationalists, was fighting an insurgency out of the Sotho-speaking Bantustan of Qwa Qwa. Cold War power-plays added an extra twist. During the early 1980s, the apartheid government backed the insurgency as a means of destabilising the Government of Lesotho, which was providing ANC guerrillas a base from which to strike South Africa. At times, these complex conflicts spilled over into Transkei's Sotho-speaking, north-eastern districts. The Transkei Defence Force was deployed into the Matatiele's mountains to quell secessionism, secure the border, stop stock theft, and trap ANC infiltrators who took advantage of the region's instability to steal across the border.[8]

Indeed, it was a picaresque cross-border political adventure that initiated a chain of events that would topple the Transkei government. In the first half of 1986, senior apartheid military officers hatched a plan named Operation Katzen to amalgamate Transkei and Ciskei into a Xhosa nation. This would, they believed, destabilise anti-apartheid forces in the Eastern Cape. The Matanzimas were willingly co-opted, as they had long wanted to expand Transkei's boundaries and rule a Greater Xhosaland. Ron Reid-Daly's Selous Scouts were also brought into the plot. Bantu Holomisa, by now a brigadier and second-in-command of the Transkei Defence Force, was the sharpest critic of this venture. He was detained in January 1987 for 'complaining that the Selous Scouts used Transkei Defence Force facilities for their private security operations'.[9] When a coup against Ciskei launched from Umtata went disastrously wrong in February 1987, the balance swung back. Holomisa's supporters forced his release. In April 1987, the Rhodesians were exiled from Transkei. The Matanzimas' position had also been undermined by their sponsorship of the scheme.

Compounding these centrifugal forces, a destabilising series of conflicts

---

[7] H. Heitman, 'The Transkei Defence Force', *Armed Forces* (August 1984), pp.7-14.

[8] *DD* 18 May 1984. SADET interview, Charles Setsubi, 19 July 2001.

[9] J. Peires, 'The Implosion of Transkei and Ciskei', *African Affairs*, 91 (1992), p.368. Cf. P. Stiff, *Warfare by other Means: South Africa in the 1980s and 1990s* (Johannesburg, 2001), pp.194-241.

unfolded over the spoils of the Bantustan system that divided Transkei's ruling party. The rush to full Bantustan 'independence' in 1976 had allowed a new round of asset-grabs. Later investigations surmised that at least R260 million had been misappropriated or misspent in the decade after independence. The stench of illicit financial gain tore apart the fragile ruling coalition, starting with a rift between Kaiser Matanzima and his younger brother, George. Fearing he was 'losing his strength and vitality', the apartheid government eased Kaiser Matanzima upstairs into the President's post, pushing his brother 'into the proverbial hot seat as Prime Minister' in 1979. However, the younger man 'more and more assumed the image of the dandy. I lost count of the many, very expensive suits he wore', reminisced an old Umtata journalist.[10] Kaiser Matanzima transformed his presidential offices, on the top floor of the eleven-storey Botha Sigcau building, into a rival seat of power. 'He [Kaiser Matanzima] has on occasion reduced George to tears about his inept handling of the government', the Pretoria's Ambassador reported from Umtata. [11] But George bested his brother, forced Kaiser Matanzima out of office in 1986, and launched commissions of enquiries into his brother's business affairs. The inquiries were backed by the apartheid government, determined to clean up the morass of corruption enveloping the state. Then a series of counter-revelations implicated George Matanzima himself, leaving the entire government in disarray.

In the final quarter of 1987, the Transkei Defence Force used allegations of corruption to overthrow two successive Bantustan governments. In September 1987 they toppled George Matanzima and then in December 1987 deposed his successor, Stella Sigcau, replacing her with Bantu Holomisa. Indeed, the plotters moved against Sigcau after intelligence sources uncovered her involvement in a web of corrupt transactions related to the Wild Coast Casino development. Cheques paid to her were the central weapon of the plotters. 'We called almost everyone in the Transkei Defence Force to Umtata on [the day of the coup]... when the politicians were sunning themselves on the beaches,' remembered Holomisa. 'We made thousands of copies of the bank documents and distributed them so that all soldiers, from top officers down to the most junior ranks, could read them for themselves.'[12] On December 30 1987 'General Holomisa announced over Radio Transkei that martial law had been declared.'[13]

A week later, on 6 January 1988, Bantu Holomisa announced the members of his government at a Great Indaba held at Umtata City Hall to a crowd of 'four thousand people who packed the hall and overflowed through the streets'. It was a tense speech. All the main politicians in Transkei turned up; even 'Miss Sigcau [who] arrived with her two brothers and other Pondo councillors to a muted reception.' Flanked by allies and opponents, Holomisa suspended the Transkei Legislature indefinitely and announced decrees consolidating authority in a Council of Ministers that reported to a ruling Military Council

---

[10] *DD* 16 November 2000. Cf. BTS1, 'Foreign Political Situation', p.56. BTS20, Umtata Ambassador to DG/DFA, 21 November 1984. Southall, 'Rethinking Transkei Politics', p.5.

[11] BTS12, Umtata Ambassador to S/BTS, 20 September 1979. Cf. *DD* 6, 22 May, 3 October 1987.

[12] Holomisa and Meyer, *A Better Future*, pp.9-10. Cf. BTS24, 'Minutes of Meeting with Transkei Ambassador', 7 January 1988.

[13] *DD* 4 October 1988.

of which he was leader. 'The one time the public burst into laughter was when 'General Holomisa [wryly] thanked the previous governments "only for the good things that they did for our beloved country".'[14] Rumours soon spread that the 'Council of Ministers included people quite close to Kaiser Matanzima.'[15] Holomisa was forced to deny stories that the Council of Ministers had been chosen at a gathering at Matanzima's Great Place at Qamata.

The pro-apartheid security services also continued to operate with impunity. Close links continued between South African securocrats and their Bantustan counterparts in the security police and military intelligence. Later that January, a young political activist was murdered by two Transkei Security policemen who were well known as being close to apartheid counterinsurgency forces.[16] On Friday 5 February, an apartheid hit squad assassinated three young men, who were suspected of MK membership, at traffic lights in the middle of Umtata. Called to the hospital mortuary, Dumisa Ntsebeza was presented with 'a scene that would haunt him for years. The death squad used exploding dumdum bullets.' Together with other friends and family, Dumisa Ntsebeza cast caution aside and tracked down the murder vehicle to an Umtata police station. They could do no more: the hit squad radioed for help and suddenly the street was swarming with police reinforcements and white, South African operatives.

> His fists clenched in frustration and anger, Dumisa... drove straight to the home of his former student... Bantubonke Holomisa... Holomisa was pleased to see 'Cat' [as Dumisa was affectionately known]. He was not at all pleased with what he was told. 'He would do what he could,' he said, 'but things were not so straightforward.'[17]

This killing proved the turning point. The Military Council 'read the riot act to the Transkei Security Branch.' They also looked for new allies.[18] Although Holomisa did not have close connections with the liberation movements, a number of other senior officers could oblige. General T.T. Matanzima was probably the most senior officer inside the Transkei Defence Force to have close connections to the ANC underground. He had joined the first draft of officers recruited into the Defence Force in 1975, but when he had been sent to Fort Hare University on study leave he had got involved on the fringes of student politics. Apparently, he had even held a position on the strike committee that brought Fort Hare to a standstill in 1980. Throughout that decade, he kept in contact with a few of the senior MK cadres based in Lesotho, even though he was an officer in the Transkei Defence Force's counterinsurgency battalion tasked with fighting the guerrillas. T.T Matanzima's brother, Chief Ngangomhlaba, was also sent to see Nelson Mandela on Robben Island on 'family business'.[19]

---

[14] All above quotes from *DD* 7 January 1988.

[15] D. Koyana, 'A Constitutional History of Transkei' (Pretoria University, Ph.D. thesis, 1994), p.194. Cf. *DD* 11 February 1988.

[16] *Truth and Reconciliation Commission Report, Volume III*, pp.120-1.

[17] Bell and Ntsebeza, *Unfinished Business*, p.166.

[18] Author interview, BH, Pretoria, 2 September 2008.

[19] NMPF A27, 63, T.T Matanzima to Commanding Officer, Victor Verster Prison, 5, 7 April 1989. Cf. BTS3, Zondwa Mtirara to RSA State President, (n.d. 1989?). NMPF 46, 94, T.T Matanzima to Mandela. Author interviews with Mafu, Ntsubane, and Thembile Templeton (T.T.) Matanzima, Pretoria, 2 September 2009.

Bantu Holomisa sent his most trusted, senior officers to the Wavecrest Hotel on Transkei's Wild Coast to plot a new political course. South Africa was preparing for negotiations that might usher in some form of democratic rule. The Military Council 'did not want to appear as mere stooges' even if this forced them into confrontation with the powerful, pro-apartheid, security forces in the Eastern Cape.[20]

Reburying Sabata, returning to the ANC family

Bantu Holomisa started to inch towards the liberation movements whilst easing out Matanzima's supporters in a series of gambits that would reveal the enduring weight of Transkei's notable families in the region. Holomisa had risen through the security services because he came from the Thembu chieftaincy; now he reached out to the most senior ANC leaders who came from Thembuland. The centrepiece of Holomisa's new strategy was the posthumous rehabilitation of the exiled Thembu king, Sabata Dalindyebo.

During the 1980s, Kaiser Matanzima had attempted to consolidate his control over Thembuland by extinguishing Sabata's line of kingship and banishing the Comrade-King's pro-ANC supporters. The first set-piece clash came when Sabata died in Lusaka in the autumn of 1986. His followers had brought their king's body home from Lusaka to Umtata, on the understanding that a royal funeral was guaranteed. A grave had even been dug at the family's burial yard. But the night before the funeral was due to take place, Winnie Mandela, who had come to Umtata to help the young heir, Buyelekhaya, with the handling of political sensitivities, saw early signs of government interference. She tried to take out a court order to stop the funeral and have Sabata's body returned to Lusaka. Instead, the King's body was stolen in the night from the funeral parlour by Matanzima, and hastily buried in the 'female section of a pauper's burial ground'.[21] Busloads of Sabata's supporters coming home to Thembuland from as far as Gauteng and Cape Town were turned back at Transkei's borders. Security forces filled Umtata's streets.

Winnie Mandela was furious and brought a court action against Matanzima. Nelson Mandela was also angry. Prison guards recorded his comments: 'Kaiser Matanzima was never a dignified man. Nobody recognises him or Transkei... He is a stooge for the Afrikaners... He is a just junior chief.'[22] Matanzima followed up this victory a year later upon the death of Acting-Paramount Chief Bambilanga Mtirara, who had acted as Thembu regent after Sabata was exiled. Kaiser Matanzima was determined to make Bambilanga Mtirara's heir, Zondwa Mtirara, the next king. Any attempts

[20] Author interview, BH.

[21] G. Dennie, 'One King, Two Burials: The politics of funerals in South Africa's Transkei', *Journal of Contemporary African Studies*, 11, 2 (1992), p.79.Cf. BTS22, F.G. Conraadie to G.P. Pretorious, 7 May 1986, Umtata Ambassador to S.J.M. Steyn, 11 September 1986. *DD* 21, 22 April, 16 May 1986. KGC88. *Southscan* 17 May 1989

[22] NMPF A14, 37, Munro to Commissioner Prisons, 2 May 1986.

to install Sabata's ANC-educated son as king were 'conceived and nurtured strictly in line with the plans of revolutionary politics in southern Africa', he claimed.[23] A series of meetings of the Dalindyebo Regional Authority and the Dlomo Inner Council of the Thembu Ruling Houses secured a decision in Matanzima's favour. Zondwa's installation was set for 15 April 1988.

However, the political mood was shifting in Transkei. A day or two before Zondwa's installation the Military Council intervened: the Chief Magistrate cancelled the meeting of the Thembu Regional Authority, which would have made Zondwa Mtirara the Paramount Chief of Thembuland. Kaiser Matanzima publicly demanded that Holomisa stay out of Thembu affairs. Holomisa's reply was robust:

> Whereas the Military Government would out of sheer respect avoid confrontation... Matanzima should take note that the Military Government's patience is wearing thin... My brother thinks he is above the law... I would not like to do what he did to Sabata Dalindyebo.[24]

Holomisa's new-found assertiveness was clearly worrying the apartheid government. At about the same time, the South African Minister of Foreign Affairs summoned the Transkei Military Council 'to talk very frankly with General Holomisa about the rumours he had met with Winnie Mandela... [and] might have ANC sympathies.'[25] Holomisa denied these allegations, of course. Yet suspicions remained.

Over the following year, Bantu Holomisa was pressed into declaring his sympathies ever more clearly. Paramount Chief Bambilanga Mtirara had never been popular. His reign over Thembuland had been marked with murmurs of smothered dissent. Now a newly formed Sabata Dalindyebo Trust Fund sought to capitalise on their late king's popularity and reactivate his old political networks. 'Bantu Holomisa allows political rallies under the guise of... Trust Fund meetings', Zondwa Mtirara complained to the apartheid government.[26] The Trust Fund was also a vehicle for broadening the fragmented support for the anti-Bantustan movement, which had been weakened by repression. Established ANC stalwarts such as Alfred Xobololo and Anderson Joyi pulled the strings, but they were magnanimous to opposition leaders who had fallen by the wayside. Knowledge Guzana was the first secretary of the Trust Fund; on his death in 1989, Hector Ncokazi took over.[27]

The momentum of the Great Place Gang built up until the Dalindyebo Regional Authority called a meeting in Umtata City Hall in May 1989. It removed Zondwa Mtirara as Paramount Chief-designate in favour of Sabata's son, Buyelekhaya. 'Some 2000 Thembus flocked to hear the meeting from all over the territory and even from Cape Town.'[28] Newspapers described how 'hundreds of supporters sang freedom songs and traffic in Umtata was brought

---

[23] *DD* 8 July 1989. For more details: *DD* 27 August 1987, 9, 12, 13 April 1988.
[24] *DD* 29 April 1988. Cf. *DD* 15, 20 April, 14, 20 May 1988.
[25] BTS24, Minutes of Meeting between Military Council and M/BTS, 8 June 1988.
[26] BTS3, Zondwa Mtirara to RSA State President. *DD* 2 January 1982.
[27] *DD* 25 October, 8 November 1989. Interview, Nelani.
[28] All quotes from *Southscan* 17 May 1989.

to a standstill as groups danced down the main road... Supporters cheered as the Dalindyebo Regional Authority called on Buyelekhaya – whose name means 'come home' – to return to Transkei.

The tide now turned against Matanzima and those associated with him in the Thembuland chieftaincy. A chief banished by Matanzima returned from internal exile and took the post of Thembu regent until Sabata's son returned to the throne. Chief Mvuso Joyi, the Matanzima-supporting head of Mputi Tribal Authority, was bankrupted and his flock of 100 sheep was sold at a public auction.[29] Matanzima complained that Holomisa was trying to unseat him and 'bring all glory to himself.'[30] He further claimed that:

> Bantu Holomisa instructed the police to investigate high and low for any possible acts of corruption on my part and search for arms at all my residences with a view to imprisoning me and removing me from my hereditary status of Paramountcy of Western Thembuland...[31]
>
> [The ANC] has been tacitly let loose with official support and recognition to enter and hold public meetings in Transkei, and more particularly my region of Western Thembuland, in full force, with Government servants, teachers and school children singing abusive songs against traditional leadership.[32]

Bantu Holomisa faced pressure on a second front. The ANC underground also mobilised support amongst the university students and high school pupils clustered around Umtata. They ran a campaign to 'Save the [MK] Patriots' who were facing the death sentence for the bombing of the Wild Coast Casino. It was a well chosen rallying cry given that many of the leading members of the MK had been drawn from the elite schools in the region – indeed both of the Wild Coast bombers were alumni of St Johns College, Umtata. When students disrupted the Wild Coast trial chanting freedom slogans, Holomisa disciplined the police colonel who had tried to clear them out of the court room. Another march to the town hall veered off route and erupted into angry protests. The police could only look on, 'helpless because those involved claimed that the government had allowed the organisation to go ahead.'[33] Prison warders could no longer wear their uniforms beyond the prison gate for fear of attack. 'There is a mushrooming of democratic structures in the Transkei,' Chris Hani reported back to the ANC's National Executive Council soon afterwards.[34]

Bantu Holomisa allowed the courts to sentence the Wild Coast bombers. In May 1989, Pumzile Mayaphi and Ndibulele Ndzamela, 'dressed in red tracksuits with a rosette in the colours of the ANC on their chests, stood smiling and acknowledged cheers and greetings from the public gallery' as

---

[29] *DD* 14 December 1988, 11 July 1989. BTS AJ1994, 'Transkei'.
[30] BTS34, 'Detention in Wellington Gaol and Lusikisiki Gaol', 1991.
[31] Ibid.
[32] BTS30, KD to Pik Botha, 23 January 1990. Ntsebeza discusses the unrest in Western Thembuland: *Democracy Compromised*, pp.229-55.
[33] BTS3A, letter to General J. Coetzee, 24 November 1989. Cf. BTS3, Zondwa Mtirara to RSA State President. BTS24, University of Transkei pamphlet: 'Detentions, Bannings, Killings', 1988. *DD* 3 October 1989.
[34] O'Malley files, ANC National Executive Council meeting, 27 October 1989

they were sentenced to death. [35] Some months later, they were released when the Transkei Military Council granted a political amnesty that saw half-a-dozen MK cadres walk free from Transkei's cells.

Having roused the ire of apartheid's securocrats, Holomisa announced his move into the anti-apartheid camp with a dramatic theatrical event. On 1 October 1989, Sabata Dalindyebo was symbolically reburied at Bumbane by a crowd of six thousand. 'Xhosa women in tribal dress cooked up a feast in 20 iron pots scattered across an open fire... Tribal elders, many of whom had walked miles to reach the site, rubbed shoulders with youths wearing a large variety of liberation T-shirts.' [36] Tributes from a panoply of anti-apartheid organisations were read out to the assembled crowd. Black students from the University of Natal and its sister campuses hired three buses to travel to Umtata, to the confusion of the radical white activists, who thought that the chieftaincy was a reactionary institution. Winnie Mandela and Peter Mokaba, better known for rousing township crowds, shared the stage with Thembu activists and representatives from the royal houses of Lesotho and Swaziland. 'Holomisa, who had shed his military uniform and donned a dark suit for the occasion, initially received a mixed reaction from the crowd.' [37] But when he told the 6,000 mourners of his intention to offer Transkeians a referendum on Bantustan independence, their mood changed: in effect he was burying the Bantustan system. Weeks later Holomisa formally unbanned the ANC and Pan African Congress (PAC) in Transkei. [38]

It was a virtuoso performance by 'the model of a post-modern' Bantustan general, wrote an admiring press correspondent. [39] Bantu Holomisa had outwitted the might of the apartheid security services. The ANC were more cautious: they did not know whether to be impressed or worried by his mastery of this mode of politics. 'The worry is that Holomisa did not seem to have discussed this [the unbanning of the liberation movements] with his colleagues,' Chris Hani reported to the National Executive Committee of the ANC. [40] 'There is an increasing feeling that the General has an autocratic and populist style.' Jacob Zuma concurred: 'Holomisa must be reined in.' From his perch in Umtata, Dumisa Ntsebeza took a more sympathetic view of his former pupil's predicament. Bantu Holomisa was 'walking his own tightrope, trying to consolidate his control [of the Military Council], make closer contact with the exiled ANC and PAC, while at the same time ensuring that he did not trigger too harsh a reaction from the apartheid state.' [41]

---

[35] *DD* 13 May 1989. Cf. MTA Case 34P/89, 16/1989, Transkei M/Justice to Transkei Attorney General, 13 October 1989. BTS3, Zondwa Mtirara to RSA State President. *DD* 13 May 1989.

[36] J. Battersby, 'Comrade King', *Leadership*, 8, 9 (1989) p.66.

[37] Ibid., p.67.

[38] *DD* 9 November 1989.

[39] R. Stengel, 'Cashmere Tyrant', *The New Republic* (March 1 1993), p.15.

[40] Hani and Zuma's comments: O'Malley files, ANC National Executive Committee (hereafter NEC) meeting, 27 October 1989.

[41] Bell and Ntsebeza, *Unfinished Business*, p.166.

Counterintelligence, corruption and the chieftaincy: a web exposed

Bantu Holomisa also faced apartheid's securocrats, who held formidable influence in Transkei. They had built up a small but powerful network of African informants and allies whose connections reached close to the heart of the Bantustan state. This was a key element of apartheid 'Third Forces' – a term used to describe the shadowy police, military intelligence and army units that emerged during southern Africa's interlocking counterinsurgencies, whom ANC leaders argued were behind the upsurge in violence across South Africa from the late 1980s. Yet Holomisa had one trump card. He launched a series of investigations that exposed the nexus of corrupt business interests who had benefited from the Bantustan system and were linked to apartheid Military Intelligence operatives. These investigations provide us with a rare insight into how the counterinsurgencies of the 1980s led to the criminalisation of the state. Bantu Holomisa's first stroke was to prosecute George Matanzima on charges of corruption. The former Prime Minister had fled to South Africa when he was implicated in a disastrous agricultural development deal. In the 1980s, he had bought R54 million's worth of tractors only to see most of them 'go missing' or sold off at bargain prices. The apartheid government was reluctant to see George Matanzima face prosecution, but they handed him over when Holomisa promised to pay back the remainder of the money that the Transkei Government still owed on the deal. Holomisa had driven an astonishingly good bargain. George Matanzima served two and a half years in jail and was declared insolvent. 'After his release, his health deteriorated and he disappeared from the public eye. At one stage he was reportedly staying in a backroom shack of a house in Umtata.'[42] It was a shocking fall from grace and a body blow to the Qamata clique.

Holomisa's next manoeuvre was to broaden the remit of the judicial inquiries on government mismanagement and corruption into areas that would most damage his enemies. Holomisa directed Justice Gerald Alexander, the chair of one judicial commission, to extend his investigations into the Wild Coast Casino business deals. The inquiry revealed a bitter squabble within the ruling circles in the mid-1980s. Because these gambling rights for the Wild Coast Casino were in the gift of the Bantustan government, a succession of Transkeian politicians and business impresarios, related to the Matanzima family, convinced eager South African developers that they could secure the license. A complicated web of dubious transactions and infighting touched almost every member of the former government.

Surprisingly, Stella Sigcau survived the Commission of Enquiry into the Wild Coast Casino, even though Holomisa had used these charges of corruption to launch a coup against her. Gerald Alexander only reprimanded Stella Sigcau for taking a R50,000 gift from George Matanzima: 'there was no

---

[42] *DD* 16 November 2000. Cf. BTS24, Meeting Minutes, 29 February 1988. Holomisa and Meyer, *A Better Future*, p.9. *DD* 31 August 1989.

need of further investigation.'[43] Judge Alexander accepted her arguments that 'gifts of this nature are not foreign amongst black communities... and serve to strengthen the bonds of friendship between different families of different tribes.' What convinced him was that the payment was well-known and not a secret bribe. Struggling to pay her daughter's school fees, Sigcau had believed that Matanzima's money was a Godsend, so she had her aunt bless the gift in a family ritual. She also slept on 'her good fortune', literally placing the cheque under her pillow, 'so that it would bring whatever is thought'.[44] After taking care of her family's needs, she shared the remainder throughout Mpondoland, purchasing building materials for her local church, the New Holy Apostolic Church in Zion. The pastor held a service of thanks: 'the congregation was aware of the financial hardship facing Miss Sigcau in sending her daughter to study in London, and the gift was truly an answer to everyone's prayers.'

In contrast, it was the Qamata clique that was worst hit by the Alexander Commission, as well as by another judicial enquiry, running concurrently, that probed failed housing contracts. In particular, these investigations revealed how apartheid policies promoting Bantustan economic development had spawned a squalid set of relationships between South African and Thembu-land businesses. One of the most prominent figures involved was a Cofimvaba businessman, Vusi Mbotoli, who had used his family connections to acquire a series of company directorships. Mbotoli had personally profited from being given shares in a series of gambling and construction businesses in companies doing business in Transkei.[45] The report recommended the prosecution of Kaiser Matanzima, George Matanzima, Vusi Mbotoli and half a dozen other family members.[46] Most embarrassing for the apartheid government were their connections with the former mayor of Cape Town, David Bloomberg, and the South African resort magnate, Sol Kerzner. The easy profits to be made in the Bantustans had lured many South African and foreign businessmen into a web of complicated financial transactions. Pretoria was forced to defend Bloomberg and Kerzner's involvement in the casino contracts when Transkei Government demanded their extradition.[47]

Even more importantly, Holomisa's investigations had the effect of digging up a sprawling set of military-business networks rooted around Qamata. Mbotoli was the lynchpin again, this time through his directorship of Temba Investments, a subsidiary company of JALC[48] that was part-owned by a South African businessman, Chris van Rensberg. Van Rensberg was a buccaneer, involved in a wide spread of business ventures and contracts offered by Bantu-stan governments. (His company had even printed the glossy booklet, *This is Transkei*, showcasing the newly independent Bantustan.) Like a number of

---

[43] G. Alexander, *Commission of Inquiry into the Department of Works and Engineering: Third report with particular reference to gambling rights and related matters* (Umtata, 1988), p.542.

[44] All further quotes in paragraph: Ibid., p.411,

[45] L. Harms, *Commission of Inquiry into Certain Alleged Across-Border Activities: Second report – Transkei gambling rights* (Pretoria, 1989), p.8.

[46] Alexander, *Commission of Inquiry*, pp.520, 522, 524-5, 536, 542, 548.

[47] Ibid., pp.534, 540. *DD* 15 June 1990.

[48] Named after its directors John Strong, Athis, Laurie Painting and Chris van Rensberg – TRC-AH AM0434/96, R. Moringer, 18 April, 1999.

other cross-border companies, JALC had close contacts with South African Military Intelligence. Vusi Mbotoli was allegedly a paid informer of the infamous apartheid counterinsurgency unit, Vlakplaas, named after the farm in the Johannesburg from which it operated.[49]

The main bone of contention that Holomisa used against the Military-Business networks was a R70 million housing contract granted to JALC.[50] The judicial commission revealed a poisonous mix of corruption and incompetence within the Transkei Government. Justice Van Reenen (who had taken over the enquiry from Gerald Alexander) reported: 'No complete copy of the [building] contract existed';[51] rather, it was incompetently patched together from a variety of documents, full of crossings-outs and additions. The construction of the housing developments had been even more fraught:

> There were numerous disputes; but whenever Temba [JALC] could not get what it wanted it ran, like a spoilt child, to the Prime Minister [George Matanzima] or the State President [Kaiser Matanzima], and a soothing directive was issued compelling departmental officials to comply with their demands... They [the Bantustan officials] were ignored and vilified whenever they did not promptly act in accordance with the directives given. [52]

Holomisa used Van Reenen's findings to attack the Qamata-JALC faction, refusing to make the remaining payments to JALC. In reply, 'Kaiser Matanzima made representations on their behalf [of JALC] to the State President [P.W. Botha] during the middle of 1988... South Africa [should] freeze all monies payable to Transkei'[53] until Holomisa relented. This was a suggestion tantamount to treason. In December 1988, a group of thirty malcontents– including Kaiser Matanzima, Zondwa Mtirara and Vusi Mbotoli – met the Military Council to demand that civilian rule be restored. Bantu Holomisa deftly outdebated them: 'he said he was not ready for that, he was still too busy. We waited, but we were arrested one by one.'[54] The remainder fled to South Africa, from where they plotted their return.

Holomisa replied in kind, using the type of counterinsurgency tactics used by the South African security services. Whilst most of the Transkei Defence Force was in disarray, there were still fragments that he could trust. In July 1989 Zondwa Mtirara was 'abducted from his sister's home in Daveyton' township, Johannesburg, bundled into the boot of a car and smuggled across South Africa by Transkei Defence Force operatives. Another kidnapping in Johannesburg, later organised by the Transkei Defence Force, would use a

[49] TRC-AH, Moringer. TRC-AH, E. de Kock, 18 April 1999. TRC-AD AC/2001/95, E. de Kock.

[50] This was part of a deal made to develop urban areas in Transkei with South African financial support – BAO12/151, 145/2, 'Agreement between the government of the Republic of Transkei and the Republic of South Africa relating to the continued development of certain areas in the Republic of Transkei and the resettlement of Transkeian citizens from the Republic of South Africa'.

[51] T. van Reenen, *Report of the Commission of Inquiry into the Department of Works and Energy on the Butterworth and Ezibeleni Housing Contracts* (Umtata, 1988), p.19.

[52] Ibid.

[53] L. Harms, *Report of the Commission of Inquiry into certain possible Irregularities or Illegalities: Second report – Transkei gambling rights* (Pretoria, 1989), p.25.

[54] TRC-AH, AM6361, M. Ntisana, Umtata, 31 January 2000.

hapless Austrian businessman as bait to bring a conspirator out of hiding and to a bogus business meeting. It was an indication of the extent to which military and business networks were intertwined during late apartheid.[55]

The Vlakplaas counter-coup

Bantu Holomisa's Military Council could direct judicial enquiries against their opponents and was armed with a panoply of emergency laws, but they could not control the courts when their enemies came to trial. In December 1989, the Transkei Supreme Court forced Bantu Holomisa to release five of the plotters he had indefinitely detained under the Public Security Act.[56] They immediately fled to South Africa and made contact with apartheid counterinsurgency units who were now determined to overthrow the Transkei Military Council. Eugene de Kock's infamous counterinsurgency unit based at Vlakplaas held an illicit stash of weapons and was able to arm their protégés at will. (Eugene de Kock, whose involvement in southern Africa's counter-insurgency wars went back to his military service in Namibia, would later be sentenced to 212 years in jail for crimes against humanity.)[57] A counter-coup against Holomisa's government was now inevitable.

One of the conspirators that the apartheid securocrats turned to was Colonel Craig Duli. The relationship between Holomisa and Duli reveals the complex loyalties of Transkei's notables. Both men shared the same hinterland. They were distantly related to each other as relatively minor members of the Thembu chieftaincy. Like Holomisa, Duli was rapidly promoted through the Defence Force, heading Transkei's Military Intelligence early in his career. He had been one of Holomisa's closest supporters during the first two military coups against Matanzima and Sigcau. Because of these connections, they had initially been close friends in the Military Council. Duli's wife remembered Holomisa was almost like family: someone who could come into her home whenever he pleased. Both men 'would hide together in a room [in her house] and talk over issues' for hours. Subsequently he was briefly 'regarded as the second most powerful man in Transkei.'[58] But their relationship turned sour when Duli's loyalties remained with Matanzima, to whom he would report everything. Transkei officers also wondered whether Duli had come under the influence of Pretoria's securocrats during his time in Military Intelligence – a post that was deeply embedded in the web of counterinsurgency networks.[59]

Having fled Transkei in December 1989, Craig Duli quickly made contact with Vusi Mbotoli, and brought together a group of plotters at a farm just outside Queenstown in South Africa. They pooled their contacts in Vlakplaas and JALC, gathering together weapons and vehicles for a coup scheduled for 15 January 1990, but it was called off with days to go when Holomisa got wind of

[55] BTS30, BTS to Sam Sole, no date. TRC-AH, Moringer.
[56] BTS30, 'Supreme Court Judgement: The matter between Bukelwa Duli, Ndkwanda Duli, Craig Duli, David Nomoyi, Sizeka Mtirara and the Minister of Police', 18 December 1989.
[57] TRC-AH, de Kock.
[58] TRC-VH, ECO236/96, N. Duli, Umtata, 19 June 1996. *DD* 23 November 1990.
[59] Interview, T.T. Matanzima. BTS30, J. Coetzee to A. Venter, 28 August 1988.

the plans. A few days later, Transkei Defence Forces staged an abortive cross-border raid against the plotters. Shortly afterwards, the South African police raided the Queenstown farm, arrested the conspirators and confiscated their weapons. They were soon released – an indication of the power-plays inside the apartheid security forces.[60] The conspirators regrouped and planned a second coup. Although Duli was given bin-bags full of weapons from Vlakplaas agents at a hotel, he told colleagues that the operation would be bloodless. It seems he believed 'a large section of the [Transkei] army is disenchanted because of the general disorganisation and deterioration of the army.'[61] He believed that half a dozen senior officers were in sympathy with the plotters, and Holomisa would be toppled.

Bantu Holomisa was also making preparations, reaching out to his contacts in the MK who feared that the ANC leadership might let them down. In May 1990, the ANC had signed an agreement with the apartheid government at Groote Schuur that did not provide the MK with indemnity for their activities in the armed struggle. On 18 July, Chris Hani gave a speech to 3,000 students at the University of Transkei. He warned them that the ANC was continuing to infiltrate guerrillas into South Africa and that the MK might have to seize power.[62] Already, there were rumours that MK guerrillas had returned to Transkei where they were immune from prosecution because of its status as an independent Bantustan.

In the early hours of 22 November 1990, Duli's conspirators crossed into Transkei. They mortared the Transkei Defence Force base at Ncise, just outside Umtata, killing four and routing the rest. Then they moved into the capital, where they took over the main government offices at the Botha Sigcau Building. However, in the dark hours of the night, Holomisa had phoned his allies in the ANC. Some sort of loyalist force was put together from Transkei Defence Force soldiers and MK cadres to quash Duli and his associates, who were holed up in the Sigcau building.[63] South African troops massed on the border; Vlakplaas operatives stood by their radios, ready to cross into Transkei; the South African Broadcasting Corporation even announced that their troops 'had entered Transkei to protect... property'.[64] But the South African forces never moved, 'perhaps because Pretoria had suddenly developed cold feet.' As the day drew out, crowds gathered in Umtata's streets, demanding weapons to fight Duli's rebels. Pumla Gobodo-Madikizela, then a young lecturer at the University of Transkei who would later make her name as a Truth and Reconciliation Commissioner, witnessed the scene. She later recalled:

You could see groups of people throughout the city... their eyes cast upwards towards

---

[60] TRC-AD, de Kock. TRC-AH, de Kock. *DD* 15 January 1990. BTS30, BTS to Sam Sole. *DD* 11 April 1990.

[61] BTS3 J. Coetzee to A. Venter, 28 August 1988. TRC-VH ECO236/96. S. Vhana [sic], Umtata, 19 June 1996. Southall and Woodall, 'Control and Contestation', p.76.

[62] Simpson, 'Toyi-Toying to Freedom: The endgame in the ANC's armed struggle', *JSAS*, 35, 2 (2009), pp.516-7.

[63] Ntsebeza, 'The Re-incorporation of Transkei', p.30

[64] Both quotes from R. Southall and G. Woodall, 'Control and Contestation: State security in South Africa's Homelands', (Grahamstown, Report to the TRC, n.d.), p.76.

Holomisa's office on the eleventh floor of Botha Sigcau, the tallest building in that small city... Gunfire echoed through the streets and over our heads, and the smoke and dust pouring from the windows... were visible signs of the battle being fought inside.'[65]

Hours later, after apparently making desperate phone calls to the South African Ambassador in Umtata and contacts in the South African security services, Craig Duli gave up. He had been seriously wounded in the gunfight. Ten of his associates had been killed, and a total 47 Transkei Defence Force soldiers were dead or wounded.[66] 'There was jubilation throughout the streets of Umtata,' remembered Gobo-Madikizela. 'My car was full to the brim [with soldiers who]... hoisted their R1 rifles in the air through the [vehicle's] windows' in a convoy of cars circling the city centre, honking their horns and singing songs of victory against Craig Duli, 'the puppet of the Boers'.[67] They made their way to the Independence Stadium for a victory celebration led by General Holomisa, who spoke to the 15,000 strong crowd flanked by ANC stalwarts, Pumzile Myaphi and Ezra Sigwela.[68]

Across town, Craig Duli's wife received the news that her husband had been killed, fighting against their former family friend. That morning, she had gone to check in on her daughter who was taking exams at the elite Holy Cross secondary school, when she heard news of the coup on the radio. 'My child was writing her exams in tears. They kept giving my child coffee, just to sustain my child.' [69] Later in the day, T.T. Matanzima came on Transkei radio to announce the Transkei Defence Force was negotiating the rebels' surrender. At that moment, a friend told Mrs. Duli: 'You are the only person who can save Craig's life; stand up; go to General Holomisa.' So they drove to his offices, only to be 'sent to the army camp [at Ncise]. It was utmost chaos... I didn't get a chance to speak to the General.' Instead, soldiers beat her friend to the ground. They were saved by a senior officer, who knew Mrs. Duli well. 'We were put into a car and taken back home. On the way back, one of the soldiers tried to console me. He said: "Topsy, don't cry so much; we know Craig"... That consoled me.'

But when Craig Duli was captured and taken from the Sigcau Building, he was 'thrown into the trunk of an army vehicle', despite his severe injuries. [70] He died later that day, possibly of his wounds, although rumour rapidly spread that he was hastily executed. Bantu Holomisa would later vehemently deny all allegations of wrong-doing. He 'could confirm Duli was a friend of mine and a highly respected officer'; he had sent bodyguards to East London to try to broker reconciliation; he was even 'seen to shed tears... when told that Duli was dead.'[71]

[65] P. Gobodo-Madikizela, *A Human Being Died That Night: A story of forgiveness* (Cape Town, 2003), pp.10-1.
[66] *Truth and Reconciliation Commission Report, Volume III*, p.127. BTS AJ1990, 'Position Paper on Transkei', 3 December 1990.
[67] Gobodo-Madikizela, *A Human Being Died*, p.11.
[68] *DD* 23 November 1990.
[69] All quotes in paragraph from TRC-VH, Duli.
[70] Ibid.
[71] B. Holomisa, *Comrades in Corruption* (Johannesburg, 1997), p.15.

Fearful of a third coup attempt, the Military Government launched a series of cross-border kidnappings of the remaining plotters. The most daring foray abducted Vusi Mbotoli from Johannesburg. In June 1991, he was put on trial with 16 other defendants. It was an almost all-Thembu affair, with the vast majority from Kaiser Matanzima's Cofimvaba district. (The only four who were not from Thembuland were from a faction of the Lesotho Liberation Army. They had joined the coup attempt with the promise that, on its successful completion, they could use Transkei as a base for their own guerrilla war into Lesotho.) They were found guilty and sentenced to a total of eight hundred years' imprisonment. The prosecutor had asked for death sentences.[72]

The militant moment

Bantu Holomisa now moved to consolidate his position by providing support to the nationalist movements during the final tumultuous years of apartheid. Holomisa found himself in a powerful position. In the words of one senior American diplomat, it was 'high noon in Southern Africa'. The rival insurgencies and counterinsurgencies had stalemated each other. However, the apartheid state was still strong and its security forces had not been militarily defeated.[73]

Indeed, the apartheid president, FW de Klerk, believed that the stalemate strengthened his position at the constitutional negotiations, the Convention for a Democratic South Africa (CODESA), which opened in Johannesburg in December 1991. The ANC also faced organisational crisis. During the most critical years of the political transition, the MK 'was in a state of absolute chaos'. Morale inside its camps was low and its supply lines into South Africa were under strain.[74] The release of Mandela and the unbanning of the liberation movements had been a long-held dream, but it was fast becoming a nightmare. Padraig O'Malley writes that the swift-flowing course of events 'almost overwhelmed the ANC':

> It struggled to establish itself inside South Africa, to set up national and regional offices and structures, deal with the return of exiles, the dismantling of [MK] camps in Tanzania, the future of the MK, negotiations, build a parallel underground, and introduce Mandela to the international community.[75]

Most important was the support that Holomisa gave to the ANC in three key areas. Firstly, he was part of the Patriotic Front coalition that the ANC had been trying to build since 1991 against the apartheid government from the nine political parties and ten Bantustans present at the CODESA constitutional negotiations. The ANC knew that their party organisation was weakest in the Bantustans, the home of around 50% of the African population; they worried

---

[72] DD 26 June 1991, 15 December 1993. TRC-AH, Moringer.
[73] H. Giliomee, 'Surrender without Defeat: Afrikaners and the South African "miracle"', *Daedalus*, 126, 2 (Spring 1997), pp.113-146.
[74] Simpson, 'The Endgame', p.508.
[75] O'Malley, *Shades of Difference*, p.344.

that many Bantustans leaders were in hock to Pretoria. They reached out to the Bantustans by drawing on their Homeboy connections. Oliver Tambo made preparations to build a homestead at his birthplace in Eastern Mpondoland. Nelson Mandela's closest friend on Robben Island, Walter Sisulu, spoke at a Welcome Home rally in Umtata (for he was born in Thembuland) shortly after he was released from jail. Sisulu's speech revealed the extent to which the ANC had placed their bets on the Transkei Military Government: 'Today we call on all our people in other Bantustans to follow General Holomisa's example... You are proudly carrying forward the struggle against tribalism as you fight to re-unite our people into a single and undivided nation.'[76]

Second, Holomisa's entanglement in apartheid Military Intelligence networks gave him access to documents that contained explosive revelations. The apartheid government and the ANC blamed each other for the violence that was sweeping across South Africa, undermining the course of the negotiations. Nelson Mandela strengthened his hand by taking Holomisa to London, where he told a UN International Hearing about the Third Force hit squads. Under the spotlight were the deaths of four Eastern Cape political activists who had disappeared in 1985. Amongst the four was Matthew Goniwe, the old friend of Dumisa Ntsebeza, who had once taught at Holomisa Secondary School in Transkei. Foul play was widely suspected, but it had not been proven because their bodies had disappeared (later found burnt and buried in an unmarked grave).[77] Holomisa made public the notorious 'Goniwe death signal' – a message sent within the highest echelons of the government, three weeks before the four men died, recommending Matthew Goniwe's 'permanent removal from society, as a matter of urgency'. It was the closest investigators would ever get to establishing the complicity of the most senior members of the apartheid government in Third Force violence. Later, Holomisa explained how 'President Mandela asked me to keep the files and leak them periodically to the editor of the *New Nation*... [so] to pressurise FW de Klerk for more concessions and progress in the negotiations.'[78]

Third, Transkei provided the ANC and MK with a base area in which they could build up their forces. South Africa was close to civil war. Hundreds of people were being killed every month despite the National Peace Accord that had been signed between the apartheid government and ANC in September 1991. Whilst FW de Klerk had brought the National Party into negotiations, hardliners within the counterinsurgency forces instigated a series of bloody conflicts. The ANC was caught on the horns of a dilemma. The MK stocked arms as an insurance policy and trained Self Defence Units. At the same time, however, the ANC's doctrines of 'people's power', which urged revolution from below, were faltering in the face of the resistance put up by Bantustan leaders and their allies in Pretoria's security services. In the Ciskei Bantustan, an ANC-organised mass demonstration, intended to overthrow General Oupa Gqozo's pro-apartheid regime, was massacred by security forces. KwaZulu Natal and

[76] *The Citizen* 27 November 1989.
[77] *Report of the International hearing on political violence in South Africa and the implementation of the national peace accord* (London, 1992) – attached document: BH to D/Transkei Military Intelligence, (n.d. 1992?).
[78] Holomisa, *Comrades in Corruption*, p.13.

Johannesburg's southern townships were consumed by 'tribal' violence.

Transkei provided a transit point for ANC exiles repatriating to South Africa, a sanctuary for the 'high-risk' cadres who were refused entry by the apartheid government, and a refuge for victims of political violence in neighbouring KwaZulu Natal. Kenny Jafta had fled into exile in the mid-1980s (see Chapter Six). He was now one of the many MK cadres who returned to Transkei and was drawn into this work around Umtata. 200 kilometres away in Eastern Mpondoland, Zoleka Langa was involved in another MK cell. She had been drawn into ANC activism after her brother, Chief Babini, died in Matanzima's jails in the early 1970s (see Chapter Three). During the early 1990s, she hid scores at her family home or in her workplace, Holy Cross Hospital. Holy Cross even acted as a dressing station for wounded militants who were smuggled out of KwaZulu Natal by a cell operating out of a Durban hospital.[79]

The apartheid government suspected that Bantu Holomisa had far more systematic ties to the MK: that the MK was training Self Defence Units and that Transkei was a rear-operating base from which attacks into KwaZulu Natal were launched. Apartheid police told the press that the MK had moved 22,000 tons of weaponry from Angola to Namibia and Transkei. These rumours were fuelled by a trickle of arrests. In 1991, senior MK cadres (including two who had bombed Umtata in 1986) appeared in a magistrate's court close to the Transkei border on the charges of carrying unregistered arms. Their defence – which was successful – was that the Transkei Military Government had given them permits to carry weapons. A year later, South African police stopped a car driven by MK cadres and stocked full with small arms close to the Transkei border. Once again the cadres escaped jail – receiving fines.[80]

In one sense, these ties consolidated Bantu Holomisa's position. 'Mr [Chris] Hani lived in the ministerial complex, in the midst of the members of the Military Council, occupying the house that used to belong to George Matanzima.'[81] The ANC's armed wing celebrated their 30th anniversary at a rally in Umtata. It was a brave sight: a spectacle of the MK's security consciousness and celebrity status. 'A siren-wailing Ford Sierra leading a swift convoy of Mercedes-Benz cars screeched into the [Umtata] Independence Stadium... before broad-siding in front of the crowds.' A Transkei Defence Force band played *Nkosi Sikelel' iAfrica*. Chris Hani's speech praised Bantu Holomisa for running 'a unique Bantustan... whose army is part of our people's aspirations for power'. T.T. Matanzima's reply was equally emphatic. The 'Transkei Defence Force and the MK would go back to the bush together in the struggle for freedom if negotiations failed', he promised.[82]

At the same time, Bantu Holomisa's position was tenuous. One reason was that the Transkei government hosted two rival liberation movements – the Pan African Congress (PAC) as well as the ANC. As discussed in Chapter Two, the PAC had been a presence in western Transkei and their insurgents had organised a series of attacks in these districts during the early 1960s, until

---

[79] Interviews, Langa (2009), Jafta.
[80] Jeffrey, *The Natal Story*, pp.391, 491, 709-10. *DD* 17 July 1991, 20 June 1992. Gibbs, 'Chris Hani's "Country Bumpkins"', p.689.
[81] Koyana, 'History of Transkei', p.23.
[82] *DD* 16 December 1991.

they were crushed by the apartheid state. The experience of the PAC in exile in the 1960s, 1970s and 1980s had been exceptionally troubled, and they had dwindled into insignificance compared to the ANC. Nevertheless, they retained support and sympathy in parts of Transkei. Indeed, the leader of the PAC in the 1990s, Clarence Makwetu, who had been born in Western Thembuland, had returned to his home on release from Robben Island. Holomisa took great pains not to favour the ANC over the PAC or vice versa. This placed him in a quandary when the PAC rejected all negotiations with the apartheid government. Instead, the PAC's guerrilla wing, the Azanian People's Liberation Army (APLA) mounted a series of attacks from their base in Transkei. One attack on St James' Church in Cape Town killed eleven and wounded 56. The grenades used in the attack were apparently traced back to a batch supplied to the Transkei Defence Force.[83]

Pretoria responded to the series of attacks by throttling Bantu Holomisa's government. During 1993, Pretoria temporarily closed the border with Transkei. Apartheid forces also mounted a disastrous helicopter raid on an Umtata suburb that killed four youths. (They claimed their raid was targeting a PAC training camp.)[84] Many more haphazard attacks were carried out by local security forces. Zoleka Langa's Mpondoland home was attacked after her cell was betrayed by a turncoat. She was not at home, but the two MK cadres eating breakfast only survived by escaping out of the back window through a hail of gunfire.[85]

Transkei was also awash with weapons as a result of the low intensity war fought in the region. PAC cadres robbed the University of Transkei, wounding students in the cross-fire. The MK soldiers, squatting in camps around Umtata and facing miserable conditions were restless too. Even a few senior MK cadres became involved in the mayhem. One of Chris Hani's bodyguards was jailed for robbing a Cash and Carry supermarket in Engcobo. In an 18-month period, 198 armed robberies netting R6.2 million were carried out in Western Thembuland alone.[86] The MK's strategy of arming Self Defence Units willy-nilly stoked violence when one unit fought the PAC.[87] Even as South Africa edged towards the first democratic elections in 1994, Bantu Holomisa's regime remained fragile.

Bantu Holomisa's fall and the new South Africa

With South Africa's democratic elections approaching, Bantu Holomisa manoeuvred to position himself within the ANC family. Having received the

[83] *Truth and Reconciliation Commission Report, Volume III*, p.510.
[84] Bell and Ntsebeza, Unfinished Business, pp.168-9. CKC94, Lawyers Committee for Human Rights to FW De Klerk (hereafter FWDK). *Truth and Reconciliation Commission Report, Volume III*, p.600
[85] Interview, Langa (2008).
[86] SAPA 15 December 1993. TRC-AD, AC/99/0227, Pumlani Kubukeli, Themba Mnguni, Mtutuzeli Ngozwana.
[87] TRC-AD, AC/2000/045 The participants were Lusindiso Poyo, Templeton Pato, Funisile Guleni, Dumisa Mdlulwa, Mfanelo Matshaya, Pumelele Hermans.

assent of the Transkei Military Council, he joined the ANC in December 1993.

Initially, Holomisa seemed well placed. He sided with Chris Hani in aligning himself with the militants in the struggle for the soul of the ANC against the group in favour of compromise and negotiations clustered around Thabo Mbeki. Hani and Mbeki had been the brightest, most successful cadres within the ANC in exile, so perhaps it was inevitable that they would become rivals. What made their enmity so crucial was that their personal styles embodied searing political debates within the ANC. Mbeki's biographer writes that Hani became the lightning rod for mass-based militancy, particularly as '[he] appeared to find himself more at home on the streets... than he had ever been among the ANC oligarchs in Lusaka.' (In one of his last interviews Hani talked about his dream of farming at his father's home in Thembuland.)[88] By contrast, Mbeki was seen as a turncoat who joined the South African Communist Party when it had been a vehicle for personal advancement amongst the exiles, but was now making friends with South Africa's corporate sector.

In the ANC's internal battles, Holomisa used his intelligence sources to smear rivals. For instance, he revealed to the press that Sol Kerzner, who had been investigated for corruption in the Transkei, footed the bill for Mbeki's 50th birthday party. Holomisa was firmly in the Hani camp and almost as popular. One academic researcher marvelled: 'In a five minute walk [across the street in Johannesburg], fifteen people stopped to shake his [Holomisa's] hand.... It was like a celebrity had arrived.'[89] In part it was because of his militant reputation; but much was also due to his popular manner which resembled Chris Hani's political style. Holomisa was a man who answered his own phone, received uninvited petitioners into his office, lived in a 'modest suburban home' rather than taking over Kaiser Matanzima's presidential palace, and who helped ordinary people put out chairs at a wedding whilst other dignitaries remained in the VIP marquee.[90]

When Chris Hani was assassinated on Easter Saturday in 1993 – a plot by two men from white supremacist circles to derail the constitutional negotiations – Bantu Holomisa told journalists of how he wept. Known to the press corps as a notoriously guarded and unemotional politician, it was perhaps a sign of how Holomisa had lost a close colleague and protector. Nonetheless, Holomisa was still powerfully positioned as the protégé of Nelson Mandela. The two men struck up a close, familial-like relationship. Holomisa told journalists that, 'he [Mandela] treats me like a son. And I treat him as I would my father... He phones me early in the morning or late at night. I'm learning a great deal from him.'[91]

Holomisa was a late convert to the ANC. Nonetheless, on the back of this patronage and popular support, he was placed high on the ANC's election list in 1994. He was also chosen by the party's Election's Committee to campaign the length and breadth of the country. At the ANC National Conference held at the end of 1994, Holomisa capped his year by winning the party's

[88] Gevisser, *Mbeki*, p. 596. Cf. W. Kodesh interview Chris Hani, 1 April 1993.
[89] O'Malley interview, Jac Buchner, 12 November 1996. Cf. Gevisser, *Mbeki*, p.581.
[90] Stengel, 'Cashmere Tyrant', p.15. Author interview, Valerie Viljoen, East London, 20 October 2008.
[91] Stengel, 'Cashmere Tyrant', p.15. Cf. Smith and Tromp, *Hani*, p.274.

'beauty pageant': coming top of the list in elections to the National Executive Committee.[92] Holomisa's meteoric rise was extraordinary given that he had only joined the ANC a year earlier. It also speaks of the power that charismatic militant figures held within the ANC at a time when party structures were in chaos, and shadowy exile figures – like Thabo Mbeki – were not well known.

Reincorporating the Bantustans also meant attending to family business. When Mandela rebuilt his ancestral home at Qunu it was 'Holomisa who took control of the project'.[93] It was also time to settle scores. After the defeat of the Duli coup, Kaiser Matanzima was a spent force.[94] Mandela now sought reconciliation with the political rival who had once been his university friend. One morning in the later summer of 1993, Holomisa and a coterie of bodyguards accompanied Mandela on a visit to meet Matanzima at Qamata:

> Matanzima, tall, lean and resplendent in a white linen suit met us at his windswept kraal... Under a stifling late morning sun, they greeted each other solemnly; each made brief remarks to a small crowd. Then, while Holomisa, Mandela and their entourage had lunch, Matanzima... dozed on a carved wooden throne that sat on a grizzled lion-skin rug.[95]

▲ ▲ ▲

But if a reputation as a militant and populist made Bantu Holomisa a household name, it would be a hindrance as the ANC consolidated power. In 1996, only two years after his triumph at the ANC party conference, Holomisa would be pushed out of the ANC. In one sense, he was a creature of the years of flux during the political transition. To outwit the might of the apartheid state he had developed a mode of political brinkmanship that was ill-suited to the ANC's brand of party politics, which stressed a style (if not always the substance) of internal consultation and deliberation. Perhaps Holomisa sensed this in the first months of 1994. He vacillated over whether to take a post in the army, where he would fall under senior MK leaders who had feuded with Chris Hani since the late 1960s (see Chapter Six). The alternative was to chance his hand in politics at the mercy of the party machine run by Thabo Mbeki. In the end he chose politics and was given the paltry position as Deputy Minister of Environmental Affairs, outside the cabinet.

Worse, Holomisa's rivals prospered. During the hiatus, Stella Sigcau took a post in the ANC Women's League in the Transkei. Stella Sigcau's family and schooling connections gave her stature at the national level and she was appointed into the first democratic government as a full cabinet minister, senior to Bantu Holomisa. Thabo Mbeki was also settling scores. Holomisa faced a corruption investigation after the reincorporation of Transkei into South Africa revealed the full extent of Bantustan mismanagement and debt. In one sense, some sort of enquiry was necessary, given that Bantustan government

---

[92] KGC88, BH CV.

[93] Stengel, 'Cashmere Tyrant', p.16.

[94] See, for instance, the apartheid government's offhand dismissals of Matanzima's demands – BTS34, KD to Pik Botha, 1 July 1991, Pik Botha to KD, 10 July 1991.

[95] Stengel, 'Cashmere Tyrant', p.16.

processes had descended into chaos in the early 1990s. In one district office visited by journalists, officials were housed in a garage and used a zinc shack as an office. Cattle strayed into the compound after hours and the 'garden was littered with human faeces'. [96] However, the enquiries into graft took on the appearance of a witch hunt given the time spent investigating Holomisa's pay rises.

Mbeki's allies in the intelligence services were also probing the murky dealings of the Transkei Defence Force. Police arrested two senior officers and questioned Holomisa's bodyguard over allegations that he had ordered the cold-blooded killing of Craig Duli.[97] Holomisa struck back, using his appearance in front of the Truth and Reconciliation Commission to remind the press of how Stella Sigcau had taken a R50,000 gift that could be traced back to Sol Kerzner. Mbeki seized his opportunity: Holomisa was hauled in front of a disciplinary committee and forced out of the ANC. Not even Mandela could save him – although the two later reconciled.

Beinart and Gumede suggest that Holomisa's fall epitomised the centralisation of power under Thabo Mbeki. Soon after Holomisa's fall, Winnie Mandela and Peter Mokaba would face censure. 'These were exemplary lessons in party discipline and helped curtail populist and militant rhetoric', Beinart argues.[98] But this was not a straightforward centripetal consolidation of power. Mbeki proved the master at using the internal conflicts within fragmented state institutions to engineer his enemies' downfall. Over the coming months, Holomisa and his rivals raked over and rekindled the embers of the political transition. The ANC printed a pamphlet, *The Rise and Fall of Bantu Holomisa*, linking him to the infamous apartheid counterinsurgency units. Holomisa's riposte was equally apposite. He released a pamphlet against the ANC, *Comrades in Corruption*. These tactics – particularly the use of smears, corruption investigations and intelligence dossiers – would feature in many more of the ANC's internecine struggles.

If Holomisa's downfall provides a dramatic example of how the fragmented histories of the old regime persisted within the new dispensation, others, more quietly, used these turbulent legacies to their advantage. T.T. Matanzima was the most successful of the Transkei Defence Force officers. In the mid 1990s, he served on a coordinating committee, in charge of integrating the fragmented apartheid, Bantustan and MK security services. He put senior white officers at ease by joking how, just a few years ago, they had plotted against him. Matanzima then steadily rose through the ranks of the South African National Defence Force. In a military service racked by trouble and conflict, his administrative skills (thanks to his Transkei Defence Force training) gave him an unusual reputation for competence. He was even briefly made the Acting-Secretary of Defence, the highest administrative post in the military, until the ANC found a civilian to fill his place.[99]

---

[96] *DD* 13 October 1995. Cf. *DD* 17, 18, 24 February, 18 October 1995, 20 May 1997.

[97] *DD* 30 December 1994, 28 November 1995, 15 March 1997.

[98] Beinart, *South Africa*, p.294. Cf. W. Gumede, *Thabo Mbeki and the Battle for the Soul of the ANC* (Cape Town, 2005), pp.44, 62.

[99] Statement by the Democratic Alliance, 3 March 2010. Statement of the Presidency, 6 April 2010.

With the reincorporation of the Bantustans, many more of the Eastern Cape elite took senior positions in post-apartheid government and business circles. These journeys to the national centres of South Africa were expedited through regionally rooted networks. Because the South African state comprises a set of 'relatively closed institutional spaces' it is held together by 'complex networks of relations that stretch well beyond territorial boundaries'.[100] In 1999, for instance, 40 per cent of the African Director-Generals heading government departments in Pretoria had passed through the Transkei's schools or university.[101] Others had taken parallel paths through the institutions clustered around the other Homeland states. In this way, several regional histories of African education success, professional achievement and political connection were interwoven into the fabric of the new South Africa. The ghosts of the Bantustans lived on.

[100] W. Pansters, 'Goodbye the Caciques', in A. Knight and W. Pansters (eds), *Caciquismo in Twentieth-Century Mexico* (London, 2005), p.359.

[101] Of the 31 Director Generals heading national departments in 1999, 15 were African. They included: Chabani Manganyi, a former lecturer at the University of Transkei, born in Limpopo; Sizakele Sigxashe, Ayanda Ntsaluba and Mthobi Tyamzashe, alumni of St Johns College; Zam Titus had served the Transkei Bantustan administration, as had Sandile Nogxina, a contemporary of Dumisani Mafu who also fled into exile in the mid-1980s. At least two more had attended Fort Hare. *Who's Who* (Johannesburg, 1999).

8.   The New South Africa & Transkei's Collapse, 1990 Onwards

Mandela's moral homilies

If the democratic transition allowed many of the region's elite to secure high office in the new South Africa, Transkei itself imploded. Ironically, some of the greatest challenges to Bantu Holomisa's military government in the early 1990s came from the more disorderly elements within the broad nationalist alliance. After Holomisa unbanned the liberation movements, a plethora of organisations, political groups and local initiatives mushroomed. From their base in Umtata, a hastily formed Interim Regional Executive Committee, nominated in early 1990 by the ANC national leadership, struggled to gain some control of events. The ex-Robben Islander, Alfred Xobololo, was made chair of the Transkei Regional Executive. Samson Fadana, aged 69, one year older than his friend in the chair, was the most senior figure in the committee. Below them were the next generation of stalwarts in the struggle – including Zoleka Langa, Mzolisi Mabude, Prince Madikizela, Harris Majeke and Ezra Sigwela. Then there was a smattering of Soviet-trained thirty-somethings such as Pumzile Mayaphi, who had risen rapidly in the MK during the 1980s.[1] They would struggle to establish control over many of the organisations that were notionally aligned to the ANC.

South Africa's historians typically have seen these conflicts as expressive of the deep social divisions within the Bantustans. Rural society had been transformed by the burgeoning ranks of youth – both unemployed miners returned from urban centres and disaffected students – who brought new styles of political action into the rural areas. Insurgents struck out from below against the corrupted Bantustan authorities. At the same time, the beneficiaries of the Bantustan system also mobilised to maintain their privileges.[2]

Yet we should add a significant caveat to this picture. Many ANC leaders, struggling to contain and channel the forces released by mass mobilisation, took inspiration from older patterns of social authority. At the very highest level, Nelson Mandela made great show of the consensual values of African leadership that he had learnt as a child by watching his guardian, Jongintaba, the Thembu Regent, hold *inkundla* meetings at Bumbane Great Place. His biographer, Tom Lodge, notes that this consensual rhetoric was admirably

---

[1] *DD* 15 October 1991. Interview, Jeff Peires, King Williams Town, 10 August 2007.
[2] Delius, *A Lion Amongst the Cattle*, pp.204-11. Van Kessel, 'From Confusion to Lusaka'. Van Kessel and Oomen, 'One Chief, One Vote'. P. Lekgoathi, 'Teacher Militancy in a Rural Northern Transvaal Community of Zebediela, 1986-94', *South African Historical Journal*, 58, 1 (2007), pp.226-52.

suited to the tumultuous years of the early 1990s when South Africa came so close to fragmentation and civil war.[3] In the Transkei, it was the same. Local politicians often imagined a bygone era in which the African elite had been leaders of local communities. They even brought back ageing activists to chastise and encourage the younger generations. In these earlier periods (so the discourse went), Transkei's political elite had also been community leaders – able to heal the divisions of society. Thus there were significant continuities in communitarian ideology despite the dramatically changed political and social circumstances.

The heirs to Fort Hare University

A surge of student and pupil protest was most apparent. The University of Transkei was the epicentre as it had been the main source of open dissent during the 1980s. The student leaders saw themselves as the progenitors of political activism in the schools across the region and heirs to the traditions of Fort Hare University, which had been the *alma mater* of Nelson Mandela and other nationalist leaders. Yet their militancy also tore apart the Umtata campus.

Bantu Holomisa had actually tried to make peace with the student activists when, in March 1988, he forced Kaiser Matanzima to relinquish the Chancellorship of the university and appointed Wiseman Nkhulu as the new Vice-Chancellor in charge of campus affairs. It raised hopes that the destructive conflicts which had wracked the campus ever since the 1984 student boycott might finally end.[4] Nkhulu had respected credentials; he had spent two years imprisoned on Robben Island in the 1960s. Although he had subsequently left the political arena to pursue business interests – becoming the first black chartered accountant in 1976 – he had been associated with the protests that shook the University of Transkei in 1984. Once in post, Nkhulu made moves to mollify the student body. He invited Dumisa Ntsebeza to give a public lecture on security trials under Transkei's notorious Public Security Act. He raised eyebrows in Umtata when he allowed the students to commemorate the Sharpeville massacre and the Soweto uprising.[5]

However, the Vice Chancellor faced a Student Council who had been hardened by the bitter conflicts of the 1980s. Indeed, a bumper intake of 2,600 students arrived at the University of Transkei in 1988, having been banished from the Ciskei Bantustan for their role in the tumult at Fort Hare University the previous year.[6] The conflicts of the 1980s had reinforced student attitudes against all authority thought to be synonymous with the 'apartheid system'. The Student Council almost immediately clashed with Nkhulu, when, in June 1988, they held a three-day boycott of all classes. In part, it was in support

[3] Lodge, *Mandela*, pp.15-16.
[4] *DD* 5 March 1987, 15 March 1998. Russell, 'UNITRA: Profile of a Bantustan University', *Sechaba* (February 1988), pp.18-24.
[5] KGC3, G. Gerhart and T. Karis interview, Wiseman Nkhulu, Umtata, 28 October 1985. *DD* 9 September, 11 October 1988. Barron, 'Teaching Training', p.59.
[6] Author interview, Mcebisi Magadla, East London, 21 October 2008.

of an anti-apartheid action running in South Africa. It was also a protest against mid-year exams. For Nkhulu, the principle of academic excellence was paramount. He believed that the culture of learning had been shattered by the violence that the security police had brought onto the campus in 1984. Indeed, exam results had dropped disastrously. He argued that new mid-year tests were necessary to improve pass rates. However, the Student Council was suspicious of the extra exams: 'We always believed that the education system was structured in such a way to make it difficult to get through... Some courses were just impossible for black students', one student leader later reminisced. They also feared that test results would be used punitively to exclude students who were preoccupied with political activism.[7]

During their three-day boycott in June 1988, 400 students marched through the campus, forcibly stopping lectures, smashing windows, breaking up exams and burning exam papers, until they were chased away by police. The detritus of the clashes – 'stones, broken bottles and iron bars' – were found 'scattered all over campus the next day.'[8] The students won a partial victory as the tests were watered down, but this was not enough. In 1989, 250 protesters, chanting 'We belong to the MK,' violently blocked entrance to the university for fellow students who wanted to sit the mid-year exams. The police tear-gassed and then charged the marchers, shooting one in the hand. The university was forced to shut down the residences for a few months and to close the site early for the mid-year winter holidays.[9]

Wiseman Nkhulu argued that these disruptive demonstrations were unconscionable and that liberal freedoms should prevail: 'Education is the common objective which should unite students and staff... You [the Student Council] cannot direct punitive action against innocent people [i.e. prevent other students from taking exams] in the name of freedom and justice.' In the wake of the strikes he announced that: 'Effective measures were to be introduced to restore discipline in residences – the disregard of the authority of house directors, the accommodation of squatters, and the deliberate damage of university property has to stop.'[10] However, bringing police onto campus entangled university affairs with anti-apartheid politics. During 1989, elements of the security police still loyal to the apartheid order mounted midnight raids on student residences, and detained Student Council leaders.[11] These measures to restore discipline in the residences also strengthened the hand of the senior university staff who had been responsible for the crackdown on students in 1984.

The conflict on campus took a sinister turn when university officials hired a shadowy contractor, Pierre Bezuidenhout, as the Head of Campus Security. A special Commission of Inquiry later concluded that Pierre Bezuidenhout and his cousin, employed by the university as a maintenance technician, were former spies who had probably worked for the apartheid government Military Intelligence. Witnesses alleged that Bezuidenhout 'was saluted by members of the Transkei Security police' who addressed him as 'major'. The cousins had

---

[7] *DD* 10, May 1988, 16, 30 May 1989. Interview Magadla.
[8] *DD* 23 June 1988.
[9] *DD* 30 May, 1, 8 June, 8 August 1989.
[10] *DD* 23 June 1988.
[11] *DD* 9 August 1989.

compiled security profiles on suspicious students and staff. They kept a secret arms cache in the university strong-room. They had even planted explosive charges around the security fence that they threw up round the campus – to which students were apparently alerted after a wandering horse was blown up.[12]

This secret war between campus security and the student leadership galvanised some parts of the student body. Many student activists believed that the struggle demanded a new, militant type of political authority and control. The Student Council operated in secret cells. 'If ever you had a conversation on campus you had to whisper.... They had a complete security network that was linked to South African intelligence.'[13] The university residences were an ANC bastion. University resources were siphoned off for the struggle. Student Council funds were stretched to find food and transport for political groupings mushrooming up all over Transkei. Members of the Student Executive concurrently held posts in the South African National Student Congress and gave themselves responsibilities that reached far beyond campus affairs into political matters.

Indeed, the Student Council had long been preparing for political mobilisation, 'encouraging students to go home at weekends' and form youth groups. Impromptu groups of university activists would make three-day road trips around the Transkei in borrowed cars, distributing political literature to schools and colleges.[14] The Student Council broke away from the Natal region of the South African National Student Congress. Instead of playing sports at the University of Natal and Rhodes University, they concentrated on arranging fixtures with Transkei's teacher training colleges. Some disdained the dilapidated training college facilities, but the student leadership held firm. 'Our brothers and sisters were in awful conditions' and if they were 'lifted up, the whole countryside [around them] was converted'. Before each sports match there would be speeches of welcome which were turned into political addresses by the sportsmen-turned-political activists. Later, over a barbecue and beers, political conversations would continue well into the night.[15]

Many parts of the ANC supported the students against the authorities. Chris Tapscott had once cautiously supported Wiseman Nkhulu. Now based in London, he wrote an angry article, published anonymously in the ANC's magazine *Sechaba*, condemning the Vice Chancellor as an apartheid stooge:

> Despite his outpouring of Africanist rhetoric, Nkhulu has been thoroughly co-opted by the apartheid regime, serving as a director on the board of the Development Bank of South Africa. A purveyor of Pretoria's new apolitical language of technocracy... his impact on student opinion is likely to extend only to the most politically naïve.
>
> The struggle of the student activists in the past five years has been a heroic one. Despite appalling repression from the Bantustan police, they have refused to submit and have steadfastly persisted in their fight to expose the sham of independence in the Transkei... In doing so, they have carried the torch for freedom fighters in the

---

[12] *DD* 3, 6, 12 October 1990, 14 March 1991. Interview, Mojo Mdikane Umtata, 3 November 2008.
[13] Interview, Mdikane.Cf. *DD* 6 June 1990.
[14] Barron, 'Teacher Training', p.23.
[15] Interviews, Magadla, Mdikane.

region. Through their courage they have inspired others – brothers, sisters, parents and elders – to take up the struggle [16]

Yet the all-embracing demands of political activism hardened the Student Council against those classmates who lay outside their charmed circle. In 1990, the student leadership was forced to resign by their peers, as a clamour of voices rose against them, and a petition alleging corruption was sent to the university authorities.[17] The findings of the subsequent Commission of Inquiry that delved into their affairs painted a picture of a campus run by a small clique, who dominated all the student societies and viewed the campus as their fiefdom:

> The Student Council came to mass meetings with 'cooked' suggestions and was negative to speakers with opposing views – allowing intimidation and humiliating howling against them... Insufficient notice was given for meetings and .... majority decisions were determined by volume of noise rather than voting.[18]

Vice-Chancellor Nkhulu attacked the Student Council, claiming it was out of control. Certainly, the redirection of funds for political causes all too easily led to claims of corruption and theft. There was no control over tuck-shop takings; money was kept in students' rooms and rarely banked. R5,000 was allegedly stolen from the tuck shop, although this was impossible to prove as few records were kept. The Student Council hid liquor that had been donated for the Freshers' Ball. There were also more sinister claims: 'violence caused by excess drinking [was] endemic'; and that 'there had been friction among women students over the number of girlfriends Council members had.' There were even allegations that one student had been assaulted after she rejected the advances of a Council member. No evidence was found to support these charges, although the Commission of Inquiry's chair, Professor Alex Gumbi, noted that the 'intimidation of witnesses might have affected these findings'.[19]

The older generations of ANC members in the Regional Executive Council in Transkei were caught in a dilemma. The ANC's organisational efforts benefited from the students' dynamism and some embattled members of the Regional Executive were inclined to see conspiracies around every corner (often with good reason). A group of ANC aligned lecturers formed a rival committee to protest the findings of the Gumbi Commission. Mzolisi Mabude dismissed the inquiry out of hand: it was motivated by political malice.[20]

▲ ▲ ▲

Stoked by activities of the university activists, long-standing grievances sparked into politicised protests in the schools throughout Transkei. The Transkei branch of the Congress of South African [Secondary School] Students (COSAS) held a series of sit-ins in the offices belonging to the Department of Education. They demanded that misspent school fees should be refunded,

[16] Russell, 'UNITRA', p.22.
[17] *DD* 4 May, 11 July 1990.
[18] *DD* 6 June 1990.
[19] *DD* 23 June 1988, 6 June 1990. Interview Magadla.
[20] *DD* 11 July 1990.

exam fees abolished, and buildings renovated.[21] Hundreds more pupils held protests at the district offices of local schools inspectors. Very often local inspectors could successfully conclude negotiations with the student leaders and their followers,[22] but there were times when protests spilt into the local community, causing wider conflicts.

At Nyanga Senior Secondary School, in Engcobo district, trouble started when a hostel housing 390 pupils was destroyed by matriculating students. The pupils had claimed their indemnity deposits were not paid back; the School Governing Council argued that the funds were needed for urgent repairs. The hostel was then declared uninhabitable by a circuit inspector and senior community members, forcing many boarders to take even more squalid accommodation in the locality. Many pupils returned to squat in the school, complaining 'living in the village was proving far more expensive.' As many as 25 pupils slept in each classroom and lessons became impossible, but the youths refused to budge because they claimed that the School Council was corruptly appointed by the principal. With the local Department of Education officials unable or unwilling to resolve the dispute, 'the chief of the area, Chief Zanegqele Dalasile, called the community together' and took charge. He 'had the authority to approach the pupils on school matters because the school belonged to the community.' The chief led a delegation of villagers and parents, armed with sticks and guns, to the school. After negotiations failed, the villagers threw the pupils out of the school, killing one child in the process.[23]

The Regional Executive of the ANC in Transkei struggled with this turn of events. Prince Madikizela and James Kati were prompted to form an ad hoc Crisis Committee, a few days after 200 pupils from Buntingville College 'swarmed into' Madikzela's office 'reporting they had been beaten up by police'. Madikizela accommodated the stranded pupils in his office, house and a local church hall, whilst his committee tried to broker a peace deal. He told the press that 'the police displayed a clear disrespect for the youth who were the future leaders of the country.'[24] The chair of the Regional Executive, Alfred Xobololo, sent the younger members of the ANC underground who had spent time in prison and carried a whiff of glamour, 'to put out the fires [in the schools] and educate them [the pupils]'. Sometimes they would get phone calls from principals who could no longer handle the pupils in their charge.[25] Yet for every conflict that they resolved, there were many more wildfire protests in Transkei's schools.

Civic organisations against the chieftaincy?

There was also a mounting crescendo of local protests across the Transkei. At times these protests pitted insurgent civic organisations against the authori-

---

[21] *DD* 2 March 1990, 17 February 1993.
[22] *DD* 27 October 1988.
[23] *DD* 15, 16, 20 March 1990. Government directives had urged chiefs to take control of school unrest in their localities – BAO11/33, 219/22/39, 'Circular 4 of 1976'.
[24] *DD* 14 October 1989.
[25] Interview, Saliwa.

tarian rule of the chieftaincy and Bantustan officials. (This narrative of repression and resistance is also reflected in many writings on these conflicts.) Yet a closer examination of the local dynamics often reveals a far more diverse range of forces and ideas; a set of conflicts in which communitarian ideology was often as important as insurgent protest.

Most importantly, it was the national political situation that framed the conflict between the chieftaincy and grassroots protests. In KwaZulu and Natal in particular, civic organisations were engaged in a struggle with the chieftaincy – who, backed by apartheid security forces, threatened to undermine the constitutional negotiations. Given the fear of a civil war that would pit insurgents against the chieftaincy, a significant section of the national ANC leadership level resolutely courted traditional leaders. There was *realpolitik* in this line. In an attempt to ease the chieftaincy away from the clutches of the apartheid government and its allies, the ANC created the Congress of Traditional Leaders of South Africa (Contralesa).

The Congress of Traditional Leaders of South Africa was Pathekile Holomisa's route into the upper ranks of the ANC. After leaving St Johns College (see Chapter Four), he had taken a law degree at the University of Natal, where had been involved on the margins of student politics. Graduation posed a dilemma. Pathekile's student fees had been paid by the Hegebe community; but he did not want to be a traditional leader under the Bantustan system. His old school friend, Oyama Mabandla, suggested he should meet Oliver Tambo in Lusaka. Holomisa was surprised to find that Tambo urged him to accept the chieftainship, even 'join the ruling party in Transkei... so that the ANC would have one of its own inside the system'. Instead Holomisa stalled. He took articles in East London and joined the National Association of Democratic Lawyers, before returning to Umtata to train as a barrister. 'In the end Pathekile Holomisa got off the hook when his uncle [Bantu Holomisa] seized power.' He took up the Hegebe chieftainship, and in 1990 the ANC turned to him again, asking him to lead Contralesa. [26]

Pathekile Holomisa was thrown head first into a messy situation. The first executive of the Congress of Traditional Leaders had collapsed amid claims of corruption. The organisation was also side-lined and at odds with the rest of the ANC alliance at the negotiations taking place in Johannesburg. Contralesa's arguments in favour of preserving the patriarchal privileges of the chieftaincy deeply angered other parts of the ANC alliance, not least because they resembled the arguments made by the Inkatha Freedom Party. For a number of years, Pathekile Holomisa was unpopular within the ANC; he was almost suspended for not following the party line. However his legal nous and close relationship to Winnie Madikizela-Mandela (as well as the ANC's uncertain handling of the chieftaincy) ultimately entrenched Contralesa in the post-apartheid landscape. [27]

'The One who Moves Mountains' is the most literal translation of Pathekile

[26] Gerhart interview, O. Mabandla. Cf. Author interview, P. Holomisa.
[27] A. Mokvist, 'Democratisation, Traditional Leadership and Reform Politics in South Africa', (Uppsala University, PhD thesis, 2006), pp.51-88. Gerhart interview, O. Mabandla. P. Bell, 'The Wild Coast', *Millenium* (October-November 1996), pp.56-9.

Holomisa's praise name, *Ah! Dilintzaba!* It is an appellation full of patriarchal power and might. Intriguingly, Holomisa prefers another translation: 'the one who breaks down barriers'.[28] In this more sinuous rendering of his praise name, we have a glimpse of the fraught negotiations through which well-educated traditional leaders, such as Pathekile Holomisa, secured their place in the post-apartheid order.

Transkei mirrored the national situation in that it seemed that the chief-taincy might stymie the democratic transition in the early 1990s. The chiefs were being courted by the Transkei Traditional Leaders Association, which had strong links to Kaiser Matanzima and thus the apartheid government. Nelson Mandela told the crowd of 100,000 at his Welcome Home event in 1990 that, contrary to rumours, 'the ANC had always respected the chiefs' who were 'an important part of the community,' especially as 'some ... had played a crucial role in the freedom struggle.'[29] Even so, he called for 'the formation of civic and village structures' and warned that 'those chiefs who worked against the aspirations of their subjects would not be protected by leaders and organisations of the people.' In a similar vein, the Transkei Military Government argued, 'any attempts to oppose or bypass them [Traditional Authorities] are unlikely to succeed and a much more effective approach is to augment them with other local development bodies... [and] make them more representative by having a majority of elected members.'[30] This diplomatic approach worked, as the Transkei Traditional Leaders Association faded away – most specifically following the murder of the organisation's leader, and more generally because of the waning influence of Kaiser Matanzima. Transkei's chiefs then drifted into the ANC-aligned Congress of Traditional Leaders.[31]

At a local level the picture was much more mixed. Sometimes the chieftaincy lined up against insurgent demands of grassroots organisations. Mobilising in Transkei's rural areas, ANC organisers found 'there were many chiefs that did not want us... Once you organise [party branches] people worry because you are tampering with the status quo.' Bolstered by senior party leaders Mzwai Piliso and Ambrose Makiwane, an organising team from the ANC crisscrossed the Transkei. They borrowed cars, caught minibuses and slept in villages where they found a welcome. They found some traditional leaders loath to relinquish the powers granted to them by the apartheid and Bantustan governments. For Mojo Mdikane, one of the University of Transkei's young activists who had helped on the ANC's organisation campaign, this was a particular irony. His father was a brother to King Sabata Dalindyebo and, 'as an African', he valued traditional leaders 'as custodians of our traditional and cultural makeup' and 'part of our history.'[32] Now, despite his best efforts to introduce the message of the ANC respectfully, 'there were villages where we were actually chased away' by the local chief.

At other times, civic organisations vied with local chiefs for leadership of the community. This was the experience of the Lusikisiki branch of the ANC.

[28] P. Holomisa, *According to Tradition: A cultural perspective on current affairs* (Somerset West, 2009).
[29] *DD* 23 April 1990,
[30] *Transkei Agricultural Development Study*, p.94.
[31] Peires, 'Transkei on the Verge of Emancipation', p.198.
[32] All quotes from author's interview with Mdikane.

Local ANC leaders complained that 'there was strong collaboration between local police, state officials and reactionary chiefs to undermine party growth in the area.'[33] Three hundred ANC activists were detained by police in one year alone. Among them was Veli Ntsubane, a longstanding member of the ANC underground who had become the vice-chairman of the ANC in the area and the General Secretary of the Transkei Congress of Civic Organisations. His own organisation had urged its members to consolidate their authority over the rural areas and help local communities by starting up small-scale projects: piggeries, vegetable gardens, and school building schemes. In response, Ntsubane had been arrested by local police, accused of 'interfering in [rural] administrative areas' and 'destabilising the government,' when he constructed a community clinic in Lusikisiki that must have undermined the authority of a local chief. This was a communitarian conflict over who commanded the resources and leadership of the community.[34]

Elsewhere, the patterns of conflict and cooperation on the ground were much more messy.[35] Sometimes strong local leaders managed to conciliate those in conflict. This was seen in a march on Mkambati Nature Reserve, led by Zoleka Langa. Drawing on her authority as the daughter of a chief, an MK operative and a respected local nurse, Zoleka Langa headed a protest action demanding the return of land that had been expropriated from the community in the early 20th century (see Chapter Three). The Transkei Military Government had already released back 3,500 hectares to the local community in the late 1980s; but a large chunk of land was still designated a nature reserve, which was a holiday playground for white tourists.[36] These protests had the potential to spark off a power struggle with the local chieftaincy. However, most local headmen happily fell in behind the civic organisations. A number of chiefs and headmen readily conceded power to civic movements: they simply stopped performing duties that were required them of them by the government. 'Why should I allow myself to be hated by my neighbours?' one explained to an academic researcher.[37] Zoleka Langa's royal name and her well-known struggle history also bridged divides as did her carefully chosen mobilising slogan: 'The land... belonged to the people and their chiefs, who deserved a say in how it was utilised.'[38]

The march itself provoked a moment of crisis. 'Thousands of protestors converged on the [holiday resort] area [of the Nature Reserve] and hoisted an

---

[33] *DD* 23 August 1991.

[34] *DD* 11 January 1991. BTS34, 'Press Statement of the Transkei Congress of Civic Organisations', 15 July 1991.

[35] S. Fikeni provides half-a-dozen case studies that show the complex patterns of co-operation and conflict between civic leaders and local chiefs in the Transkei: 'Conflict and Accommodation: The politics of rural local government in post-apartheid South Africa', (Michigan State University, Ph.D. thesis, 2008).

[36] Similar conflicts occurred at the Dwesa-Cwebe nature reserve in western Transkei: R. Palmer, H. Timmermans and D. Fay, *From Conflict to Negotiation: Nature-based development on South Africa's Wild Coast*, (Pretoria, 2002).

[37] Kepe, 'Grassland Vegetation and Rural Livelihoods: A case study of resource value and social dynamics on the Wild Coast, South Africa', (University of the Western Cape, PhD thesis, 2002), p.68.

[38] *DD* 12 August 1992. Cf. Interview, Langa (2009),

ANC flag, while others manned a roadblock at the gate', effectively holding the holidaymakers hostage. In the violent climate of the time, there were widespread fears that the hostages would be killed. [39] The Military Council hurriedly sent a senior minister, Chief Ngangomhlaba Matanzima, in a specially chartered helicopter to negotiate with the protestors. South African authorities even sent in rescuers; but the protest action was well disciplined and in good spirits. A few of the 'hostages', interviewed by the newspapers, even gave their support to the protestors' demands. Interviewed nearly 20 years later, Zoleka Langa remembered the march as a triumph of cooperation and communitarian spirit. 'Even the tourists were with us, they assisted us with food. They really strengthened us... We were in control because we didn't burn anything.'[40]

In contrast, other civic leaders engaged in a far more divisive mode of politics. This was seen in the neighbouring Flagstaff district, through the convoluted relationship between Mwelo Nonkonyana and his cousin-brother, Elliot Nomazela Bala, who ran the local civic movements. Mwelo Nonkonyana was a young chief from Eastern Mpondoland, who (like Pathekile Holomisa) had been educated at St Johns College, become an advocate in Umtata, and then joined the Congress of Traditional Leaders of South Africa. Elliot Bala is one of those characters, thrown up during the intense political conflicts of the time, whose name still carries many turbulent stories in his wake. Bala had made a name for himself as a mid-ranking but very charismatic, violent, and influential shop steward in the National Union of Mineworkers (NUM) during the tumultuous strikes on South Africa's goldfields in the 1980s. In the late 1980s, he went back to Transkei, one of the thousands of miners who returned home from South Africa's mines after the huge NUM strike of 1987.[41]

Back in Transkei, Elliot Bala initially made an alliance with Mwelo Nonkonyana to ease his way into local politics. (Indeed, the brothers had grown up together in the same household.) Bala gained control of the cooperative projects that were set up by the NUM to provide livelihoods for their unemployed members by Bala's advertising his relationship to Chief Nonkonyana. He located the first cooperative scheme in his home area of Flagstaff, 'to reinforce his power in the community as well as the cooperative.'[42]

He used the claim... [that] he was related to the chief [Nonkonyana]... to further assert his power in the NUM... [And] he travelled through the Transkei, promising ex-mineworkers that the union was going to employ them, paying them all over R400 a month... [This] convinced ex-mineworkers that there was no other choice; it was up to him to get the projects going.[43]

When these cooperatives collapsed, Elliot Bala adjusted his political

---

[39] *DD* 12 August, 8. Cf. *DD* 11 December 1992.
[40] Interview, Langa (2009).
[41] R. Malan, *My Traitor's Heart* (New York, 1990), pp.236-63. Cf. T.D. Moodie, 'The Rise and Demise of Lira Setona? Questions of race and how the NUM became a social movement', (typescript, n.d.), pp.1, 18 and also T.D. Moodie interview, M. Mlungwana, Umtata, 1 July 1995.
[42] Michelle Adato, '"They Have Been Given Democracy": Mediated models, democratic meanings and co-operative development in the Transkei', (History Workshop Conference, Witwatersrand University, 13-5 July 1994), p.9.
[43] Ibid., p.10.

alliances. He took a heavily armed group of unemployed miners from Transkei to Johannesburg to demand funds from Cyril Ramaphosa and James Motlatsi, the leaders of the National Union of Mineworkers. He told his followers that the union was dominated by Sothos and a threat to the ANC. [44]

Back in Flagstaff, Elliot Bala also reinvented himself as the scourge of the chieftaincy and the leader of a local branch of the South African National Civic Organization (Sanco). His challenge to the chieftaincy drew on an intriguing set of ideas and discourses. He burnt down the forests controlled by the Tribal Authority. Sanco allocated fields and sold thatching-grass, usurping the chieftaincy's power. Bala also mobilised a rural youth association behind him. They stirred up trouble throughout the area, weighing into a murderous dispute between local taxi owners and bus drivers in Flagstaff. (This clash would cost Bala his leg – apparently cut off as a punishment and warning.) Mwelo Nonkonyana mobilised a rag-tag collection of bodyguards in response, who also claimed affiliation to the ANC. Eventually Nonkonyana prevailed and Bala's supporters were routed. [45]

As many of Transkei's localities fragmented along myriad lines in the early 1990s, the authority of the Bantustan government also fractured. These tensions came to a head in the middle of 1992 when the national ANC leadership called for a 'Week of Mass Action' against government structures following the breakdown of the constitutional negotiations. Transkei posed a delicate problem. The Week of Mass Action prompted widespread, coordinated demonstrations across Transkei for the first time ever; yet the ANC did not want to undermine the authority of Bantu Holomisa's government. Trying to avoid trouble, the local ANC produced a 'list of positive and constructive' demands and Bantu Holomisa called a public holiday. Nonetheless, there were incidents in a number of districts. Roads were blocked in the town of Butterworth. In Umtata, Bantustan civil servants, 'including director generals, [were] pulled out of their offices and forced into the street.' [46] At Lusikiski, Flagstaff and Qumbu (an even more troubled district, where the social fabric had been shattered by widespread stock theft and car-jacking) the flag of the Republic of Transkei was lowered or burned.

The Transkei Government was obsessed with maintaining order. 'The Boers would like to destroy Transkei... They are looking for chances... The security of the roads must be maintained', they explained in one fraught meeting. [47] Holomisa contacted the ANC national leadership, who sent Walter Sisulu down to chastise the local party leaders who were caught in this Catch-22.

---

[44] T. Philip, 'Enterprise Development on the Margins: Making markets work for the poor', (PhD thesis, Witwatersrand University, 2006), pp.57-66.

[45] Author interview, Advocate Mdutshane, Umtata, 19 November 2008. Interview, Peires (2007). Author interview, Mwelo Nonkonyana, 18 September 2009. Peires, 'Transkei on the Verge of Emancipation', p.198. TRC-VH Lusikisiki , Nomgwena Mancaneni, Nkebe Mdutshane, Mwelo Nonkoyana, Sipho Phangomso, Elliot Skhosana, 25-26 March 1997.

[46] *DD* 1 August 1992. Cf. *DD* 23, 29, 31 July 1992 and 5, 6, 7, 8 August 1992. J. Peires personal collection, 'Minutes of meeting between Deputy President Walter Sisulu and Transkei ANC Regional Executive Committee and Transkei ANC Youth League', 1 August 1992.

[47] J. Peires personal collection, 'Minutes of meeting held in General Holomisa's office, Botha Sigcawu building', August 1992. Cf. 'Minutes of meeting between Deputy President Walter Sisulu and Transkei ANC'.

'Ancient teacher prestige down the drain'

The foundations of the Bantustan state were also exceptionally vulnerable during this period of political transition. In the early 1990s many of Transkei's professionals joined public sector trade unions and embarked on a series of strikes that often brought the Bantustan bureaucracy to a standstill. The teacher's strikes were particularly damaging, given the growing spread and importance of schooling during the Bantustan era. The strikes also raised fundamental questions about the transformation of the professions. As discussed in Chapters One and Two, teachers and professionals had historically played a leadership role in African politics. Their professional status and moral legitimacy rested on their claim to be leaders of the community. However, the expansion of the teaching profession and the troubles experienced in many schools during the Bantustan era had watered down this claim to authority. In the 1990s, the militant mode of trade union mobilisation would mark an even more turbulent phase in the transformation of the profession. Nevertheless, residual ideas about the role of the teacher as community leader would continue to have remarkable purchase in Transkei's politics. Paradoxically, communitarian ideas about the nature of moral authority gained in strength during times of trouble.

Most directly, it was tactical political considerations that led to the growth of ANC-aligned trade unions. The ANC leadership wanted to create a broad church by uniting the country's fragmented teaching associations under the party's banner in order to strengthen their hand. In the Transkei, it was Mkangeli Manford Matomela (b.1957) who skilfully brought Transkei's teachers into the ANC-aligned South African Democratic Teachers' Union (Sadtu). Matomela had been detained and tortured in the early 1980s because of his involvement in the ANC underground. Subsequently he became a teacher and in the late 1980s the ANC instructed him to join the Transkei Teachers' Association, a meek professional body cowed by decades of Matanzima's rule. His directive was to 'work within the Association to change its direction.' For two years, Matomela attended hours of meetings convened by the Teacher Unity Forum, shuttling between Port Elizabeth, East London, Umtata and Transkei's outlying districts. In 1990 he carried the floor, bringing the entire Transkei Teachers Association – its members, its bank accounts and assets – into the ANC-aligned teachers' union. [48]

In one very immediate sense, Transkei's teachers strengthened the ANC alliance. The national leadership of Sadtu faced financial crisis. The apartheid government 'were not processing... [Sadtu] membership applications [in apartheid-controlled South Africa so as] to throttle the growth of the union', Matomela recalled. 'We signed a cheque and transferred it all to Sadtu... For a long time, Sadtu's affairs were financed because of Transkei.' [49]

Moreover, the ferment of mobilisation sometimes brought professionals into

[48] Interview, Matomela.
[49] Ibid.

the ranks of the political leadership, where their expertise was badly needed. This was the case with Bukhosi Bigglesworth Mabandla, who was Matomela's closest colleague in the Transkei region of the South African Democratic Teachers' Union. Mabandla was not a political firebrand. Whilst Matomela was in jail, Mabandla was quietly rising through the ranks of the Transkei Teachers Association. Nonetheless, Mabandla strongly believed that teachers had 'a calling to serve the local community.' This belief in the principles of public service was born of his deep Christian faith and his lineage in the Bhele clan, where he had been taught that chiefs were the voices of their community. These were values that brought Mabandla closer to Matomela, who was also an active Christian. Bukhosi Mabandla would rise through the union hierarchy to become the president of Sadtu and a senior official in the post-apartheid government. In retirement he was ordained as an Anglican priest.[50]

Even in the early 1990s, when so many schools and colleges were in turmoil, it was possible to believe that the social values of the previous generation still had significance – that professionals had a role as community, and political leaders. Fred Barron, an education researcher touring Transkei's teacher training colleges, noted that despite the general breakdown of morale, a core of committed teaching staff remained. The principals who showed 'an attitude of extreme paternalism' managed to quell the most disruptive protests, Barron noted, 'Where lecturers are open, relating in a "firm and parental manner", arranging venues for meetings and paying for parties, ensuring the budgets stretch to provide adequate food and decent living conditions, no student action has been targeted at such rectors.'[51]

On his return to Transkei after decades of exile, Wycliffe Tsotsi (whose story was narrated in Chapter Two) emphatically underscored these themes when he gave the keynote address to the teacher's annual conference. It was the duty of the teachers, 'who constitute the most numerous and most powerful intellectual force in the territory [to] guide the masses', he explained. '*Hic Opus; Hic labor Est! Asiyo Ndlwana Iyanetha Ke Leyo!*' [Here is toil; here is labour! Here is no child's play!]. The fact that Wycliffe Tsotsi chose both Latin and Xhosa proverbs was significant: it was a reminder of an earlier era when elite mission schools in Transkei taught the Classics.[52]

Yet Manford Matomela and Bukhosi Mabandla found themselves presiding over a wave of damaging strikes. One issue at stake was the ethos of trade unionism. Transkei's teachers were caught up in the conflicts that had engulfed schools and local communities. The growth of Sadtu suddenly transformed these problems into political grievances. These troubles were compounded by tensions that had stoked teachers' resentment of government: they spoke out against unpopular systems of school inspection and of their frustration with persistent shortages of books and equipment. At a number of schools, trade unionists were embroiled in internecine factional conflicts; some forced inspectors out of school; others disappeared from the classrooms on spurious

---

[50] Author interview, Bukhosi Mabandla, King Williams Town, 17 November 2008. *DD* 1 December 2000.
[51] Barron, 'Teacher Training', pp. 52, 64.
[52] W. Tsotsi, 'Keynote Address', (Transkei Teachers Association annual conference, Umtata, 9 July 1990).

'union business' during school hours.[53]

The rhetoric of the conflict turned on the question of whether teachers were professionals or radical trade unionists. 'The new teacher protested against the authorities... because he wanted a say... Principals could not handle these upstarts.'[54] The charge of many politicised teachers was that professional standards were synonymous with the sycophantic leadership of the old professional teacher's associations, who had remained 'politically neutral and cultivated an ethos of working collaboratively with the educational authorities'. Yet too few trade-unionist teachers attempted to create an alternative code of conduct and morality. [55] For many, the trade union's job was simply to fight for better salaries suitable to their status. One teacher later explained: 'we are not demanding to be rich, but we want to live and maintain a certain lifestyle as professionals.' [56] In 1990 Sadtu started an indefinite strike in Transkei just weeks before the end-of-year exams. The teachers won a significant pay rise from the Transkei Military Government, so repeated the same tactics in 1991 and 1992.[57]

The strikes over salaries raised troubling questions about the fragility of the Bantustan state. Teachers' salaries were a significant item of government expenditure: the Department of Education accounted for one-quarter of Transkei's budget, of which wages made up 75 per cent. Holomisa had come to power promising he would control the civil service wage bill, but was soon forced into an abrupt reversal by trade union militancy. He raised salaries twice and slashed taxes on wage earners, sacking officials who disagreed with him.[58] The figures are complicated and were bitterly contested at the time; but it seems that his policies reversed the financial position of Transkei's teachers and officials. From being the worst paid in South Africa, they were now very well remunerated. [59] Holomisa's finances fell apart. The Military Government's expenditure doubled between 1987/8 and 1990/1 from R1.6 Billion to R3.2 Billion, whilst its debts piled up to over R2 Billion. This incensed Pretoria, whose officials argued that 'the spending was 'unauthorised, unjustified and... funding had not been provided'.[60]

Expenditure was a weapon of war. Although the union leadership backed Holomisa, the apartheid government was well aware that restive teachers and civil servants might turn against the Transkei Military Government. 'We

---

[53] *DD* 1 May 1991, 20, 22 February, 25 May 1992. Interviews, Matomela, B. Mabandla.

[54] Interview, B. Mabandla

[55] Lekgoathi is sympathetic to the 'unionist' side of the argument, but also notes these issues: 'Teacher Militancy'. *DD* 15 January 1987.

[56] *DD* 5 June 1993.

[57] *DD* 11, 23 August, 4, 6, 7 September 1991.

[58] *DD* 22 April 1988. BTS30, 'Holomisa speech to Cape Town Press Club', 15 October 1990. BTS30, 'Background brief on the issues likely to be raised by BH if the State President agrees to see him', n.d. (1990?).

[59] Andrew Donaldson, a politically astute economics lecturer, thought civil servants were 'earning more that they ought' – *DD* 27 November 1990. Cf. BTS35, Forum of Transkei Progressive Structures to FWDK, 22 August 1991.

[60] BTS AJ1990B, 'Financial Accountability of the Transkei Government'. Cf. *DD* 3 June 1988, 20 September 1991; BTS30, 'Background brief', n.d. (1990?); BTS34, 'Minutes of meeting between RSA and Transkei re. the Transkei Financial Crisis', 3 June 1991.

tried to throttle him [Bantu Holomisa] financially', the South African Foreign Minister of that era, Pik Botha, later conceded. 'He had resilience, believe me.'[61] The apartheid government delayed financial negotiations and froze budget aid provided to the Transkei Government. Holomisa held on – plundering Transkei's civil service pension funds to pay government officials' salaries. Eventually, Nelson Mandela successfully lobbied Pik Botha on behalf of Holomisa's government. He angrily demanded that the apartheid government honour payments to the Bantustan states or else South Africa would fall apart.[62] Holomisa was also winning the war of words. Apartheid officials complained that 'a negative perception of the South African government is being created among the Transkei public and the black public in general.'[63] Pretoria unfroze the financial flow and development aid rose sharply again, climbing to R2.7 billion in 1992/3.

Relations between Holomisa and Pretoria hit a new low in March 1993 when the Goldstone Commission concluded that Transkei was being used as a base from which guerrillas mounted attacks on the rest of South Africa. 'The State President was reported to be... weighing financial pressure against military action as the best course to regain administrative control of the Homeland.'[64]

That same month, Sadtu mounted their most disruptive strike in Transkei. Five hundred protestors occupied the Head Office of the Department of Education in Umtata. 'That occupation was like a coup', remembered Matomela. 'It was very embarrassing for Bantu Holomisa.'[65] One teacher involved in the strike thought it was well disciplined – initially, at least. When his district took part in the sit-in, sleeping in the Botha Sigcau Building for a few days, they obeyed Sadtu-issued guidelines, but tensions apparently flared when another group of teachers from Qumbu took over. 'These guys were hoping to provoke conflict', one witness recalled.[66] 'They arrived armed with *knobkerries* and vandalised the building.' Some officials 'were virtually held hostage' and were only released after a lengthy negotiations.[67]

On 3 June, Holomisa's Government struck back, deploying policemen to prevent the 250-strong crowd of Sadtu reinforcements from entering the Sigcau building. The teachers withdrew and 'resorted to playing a dangerous game of taunting the police: hurling insults, toyi-toying, and singing.' Their slogans were a peculiar mix of trade unionist anger and claims to professional privilege. They were particularly angry that 'mere clerks and people without university education were getting better pay' than them. One chant claimed: 'Officials of the Department of Education have no worries, have big bulky stomachs and were fat swines.' The policemen on duty were excoriated as: 'uneducated things, with only [a] Standard Six [education]... employed by the Mantanzima regime.'

[61] O'Malley interview, Pik Botha, 13 December 1999. Cf. BTS3, Zondwa Mtirara to FWDK.
[62] Interview, T.T. Matanzima. Cf. BTS AJ1990A. 'Transcript of the meeting between FWDK and T.N. Ndamase', 3 December 1990. BTS30, 'Background brief'.
[63] BTS43, T.F. Wheeler to A. Venter, 12 June 1991. Cf. BTS AJ1994, 'Transkei'.
[64] *DD* 29 March, 21 Cf. 27 April, 13, 20 May 1993.
[65] Interview, Matomela.
[66] Interview, Magadla.
[67] A. Lugaju, *Report of the Commission of Inquiry into activities of police and military relative to the teachers strike* (Umtata, 1993), p.10.

The police replied in kind, accusing the teachers of laziness and deserting their communities: 'go back and teach the children you left behind.' [68]

Suddenly, the tension snapped. The police baton-charged the teachers. One group of middle-aged, female teachers were especially badly injured. Running away, they 'tried to escape... [but] a high cement wall' blocked their retreat. 'They found themselves like... sheep in the kraal. The police dealt with them, beating them one by one.' The *Daily Dispatch* reporter spoke to a fifty year old teacher, the mother of eleven, whose 'eyes were swollen and closed.' Another teacher, Ms Lindergirl Mfithi, pressed charges against the police as she had 'suffered severe injuries and humiliation.'[69]

The Military Government was in no mood for conciliation. Eight days later, at 5pm on 11 June 1993, riot police 'surrounded the [Sigcau] building and fired in tear gas canisters' through open windows. The teachers had no more stomach for a fight, and slipped away in the fading evening light, 'carrying suitcases and duvet covers'. Explaining his actions, Holomisa argued: 'there was a pervasive feeling that the Sadtu sit-in was degenerating into anarchy which would surely threaten the security of the whole of Transkei.'[70]

The rest of the ANC alliance was appalled. Jeff Peires, who combined lecturing at the University of Transkei with committee work in the ANC's Regional Executive, wrote an academic article excoriating the sectional self-interests of the public sector trade unionists. In his view, many of the Bantustan government officials who had suddenly discovered militant trade unionism constituted little more than a parasitic comprador bourgeoisie. Other members of the ANC Regional Executive criticised the teachers using a more communitarian ideology.[71] The Black Consciousness activist, Vuyani Mrwetyana, concurred. His newssheet brought in an old political activist to write a column titled: 'Ancient Teacher Prestige down the Drain.' [72]

> Traditionally, teachers are held in very high esteem in our communities. It is generally understood that teachers are the makers of all categories of manpower that the modern state needs to run its affairs. They virtually sit next to the Almighty...
>
> [But now] this trust and confidence are fast wearing away. Behind our backs people more often than not are calling us cheaters... It will be very sad if the only contribution the teachers of Transkei make to the formulation of a progressive education policy for the new South Africa would be the display of parity in their pay packets. Rather than staging sit-ins, we should be staging work-ins... It is high time we teachers of Transkei became community orientated. If we shine our light on the communities we serve, these communities would soon identify us as torchbearers.[73]

Popular anger against the teachers was also on Holomisa's side. Although

[68] Lugaju, *Report*, pp.10-12, 16. Cf. Interview, Magadla.

[69] Lugaju, Report, pp.10-12, 16.

[70] Lugaju, *Report*, enclosure: letter from BH – 'Brief outline of discussion between SADTU and me.' *DD* 12 June 1993.

[71] *DD* 7 September 1990. Cf. J. Peires, 'Transkei on the Verge of Emancipation', pp.192-221; Peires, 'The Implosion of Transkei and Ciskei', pp.365-87; Southall, 'Rethinking the Bantustans', pp.8-10.

[72] A. Songca, 'Ancient Teacher Prestige Down the Drain', *Isizwe*, 15 (October/November 1993), p.9.

[73] Ibid.

the school strikes rumbled on, their action had already largely 'buckled under the pressure from community organisations'. By the year's end, the protests had petered out.[74]

▲ ▲ ▲

Transkei's troubles continued into 1994. There were crippling strikes in the other government bureaucracies which had been unionised by the ANC-aligned public sector trade unions. There was also outrage when the ANC announced that Transkei would be incorporated into a wider Eastern Cape Province, and that the new provincial capital would not be Umtata but Bhisho, in the Ciskei Bantustan. The rival Pan African Congress capitalised on this response, claiming that Umtata would lose 18,000 jobs. In addition to its long-standing support amongst Transkeian migrant labourers who worked in Cape Town, the party was making inroads amongst 'the old Matanzima faction among the chiefs and the civil service'.[75] In January 1994 the PAC suspended its armed struggle and prepared for the elections. T.T. Letlaka, the cabinet minister from the old Bantustan government, was their nominee for the premiership of the Eastern Cape Province in the upcoming elections.

With elections approaching, the ANC leadership even had a minor scare that they might lose the region to the PAC. Govan Mbeki was sent down to rejuvenate the election campaign in Transkei. He reported back to headquarters that he had found a mess.[76] Jeff Peires saw matters differently. Powerful individuals, worried about their place in the post-apartheid order, had pulled rank when they had been left off the election lists organised by the ANC Regional Executive in Transkei. They had complained directly to Nelson Mandela: the ANC was 'staffed by children; responsible people would not vote for the party.'[77]

Finally, Election Day came. Despite a series of mutinous, debilitating strikes in the preceding month, the region delivered a thumping majority to the ANC. In April 1994, the Transkei Bantustan flag was lowered one final time at the Independence Stadium in Umtata. The crowd derisively chanted: '...take it [the flag] back to Daliwonga [KD Matanzima]!' Walter Sisulu's address was more ambivalent: 'apartheid and the Homeland system had been buried for ever', he declared, but 'the most difficult part of the struggle' would come 'when one [the ANC government] takes over.'[78]

After 1994: Traditions reasserted

The years after 1994 were every bit as difficult as Walter Sisulu had feared. Viewed from the regions, it seemed that the national government in Pretoria could barely contain powerful centrifugal forces that had emerged during

---

[74] *DD* 11 May, 5 June, 28 August, 28 October 1993.
[75] Peires, 'Transkei on the Verge of Emancipation', p.205.
[76] Govan Mbeki Collection, 19, 48, Matjie to ANC Secretary-General, (n.d.), Mbeki to Mandela, (n.d.).
[77] Interview, Peires (2008).
[78] *DD* 15 April 1994.

the final years of the Bantustan era. Most prominent in academic and policy debates was the tenacious survival of the chieftaincy. A great number of studies pointed to the weak grasp of democratically-elected, local government structures, which created a space that was filled by a plethora of actors who claimed that their authority came from tradition.[79] But far more important than grassroots politics was the linkage between government and local communities. 'It is important to understand that wealth and power in the rural Eastern Cape no longer derives from control of land but rather from control of government funds', Jeff Peires noted.[80]

In the period immediately after 1994, the ANC government presided over an austere period of local government reform that threatened to further unravel the relationship between the state and rural communities. In one sense, the impact of government reorganisation and austerity is far too complicated to detail here. We see this in the wildly differing fates of two of the grand old mission colleges after 1994. St Johns College no longer educated the African elite, who had left Transkei for the centres of power in Cape Town, Johannesburg and Pretoria. Nevertheless, it was still over-subscribed, teaching the children of upwardly mobile local government officials, who were clustered in Umtata. In contrast, Nelson Mandela's *alma mater*, Clarkebury College, which had latterly trained teachers, struggled after a central government fiat closed teacher training colleges countrywide. Attempts to revive the school faltered until wrangles with the principal, who was a Matanzima appointee, had been ironed out.[81]

Indeed, South African political scientists and policy experts have hardly begun to investigate the wrenching changes made to South Africa's institutional landscape after 1994 – although some specific sectors, such as agriculture and education, have been better researched.[82] The fate of the various mission schools, the Universities of Transkei and Fort Hare, the agricultural college at Tsolo, the different chieftaincies (who had their genealogies investigated by a ham-fisted government commission), the nature reserve at Mkambati, and the irrigation schemes at Qamata each have their own complex histories.

Nonetheless, the broad outlines of the crisis that struck the former Bantu-stans in the mid-1990s, as they responded to the withdrawal of government funds, can be sketched out quite clearly. Viewed from Pretoria, which held the purse strings, economic shock therapy made sense in one respect. In the last years of apartheid, Bantustan structures fell apart, leaving Transkei's communities in crisis as the lower levels of government collapsed. Creating a joined-up bureaucracy from the bloated remnants of the old Bantustan regimes was a nightmarish task. Transkei was incorporated into a new Eastern Cape province together with part of the old Cape province and the

---

[79] Ntsebeza, *Democracy Compromised*, p.294. Cf. P. Jones, 'From Nationhood to Regionalism in the North West Province', *African Affairs*, 98 (1999), pp.509-34. J. Williams, 'Leading from Behind: Democratic consolidation and the chieftaincy in South Africa', *Journal of Modern African Studies*, 42, 1 (2004), pp.113-36. B. Oomen, *Chiefs in South Africa*.

[80] J. Peires, 'Traditional Leaders in Purgatory: Local government in Tsolo, Qumbu and Port St Johns, 1990-2000', *African Studies*, 59 (2000), p.108.

[81] Field notes, Umtata, 15 August 2009. Cf. P. Harrison, *South Africa's Top Sites: Struggle* (Cape Town, 2004), p.24 and J. Peires, pers. comm. 29 January 2013.

[82] For example, T. Kepe's research on Mkambati and Magwa.

Ciskei Homeland. Below that, government taskforces attempted to create viable structures of local government from a patchwork of Tribal Authorities and municipalities that were bankrupt and sometimes corrupt. Furthermore, the ANC government inherited an insolvent state and a struggling economy. Because the ANC wanted to expand education and social welfare expenditures, other spending departments had to make deep cuts.

It was the former Bantustans that often bore the brunt of declining infrastructure budgets in the Eastern Cape. Ironically, Ezra Sigwela, a staunch advocate of rural community development when he worked for the Transkei Council of Churches in the 1980s, was one of the provincial politicians forced to make spending cuts when he headed the Eastern Cape Department of Agriculture and Land Affairs.[83] Such budget cuts particularly hit the old Transkei Bantustan bureaucracy, which had contributed 85% of the personnel to the new provincial departments.[84] Many other institutions faced crisis. The University of Transkei's accounts, for instance, went into the red when it lost both government subsidies and student fees, leading to a vicious cycle of high staff turnover, student failure and, eventually, the resignation of the entire senior management.[85] Jeff Peires coined an apt phrase to describe the disillusionment with democracy, and even the nostalgia for the past, when he wrote: 'the old [Bantustan] government structures were corrupt and inefficient, but a bribe in the right place could always get your road fixed in time for a wedding or a funeral.'[86]

During the crisis, ANC activists-turned-officials often stepped in to play their roles as mediators and community leaders. Kenny Jafta, the former student activist and MK cadre, used his ANC connections to help rural communities reschedule their debt payments when their loans were suddenly called in by the provincial government. As a result, he prospered as a local government councillor. 'Hundreds of [ordinary] people attend my meetings without [the inducement of] free food,' he boasted.[87] At other times, mediators capitalised on their connections with the traditional leadership. Bukhosi Mabandla (by now a senior government official) acquired private money through Nelson Mandela to build a health clinic for his amaBhele community in Transkei. Mabandla eventually preferred to retire to King Williams Town rather than live in Transkei, yet he retained close contact with the amaBhele chieftaincy. He often made the three-hour drive to participate in ceremonies and attend gatherings. He also made several trips to the Cape Town archives to research the history of the amaBhele.[88] Even provincial politicians who had few connections to the chieftaincy played the politics of locality. One Eastern Cape minister faced a minor scandal when it emerged that his family's 'home' region was receiving scarce resources. By these means, the discourse of ethnicity and local identity was used to mediate the relationship between the state and those marginalised communities facing crisis.

---

[83] T. Kepe, 'The Magwa Tea venture in South Africa: Politics, land, economics', *Social Dynamics*, 31, 1 (2005), pp.215-30.
[84] *DD* 24 February, 20 April 1995.
[85] Habib, *University of Transkei*.
[86] Peires, 'Traditional Leaders', p.109.
[87] Interview, Jafta. Cf. Author interview, Simphiwe Somdyola, East London, 18 November 2008.
[88] *DD* 1 December 2000. Cf. interview, B. Mabandla.

Nevertheless, Transkei's' rural communities reacted to the withdrawal of state patronage as they had fifteen years previously, when the Bantustan state had cut expenditures in the late 1970s (see Chapter Three). They punished the ruling ANC government, although this time it was through the ballot box rather than with threats of rural revolt. After his expulsion from the ANC, Bantu Holomisa formed a party of malcontents, and in the 1999 elections his United Democratic Movement picked up some 14% of the vote in the Eastern Cape, winning control of a large municipality centred on Umtata. In one sense, Holomisa's foremost supporters were reactionary remnants of the old Bantustan regime. 'Those who supported the United Democratic Movement in 1999 were precisely those who opposed the General [i.e. Holomisa] when he was still in power', Peires noted. [89] But the broader discontents were worrying. There had long been rumblings of discontent in Transkei. In the mid-1990s a Tenth Province Movement had emerged, claiming that Transkei's special problems demanded separate governance. Holomisa tapped into these complaints:[90] in his political party, the ANC saw a centrifugal form of localist politics, which threatened the fragile nation-building project.

The worst years of the crisis eventually passed. With South Africa's economy and treasury budgets improving in the early 2000s, a centripetal form of localist politics emerged. The national government embarked on new spending programmes to assuage the discontents of the populous rural regions. This opened up new opportunities for local leaders to play the role of intermediaries, and to channel state expenditure. Bulelani Ngcuka, the urbane National Director of Public Prosecutions, well known for his involvement in the Johannesburg Stock Exchange, sourced money through a public-private partnership to bring an irrigated dairy farm to his mother's home village of Middledrift, just down the road from Fort Hare University.[91] Zoleka Langa, the mayor of OR Tambo District Muncipality, which was formed from the rump of the old Transkei Bantustan, took advantage of the Eastern Cape's 'Green Revolution' programme (which essentially reintroduced the agricultural services that were cut in the 1990s) to start a series of rural development projects. She started a maize project on 340 hectares near her home town of Flagstaff that was run by a local chief and an unemployed school teacher. It was one of the government's new Massive Food Production Schemes – a policy that had close resemblance to the Bantustan government's ploughing schemes. 'Arm-in-arm with the provincial agriculture minister', she handed over dozens of tractors to 'happy groups of farmers' from around the region at key-giving ceremonies. [92]

As the mayor of the populous OR Tambo District, which carried more votes in ANC caucuses than the whole of Cape Town and the Western Cape Province, Zoleka Langa was a powerful figure in party circles. A member of the senior chieftaincy in the Eastern Mpondo kingdom, she spent significant amounts of time at her rural homestead, on ancestral land. At weekends she spoke

[89] Peires, 'Traditional Leaders', p.111.
[90] *DD* 7 September, 7 October 1995.
[91] *Engineering News* 12 October 2007.
[92] *DD* 4 April 2003.

at funerals and weddings in the region – an arena for public gathering and discussion. Langa even set up an NGO, temporarily housing AIDS orphans and battered wives in her rural homestead. In spring, her yard was full of stumbling toddlers, bleating lambs and tiny chickens. However, she landed in hot water when newspapers revealed that her municipality had spent its budget driving a motorcade to Lusaka to hold ceremonies for ANC guerrillas who had died in exile. 'We can't have a person running the municipality like it is her own *spaza* [small] shop,' railed a political rival.[93] It was an intriguing insight into how personal and political networks were interwoven with state structures; a sign of how localist politics might flourish as state expenditure expanded in the rural regions.

If the injection of government resources allowed some sectors to burgeon, it was clear that others were in a state of perpetual crisis. For instance, the education sector performed particularly poorly, to use the language of policy experts, who noted that expenditures had exponentially increased whilst pupil attainment stagnated and teacher absenteeism was rife. Rural provinces, such as the Eastern Cape, were worst afflicted by these troubles. Academics noted the institutional ruptures that had demoralised and de-skilled the longstanding black professions, such as nursing and teaching.[94] Public debates framed this far more straightforwardly as a crisis of public service morality and imagined an older era when black professionals were held in high esteem by local communities. One Eastern Cape premier, Nosimo Beauty Balindlela, tried to articulate the values of *Batho Pele* ('people first') by turning up to public gatherings and school openings bare footed, in traditional dress. Elderly grandmothers would greet her with shouts of 'welcome our mother'. Balindlela, a former Eastern Cape teacher who had briefly lectured at the University of Transkei in the mid-1980s, attempted to revitalise the lethargic provincial bureaucracy by meeting senior civil servants at dawn, for villagers were already working at this hour. 'A civil servant should ask: "Have I done something for the poor today?"' she explained. This invocation of older traditions of social authority and integrity tapped into a popular vein. Nosimo Balindlela's political style briefly made her the most popular provincial premier in South Africa, but she was soon forced out of office, a victim of internal party machinations.[95]

In these new developments we are perhaps witnessing a novel use of local traditions. 'The barefoot premier', Nosimo Balindlela, tried to use communitarian rhetoric as a glue that could repair the shards of an impoverished, fragmented society and address the failures of government to deliver public services. In contrast, Zoleka Langa has revealed how a centripetal form of local politics works in post-apartheid South Africa, with ANC figures invoking 'tradition' as they redistribute wealth from the national centre to the country's poorest rural regions.

---

[93] *DD* 19 November 2009. Cf. *Times* 11 September, 15 November 2009; Interview, Langa (2009).
[94] Delius *A Lion amongst the Cattle*, pp.157-9. The transformation of other professions is suggested by J. Steinberg, *The Thin Blue Line: The unwritten rules of policing South Africa* (Johannesburg, 2008). Cf. S. Marks, *Divided Sisterhood: Race, class and gender in the South African nursing profession* (Basingstoke, 1994).
[95] *Sowetan* 21 May 2007. Cf. *DD* 31 December 1994, 26 August 1997.

Conclusion
African Nationalism
& its Fragments

Commemorating Mandela's kinsmen

On 1 October 2008, South Africa's new National Heritage Council laid on a feast at Bumbane to commemorate the memory of Sabata Dalindyebo, a close relative of Nelson Mandela, whose story has threaded through the pages of this book. National politicians and well connected chiefs flew in from Cape Town and Johannesburg; the cow to be slaughtered was apparently trucked across the Transkei, having been donated by the Zulu king.[1] The social landscape of Transkei has changed hugely since Sabata Dalindyebo and Nelson Mandela grew up in rural Thembuland in the first decades of the 20th century. A dignitary driving from Umtata Airport to Bumbane in 2008 might have passed through Umtata's town centre, congested with businessmen buying groceries and bottled beer to transport out to the rural locations, where they would be sold on in smaller *spaza* shops and drinking *shebeens*. (This vibrant consumer market almost entirely depends on pensions and welfare grants that play a vital role in the Bantustans, where jobs are scarce.) The route then leaves Umtata and passes a dozen small settlements strung along the roadside, where smart brick houses with satellite TV stand next to small zinc shacks; some with electricity, piped water and government-issued pit latrines, others without. Even Qunu – so evocatively described in Nelson Mandela's autobiography – has become one of these ribbon settlements, favoured because it lies close to a busy, national road. Finally, the route cuts off onto a gravel road leading to Bumbane. For a moment, one might recall the beautiful steep-sided valley that visitors described when they visited Sabata Dalindyebo in the late 1950s. Yet this too has changed. The fields in the valley bottom lie fallow. A couple of junior secondary schools lie across the ridge.

In recent years, the ANC government has made concerted attempts to symbolically connect itself to South Africa's populous rural areas through commemorations and memorials of local figures such as Sabata Dalindyebo. In one sense, these have been very successful. ANC party membership has grown to more than one million, most rapidly in the rural regions. The largest delegations to the 2012 ANC elective conference come from three provinces that have incorporated the old Bantustans – the Eastern Cape, Limpopo and KwaZulu Natal. Gauteng, the mega-city conurbation made up of Johannesburg and Pretoria, provided the fourth largest delegation, just pipping Mpumulanga, yet another province that includes the old Homelands.[2]

---

[1] Fieldnotes, 1 October 2008.
[2] *M&G* 13 December 2012. *Business Day* 3 October 2012.

The weight of the rural regions within the ANC today challenges us to think about the dynamics of South African nationalism, which has typically been seen as an urban and industrial phenomenon. There is also the paradox of the ANC's increasing membership in an age that is very sceptical of nationalism, particularly in Africa. This scepticism runs deep. Take the ANC's centenary celebrations in January 2012, which brought political leaders from across the continent to celebrate the oldest nationalist movement in Sub Saharan Africa. Journalists seized on the corporate-style golf tournament which teed-off the celebrations as emblematic of how the 'ANC's reputation was being tarnished by corruption scandals, political infighting and reports of officials leading flashy lifestyles'.[3] Many academic researchers have gone further, arguing that nationalism is irrelevant; they prefer to research the more immediate, often centrifugal, fragmentary networks through which Africa so often works. Even the recent history writing that revisits the moment of nationalist independence looks not so much to resurrect the nationalist hopes of the time, as to consider the alternative routes that were not taken.[4]

This final chapter considers how we might place the post-apartheid growth of ANC membership and the significance of the nationalist project into a wider historical perspective. Certainly, the ANC witnessed at first hand and was entangled in the internecine conflicts that shook the hopes of post-colonial nationalism. The following sections discuss two of the ruptures that fractured the prospects of nationalist politics both in rural South Africa and elsewhere on the continent. Nevertheless, I conclude with a discussion of how the ANC sought to construct a nationalist political project from these fragments, and I suggest that the Bantustans played a crucial role in this.

Fractured legacies – *The Peasants' Revolt*

Terence Ranger's 1985 book on *Peasant Consciousness and Guerrilla War*, comparing insurgencies in Kenya, Mozambique and Rhodesia, turned out to be the swansong of studies that celebrated the revolutionary potential of the peasantry. Almost two decades earlier, Govan Mbeki's celebration of the rural rebellion in the Eastern Mpondoland districts of Transkei had placed South Africa firmly in this revolutionary trajectory. The Penguin series in which Mbeki was published also put out Basil Davidson's journalistic account of *The Liberation of Guinea*. In the hungry aftermath of World War II, imperial powers squeezed their colonies for resources. The forcible agricultural 'betterment' schemes that stirred rural Kenya into revolt were like a 'second colonial occupation,' wrote two historians.[5] Not since colonial conquest had African peasantries been so stirred. The apartheid regime pursued its plans to forcibly improve African agricultural production and impose government-appointed chiefs on the Native Reserves for its own ideological reasons; nonetheless, events in rural South Africa were certainly paralleled elsewhere on the continent. All

---

[3] 'The ANC at 100', *BBC News* (online), 6 January 2012.
[4] Cooper, 'Possibility and Constraint', p.168.
[5] Low and Lonsdale, 'Introduction', p.12.

across South Africa and the rest of the continent, there was a wildfire series of revolts which sometimes spread into broader conflagrations.

As a good communist, Govan Mbeki wanted revolution to overthrow apartheid and overturn the old social order, of which he was a member within the rural African elite. However, he was unsure whether the rural protesters agreed with his aims. In a wonderfully equivocal passage, he admitted that the chieftaincy retained its legitimacy in many areas of Transkei, even if individual chiefs were unpopular. Mbeki nevertheless hopefully concluded that 'when a people have developed to a stage which discards chieftainship... then to force it on them is not liberation but enslavement.'[6] Recent research tends to support Mbeki's observations, not his doctrines. Peter Delius' study of rural Sekhukhuneland, in the north, provides us with the most detailed research on South Africa's mid-century revolts. The revolts were epitomised by Flag Boshielo, a migrant worker who returned home to defend his rural homestead from government encroachment. Boshielo's migrant worker movement did not condemn the chieftaincy outright; it supported traditional leaders amenable to its cause. John Lonsdale finds something very similar in his detailed study of the Mau Mau revolt in Kenya. Mau Mau insurgents demanded that rich chiefs and patrons honour redistributive customs that were threatened by colonial intrusion. These rebellions were 'a last ditch defence of land, livestock and chieftainship' and the moral economy of the rural regions.[7]

The irony was that revolts which were defensive in nature often led to great ruptures in rural society. In Kenya, the Mau Mau insurgents, many of whom were marginalised, angry younger men, frightened the older, richer, and more established nationalist leaders. The British claimed that Jomo Kenyatta was the leader of the revolt, imprisoning and then detaining him in a remote location for a total of eight years. Actually, Kenyatta feared the insurgents too. His vision of a prosperous, hardworking peasant society disdained the grubby, Mau Mau freedom fighters. The British defeated the ill-equipped Mau Mau insurgents and hastily transferred power to rich Kenyan moderates, including Jomo Kenyatta, whom they brought out of detention. Jomo Kenyatta styled himself as *Muigwithania* (the Reconciler), but his vision of a prosperous society favoured 'big men', particularly those from his Kikuyu inner circle. 'Political tribalism' reigned as powerful patrons distributed land to their clients, squeezing out many of the poor. The demands of marginalised Mau Mau veterans for *uhuru na wiathi* (freedom and land/self mastery) would remain a subversive counter-cry.[8]

In Zimbabwe, the insurgents emerged victorious. Guided by spirit mediums and divine 'voices from the rocks', many guerrilla bands remained close to rural society. Some resettled rural communities onto land vacated by fleeing white farmers. Others dispensed rough justice: they 'hammered the [African] entrepreneurs and killed some of the ordinary peasants as sell outs and witches.'[9]

---

[6] Mbeki, *The Peasants Revolt*, p.47, quoted by van Kessell and Oomen, 'One Chief, one vote', p.565.

[7] Delius, *A Lion Amongst the Cattle*, p.221 as well as pp.108-38. Cf. Lonsdale, 'The Moral Economy of Mau Mau', pp.332-53.

[8] D. Branch, *Defeating Mau Mau, Creating Kenya: Counterinsurgency, civil war and decolonisation* (Cambridge, 2009), pp.179-207. Lonsdale, 'The Moral Economy of Mau Mau', pp.466-68.

[9] T. Ranger, *Voices from the Rocks: Nature, culture and history in the Matopos Hills of Zimbabwe*

Yet the violence and coercion of guerrilla warfare often exacerbated divisions in rural communities. Further, the spiral of violence became a motive force itself during the final years of the insurgency when rival guerrilla factions took a short-cut to power, gaining ground by brute force rather than persuasion. Then the expected fruits of victory turned bitter, when Robert Mugabe's government decided that white commercial agriculture was too profitable to sacrifice on the altar of land redistribution. Within this limited room for manoeuvre, Mugabe's regime tried to establish its nationalist legitimacy by resettling the remaining land and establishing Village Development Committees, but by the end of the 1980s, the state was in retreat, conceding powers back to local chiefs. In the late 1990s, land invasions mounted by angry 'war veterans' dominated the headlines. Zimbabwe was still an unsettled land.[10]

Perhaps the greatest ruptures were felt in South Africa. Flag Boshielo's 'last ditch defence of land, livestock and chieftainship' was crushed, as were all the other South African revolts. Rural insurgents would play a critical role in turning the ANC towards armed struggle in the early 1960s, but their efforts did not topple the apartheid government. Flag Boshielo would flee into exile, join the ANC's guerrillas, and die fighting Rhodesian security forces.[11] The next wave of revolts in Sekhukhuneland, in the 1980s, was led by a very different generation of alienated youth. With the decline of black agricultural production, rural life had fundamentally changed. Children no longer herded their father's cattle on remote cattle stations; instead they attended poorly funded, substandard, secondary schools. The political centre of gravity shifted away from a tiny network of elite rural schools to the burgeoning, discontented secondary schools. The runaway revolts of the 1980s that emanated from South Africa's townships spread outwards to the rural areas, along apartheid's social faultlines. A poem of the time, written in Sekhukhuneland, lamented:

There is a confusion between the father and mother... between the parents and daughters... between the parents and the sons... between the tribal authority and the community... between the principal and the teachers... [and] among the students... There is a confusion.[12]

These confusions would leave a long legacy. In 1999, Govan Mbeki's wife, Epainette, revisited the Transkeian village of her birth with the family biographer, Mark Gevisser. 'We drove for hours without seeing an electrified homestead... Rattling old buses, jam packed with migrants bound for Cape Town or Durban, came careering round the sandy mountain passes' along pot-holed roads. They discovered a village 'filled with the jetsam of rural poverty.' Epainette Mbeki pointed out her family's lost lands – the sorghum fields, the dairy, the apple orchards, the maize fields, the wheat fields, the sheep kraal. From 130 cattle, the remaining family were down to six; they had no other

^(contd) (Oxford, 1999), p.235.
[10] J. Alexander, *The Unsettled Land: State-making and the politics of land in Zimbabwe, 1893-2003* (Oxford, 2006). B. Raftopoulos, 'Problematising Nationalism in Zimbabwe: a historiographical review', *Zambezia*, 26, 2 (1999), pp.115-34.
[11] Delius, *A Lion Amongst the Cattle*, p.221. Magubane et. al., 'Armed Struggle', pp.53-145.
[12] I. van Kessell, '"From Confusion to Lusaka": The youth revolt in Sekhukhuneland', *JSAS*, 19, 4 (1993), p.593. Cf. Delius, *A Lion Amongst the Cattle*, pp.218-20.

livestock and did not grow crops. '*Rilithithi*', pronounced her nephew, a security guard, recently retrenched from his Johannesburg job and now uncertain of his future: *rilithithi* – 'pitch blackness,' 'darker than dark'.[13]

Fractured legacies – 'For the nation to live'

During the first heady years of Africa's guerrilla wars it was fashionable to argue that insurgent war would forge national unity. In the opening half of 1962, Nelson Mandela enjoyed a high profile revolutionary tour around Africa. A photograph from the time shows him at the headquarters of the Algerian *Front de Libération Nationale* in Morocco. Mandela was one of many leaders who travelled round the continent to learn guerrilla tactics and imbibe the heady theories of revolution. (Half a century later, President Thabo Mbeki would quote his favourite texts from the figurehead of Algeria's revolution, Frantz Fanon, in the foreword he wrote to a multi-volume celebration of South Africa's liberation struggle: *The Road to Democracy*.) Many African leaders, well versed in the lessons of history, quoted the examples of the revolutionary wars in France and Russia. 'For the nation to live, the tribe must die', argued Samora Machel, the leader of revolutionary forces in Mozambique.

'Contrary to Fanon's hopes, liberation war proved to be Africa's most divisive form of anti-colonial nationalism.'[14] Guerrilla movements rarely constructed a sense of national unity that incorporated and transcended more immediate local loyalties. Some barely tried. John Lonsdale notes that 'Angola's fighters began from three regional bases and never escaped their ethnic origins; civil war continued long after independence.' Samora Machel imposed his vision of a Marxist command state on Mozambique, and immediately faced a revolt of the regions which was backed by apartheid government. In Zimbabwe, the nationalist leader and trade unionist, Joshua Nkomo, had long believed that Ndebele ethnicity could be harnessed to a wider project of building a Zimbabwean nation. During his time in the southern city of Bulawayo, he 'visited Ndebele royal praise singers... and advocated pilgrimages to the grave of Mzilikazi', the great 19th-century king. However, Nkomo's forces never attracted much support in the more populous, Shona speaking, northern regions of the country, which was the stronghold of his rival, Robert Mugabe. Robert Mugabe's party emerged victorious in Zimbabwe's inaugural elections in 1980, winning almost three-quarters of the parliamentary seats. Mugabe's 'state tried to equate Zimbabwean identity with a Shona cultural heritage.'[15] After a few years of wary cohabitation, Mugabe's soldiers crushed dissidence in the Matabeleland areas; some 20,000 people died.

The ANC was sucked into these internecine struggles that convulsed southern Africa. In Angola they fought with the FNLA (*Frente Nacional de Libertação de Angola* – the National Front for the Liberation of Angola) against UNITA (*União Nacional para a Independência Total de Angola* – the National Union

[13] Gevisser, *Mbeki*, p. 27.
[14] J. Lonsdale, 'Anti-Colonial Nationalism', p.333.
[15] T. Ranger, 'The Invention of Tribalism Revisited', p.99.

for the Total Independence of Angola). In Mozambique they witnessed civil war between FRELIMO (*Frente de Libertação de Moçambique* – the Mozambican Liberation Front) and RENAMO (*Resistência Nacional Moçambicana* – Mozambican National Resistance). In Zimbabwe, they were so close to the forces of Joshua Nkomo's ZAPU (Zimbabwe African Peoples' Union) that Robert Mugabe became suspicious of them. Thabo Mbeki tried to broker an agreement that would allow the ANC to operate out of the newly independent Zimbabwe, but the agreement was never properly implemented. Worse was to follow. When Mugabe's troops struck out against rival ZAPU commanders, they also rounded up the entire MK command in Matabeleland: a score or more people who were detained, imprisoned and tortured. 'The ANC's infrastructure in Zimbabwe was destroyed: its properties and weapons were confiscated, and its permission to move cadres through the country or even set up minimal bases was withdrawn.'[16]

The nightmare of civil war emerged in South Africa during the early 1990s, particularly in the Bantustans where local chieftaincies set themselves up as rivals to the nationalist movement. In the province of KwaZulu Natal the ANC found itself fighting against the Inkatha Freedom Party. Inkatha was formed in 1975 by Mangosuthu Buthelezi, the Chief Minister of the KwaZulu Homeland, who initially argued that the Bantustans could be a vehicle to oppose apartheid. The ANC in exile, looking for ways back into South Africa, were impressed. Furthermore, Buthelezi came from the same ranks as the nationalist elite: he had joined the ANC Youth League when he studied at Fort Hare University in the late 1940s. During the 1970s, the ANC established contact with Inkatha leaders, trying to draw them into a broad alliance. For many from the older generation, brought up in the first decades of the 20th century, the links of family and friendship remained significant. Yet these tentative ties were soon broken when the 'young lions' of the trade unions and civic movements challenged the KwaZulu Bantustan establishment. These clashes had turned into a bloody conflict which would claim 14,000 lives across South Africa between 1990 and 1994. Guns flooded the region, as apartheid counter-insurgency forces and ANC guerrillas aided the rival camps. Political activism sometimes shaded into warlordism and even outright gangsterism. With the Inkatha Freedom Party refusing to participate in the 1994 democratic elections, South Africa was close to outright civil war.

Weeks before the democratic elections, Nelson Mandela and Mangosuthu Buthelezi patched together a deal, yet the costs of civil war were high. First, many discussions about contemporary South Africa are haunted by the notion that the democratic settlement in 1994 was the result of painful compromises similar to those faced by Africa's other guerrilla liberation movements. Just as FRELIMO was forced to make concessions to RENAMO-aligned chiefs, many academics and activists fear that the ANC made extravagant concessions to Inkatha. The ANC conceded the province of KwaZulu Natal to the IFP in the 1994 elections. Autocratic chiefs did not have their powers immediately curtailed, while many Bantustan bureaucrats also did very well for themselves

---

[16] Gevisser, *Mbeki*, p.437.

in the new democratic dispensation.[17] Second, the criminal gangs that flourished on the fringes of political activism continued to be a significant force in the new South Africa. Mozambican ex-combatants, who once smuggled AK47s into South Africa, now receive stolen cars smuggled out of South Africa. These 'new frontiers of crime' and corruption, which are sometimes woven into wider political webs, have become a staple of South African investigative journalism in recent years.[18] Third, South Africa has its own association of marginalised war veterans as well as what may termed an unruly 'lost generation' of combatants turned criminals. [19]

While there are persistent fears that the centre cannot hold and things will fall apart, others praise the fragments of the nation. In a recent book, Barbara Oomen celebrates 'the resurgence of traditional authority, custom and culture in South Africa...If South Africa was grappling for a post-apartheid identity, it seems to have found two central elements in tradition and cultural diversity', she argues. These events are in line with 'global developments: the fragmentation of the nation state, the embracing of culture, the applauding of group rights.'[20]

A nationalism of fragments

Nevertheless, to bewail or celebrate South Africa as a society of scattered shards is to miss how the ANC has sought to construct a nationalism from the fragments. Ironically, it was the weakness of the incoming ANC government during the crucial years of South Africa's democratic transition that forged this form of statecraft. Unlike Robert Mugabe in Zimbabwe or Samora Machel in Mozambique, the ANC lacked the brute force to stamp their authority over dissident regions. Instead, negotiation brought an end to South Africa's conflicts. Whereas many other nationalist elites (both in Africa and South Asia) could afford to overlook diverse constituencies, Nelson Mandela built his career as an elder statesman by calming the centrifugal conflicts that threatened to tear apart South Africa during apartheid's final years. The reintegration of the Bantustans into the post-apartheid polity (problematic as this has been) was a vital part of this process. In preceding chapters I have argued that a crucial part of this history can be followed by tracing the course of elite politics in the Native Reserves through the 20th century. Because men and women of the African elite, like Nelson Mandela, had been born and schooled in South Africa's rural regions, there were close, complex, ambivalent relationships between nationalist leaders, the Bantustan bureaucracy and the chieftaincy even at the height of apartheid. For better and worse, these relationships would shape the apartheid endgame and the making of the new South Africa.

Looking at the growth of the South African state after 1994, one might

[17] Ntsebeza, *Democracy Compromised*, pp.256-94.
[18] S. Ellis, 'The New Frontiers of Crime in South Africa', in J.-F. Bayart, S. Ellis and B. Hibou (eds.), *The Criminalisation of the State in Africa*, p.49.
[19] See also C. Campbell, 'Learning to Kill? Masculinity, the family and violence in Natal', *JSAS*, 18, 3 (1992), pp.614-28.
[20] Oomen, *Chiefs in South Africa*, p.2-3.

suggest that post-apartheid statecraft has largely concerned the incorporation of the marginal, discordant fragments. The scale of the enterprise is significant. Expenditure on social assistance programmes doubled in real terms between 1994 and 2004. For the size of its economy, South Africa has the largest welfare state in the world by some measures. There were similar increases in infrastructure expenditures – in programmes of school building, road improvements, electricity connections and the like. Government expenditure is now central in the lives of even the most remote rural homesteads: pensions and welfare grants now matter far more than migrant remittances or agricultural production. In 1994 only 35% of South African households were electrified. By 2007 around three-quarters of South African households were electrified.[21] When Epainette Mbeki and the family biographer returned to her village of birth in the late 1990s they apparently drove for hours without seeing electrified homesteads. If they had driven down the R56 a decade later they would have seen electricity lines leading from the road towards the mountains. The networks of the state were expanding even towards the most outlying communities.

The political economy of and prospects for this mode of state-building are questions that lie beyond the scope of this book. This is an effervescent debate in South Africa. Some are troubled by the expansion of the state, by the corrosive effects of persistent corruption and fruitless expenditure, by the narrowness of the tax base on which the entire edifice rests. By contrast, a left-wing critique of the ANC government argues that welfare transfers have not overturned the structural inequalities inherited from apartheid; that neoliberal policies have failed to bring broad-based economic growth. Somewhere in between these two poles lie another set of arguments about the politics of South Africa's 'welfare state'.[22]

Instead, I wish to draw a different set of conclusions about the delicate balance between state and society, and the fragmentary forms of citizenship and identity underpinning this relationship.[23] Take the growth of the state. At a central level, ANC ideology stresses 'nation-building', abhorring the centrifugal forces generated by Bantustan era 'tribalism'. They defend the importance of the unitary state in righting the inequalities of apartheid, especially its redistributive function of spreading the wealth generated in the mines and a small cluster of wealthy regions to the impoverished hinterlands. Nevertheless, the expansion of the centre has not been to the detriment of the regions. Formally, the national centre has given administrative powers to the provinces, who work through a third and fourth tier of districts and municipalities. And in any case everyone knows that the state does not operate through impersonal bureaucratic institutions, but rather through personal

---

[21] National Planning Commission, *Material Conditions Diagnostic* (Pretoria, 2011), p.41-2. A. Marquard, B. Bekker, A. Eberhard, T. Gaunt, 'South Africa's Electrification Programme: Overview and assessment' (Working paper, University of Cape Town, 2007) p.34.

[22] As Fredrick Cooper notes, the debates about the political economy of independent Kenya are now repeated in South Africa: 'Possibility and Constraint', pp.180-81.

[23] For a survey of Africa: P. Nugent, 'States and Social Contracts'. For parallel debates in Latin America and South Asia: Knight and Pansters, *Caciquismo*, P. Chatterjee, *The Nation and its Fragments* (Princeton, 1993), S. Khilnani, *The Idea of India* (London, 1997).

networks. As I have argued in Chapters Seven and Eight, regional elites have played a vital role in these developments – they are the filaments through which these currents flow. Again and again one sees national government ministers taking calls from school principals and municipal councillors back in Transkei, begging favours and asking for advice. In these new developments we perhaps are witnessing a national state being assembled from regional fragments.

'In this terrain, where state and society are increasingly difficult to distinguish ... local cultural forms... shape the state.'[24] Take, for instance, the ANC's appropriation of indigenous symbols. Researchers who have done fieldwork in Transkei for decades say they have never seen so many animals slaughtered in government ceremonies. Opposition parties complain at the amount of government money spent on ceremonies and *izimbizo* (gatherings).[25] From above, the ANC encourages identity politics only in so far as it promotes 'unity through diversity'. Intriguingly, most local forms of political protest prevalent in South Africa today take a mirror image: they do not demand autonomy but rather incorporation. South Africa is not like Kenya, where smallholder subsistence farming is still perceived to be a viable possibility, and local communities make demands for land and self-mastery. Rather, the assertions of local identity that we see in South Africa might be termed 'the politics of recognition' in which impoverished localities make claims on central government in the name of their community.

This chapter can only call attention to the ways in which the relationship between state and society has developed since 1994, rather than explore these issues in any depth. What we can be more certain of is that there has been a remarkable transformation in South African politics. In the early 1990s, senior ANC leaders were uncertain as to whether they commanded support inside South Africa's Bantustans. Today, these densely populated, rural areas have become a dominant part of party caucuses.

If this book opened with Nelson Mandela's account of his birth and early years in Transkei, so it should close with Madiba's death on 5 December 2013. A week later he was laid to rest at his place of birth at Qunu. In one sense this was the end of an era. Born, raised and schooled in the rural Eastern Cape during the first decades of the 20th century, Mandela was among the last of his generation. His close friends, Walter Sisulu and Oliver Tambo, had died in 2003 and 1993; his rival, Govan Mbeki, had passed in 2001. Nevertheless, these regional networks continue. South Africa's current crop of politicians and businessmen, many of whom were educated at South Africa's best schools in the Bantustans during the apartheid era, are in their political prime. Indeed, a number played a prominent role in the funeral ceremonies. And whilst the gathering at Qunu was a unique, global media event, driving through rural South Africa one sees scores of weddings and funerals every weekend, which are attended by prominent politicians and notables. Mandela's kinsmen remain deeply embedded within the political and social landscape of the country.

[24] W. Pansters 'Goodbye the Caciques', pp. 362-3.
[25] *Business Day* 5 May 2008. *Natal Mercury* 26 April 2012.

Bibliography

Note on abbreviations used in the footnotes: The abbreviations that are used in the footnotes are indicated below. The abbreviations/call-numbers given in brackets that are not starred ("*") are the ones used by the archivists. The abbreviations that are marked with stars are ones that I have made up for the sake of convenience.

The long form of box, file and reel references have also been abbreviated: for example, 'Flagstaff Magistrate, Box 6/42, File N1/1/5/6' is abbreviated to '1/FSF6/42, N1/1/5/6'; 'Department of Foreign Affairs, Transkei, Political Situation and Developments, BTS 1/226/1, Box 14' to 'BTS14'; 'Carter-Karis Collection, Reel 18' becomes 'CKC18'.

A number of journals have been abbreviated: The *Journal of Contemporary African Studies* becomes *JCAS* and the *Journal of Southern African Studies* becomes *JSAS*.

Manuscript and Archival Sources

Government Collections (printed)

Cape Archives, Cape Town
Chief Magistrate, Transkei – abbreviated to CMT
Magistrate, Cofimvaba – abbreviated to 1/COF
Magistrate, Engcobo – abbreviated to 1/ECO
Magistrate, Flagstaff – abbreviated to 1/FSF
Magistrate, Bizana – abbreviated to 1/BIZ
Magistrate, Mqanduli – abbreviated to 1/MQL
Magistrate, Umtata – abbreviated to 1/UTA
Magistrate, Xalanga – abbreviated to 1/XAL
Regional Director of Bantu Education, King Williams Town – abbreviated to BEK
Regional Director of Bantu Education – abbreviated to ERD

National Archives, Pretoria
Department of Foreign Affairs, Transkei, Political Situation and Developments – abbreviated to BTS
Department of Native Administration and Development – abbreviated to BAO
Department of Native Affairs – abbreviated to BO
Commissioner General, Transkei – abbreviated to KGT
Nelson Mandela Prison Files – abbreviated to NMPF*

Transkei Government Archives, Umtata – abbreviated to MTA*
Transkei Education Department:[1] 'Box 5: 9/1/10 Vol 1 – 9/3/3 Vol 2' and 'Box 7: 12/1/4 Vol 12 – 12/1/4-17'

Umtata High Court[2] – abbreviated to UHC*
CASE 168/1980: State vs. Thembile Handsome Magxinga and Zoyisile William Nelani
CASE 15/1982: State vs. Zamiwonga James Kati, Mveleli Junior Saliwa, Mzandile Mbethe, Mkangeli Manford Matomela, Fikile Alfred Marwangana and Bawose Peter King
CASE 58/1988: State vs. Ndibulele Ndzamela and Phumzile Mayaphi
CASE 158/88: State vs. George Matanzima
CASE 34P/89, 16/1989: State vs. Mzwandile Vena, Mzimkulu Tukela, Sonwabo Mbekela

Government Collections (online)

Truth and Reconciliation Commission – published (n.d.), accessed May 2007
http://www.justice.gov.za/trc/

Amnesty Decisions – abbreviated to TRC-AD*:
AC1998/34, AC1999/220, AC1999/227, AC2000/18, AC2000/36, AC2000/42, AC2000/45, AC2000/57, AC2000/76, AC2000/231, AC2000/240, AC2001/95, AC2001/231

Amnesty Hearings[3] – abbreviated to TRC-AH*:
East London, April 1999
Umtata, April 1999
Umtata, February 2000
Umtata, March 2000

Human Rights Violations Hearings[4] – abbreviated to TRC-VH*:
East London, April 1996
Lusikisiki, March 1996
Port Elizabeth, May 1996
Port Elizabeth, June 1996
Umtata, June 1996

Other Collections (printed)

Jeff Peires personal collection
'Minutes of meeting between Deputy President Walter Sisulu and Transkei ANC Regional Executive Committee and Transkei ANC Youth League', 1 August 1992
'Minutes of meeting held in General Holomisa's office, Botha Sigcawu building', August 1992

[1] The Umtata archives are in disarray. These were the markings on the boxes.
[2] The cases archived at Umtata High Court are relatively well ordered, but there is not a consistent indexing system so I provide full details of the cases.
[3] Reference numbers are inconsistent so are not listed.
[4] Reference numbers are inconsistent so are not listed.

South African Democracy Education Project – abbreviated to SADET
Interview, Charles Setsubi, 19 July 2001

T.D. Moodie personal collection
Interview, M. Mlungwana, Umtata, 1 July 1995

University of Cape Town, Manuscripts and Archives Centre
Carter-Karis Collection – abbreviated to CKC*
Karis-Gerhart Collection – abbreviated to KGC*

University of Fort Hare, Alice, Liberation Archives
Govan Mbeki Accession
Lusaka Accession

University of Fort Hare, Alice, National Heritage and Cultural Studies Centre,
Livingstone Mqotsi Collection – abbreviated to LMC*

University of KwaZulu Natal, Pietermaritzburg, Alan Paton Archives
Liberal Party of South Africa – abbreviated to PC2
Magnus Gunther – abbreviated to PC170
Randolph Vigne – abbreviated to PC86

University of South Africa, Pretoria – abbreviated to UNISA
D.A. Kotze Accession
Ntonjeni Accession
Transkei Council of Churches Accession – abbreviated to ACC318
Transkei Government Accession – abbreviated to AAS45

University of Witwatersrand, Historical Papers
Anglican Church of Southern Africa, Diocese of St Johns – abbreviated to AB1886

Other Collections (online)

Nordic Documentation Centre on the Liberation Struggle in Southern Africa
Interview, Mzolisi Mabude – published n.d., accessed March 2009
http://www.liberationafrica.se/intervstories/interviews/mabude/?by-name=1

O'Malley collection – published (n.d.), accessed May 2007
www.nelsonmandela.org/omalley
African National Congress, National Executive Council meeting, 27 October 1989
African National Congress, National Working Committee meeting, 11 May 1990
African National Congress, Interim Leadership Core meeting, 20 June 1990
Interview, Pik Botha, 13 December 1999
Interview, Jac Buchner, 12 November 1996
Interview, Bantu Holomisa, 22 July 1990
Interviews, Pathekile Holomisa, 22 August 1993, 19 October 1996

Author's Field-notes and Interviews

Author's Field-notes, Bumbane, 1 October 2008, Umtata, 27 September 2008
John Allwood, East London, 30 October 2008, King Williams Town, 14 November 2008
Reg Barry, Bhisho, 17 November 2008
Sakhela Buhlungu, Johannesburg, 26 August 2009
Richard Canca, Dutywa, 7 November 2008
Buyelekhaya Dalindyebo, Bumbane, 1 October 2008
Patrick Dalindyebo, Port Elizabeth, 22 November 2008
Somadoda Fikeni, Pretoria, 24 July 2008
Glen Fisher, phone interview, 1 October 2009
Anderson Ganyile, Bizana, 3 April 2008
Daniel Ganyile, Bizana, 5 April 2008
Bantu Holomisa, Pretoria, 2 September 2008
Pathekile Holomisa, Cape Town, 18 September 2009
Greg Houston, Pretoria, 21 July 2008
Mangaliso Kenny Jafta, Dutywa, 10 November 2008
Mike Kenyon, East London, 20 October 2008
Joseph Kobo, Umtata, 10 November 2008
Zoleka Langa, Flagstaff, 9 November 2008, 23 September 2009
Bukhosi Mabandla, King Williams Town, 17 November 2008
Oyama Mabandla, Johannesburg, 1 September 2009
Prince Madikizela, Umtata, 30 September 2008
Dumisani Mafu, King Williams Town, 19 October 2008
Mcebisi Magadla, East London, 21 October 2008, 31 October 2008
Ngangomhlaba Matanzima, Qamata, 15 November 2008
Thembile Templeton (T.T.) Matanzima, Pretoria, 2 September 2009
Nomonde Matiso, Umtata, 22 September 2009
Mkhangeli Manford Matomela, East London, 30 October 2008
Pumzile Mayaphi, East London, 11 November 2008
Kaiser Mbete, East London, 25 September 2009
Mda Mda, Viedgesville, 3 November 2008
Mojo Mdikane, Umtata, 3 November 2008
Leonard Mdingi, Bizana 2 April, 3 April 2008
Israel Mdingi, Bizana, 4 April 2008
Advocate Mdutshane, Umtata, 19 November 2008
Rob Morrell, Durban, 8 September 2008
Livingstone Mqotsi, East London, 13 November 2008
Mashwaba Melville Msizi, Bhisho, 17 November 2008
Mvula Mthimkulu, East London, 13 November 2008
Lindi Ndabeni, Johannesburg, 31 August 2008
Lungi Ndamase, Bhisho, 20 November 2008
Zoyisile William Nelani, Umtata, 6 November 2008
Mwelo Nonkonyana, Cape Town, 18 September 2009
Dumisa Ntsebeza, Johannesburg, 26 August 2009
Velile Ntsubane, Libode, 19 November 2008
Cas Paulsen, Umtata, 21 September 2009
Jeff Peires, King Williams Town, 10 August 2007, 22 October 2008
Glen Robbins, Durban, 28 July 2007
Mvelile Junior Saliwa, Umtata, 21 September 2009
Sandy Shell, Cape Town, 16 May 2008
Ezra Sigwela, Pretoria, 27 August, 1 September 2009

Simphiwe Somdyala, East London, 18 November 2008
Chris Tapscott, Cape Town, 7 September 2009
Wolfgang Thomas, Cape Town, 11 September 2009
Andrew Trench, East London, 12 November 2008
Zweliyanika Vena, Grahamstown, 27 October 2008
Val Viljoen, East London, 20 October 2008
Peter Wakelin, Kimberly, 30 August 2009
Richard Wicksteed, Cape Town, 12 June 2008

Printed Primary Sources

Printed Sources Held in Libraries and Personal Archives

African Studies Library, University of Cape Town
Black Community Programmes, *Transkei Independence* (Black Viewpoint 4, Durban, 1976)

Authors Collection
Debates of the Legislature of the Eastern Cape (King Williams Town, 1994-2008)
Department of Agriculture and Lands Affairs, *Annual Reports* (King Williams Town, 1995-2008)
Department of Agriculture and Lands Affairs, *Green Revolution,* (King Williams Town, 2006)
Mqingwana V. and J. Peires, *Chris Hani Municipality Liberation Heritage Route: Icon Site Guide* (n.d., 2008?)

Rhodes University, Cory Library
E.G. Sihele, *Ngobani na abaThembu, bevela phi na?*
Praise poems in honour of King Sabata in *Umthunywa* (PR 3669)
Making Government Work for Poor People in the Eastern Cape: A report for the Department for International Development, UK (Pamphlet Box 226)

South African Parliamentary Library, Cape Town
Eastern Cape Department of Agriculture and Land Affairs, *Annual Reports* (King Williams Town, 1995–)
Eastern Cape Department of Agriculture and Land Affairs, *Strategic Plan, 2004 – 7,* (King Williams Town, 2004)

University of Cape Town, Government Publications Library
African National Congress, *The Rise and Fall of Bantu Holomisa* (Johannesburg, 1997)
Alexander G., *Interim Report of the Commission of Inquiry into the Department of Works and Engineering* (Umtata, 1987)
Alexander G., *Commission of Enquiry into the Department of Works and Engineering: Third report with particular reference to gambling rights and related matters* (Umtata, 1988)
Cingo M., *Report of the Commission of Inquiry into the teaching of the official languages and the use of the Mother Tongue as medium of instruction in Transkeian primary schools* (Pretoria, October 1962)
Department of Agriculture and Forestry, *Annual Reports* (Umtata, 1964-94)
Department of Education, *Annual Reports* (Umtata, 1964-94)
Habib A., *Structural constraints, managerial ineptitude, and stakeholder complicity: a study*

Bibliography

of the institutional crisis of the University of Transkei (Pretoria, 2001)

Harms L., *Report of the Commission of Inquiry into Certain Possible Irregularities or Illegalities – second report – Transkei Gambling Rights* (Pretoria, 1989)

Hawkins Associates, *The Physical and Spatial Basis for Transkei's First Five Year Development Plan* (Salisbury, Zimbabwe, October 1980)

Holomisa B., *Comrades in Corruption* (Johannesburg, 1997)

Kakana G.L., Ntusi D.M., Nkungu T.M., *Report on the Standards of Education in the Transkei* (Umtata, 1973)

Lugaju A.V.M., *Report of Commission of Inquiry into Activities of Police and Military relative to the Teacher's Strike', 24 September – 20 October 1993* (Umtata, 1993)

Office of the Auditor General, *Report of the Auditor General on the Appropriation and Miscellaneous Accounts and on the Accounts of Lower Authorities* (Umtata, 1964-94)

Republic of Transkei, *Development Strategy, 1980-2000* (Umtata, 1979)

Republic of Transkei, *Estimates of Expenditure to be defrayed from the Transkeian Revenue Fund* (Umtata, 1964-94)

Republic of Transkei, *Transkei Agricultural Development Study* (Umtata, 1991)

Taylor A., *Report of the Commission of Inquiry into Education in the Republic of Transkei* (Umtata, 1979)

Tsotsi W., *Keynote Address delivered at the annual conference of the Transkei Teachers Association held at Umtata on 9-11 July 1990*, (Umtata, 1990)

Van Reenen T.H., *Report of the Commission of Inquiry into the Department of Works and Energy on the Butterworth and Ezibeleni Housing Contracts* (Umtata, 1988)

University of Fort Hare, East London Campus, Government Publications Section

Government of Transkei, *Standards within the civil service of Transkei with particular regard to co-ordination, efficiency and effectiveness*, (Umtata, March 1991)

Government of Transkei, *Financial Transfers from the RSA to Transkei, 1990/1 to 1992/3, in the context of the interdependent nature of the Southern African economy: Position paper of the Transkei Government, presented at the 7th December 1989 discussions with the RSA Government and the DBSA*, (Umtata, December 1989)

Government of Transkei, *Transkei Government Finance: Motivations to JFAC in March and September 1988*, (Umtata, 1988)

University of Oxford, Rhodes House Library

Debates of the Transkei Legislative Assembly (Umtata, 1964-76) – abbreviated to *TLA*

Debates of the National Assembly, Republic of Transkei (Umtata, 1977-87) – abbreviated to *TNA*

Holomisa B. and R. Meyer, *A Better Future: United Democratic Movement towards a winning nation in ten years* (Pretoria, 1999)

Truth and Reconciliation Commission Reports (Cape Town, 1998)

United Nations, *Report on the International Hearing on Political Violence in South Africa and the Implementation of the National Peace Accord* (London, 1992)

Who's Who of Southern Africa (Johannesburg, 1994, 1997)

University of Witwatersrand, Government Publications Library

Laborateur (Umtata, 1980-85)

Transkei Development Review (Umtata, 1980-85)

Wolfgang Thomas Private Collection

Information about the Institute for Development and Management Studies, (September 1980)

Report on Institute for Development and Management Studies Activities, September 1980 –

December 1981, (February 1982)

Thomas W., *Faculty of Economic Sciences: Proposal for steps to improve student performance*, (February 1981)

Thomas W., *The Hawkins Report: First of a new type of planning report*, (February 1981)

Thomas W., *The Homeland Dimension to the Fiscal Restructuring of South Africa*, (December 1992)

Online Printed Sources

ANC Documents

ANC 49th National Conference: National Executive Committee voting results
http://www.anc.org.za/show.php?doc=ancdocs/history/conf/conference49/necvot49.html

'Further Submissions and Responses by the African National Congress to Questions Raised by the Commission for Truth and Reconciliation', 12 May 1997 www.anc.org.za/ancdocs/misc/trc2.html

Politicsweb

'Statement by the Democratic Alliance' – published 3 March 2010, accessed 16 December 2012 http://www.politicsweb.co.za/politicsweb/view/politicsweb/en/page71651?oid=163714&sn=Detail.

'Statement of the Presidency', published 6 April 2010, accessed 16 December 2012 http://www.politicsweb.co.za/politicsweb/view/politicsweb/en/page71656?oid=169605&sn=Detail

South African Constitutional Court

'Current constitutional court judges' – published (n.d.), accessed 18 December 2012 http://www.constitutionalcourt.org.za/site/judges/currentjudges.htm

South African History Online

'Richard Canca biography' – published (n.d.), accessed 12 February 2012 http://www.sahistory.org.za/people/richard-s-canca

'Joe Modise biography' – published (n.d.), accessed 12 March 2013 http://www.sahistory.org.za/people/johannes-joe-modise

Newspapers and Periodicals

Note: I used a number of press clippings archives, most notably: Barry Streek Collection, Mayibuye Centre, Cape Town; *Daily Dispatch* archive, East London; Digital Innovation South Africa (DISA). A number of Government files – particularly CMT and BTS 1/226/1 – archived clippings. I provide details of the location of the less accessible publications.

Africa Confidential
African Communist
Armed Forces (found at Lusaka Accession, Liberation Archives)
Cape Argus
Cape Times
City Press
Daily Dispatch– abbreviated to *DD*
Drum

Financial Mail
Instimbi Xhosa News (found at Ntonjeni Accession, UNISA)
Isizwe (found at National Library, Cape Town)
Izwe Lomzi (found in CMT and KGT)
Johannesburg Star – abbreviated to *Star*
Leadership South Africa
Mail and Guardian – abbreviated to *M&G*
Millennium
New Age
New Republic
Pretoria News
Rand Daily Mail – abbreviated to *RDM*
Reality (found in CKC)
Sechaba (found in GKC and DISA)
South African Press Association – abbreviated to *SAPA*
Southscan (found in KGC)
Sunday Independent
Sunday Times
Transkei Liberal News (found in PC2 and PC86)
Weekly Mail

Newspapers and periodicals (online)
BBC News, 'The ANC at 100' – published 6 January 2012, accessed 10 January 2013
　　http://www.bbc.co.uk/news/world-africa-16442287
Daily Telegraph, 'Obituary, Lieutenant Colonel Ron Reid-Daly' – published 20 September
　　2010, accessed 2 February 2013
　　http://www.telegraph.co.uk/news/obituaries/military-obituaries/special-forces-
　　obituaries/8014261/Lieutenant-Colonel-Ron-Reid-Daly.html
Molotov Cocktail – published March 2008, accessed 10 May 2009 (subsequently taken
　　off the web – a copy is in the possession of the author)
　　http://www.molotovcocktail.co.za/pdf/edition4.pdf

Unpublished Theses, Typescripts and other Grey Literature

Adato M., '"They Have Been Given Democracy": Mediated models, democratic meanings
　　and co-operative development in the Transkei', Witwatersrand University, (History
　　Workshop Conference, 13-5 July 1994)
Ainslie A., with T. Kepe, L. Ntsebeza, Z. Ntshone and S. Turner, 'Cattle Ownership and
　　Production in the Communal Areas of the Eastern Cape', (University of the Western
　　Cape, Research Report No. 10, 2002)
Andrew M. and R. Fox, 'Cultivation Trends in the Transkei and Ciskei, 1940-96', (Fort
　　Hare Institute of Social and Economic Research conference paper, 2003)
Barron F., 'The Trouble with Teacher Training in Transkei', (University of Cape Town,
　　Honours thesis, 1991)
Bembridge T., 'Aspects of Agriculture and Rural Poverty in Transkei', (Cape Town,
　　Carnegie Inquiry paper, 1984)
Bembridge T., 'Problems of Agricultural Development in the Republic of Transkei:
　　A preliminary summary', (Stellenbosch, Research report for the Urban-Rural
　　Workshop, 1982)
Bundy C., 'Schooled for Life? The childhood and education of Govan Mbeki', (Yale
　　University, Seminar Paper, 2 December 1992)

Bibliography

Bundy C., 'Breaking the Midnight Slumber: Govan Mbeki in the Transkei, 1940-48,' (Institute of Historical Research seminar paper, 28 September 1998)

Donaldson A., 'Aspects of the Economics of Education in Transkei', (University of South Africa, M.A. thesis, 1984)

du Preez J.N., 'The Educational System in Transkei: A needs assessment', (University of Orange Free State, M.A. thesis, 1980)

Fikeni S., 'Conflict and Accommodation: The politics of rural local government in post-apartheid South Africa', (Michigan State University, Ph.D. thesis, 2008)

Groves Z., 'Malawians in Colonial Salisbury: A social history of migration in central Africa, c.1920s-1960s' (Ph.D. thesis, Keele University, 2011)

Hadfield L., 'Restoring Human Dignity and Building Self-Reliance: Youth, women, church and Black Consciousness community development, South Africa, 1969-1977', (PhD thesis, Michigan State University, 2010).

Hendricks F., 'Preliminary Notes on Land and Livestock in Libode', (Carnegie Conference paper 294, Cape Town, 1984)

Kepe T., 'Grassland Vegetation and Rural Livelihoods: A case study of resource value and social dynamics on the Wild Coast, South Africa', (University of the Western Cape, Ph.D. thesis, 2002)

Koyana D., 'A Constitutional History of Transkei', (Pretoria University, Ph.D. thesis, 1994)

Manona S. 'Smallholder Agriculture as Local Economic Development Strategy in Rural South Africa: Exploring prospects in Pondoland, Eastern Cape', (University of Western Cape, M.A. thesis, 2005)

Marquard A., B. Bekker, A. Eberhard, T. Gaunt, 'South Africa's Electrification Programme: Overview and assessment' (University of Cape Town, Working Paper, 2007)

McAllister P., 'Xhosa Co-operative Work Groups', (Fort Hare Institute of Social and Economic Research, Working Paper 12, 2003)

Mokvist A., 'Democratisation, Traditional Leadership and Reform Politics in South Africa', (Uppsala University, Ph.D. thesis, 2006)

Moodie T. D., 'The Rise and Demise of Lira Setona? Questions of race and how the NUM became a social movement', (typescript, n.d.)

Moreku C., *Community and Church during the Apartheid Era: A focus on the projects of the Transkei Council of Churches*, (University of South Africa, M.A. thesis, 2003)

Murphy O., 'Race, Violence and Nation: African nationalism and popular politics in South Africa's Eastern Cape, 1948-1970' (Oxford University, D.Phil. thesis, 2013)

National Planning Commission, *Material Conditions Diagnostic* (Pretoria, 2011)

Ngubentombi S., 'Teacher Education in Transkei', (University of Natal, Ph.D. thesis, 1984)

Ntsebeza L, 'Land Tenure Reform, Traditional Authorities and Rural Local Government in Post-Apartheid South Africa', (University of the Western Cape, Research Report No. 3, 1999).

Philip T., 'Enterprise Development on the Margins: Making markets work for the poor', (Witwatersrand University, PhD thesis, 2006)

Simpson T., 'The People's War of Umkhonto we Sizwe' (University of London, PhD thesis, 2006)

Southall R. and Woodall G., 'Control and Contestation: State security in South Africa' Homelands', (Grahamstown, Report to the TRC, n.d.)

Tapscott C., 'The Rise of Development as a Policy Theory in South Africa, 1978-88: A critique', (London School of Economics, Ph.D. Thesis, 1992)

Tapson D., 'Proposals for a Cattle Marketing Strategy for Transkei', (Agricultural and Rural Development Institute, Fort Hare, Report No. 1/82, Alice, 1982)

Wotshela L., 'Homeland Consolidation, Resettlement and Local Politics in the Border and Ciskei Region of the Eastern Cape, 1960-66', (Oxford, D.Phil. thesis, 2001)

Books and Articles

Alexander J., *The Unsettled Land: State-making and the politics of land in Zimbabwe, 1893-2003* (Oxford, 2006)

Allman J., *The Quills of the Porcupine: Asante nationalism in an emergent Ghana* (Madison, 1993)

Anderson B., *Imagined Communities: Reflections on the origin and spread of nationalism,* 13th edn. (London, 2003)

Anderson D., *Histories of the Hanged: Britain's dirty war in Kenya* (London, 2005)

Bank L. and R. Southall, 'Traditional Leaders in South Africa's New Democracy', *Journal of Legal Pluralism and Unofficial Law,* 37-8 (1996), pp.407-30

Barrell H., 'The Turn to the Masses: The ANC strategic review of 1978-9', *Journal of Southern African Studies,* 18, 1 (1992), pp.64-92

Bayart J.-F., S. Ellis and B. Hibou (eds.), *The Criminalisation of the State in Africa* (Oxford, 1999)

Beall J., S. Mkhize and S. Vawda, 'Emergent Democracy and "Resurgent" Tradition: Institutions, chieftaincy and transition in KwaZulu Natal', *Journal of Southern African Studies,* 31, 4 (2005), pp.755-71

Beinart W., 'Agrarian Historiography and Reconstruction', in Lonsdale J. (ed.), *South Africa in Question* (Cambridge, 1988), pp.134-53

Beinart W., 'Beyond the Homelands: Some ideas about the history of African rural areas in South Africa', *South African Historical Journal,* 64, 1 (2012), pp.5-21

Beinart W., 'Chieftaincy and the Concept of Articulation: South Africa, 1900-50', *Canadian Journal of African Studies,* 19 (1985), pp.91-8

Beinart W., *The Political Economy of Pondoland* (Johannesburg, 1982)

Beinart W., *Twentieth Century South Africa* (Oxford, 2001)

Beinart W. and Bundy C., *Hidden Struggles in Rural South Africa: Politics and popular movements in Transkei and the Eastern Cape, 1890-1930* (London, 1987)

Bell T. and D. Ntsebeza, *Unfinished Business: South Africa, apartheid and truth* (London, 2003)

du Preez Bezdrob A., *Winnie Mandela: A life* (Cape Town, 2003)

Blair D., *Degrees in Violence: Robert Mugabe and the struggle for power in Zimbabwe* (London, 2002)

Bonner P., *Kings, Commoners and Concessionaires: The evolution and dissolution of the nineteenth-century Swazi state* (Cambridge, 1983)

Bradford H., 'Highways, Byways and Cul-de-Sacs: The transition to agrarian capitalism in revisionist South African history', *Radical History Review,* 46, 7 (1990), pp.59-88

Branch D., *Defeating Mau Mau, Creating Kenya: Counterinsurgency, civil war and decolonisation* (Cambridge, 2009)

Bundy C., *Govan Mbeki* (Athens OH, 2013)

Bundy C., *The Rise and Fall of the South African Peasantry,* 2nd edn. (London, 1988)

Callinicos L., *Oliver Tambo: Beyond the Engeli Mountains* (Claremont, 2004)

Campbell C., 'Learning to Kill? Masculinity, the family and violence in Natal', *Journal of Southern African Studies,* 18, 3 (1992), pp.614-28

Carter G., T. Karis and N. Stultz, *South Africa's Transkei: The politics of domestic colonialism* (London, 1967)

Chandarvarkar R., 'Imperialism and the European Empires', in J. Jackson (ed.), *The Short Oxford History of Europe, 1900-45* (Oxford, 2002), pp.138-72

Charton N., 'Black Elites in the Transkei,' *Politikon*, 3, 2 (1976), pp.61-74

Chatterjee P., *The Nation and its Fragments* (Princeton, 1993)

Cherry J. and Bank L., 'A Tale of Two Homelands: Transkei, Ciskei', *Southern Africa Report*, 9, 1 (1994), pp.25-30

Cobley A., *Class and Consciousness: The black petty bourgeoisie in South Africa, 1924-50* (London, 1990)

Comaroff J., 'Reflections on the Colonial State in South Africa and Elsewhere: Factions, fragments, facts and fictions', *Social Identities*, 4, 3 (1998), pp.321-61

Cooper F., 'Possibility and Constraint: African independence in historical perspective', *Journal of African History*, 49, 2 (2008), pp.167-96.

Cope N., 'The Zulu Petit-Bourgeoisie and Zulu Nationalism in the 1920s: the origins of Inkatha', *Journal of Southern African Studies*, 16, 3 (1990), pp.431-51

Coplan D. and Quinlan T., 'A chief by the people: Nation and state in Lesotho', *Africa*, 67 (1997), pp.27-60

Cousins B. and Kepe T., 'Decentralisation When Land and Resource Rights are Deeply Contested: A case study of the Mkambati eco-tourism project on the Wild Coast of South Africa', *European Journal of Development Research*, 16, 1 (2004), pp.41-54

Couzens T., *The New African: A study of HIE Dhlomo* (Johannesburg, 1985)

Crais C., *The Politics of Evil: Magic, state power and the political imagination in South Africa* (Cambridge, 2002)

Crais C., *White Supremacy and Black Resistance in pre-industrial South Africa* (Cambridge, 1992)

Delius P., *A Lion Amongst the Cattle: Reconstruction and resistance in the Northern Transvaal* (Oxford, 1996)

Delius P., *The Land Belongs to Us: The Pedi polity, the Boers and the British in the nineteenth-century Transvaal* (London, 1984)

Denis P. and G. Duncan, *The Native School that caused all the trouble: A history of the Federal Theological Seminary of Southern Africa* (Pietermaritzburg, 2011)

Dubow S., 'Holding a Just Balance between Black and White', *Journal of Southern African Studies* 12, 2 (1986), pp.217-39

de Wet C., *Moving Together, Drifting Apart: Betterment planning and villagisation in a South African Homeland* (Johannesburg, 1995)

Dlamini J., *Native Nostalgia* (Johannesburg, 2010)

Elkins C., *Britain's Gulag: The brutal end of empire in Kenya* (London, 2005)

Ellis S., 'The ANC in Exile' *African Affairs*, 90 (1991), pp.439-47

Ellis S., 'The Historical Significance of South Africa's Third Force', *Journal of Southern African Studies*, 24, 2 (1998), pp.261-99

Ellis S. and Sechaba T., *Comrades Against Apartheid: The ANC and South African Communist Party in exile* (London, 1992)

Ferguson J., *The Anti-Politics Machine: "Development", de-politicisation and bureaucratic power in Lesotho* (London, 1996)

Geiger S., *TANU Women: Gender, culture in the making of Tanganyikan nationalism, 1955-65* (Oxford, 1997)

Gevisser M., *Thabo Mbeki: The dream deferred* (Johannesburg, 2007)

Gibbs T., 'Chris Hani's "Country Bumpkins": Regional networks in the African National Congress underground, 1974-94', *Journal of Southern African Studies*, 37, 4 (2011), pp.677-91

Gibbs T. 'From Popular Resistance to Populist Politics in Transkei', in Beinart W. and M. Dawson (eds.), *Popular Politics and Resistance Movements in South Africa, 1970-2008* (Johannesburg, 2010), pp.141-60

Giliomee H., 'Surrender without Defeat: Afrikaners and the South African "miracle"',

Daedalus, 126, 2 (Spring 1997), pp.113-146

Glaser C., *Bo-Tsotsi: The youth gangs of Soweto* (Oxford, 2000)

Gobodo-Madikizela P., *A Human Being Died That Night: A story of forgiveness* (Cape Town, 2003)

Graaff J., 'Towards an Understanding of Bantustan Politics', in Nattrass N. and E. Arlington (eds.), *The Political Economy of South Africa* (Oxford, 1990), pp.55-72

Grundy K., *Soldiers Without Politics: Blacks in the South African armed forces* (London, 1983)

Gumede W., *Thabo Mbeki and the Battle for the Soul of the ANC* (Cape Town, 2005)

Guy J., *The Destruction of the Zulu Kingdom: The civil war in Zululand, 1879-1884* (London, 1979)

Haines E., 'The Transkei Trader', *South African Journal of Economics*, 1, 2 (1933), pp.201-16

Hajdu F., 'Relying on Jobs instead of the Environment? Patterns of local securities in the rural Eastern Cape', *Social Dynamics*, 31, 1 (2005), pp.235-60

Hammond-Tooke W.D., 'Chieftainship in Transkeian Political Development', *Journal of Modern African Studies*, 2,4 (1964), pp.513-29

Hammond-Tooke W.D., *Command or Consensus: The development of Transkeian local government* (Cape Town, 1975)

Hartshorne K., *Crisis and Challenge: Black Education, 1910 – 1990* (Oxford, 1992)

Hastings A., *The Construction of Nationhood: Ethnicity, religion and nationalism* (Cambridge, 1997)

la Hausse P., *Restless Identities: Signatures of nationalism, Zulu ethnicity and history* (Pietermaritzburg, 2000)

Healy M., *'A World of Their Own': A history of South African women's education* (Durban, 2013).

Hendricks F., *The Pillars of Apartheid: Land tenure, rural planning and the chieftaincy* (Stockholm, 1990)

Hughes H., *The First President: A life of John L. Dube, founding president of the ANC* (Johannesburg, 2011)

Hunter E., 'Revisiting *Ujamaa*: Political legitimacy and the construction of community in post-colonial Tanzania', *Journal of East African Studies*, 2, 3 (2008), pp.471-85

Hunter M., *Reaction to Conquest: Effects of contact with Europeans on the Pondo of South Africa*, 2nd edn. (London, 1961)

Hyslop J., '"A Destruction Coming In": Bantu Education as a response to social crisis', in Bonner P., Delius P., Posel D. (eds.), *Apartheid's Genesis, 1935-62* (Johannesburg, 1993), pp.393-410

Hyslop J., *The Classroom Struggle: Policy and resistance in South Africa, 1940-90* (Pietermaritzburg, 1999)

Iliffe J., *Africans: History of a continent* (Cambridge, 1995)

Jeffery A., *The Natal Story: Sixteen years of conflict* (Johannesburg, 1997)

Jones P., 'From Nationhood to Regionalism to the North West Province: Bophuthatswananess and the birth of the New South Africa', *African Affairs*, 98 (1999), pp.509-34

Journal of Contemporary African Studies, 11, 2 (1992) – special issue on the Transkei

Jozana X., 'The Transkeian Middle Class: Its political implications', *Africa Perspective*, 1, 7&8 (1989), pp.94-104

Kepe T., 'Clearing the Ground in Spatial development Initiatives: Analysing "process" on South Africa's Wild Coast', *Development South Africa*, 18, 3 (2001), pp.279-93

Kepe T., 'The Magwa Tea Venture in South Africa: Politics, land and economics', *Social Dynamics*, 31, 1 (2005), pp.261-79

Kepe T. and L. Ntsebeza (eds.), *Rural Resistance in South Africa: The Mpondo revolts after fifty years* (Cape Town, 2012)

Khandlhela R., 'The Trappists in South Africa: A short overview', *Kleio*, 27, 1 (1995), pp.46-62

Khilnani S., *The Idea of India* (London, 1997)

Knight A. and Pansters W. (eds.), *Caciquismo in Twentieth-Century Mexico* (London, 2005)

Harrison P. , *South Africa's Top Sites: Struggle* (Cape Town, 2004)

Holomisa P., *According to Tradition: A cultural perspective on current affairs* (Somerset West, 2009)

Krog A., *Country of My Skull* (Johannesburg, 2002)

Kuper L., *An African Bourgeoisie: Race, class and politics in South Africa* (London, 1965)

Lekgoathi P., 'Teacher Militancy in a Rural Northern Transvaal Community of Zebediela, 1986-94', *South African Historical Journal*, 58, 1 (2007), pp.226-52

Laurence P., *The Transkei: South Africa's politics of partition* (Johannesburg, 1976)

Lodge T., *Mandela: A critical life* (Oxford, 2006)

Lodge T., 'Patrick Duncan and Radical Liberalism' in *African Seminar: Collected Papers, Volume I* (1978), pp.108-21

Lentz C., 'Home, Death and Leadership: Discourses of an educated elite from north-western Ghana, *Social Anthropology* 2, 2 (1994) pp.149-69

Lentz C., 'Tribalism and Ethnicity in Africa: A review of four decades of Anglophone research', *Cahiers des Sciences Humaines*, 31 (1995), pp.303-28

Lonsdale J., 'Anti-Colonial Nationalism and Patriotism in sub-Saharan Africa', in J. Breiully (ed.), *The Oxford Handbook of the History of Nationalism* (Oxford, 2013), pp.304-18

Lonsdale J., 'The Moral Economy of Mau Mau: Wealth, poverty and civic virtue in Kikuyu political thought', in Lonsdale J. and B. Berman (eds.), *Unhappy Valley: Conflict in Kenya and Africa* (London, 1992), pp.265-468

Low D. and J. Lonsdale, 'Introduction', in D. Low and A. Smith (eds.), *The Oxford History of East Africa* (Oxford, 1976), pp.1-64.

Magaziner D., *The Law and the Prophets: Black Consciousness in South Africa, 1968-1977* (Athens OH, 2010)

Mager A., *Gender and the Making of a South African Bantustan: A social history of Ciskei, 1945-59* (Portsmouth NH, 1999)

Makoena H., *Magema Fuze: The making of a kholwa intellectual* (Pietermaritzburg, 2011)

Malan R., *My Traitor's Heart* (New York, 1990)

Mamdani M., *Citizen and Subject: Contemporary Africa and the Legacy of Late Colonialism* (London, 1996)

Mandela N., *The Long Walk to Freedom: The autobiography of Nelson Mandela* (London, 1995)

Mare G. and Hamilton G., *An Appetite for Power: Buthelezi's Inkhata and the politics of "loyal resistance"* (Johannesburg, 1987)

Marks S., *Divided Sisterhood: Race, class and gender in the South African nursing profession* (Basingstoke, 1994)

Marks S., *The Ambiguities of Dependence in South Africa: Class, nationalism and the state in 20th century Natal* (Baltimore, 1986)

Mayer P., 'The Tribal Elite and the Transkeian Elections of 1963', in Lloyd P. (ed.), *The New Elites of Tropical Africa* (Oxford, 1966), pp.286-311

Mbeki G., *South Africa: The peasants revolt* (Harmondsworth, 1964)

Mbeki G., *The Struggle for Liberation in South Africa* (Cape Town, 1992)

McAllister P., 'Resistance to Betterment in Transkei: A case study from Willowvale district', *Journal of Southern African Studies*, 15, 2 (1989), pp.346-68

McGregor A., *Blythswood Missionary Institution, 1877-1977* (KingWilliams Town, 1977)

Morrell R., 'Books and Batons', *Work in Progress* (1984), pp.3-9

Murray C., *Black Mountain: Land, class and power in the eastern Orange Free State, 1880s-1980s* (Edinburgh, 1992)

Murray M., 'The Origins of Agrarian Capitalism in South Africa: A critique of the "social history" perspective', *Journal of Southern African Studies*, 15, 4 (1989), pp.645-65

Mwakikagile G., *Nyerere and Africa: End of an era* (Pretoria, 2010)

Mzamane M., *The Children of Soweto* (Harlow, 1987)

Ndima D., *Law of Commoners and Kings: Narratives of a rural Transkei Magistrate* (Pretoria, 2004)

Ngubentombi S., *Education in the Republic of Transkei: Some origins, issues, trends and challenges* (Pretoria, 1989)

Ngwane Z., 'Apartheid Under Education,' in P. Kallaway (ed.), *A History of Education Under Apartheid, 1948-1994* (New York, 2004), pp.270-87

Ngwane Z., '"Real Men Reawaken their Father's Homesteads, the Educated leave them in Ruins": The politics of domestic reproduction in post-apartheid rural South Africa,' *Journal of Religion in Africa*, 31, 4 (2001), pp.402-26

Noble V., *A School for Struggle: A history of the Durban Medical School and the education of black doctors in South Africa* (Durban, forthcoming).

Ntsebeza L., *Democracy Compromised: Chiefs and the Politics of Land in South Africa* (Cape Town, 2006)

Nugent P., 'States and Social Contracts in Africa', *New Left Review*, 63 (2010), pp.35-68

O'Malley P., *Shades of Difference: Mac Maharaj and the struggle for South Africa* (Johannesburg, 2007)

Oomen B., *Chiefs in South Africa: Law, power and culture in the post-apartheid era* (Oxford, 2005)

Oomen B., 'We must now go back to our History: Re-traditionalisation in a Northern Province chieftaincy', *African Studies*, 59, 1 (2000), pp.71-95

Opland J., *Xhosa Oral Poetry: Aspects of a black South African tradition* (Cambridge, 1983)

Palmer R., H. Timmermans and D. Fay, *From Conflict to Negotiation: Nature-based development on South Africa's Wild Coast* (Pretoria, 2002)

Paton A., *Hofmeyr*, (Oxford, 1964)

Peires J., *The House of Phalo: A history of the Xhosa people in the days of their independence* (Johannesburg, 1981)

Peires J., 'The Implosion of Transkei and Ciskei', *African Affairs*, 91 (1992), pp.365-87

Peires J., 'Traditional Leaders in Purgatory: Local government in Tsolo, Qumbu and Port St Johns, 1990-2000', *African Studies*, 59 (2000), pp.97-114

Peires, 'Transkei on the Verge of Emancipation', in P. Rich (ed.), *Reaction and Renewal in South Africa* (Basingstoke, 1994), pp.192-221

Power J., *Building Kwacha: Political culture and nationalism in Malawi* (Rochester, 2010)

Raftopoulus B., 'Problematising Nationalism in Zimbabwe: a historiographical review', *Zambezia*, 26, 2 (1999), pp.115-34

Ramphele M., *Mamphela Ramphele: A life* (Cape Town, 1995)

Ranger T., *Are we not also Men: The Samkange family and African politics in Zimbabwe, 1920-64* (London, 1995)

Ranger T., *Peasant Consciousness and Guerrilla War in Zimbabwe: A comparative study* (London, 1985)

Ranger T., 'The Invention of Tradition in Colonial Africa', in E. Hobsbawm and T. Ranger (eds.), *The Invention of Tradition* (Cambridge, 1983), pp.211-259

Ranger T., 'The Invention of Tribalism Revisited: The case of colonial Africa', in T. Ranger and O. Vaughn (eds.), *Legitimacy and the State in Twentieth Century Africa: Essays in honour of A.H.M. Kirk-Greene* (London, 1993), p.62-111

Ranger T., *Voices from the Rocks: Nature, culture and history in the Matopos Hills of*

Zimbabwe (Oxford, 1999)

Rathbone R., *Nkrumah and the Chiefs: The politics of chieftaincy in Ghana, 1951-60* (Oxford, 2000)

Redding S., 'Peasants and the Creation of an African Middle Class in Umtata, 1880-1950', *The International Journal of African Historical Studies*, 26, 3 (1993), pp.513-39

Redding S., *Sorcery and Sovereignty: Taxation, power and rebellion in South Africa, 1880-1963* (Athens OH, 2006)

Redding S., 'South African Blacks in a Small Town Setting: The ironies of control in Umtata, 1878-1955', *Canadian Journal of African Studies*, 26, 1 (1992), pp.70-90

Rich P., *Race and Empire in British Politics* (Cambridge, 1986)

Sachs A., *Justice in South Africa* (London, 1973)

Schuster L., *A Burning Hunger: One family's struggle against apartheid* (London, 2004)

Schmidt E., *Mobilising the Masses: Gender, ethnicity and class in the nationalist movement in Guinea, 1939-58* (Portsmouth NH, 2004)

Schmidt E., 'Top-Down or Bottom-Up? Nationalist mobilisation reconsidered', *American Historical Review*, 110 (2005), pp.975-1014

Seekings J., *The UDF: A history of the United Democratic Front, 1983-91* (Oxford, 2000)

Segar J., *Fruits of apartheid: Experiencing "independence" in a Transkeian village* (Bellville, 1989)

Shubin, *The ANC: A view from Moscow* (Bellville, 1999)

Simkins C., 'Agricultural Production in the African Reserves of South Africa, 1918-69', *Journal of Southern African Studies*, 7, 2 (1981), pp.256-83

Simpson T., 'Toyi-Toying to Freedom: The endgame in the ANC's armed struggle, 1989-90', *Journal of Southern African Studies*, 35, 2 (2009), pp.507-21

Sisulu E., *Walter and Albertina Sisulu: In our lifetime* (Claremont, 2002)

Smith J. and Tromp B., *Hani: A life too short* (Johannesburg, 2009)

South African Democracy Education Trust, *The Road to Democracy in South Africa, Volumes I, II, VI* (Cape Town, 2004, 2005, 2013)

South African Institute of Race Relations, *A Survey of Race Relations in South Africa* (Johannesburg, 1963-1994)

Southall R., *South Africa's Transkei* (London, 1982)

Southall R., 'The Struggle for a Place called Home: The ANC versus the UDM in the Eastern Cape', *Politikon*, 26, 2 (1999), pp.155-66

Spear T., 'Neo-traditionalism and the Limits of Invention in British Colonial Africa', *Journal of African History*, 44 (2003), pp.3-27

Steinberg J., *The Thin Blue Line: The unwritten rules of policing South Africa* (Johannesburg, 2008)

Stiff P., *Warfare by other Means: South Africa in the 1980s and 1990s* (Johannesburg, 2001)

Stoger-Eising V., '*Ujamaa* revisited: Indigenous and European influences in Nyerere's social and political thought', *Africa*, 70, 1 (2000), pp.118-43

Strachan H., *Make a Skyf Man* (Johannesburg, 2004)

Streek B. and Wicksteed R., *Render Unto Kaiser: A Transkei dossier* (Johannesburg, 1981)

Stultz N., *Transkei's Half Loaf: Race separatism in South Africa* (New Haven, 1979)

Tropp J., 'Displaced People, Replaced Narratives: Forest conflicts and historical perspectives in the Tsolo district, Transkei,' *Journal of Southern African Studies*, 29, 1 (2003), pp.207-33

Truth and Reconciliation Commission, *Truth and Reconciliation of South Africa: Report* (Cape Town, 1998)

Ukpanah I., *The Long Road to Freedom: Inkundla ya Bantu and the African nationalist movement in South Africa, 1938-51* (Trenton NJ, 2005)

Uys J., *Biographical Directory of South African Lawyers* (Johannesburg, 1970)

199

Bibliography

Vail L.(ed.), *The Creation of Tribalism in southern Africa* (London, 1989)

van Kessel I., *Beyond our Wildest Dreams: The United Democratic Front and the transformation of South Africa* (London, 2000)

van Kessel I., '"From Confusion to Lusaka": The youth revolt in Sekhukhuneland', *Journal of Southern African Studies*, 19, 4 (1993), pp.593-614

van Kessel I. and Oomen B., 'One Chief, One Vote: The Revival of Traditional Authorities in Post Apartheid South Africa', *African Affairs*, 96, 385 (1994), pp.561-85

Vigne R., Liberals Against Apartheid: A history of the Liberal Party in South Africa 1953 - 68 (Basingstoke, 1997)

Vilakazi H., 'Was Karl Marx a Black Man?', *Monthly Review*, 33, 2 (1980), pp.42-58

Werbner R., *Reasonable Radicals and Citizenship in Botswana: The public anthropology of Kalanga elites*, (Bloomington IN, 2004)

Williams J., 'Leading from Behind: Democratic consolidation and the chieftaincy in South Africa', *Journal of Modern African Studies*, 42, 1 (2004), pp.113-36

Wolpe H. and Unterhalter E. (eds.), *Apartheid Education and Popular Struggles* (London, 1991)

Worden N., *The Making of Modern South Africa* (Oxford, 1994)

Woods D., *Asking for Trouble: Autobiography of a banned journalist* (London, 1980)

Young C., 'Nationalism, Ethnicity and Class in Africa: A retrospect', *Cahiers d'Etudes Africaines*, 26, 3 (1986), pp.421-75

Index

Index

Honono, Nathaniel 28-9, 36, 45

Indaba eMonti newspaper 38; *see also* All African Convention; newspapers
indirect rule 5, 11, 14, 49, 59; *see also* Bantustan self-government, Transkei; Bantustan state; chieftaincy
Industrial and Commercial Union 17; *see also* trade unions
Inkatha *see* KwaZulu and Natal
Inkundla ya Bantu newspaper 37; *see also* Mbeki, Govan; newspapers
Institute of Development and Management Studies 121-3; *see also* community development projects; *Umkhonto weSizwe*; University of Transkei
insurgency 5-7, 8-9, 111, 113, 116-17, 124, 126, 129-30, 177-82; *see also* African People's Liberation Army; ANC underground; Cold War in southern Africa; frontline states; Lesotho; Lesotho Liberation Army; political repression; political violence; Poqo; Sabotage Campaign; *Umkhonto weSizwe*
intellectuals; All African Convention 28-9, 36, 167; ANC 13, 18, 115; authors 17, 19, 22, 27-8, 120, 146 n. 65, 177-8; teachers 13, 22, 33-5, 87-9, 166-71; universities 77, 119-22, 145-6, 156; *see also* African elites; nationalism; newspapers; political dissent, ideologies and discourses of; praise poets; professionals, African; tribal histories
intelligence dossiers 148, 151, 153; *see also* corruption; military intelligence
Isizwe newspaper 81 n. 43, 107, 170 n. 72; *see also* newspapers
Izwe Lomzi newspaper 34 n. 35, 41-2, 45; *see also* Mbeki, Govan; newspapers; Sabotage Campaign

Jafta, 'Kenny' Kenneth Mangoliso 76, 121, 128, 149, 173
J.A.L.C. company 142-4; *see also* corruption; counterinsurgency; military-business networks
Jongilizwe 26
Jongilizwe College 71, 85, 87, 126, 132-3; *see also* chieftaincy
Jongintaba 1, 155
journalists, African 37, 38-9, 72, 81, 88, 107-8, 158-9; *see also* intellectuals; newspapers; professionals, African
Joyi, Anderson 28, 31, 39, 43-4, 96-8, 102-4, 138
Joyi, Bangelizwe 28, 31, 39, 43-4, 98, 102-4
Joyi, Marelane 39, 102
Joyi, Mvuso 102-4, 110, 139
Joyi, Twalifeme 98-9, 102
Jozana, Xoliswa 120

Karis, Tom 29, 30, 45, 64, 82, 96
Kati, Zamiwonga James 42, 114, 117, 160
Kenya 6-7, 18-19, 177-8, 184
Kenyatta, Jomo 18-19, 178
Kerzner, Sol 142, 151, 153
Kholwa 11; *see also* African elites; KwaZulu and Natal; *Mfengu*
King Sabata *see* Dalindyebo, Sabata
kinship 1-2, 5-6, 8, 17-18, 26-30, 70-2; *see also* African elites; ceremonies and rituals
KwaZulu Homeland *see* KwaZulu and Natal
KwaZulu and Natal *see* Buthelezi, Mangosuthu; *Kholwa*; Luthuli, Albert; political violence

labour migration *see* migrant labour
land 16, 56-7, 163-5, 173, 177-9; *see also* agriculture in Transkei; Greater Xhosaland; migrant labour; rural protest
Land Acts (of 1913 and 1936) 16
land betterment; African comparisons 177-8; policies 25, 50-1; resistance to 25, 34-7, 38-40, 42-3, 48-53, 122, 114, 177-8; *see also* agriculture in Transkei; rural development projects, government; rural protest
Langa, Babini 52-3, 56
Langa, Zoleka 51-2, 149-50, 155, 163-4, 174-5
lawyers; chieftaincy disputes 30-1, 35-7, 108-10; numbers 21, 36; political activists and leaders 27, 31, 35-6, 40, 112, 125, 161; political dissent in Transkei 30-1, 35-7, 108-10, 126; practising in Transkei 23, 36, 101, 161, 164; South African Constitutional Court 5; Transkei judiciary 114, 126; *see also* African elites; Bantustan state, Transkei; magistrates;; political repression; professionals, African
Lesotho; South African exiles 35, 42-3, 45, 90, 112-13, 125; Transkei borderlands 17-18, 134, 140; *Umkhonto weSizwe* 88-90, 111-15, 117, 122-4, 127-9, 136; *see also* Basotho Congress Party; insurgency; Sotho speaking districts; *Umkhonto weSizwe*
Lesotho Liberation Army 113, 134, 147; *see also* Basotho Congress Party; insurgency
Letlaka, Tsepo Tiisetso (T.T.) 129, 171
Liberal Party of South Africa 38, 44-5, 93; *see also* *Contact* newspaper
liberalism 11-13 *passim*, 44-5, 92-4; *see also* federalism; Liberal Party of South Africa
liberation theology; Africanist politics 80-1, 82-4, 122; Bantustans, critique of 80-1, 83-4, 103-7; corruption, critique of 80-1, 105-7; *see also* Black Consciousness Movement; Catholic Students Association; Church; Federal Seminary; Transkei Council of Churches
literacy 32, 37-41 *passim*, 122; *see also* education; newspapers; praise posts
livestock; culling 25, 50-1; dipping 1, 22, 43, 55, 57-9; diseases 1, 55, 58; taxes 57, 60-2, 69; *see also* agriculture in Transkei; land; land betterment; rural protest; stock theft; veterinary services, government
local political leadership, ideologies of 4-5, 7, 22-3, 28-9, 31-7, 98-101, 155-6, 166-71, 173-5; *see also* Africanist politics; communitarianism
Lovedale College 12-13, 15, 17, 28, 74, 77, 85, 104, 112, 114; *see also* mission schools; schools
Luthuli, Albert 11, 13, 18

Mabandla, Oyama 86-7, 89-90, 114-16, 124, 161
Mabandla, Bukhosi 167, 173
Mabude, Mzolisi 120, 122, 125, 155, 159
Mabude, Saul 49, 120
Machel, Samora 8, 180, 182
Madikizela, Columbus 15-16, 21, 50-3
Madikizela, Prince 125, 129, 155, 160
Madikizela, Walter 54-5
Madikizela-Mandela, Winnie; Bantustan government ministers, relationship 93, 95, 137-40; Bantustan independence, against 95; Congress of Traditional Leaders of South Africa 161; Eastern Mpondoland hinterland 2, 21, 54, 69, 125; education 16; Holomisa, Bantu 138, 140, 153; Matanzima, Kaiser 95, 125, 137; Mpondo Revolt 53, 54; Thembu chieftaincy 137, 138, 140, 153
Mafu, Dumisani 114, 124, 125, 128
magistrates 14, 15, 31, 37, 39, 47; courts 67, 149;

Umkhonto weSizwe
Transkei Democratic Party *see* Democratic Party, Transkei
Transkei Legislative Assembly 46-7, 60, 65, 77; *see also* Bantustan state, Transkei
Transkei Military Council *see* Transkei Military Government
Transkei Military Government; ANC in Transkei 138-40, 165; apartheid government 168-9; budget deficits 168-9; chieftaincy 162-5; corruption investigations 135, 141-3, 151; coup attempt against 144-7; cross border raids and kidnappings 143-5, 147; detention 143-4; martial law 135-6; protests against and challenges to 155-6, 163-71 *passim*; reincorporation into South Africa 171-3, 181-4; Thembu chieftaincy 137-40; *Umkhonto weSizwe* 6, 136-7, 139-40, 148-50; unbans liberation movements 140, 155; *see also* corruption investigations; Holomisa, Bantu; taxation and government expenditure
Transkei Military Intelligence 133, 135-6, 144, 148, 151; *see also* military intelligence; security forces, apartheid; security forces, Transkei
Transkei National Independence Party 45, 129-30
Transkei National Progressive Party 66
Transkei security police 117, 124-5, 126, 128, 136; *see also* security forces, apartheid; security forces, Transkei
Transkei Teachers Association 166; *see also* teachers, African
Transkei Traditional Leaders Association 162; *see also* chieftaincy; Congress of Traditional Leaders of South Africa
Transkeian Territories 1, 11, 17; *see also* United Transkeian Territories General Council
Tribal Authorities 25-41 *passim*, 57-9, 63; courts 35, 102; *see also* Bantustan state; chieftaincy
tribal histories 17, 19, 98, 109; *see also* chieftaincy; intellectuals; praise poets
Tsolo College for the Sons of Chiefs and Headmen *see* Jongilizwe College
Tsotsi, Wycliffe 28, 36, 45, 167
Turfloop *see* University of the North

Umkhonto weSizwe; assassination operations 112, 117, 125; bank robbery 115, 150, 181-2; Basotho Congress Party 113; bombing campaigns 117, 124-6 *passim*; campaigns 111, 113, 116-17, 124, 126, 129-30; democratic transition 147-50, 181-2; Eastern Cape elite 114-16; frontline states 111, 115-16, 124, 127-8; Lesotho 111-16, 124-8; militancy during democratic transition 149-51; power struggles within 115-16, 152-3; Soviet support 115, 117, 155; students, recruitment of 90, 114-17; Transkei, based in 145-6, 148-50; Transkei, operations in 113-17, 124-8; *see also* ANC underground; insurgency; Sabotage Campaign
Umtata (town) 1, 15, 30, 32, 36, 45-7, 171
United Democratic Movement 174
United Transkeian Territories General Council; Bantustan self-government 23-6; chieftaincy 13-16; school building 32-5; *see also* Bantustan state; chieftaincy; government officials; taxation and government expenditure
University of Cape Town 35, 87, 101; *see also*

universities
University of Fort Hare; ANC underground 89-90, 114, 117, 124, 127; Black Consciousness Movement 63-4, 77-8, 80, 82; boycotts and protests, Bantustan era 89-90, 114, 117, 119, 156; elite formation, early 20th century 1, 8, 17, 22, 64, 112, 181; elite formation, Bantustan era 114-16 *passim*, 119, 136, 154 n. 101; nationalism, early 20th century 13, 17-18, 24, 64, 181; origins 8; *see also* universities
University of Natal 86, 117, 126, 140, 158, 161; *see also* universities
University of the North 77, 77 n. 30, 118, 121; *see also* universities
University of Transkei; ANC mobilisation 156, 158; ANC underground 122-4, 139-40; Bantustan state 118, 119, 122-3, 156; boycotts and protests 123-4, 139-40, 156-9; crisis 156-9, 173; elite formation 119; exam results (poor) 118, 157; patrimonial politics 119, 122-3, 156; political dissent 119-22; poor conditions 118; student numbers 118, 156; Student Council 119, 122-4, 156-9; *Umkhonto weSizwe* 52, 122-4, 139, 157; *see also* Institute of Management and Development Studies; universities
University of Zululand 77, 118; *see also* universities
universities; elite formation 1-2, 119; student numbers and expansion 77, 119; *see also* African elites; ANC underground; Black Consciousness Movement; education; intellectuals; nationalism; professionals, African; University of Cape Town; University of Fort Hare; University of Natal; University of the North; University of Transkei
USSR *see* Cold War in southern Africa

van Rensberg, Chris 142-3
Vena, Mzwandile 124
veterinary services, government 55-7; *see also* agriculture in Transkei; Bantustan state, Transkei; livestock; professionals, African
Vigne, Randolph 44
Vilakazi, Herbert 120
violence *see* political violence; protest and violence
Vlakplaas *see* security forces, apartheid

Western Mpondoland 95; *see also* Eastern Mpondoland; Poto, Victor
Western Thembuland; conflict within 31, 34-7, 40-1, 42, 112-13; split from Thembuland 25, 27, 30-1; *see also* Matanzima, Kaiser
Wild Coast Casino 126-7, 135, 139-40, 141-2
Woods, Donald 94-5, 108

Xobololo, Alfred Siphiwo 43, 58, 88, 96, 138, 155, 160
Xuma, Alfred 32, 38
Xundu, Mcebisi 82, 84

Yako, Mazwi 88, 116-17
youth revolt 2, 70-1, 155-6, 179-80; *see also* education protests; political dissent; protest and violence

Zimbabwe 8, 111, 133-4, 177-82
Zululand *see* KwaZulu and Natal
Zuma, Jacob 4, 140

Lightning Source UK Ltd.
Milton Keynes UK
UKOW05f1340100317

296363UK00002B/2/P